REGULATION AND POLICIES
OF AMERICAN SHIPPING

REGULATION AND POLICIES OF AMERICAN SHIPPING

ERNST G. FRANKEL
Massachusetts Institute of Technology

Auburn House Publishing Company
Boston, Massachusetts

Library of Congress Cataloging in Publication Data
Frankel, Ernst G.
    Regulation and policies of American shipping.

    Bibliography: p.
    Includes index.
    1. Shipping—United States. 2. Merchant marine—
United States. 3. Maritime law—United States.
I. Title.
HE745.F73   387.5′0973   81-12721
ISBN 0-86569-099-5   AACR2

ACKNOWLEDGMENTS

This work includes the efforts and thoughts of many colleagues, associates, and research assistants. It is possible only to name those who were involved in or contributed to specific parts of this work. Among those who have contributed substantial portions to this book and to whom much appreciation is extended include Mr. George Baker, who researched the legal issues affecting inland water and domestic shipping and contributed part of the text of Chapter 7, and Mr. Michael Flomenhaft, who researched legal and legislative issues affecting international shipping and contributed to the text of Chapters 3 and 4. Most importantly, my appreciation is extended to Ms. Maria Joy Frank, who researched the regulatory issues affecting U.S. shipping, the impact of cargo sharing on U.S. shipping, shippers, and U.S. regulatory agencies. She also made significant contributions to Chapter 6 and edited Chapters 3, 4, and 7.

For statistical material and other information, I thank the Seatrade Publications Ltd., U.S. Federal Maritime Commission, American Waterways Operators Inc., U.S. Maritime Administration, U.S. Army Corps of Engineers, United Nations Conference on Trade and Development, United Nations Statistical Office, Bureau of Census— U.S. Department of Commerce, and other organizations who willingly provided invaluable information without which this book could not have been written. Finally I would like to thank Ms. Sheila McNary for her infallible and cheerful composition, drafting, typing, and proofing of this manuscript.

Any errors or omissions are obviously the sole responsibility of the author.

E.G.F.

PREFACE

U.S. shipping policy has a long and varied history. Its development has often been affected by the conflicting objectives of furthering free enterprise in shipping and free trade in foreign commerce, and protecting U.S. shipping and defense requirements. The basic premises guiding U.S. shipping policy have not changed in over 75 years. Policy and regulatory developments were composed largely of amendments, expansions, or reinterpretations of existing shipping and other U.S. laws affecting shipping rather than any fundamental changes in their underlying assumptions and goals. The effectiveness of this approach has recently come under increasing criticism. Shipping technology, operations, and, most importantly, the structure of international shipping have undergone major changes in recent years. The U.S. role in international shipping has simultaneously continued its decline. At the same time, participation of other nations in shipping has increased, and direct government involvement in shipping has become common in many countries. International shipping has also come under increasing scrutiny by international organizations, particularly those concerned with income redistribution between developed and developing nations. A major proposal toward that end is the cargo-sharing agreement in the UNCTAD Code of Conduct for Liner Conferences. Similar or even more far-reaching proposals covering other segments of shipping have been suggested. It appears that the United States may find itself increasingly isolated and that changes in, or formulation of, U.S. shipping policy and regulation are required for effective participation in international shipping operations under new environmental conditions.

This study is an analysis of the development and effectiveness of U.S. shipping policy and regulation. It is based on an evaluation of the underlying premises and their interpretation in terms of government aid and other policies as well as their effects on the U.S. shipping industry. Its purpose is to provide an overview of policy and regulatory issues and a framework for their development.

The U.S. Federal Maritime Commission supported part of the study dealing with the "Impact of Cargo Sharing on U.S. Liner

Shipping." Numerous colleagues and students contributed to this work. Special thanks go to John Cooper, Joy Frank, Michael Flomenhaft, and George Baker for their help with various drafts of this study.

Throughout the two years of effort devoted to this study an attempt was made to continually update information, references, and data. Considering the rapid and frequent changes introduced or considered recently, though, some of the latest developments may have been omitted. Any such omission or other errors are the sole responsibility of the author.

E.G.F.

CONTENTS

CHAPTER 4

Evaluation of Economic and Regulatory Aspects of U.S. Maritime Policy

CHAPTER 5
Issues in U.S. International and Inland Shipping Policymaking

CHAPTER 6
Potential Impacts of Cargo Sharing on U.S. Shipping   213

LIST OF TABLES

LIST OF FIGURES

REGULATION AND POLICIES
OF AMERICAN SHIPPING

Chapter 1

THE CONTEXT OF CONTEMPORARY U.S. SHIPPING

The increasing participation in ship ownership and operation by large corporations and multinational or transnational companies as well as national governments greatly influences the shipping industry and its regulation. As a result, the policies, regulations, and procedures that affect shipping, as well as the framework in which shipping functions today, differ from those of the past.

Jurisdiction over coastal waters has been greatly extended. Active and passive ship traffic control and other control systems or regulation affecting ship operations are introduced with increasing frequency. Growing concern for environmental protection results in national and international regulation. Regulations also govern methods of ship ballasting, ballast, solid/liquid waste disposal, and other operating procedures. These, in turn, affect ship design, cargo planning, and ship operations management. During recent years the number of users of the oceans of the world has multiplied. Offshore resource development, fishing, and other activities compete with shipping, not only in coastal waters but, in some places, for deep ocean space as well. Shipping is consequently becoming more constrained.

The number of vessels and structures in coastal waters (the 200-mile zone of economic influence) at any one time has nearly tripled in the last ten years. The increasing number of ships under registry of flags of countries with open registry, usually called "flags of convenience," and flags of developing nations or of new maritime nations has had a major impact on the control of ship operations. It has also affected the development of procedures relating to operational requirements, such as the qualifications of shipboard staff and the condition and maintenance of ships.

The growing interest in and pressure for more international regulation of shipping management, ship design, ship operating pro-

1

cedures, and ship automation is in some ways contrary to current trends in American shipping development. Lack of availability of skilled manpower in many major shipping countries has spurred the development of long-term maintenance warranty agreements with shipyards, which will probably result in decreased shipboard repair and increased attention to effective performance monitoring and diagnosis by shipboard staff. This, in turn, may lead to the establishment of new training and skill requirements for reduced shipboard staff.

The greatest impact on shipping, however, is probably caused by the introduction of integrated and intermodal shipping, wherein shipping constitutes but one part of a multimodal, totally integrated transport system consisting of sequential land and sea transport systems such as pipelines feeding tankers. This is true even where some transport modes, such as shipping, are not under the same ownership or operational control as other modes of the integrated transport system. We note this trend with regard to container transport and liquid bulk transport now, but other modes of physical commodity transport are expected to follow. Such integrated transport may involve change of physical form of the transported commodities between transport modes to facilitate transport performance.

The growing capital intensity of transportation in general and shipping in particular, the loss of control of fixed costs, and major variable costs, such as fuel, have forced shipping operators to assure maximum utilization of their vessels as part of an integrated system. Shippers are increasingly willing to contract for the individual modal services and prefer door-to-door contracting for transport services. This implies that ship schedules, the physical form of handling cargo, ship arrival/departure conditions, sequence of port calls, speed of transit, onboard cargo maintenance, and many other shipping management functions are no longer under the sole control of shipping management. It further implies that ships are encouraged to adopt or adapt to effective interface technology.

Finally, the technological revolution in information handling, communications, and general management systems requires consistency in ship management with the requirement of fleet, company, or systems management.

We are therefore concerned today with a revolution in shipping which is the result of changes in:

- Ship technology
- Organization of shipping companies
- Role and function of ships
- Integration in transport systems
- Ship maintenance

- Congestion in ship traffic lanes
- Freedom of shipping and trade
- Jurisdiction of shipping lanes, coastal, and open waters
- Environmental impact tolerance
- Ownership of shipping
- Manning and training of ship crews

This affects the ways in which shipping is managed, ships are operated, and the financial and economic aspects of shipping.

Shipping has always offered unique challenges and opportunities and has provided a major impetus for economic development. In the past, world shipping has been largely under the control of the more developed nations. This is changing rapidly as developing nations expand their participation in world shipping at an ever-increasing rate. The role of shipping is changing and with it the requirements for shipping management.

U.S. shipping, and particularly U.S.-liner shipping, has for many years now operated under an umbrella of government aids, regulations, and restrictions resulting from government policy. Since the Shipping Act of 1916 and the Merchant Marine Act of 1936, government involvement in shipping has expanded and today comprises not only various forms of subsidies, protective operating rules, and regulations, but also measures that directly and indirectly affect the effectiveness of U.S. shipping management to meet increasing foreign and domestic competition.

Many claim that U.S. maritime policy has been ineffective in furthering the interests and competitiveness of the U.S. shipping industry, and several issues are cited. Vessel acquisition costs, even with construction differential subsidy, are not really equal to those of vessels obtained under "best-negotiated terms" available abroad; there is a lack of fuel-efficient propulsion plants on U.S.-built vessels, largely due to the historic unavailability of large U.S.-built marine diesel engines; trade route or service restrictions prevent U.S. shipping management from making astute operating decisions; and antitrust restrictions prevent U.S. operators from entering into many joint service or venture agreements which, in turn, provide their foreign competition with economic advantages (U.S.-subsidized operations, for example, cannot participate in foreign-flag feeder ownership). Comparable restrictions on vessel design, manning reductions, use of automation, and other technological factors are also noted. In brief, American shipping regulations and policies are increasingly questioned. The purpose of this book is to review the development, status, and future of U.S. shipping regulations and policies.

Whereas in past eras shipping was almost an end in itself, intimately tied to merchandising activities, it is now becoming but one stage in the process of physical production/distribution of commodities. Most bulk and parcel commodity movements travel by sea from the place of extraction to the processing sites, and distribution is often through ocean shipping. Vigorous growth has occurred in oceanborne tonnage in recent decades, accompanied by advances in ocean vehicle technology. This has affected the cost, physical form, and even the viability of transporting many categories of goods. Since an appreciable percentage of the world's gross national product (GNP), and an inordinately large percentage of the developing world's GNP, is spent on ocean transport, and since major industries are dependent on the seaborne supply of raw materials, it is evident that low-cost, adaptable shipping is a necessity for sustained economic growth and development.

Shipping also generates incomes, employment, and tax revenue. Through direct and indirect "ripple" effects, it supports a multitude of associated production and service industries, thereby contributing substantially to the GNP and growth of nations. These factors have combined to increase shipping's role in the economic development of nations. Shipping is no longer the purveyor of luxuries and innovations, but the main transport mode of the raw and semifinished materials required by industry on a daily basis. This change permits and facilitates the development of specialized ship types, which require high initial capital investment and corresponding investments in terminal facilities.

Merchant shipping was comparatively independent of government influence in the years immediately following World War II, as evidenced by the proliferation of flags-of-convenience registrations. But renewed understanding of the importance of shipping is leading to reexamination of national shipping policies in many countries and to the elaboration of regulations designed to ensure that shipping conforms to national economic objectives.

The competitive environment resulting from this trend wherein nations instead of shipping companies try to maximize their participation in world trade, combined with a mood of maritime nationalism, finds increasing expression in cargo preference laws or support of the United Nations Conference on Trade and Development (UNCTAD) "40-40-20" cargo sharing rule. Under this rule partners reserve at least 40 percent of their trade to their national shipping, subsidization of national fleets, and other distortions of the free market or competitive conditions that historically have prevailed in world shipping. One reason for this change in attitude is the development of greater understanding of the importance of ocean shipping to economic development and national defense. In consequence, ensuring shipping capacity sufficient to carry 40 to 50 percent of the country's trade and to meet defense needs is a primary objective of most national ocean shipping policies. The United States expresses this broadly in the Merchant Marine Act of 1936 (as amended).[1]

> *It is necessary for the national defense and development of its foreign and domestic commerce that the United States shall have a merchant marine (a) sufficient to carry its domestic waterborne commerce and a substantial portion of the waterborne export and import foreign commerce of the United States and to provide shipping service on all routes essential for maintaining the flow of such domestic and foreign waterborne commerce at all times, (b) capable of serving as a naval and military auxiliary in time of war or national emergency, (c) owned and operated under the United States flag by citizens of the United States insofar as may be practicable, and (d) composed of the best equipped, safest, and most suitable types of vessels, constructed in the United States, and manned with a trained and efficient citizen personnel. It is hereby declared to be the policy of the United States to foster the development and encourage the maintenance of such a merchant marine.*

Maritime shipping may be said to comprise two basic objectives. The first, the maritime contribution to national defense as expressed in U.S. shipping legislation, has two aspects. One is the provision of complementary merchant shipping operations necessary to move military cargo. The other is provision of shipping to move essential imports during periods of emergency, involving war or other critical economic contingencies. These dual aspects may be referred to as "the national security objective," the commercial trade component of which is usually less clearly defined than the military trade component.

The second basic objective provision of shipping, the development of commerce, is difficult to quantify. While this objective is related to the economic component of its national security counterpart, it is in fact separate and concerned with the import and export shipping required to support the development and growth of the economy. Most frequently it is defined in terms of the economic benefits deriving from ability to influence freight rates, trade participation, and the balance of payments.

Basic economic objectives of shipping include assurance of fair and reasonable freight rates for national imports and exports. Despite representation in the conferences (associations of liner operators designed to regulate terms of service), which serve its foreign trade, a country may still be vulnerable to rate discrimination or other,

---

1. 46 U.S.C. 101(a)(b)(1970).

subtler forms of discrimination. An explicit policy of supporting the maritime industry may prevent unilateral rate increases prejudicial to commercial development, even if a country's fleet is small. Shipping also makes an important contribution to the balance of payments, proportional to the growth of external trade. Further, it provides employment for nationals and merchant seamen who reinforce the capability for maritime mobilization in time of war. Finally, the availability of frequent, quantity shipping services promotes foreign trade.

Efforts to meet national defense and economic objectives through foreign trade are complemented by providing adequate and efficient port facilities. Because merchant ships are only one component in a complex, multimodal transportation system, attention must also be directed to the development of ports and related facilities to optimize overall system performance, so as to increase incentives for the growth of traded goods.

The demand for shipping is therefore a derived demand. That is, estimates of future shipping demand are derived from forecasts of the demand for oceangoing and inland flow of goods as a function of transport system performance. Most studies that forecast shipping demand focus on the impact of derived demand on the growth of trade of these goods.

The U.S. fleet of the future and the future of the U.S. shipping industry depend not only on the volume of goods to be moved but also on freight rates to be realized, government policy toward and legislation affecting the industry, international agreements, and advances in technology that can make U.S. shipping more competitive. Recent studies by the Federal Maritime Administration (MarAd) point out that advanced technology and favorable policy action may enable U.S.-flag U.S.-owned shipping to increase its share of the U.S. import and export markets.

Freight rates and costs are the determining factors in the shipping industry. Subsidies can result only in marginal changes, particularly if they are not tied to incentives. The number of ships, their design, and technology is usually derived in response to the volume of cargo they can expect to carry and the freight rates they expect to realize. On the other hand, freight rates respond to the demand for shipping relative to available short-term supply. If the number of ships supplied, of a given type, such as tankers, containerships, bulk carriers, or car ferries is inadequate to meet the demand, freight rates can skyrocket—as happened with tanker rates in 1967 and 1968 (or in the reverse situation, as happened in 1974 and 1975).

One of the objectives of this volume is to present the framework of the regulation of American shipping, including an analysis of government policy as it has evolved over the years and its effects on U.S. shipping. The content and format are designed for the aspiring or practicing shipping executive, regulator, or policymaker who, it is hoped, will find the content and format useful.

Chapter 1 gives an overview of the regulatory and policy issues involved in American shipping. This is followed in Chapter 2 by a summary of the structure and composition of U.S. shipping as well as U.S. waterborne trade. U.S. shipping regulation and government aids to shipping are discussed in Chapter 3. This chapter covers the role of the federal government, the regulation of aids, and the various direct and indirect aids offered to American shipping. It also presents a review of taxation of American-flag shipping and rate regulation. Economic and regulatory aspects of U.S. maritime policy are evaluated in Chapter 4. Here we discuss the economic objectives of the subsidies program and their costs and impacts. Various policy issues are reviewed and recent legislative proposals are evaluated. Policy issues affecting international and inland water shipping are discussed in Chapter 5. Here the need for new policy approaches and the changing environment of international shipping policy are established, followed by a review of the role of various United Nations and international shipping organizations. Inland water transportation policy issues such as user charges and regulation are also covered. Chapter 6 deals with cargo sharing and potential impacts on U.S. shipping, with special reference to the United Nations Conference on Trade and Development (UNCTAD) Code of Conduct for Liner Shipping. The code itself and its impact on U.S. shippers, U.S.-flag ship operators, U.S. ports, U.S. shipping regulation, and the U.S. economy are discussed.

Chapter 7 deals with U.S. inland water transportation. After reviewing the composition, capacity, and performance of U.S. inland water and Great Lakes domestic shipping, inland water policy issues and regulation of inland and domestic water carriers are discussed. Finally, in Chapter 8, we summarize the issues, challenges, and opportunities for policymakers in U.S. shipping. Also, a bibliography of the recent literature in the area of American shipping regulation and policy is provided.

Chapter 2

STRUCTURE OF
THE U.S. SHIPPING INDUSTRY

The shipping industry consists of a number of major and minor components, generally categorized under foreign, domestic, or inland water shipping. Major components of foreign shipping, for example, are liner and designated bulk shipping; a minor component would be undesignated tramp shipping. Similar designations apply to domestic and inland water shipping.

2.1. Foreign Shipping

U.S. international or foreign shipping can be divided into U.S.-owned flag vessels and U.S.-owned foreign-flag vessels. Similarly, some foreign-flag shipping, not exclusively owned by U.S. interests, is assumed to be under "effective" U.S. control, for reasons of government policy. U.S.-flag shipping is usually built, owned, and manned by U.S. citizens; it is divided into liner, proprietary, independent, and tramp shipping. Liners (general cargo, container, barge carriers, and so forth) may be subsidized or nonsubsidized. Proprietary ocean shipping is operated by or on behalf of a single economic interest and is usually employed in the trade of a particular commodity. Independent shipping generally consists of liquid or dry bulk carriers chartered by independent owners for a specific time period (or voyage) to a particular company. Tramp shipping comprises general cargo and dry and liquid bulk carriers that are for hire in the carriage of goods on particular routes, not necessarily exclusively for one commodity or cargo owner. A certain amount of overlap occurs between independent and tramp ship operations and operators.

2.2.   Domestic Shipping

This sector consists of proprietary and independent operators. Only U.S.-built, owned, manned, and operated vessels are allowed in this trade, which can be divided into coastal, contiguous, and noncontiguous trade routes. All are governed by existing cabotage and Jones Acts.

Coastal trade is primarily performed by liquid and dry bulk carriers. Contiguous and noncontiguous domestic trade also includes break bulk, container/trailer, barge, liner, and tramp services. An increasing number of domestic shipping operations are performed by oceangoing barges push-towed by oceangoing tugs.

2.3.   Inland Water Transportation

Inland water transportation is performed largely by river barges, engaged primarily in the carriage of dry and liquid bulk commodities. Many independent barge operators provide bulk cargo transportation on a contract basis. The U.S. inland water transport industry has grown very substantially in recent years and is discussed in Chapter 7.

2.4.   Types of Shipping Operators

The Federal Maritime Commission for regulatory convenience divides ship operators into four groups. In addition, it defines a freight forwarder whose business is to arrange transportation with a ship operator as an agent of the shipper.

The four groups of operators are common carriers, contract carriers, private carriers, and tramps, and are defined as follows.

Common Carriers.   The term "common carrier by water" refers to any vessel or person presenting to the general public as ready, able, and willing to engage, by water transport, in interstate or foreign commerce with passengers or property or any class or classes thereof for compensation.

Contract Carriers.   The term "contract carrier by water" refers to any person who, under individual contracts or agreements, engages in interstate or foreign commerce by water transport. The furnishings of compensation (under charter, lease, or other agreement) of a vessel to a person other than a carrier for the transportation of its own property falls within the meaning of "contract carrier by water."

Private Carriers.   The Commission also has the power to determine upon its own motion, or upon the action or request of any party or interest, whether any water carrier is engaged solely in transporting the property of a person who owns all or substantially all of the voting stock of such a carrier. If so, the Commission will issue a certificate of exemption to the carrier, thus rendering it a private carrier not subject to the provisions of the Jones Act.

Tramps. In practice a ship is termed a "tramp" if it carries no more than four cargoes on demand between two or more ports on an irregular basis. The definition of tramp does not apply to transportation in bulk where the cargo space of the transporting vessel is carrying fewer than four commodities, and applies only where bulk commodities are loaded and carried without wrappers or containers and are received and delivered by the carrier without transportation mark or count (this according to the practice of 1939).

Freight Forwarder. An "independent ocean freight forwarder" is a person carrying on the business of "forwarding for consideration"; such an individual is neither a shipper, consignee, seller, or purchaser of shipments to foreign countries, nor has any beneficial interest therein, nor directly or indirectly controls or is controlled by such a shipper or consignee or any person having such a beneficial interest.

2.5. Offshore Transportation

This is a new industry serving the transport needs of the offshore (petroleum and mining) industry and consists of proprietary and independent operators. Barges, supply ships, and specialized vessels such as pipe carriers, and so forth are used for these enterprises.

2.6. Operating Services

The U.S. maritime transportation industry also consists of shipbuilding, ship repair, and the operation of ports and terminals—all of which form a part of or are subject to government policy and regulation.

Ocean-shipbuilding is performed mostly by subsidiary companies of large corporations. In contrast, inland water shipbuilding and much ship repair are done by independent and closely held corporations. Essentially none of the shipbuilding or ship repair companies relate to maritime transportation companies, and therefore, very little shipbuilding is performed for the builder's own account. Most public-user port or terminal facilities are owned by public

Table 2–1 Federal Agencies with Important Roles in U.S. Maritime Transportation

Department of Commerce
 National Oceanic and Atmospheric Administration

Department of Transportation
 Office of the Secretary
  General Functions
  Materials Transportation Bureau
 U.S. Coast Guard
 St. Lawrence Seaway Development Corporation
 Maritime Administration

Department of Defense
 Military Research & Development
 U.S. Army Corps of Engineers
 Panama Canal Company
 Military Sealift Command

Department of State

Department of the Treasury

Department of Energy
 Environmental Protection Agency
 Federal Maritime Commission
 Interstate Commerce Commission
 Tennessee Valley Authority
 Federal Trade Commission

Department of Justice

agencies or corporations, while most single-purpose, single-user terminals are owned and/or operated by proprietary interests.

A large number of U.S. government departments have jurisdiction over various aspects of regulation, advocacy, control, and supervision related to the U.S. shipping industry. Table 2-1 presents an abbreviated list of the major agencies involved. Because some overlap in the functions of jurisdiction of these federal agencies has occurred over time, it is sometimes difficult to define the exact responsibility of a particular federal agency.

2.7. Summary Profile of the U.S. Oceangoing Shipping Vessels

In July 1981 the U.S.-flag ocean shipping industry comprised 859 vessels of 1,000 gross tons (GRT) and over, of which 578 were privately owned and 281 government owned (Table 2-2). An appreciable drop in size of the fleet has occurred, however, over the past decade.

Table 2-3 presents the development of the U.S. fleet since 1970. The general cargo and containership fleet declined from 1,466 in 1970 to 552 in 1979 with a 51 percent drop in GRT; the bulk fleet declined in number by 28 percent, but maintained its GRT, while tanker and gas carrier tonnage increased appreciably. The average size of U.S.-flag oceangoing vessels was 15,926 GRT in 1979, while over 60 percent of U.S.-flag vessels was over 14 years old (Tables 2-4 and 2-5). U.S.-flag vessel participation in U.S. foreign trade was 4.2 percent by tonnage (1977), composed of 30.7 percent liner, 2.8 percent bulk and nonliner cargo, and 3.5 percent tanker shipping (Table 2-6).

With regard to U.S.-owned foreign-flag vessels (Table 2-7), while this fleet comprises only 687 vessels, their average size is appreciably larger than that of U.S.-flag vessels, and total GRT is about three times that of the U.S.-flag component of U.S. oceangoing shipping. The relative size of the fleet of U.S.-owned, U.S.-flag, and U.S.-owned foreign-flag vessels is shown in Figure 2-1.

After languishing in the 1960s, U.S. commercial shipbuilding output has been revitalized, at least in terms of GRT output (as shown in Table 2-8). However, the number of commercial ships built has remained static at 8 to 14 per year. The manpower distribution of oceangoing personnel on U.S.-flag vessels is shown in Table 2-9 by rank and vessel type; Table 2-10 indicates the area of employment. The U.S. merchant fleet declined in total GRT by nearly 50 percent between 1952 and 1975; slight increases since then are shown in Table 2-11.

Table 2–2 United States Oceangoing Merchant Marine, July 1, 1981 (tonnage in thousands)

	Privately Owned			Government Owned			Total		
	Number of Ships	Gross Tons	Deadweight Tons	Number of Ships	Gross Tons	Deadweight Tons	Number of Ships	Gross Tons	Deadweight Tons
*Active Fleet**									
Combined passenger/cargo	5	65	45	5	58	39	10	123	84
Freighters	98	1,073	1,329	9	53	67	107	1,125	1,396
Bulk carriers	13	200	331	0	0	0	13	200	331
Tankers	247	6,888	13,346	2	14	21	249	6,902	13,367
Intermodal	138	2,871	2,945	1	19	22	139	2,890	2,966
Tug/barge	10	159	301	0	0	0	10	159	301
LNG	8	667	572	0	0	0	8	667	572
Total	519	11,923	18,869	17	144	149	536	12,066	19,017
Inactive Fleet†									
Combined passenger/cargo	2	30	13	51	530	327	53	559	341
Freighters	12	125	145	190	1,532	2,070	202	1,657	2,216
Bulk carriers	4	107	211	0	0	0	4	107	211
Tankers	22	774	1,481	16	160	256	38	935	1,738
Intermodal	13	216	209	7	102	110	20	318	314
Tug/barge	1	26	41	0	0	0	1	26	41
LNG	5	376	357	0	0	0	5	376	357
Total	59	1,654	2,457	264	2,324	2,763	323	3,978	5,218

Table 2–2 (continued)

	Privately Owned			Government Owned			Total		
	Number of Ships	*Gross Tons*	*Deadweight Tons*	*Number of Ships*	*Gross Tons*	*Deadweight Tons*	*Number of Ships*	*Gross Tons*	*Deadweight Tons*
Total Fleet									
Combined passenger/cargo	7	95	57	56	587	368	63	682	425
Freighters	110	1,197	1,474	199	1,585	2,138	309	2,782	3,612
Bulk carriers	17	307	542	0	0	0	17	307	542
Tankers	269	7,663	14,828	18	174	278	287	7,837	15,105
Intermodal	151	3,087	3,153	8	121	128	159	3,208	3,281
Tug/barge	11	185	342	0	0	0	11	185	342
LNG	13	1,043	928	0	0	0	13	1,043	928
Total American Flag	578	13,577	21,324	281	2,467	2,912	859	16,044	24,235

SOURCE: U.S. Department of Commerce, Maritime Administration, U.S. Merchant Marine Data Sheet, August 1981. Data supplied by the Division of Trade Studies and Statistics.

Note: Totals are preliminary and reflect rounding.

* Includes two vessels in bareboat charter and nine vessels in custody of other agencies.

† Includes National Defense Reserve Fleet, which consists of 264 ships, 20 of which are scrap candidates.

Table 2–3   U.S. Fleet Analysis as of July 1, 1979

Year	General Cargo/Container		Bulk		Tankers		Gas Carriers		Chemical Tanker	
	No.	GRT	No.	GRT	No.	GRT	No.	GRT	No.	GRT
1970	1,466	10,735,241	218	2,079,949	359	4,687,938	1	15,134	9	87,397
1971	1,217	8,538,479	206	1,981,172	345	4,644,780	1	15,134	9	84,831
1972	891	6,934,175	204	1,983,313	327	4,589,455	1	15,134	9	84,831
1973	773	6,483,574	213	2,139,692	320	4,721,228	1	15,134	9	84,831
1974	670	5,808,011	196	2,033,720	314	4,882,598	1	15,134	9	84,831
1975	644	5,611,838	191	1,901,067	318	5,167,259	1	15,134	9	84,331
1976	633	5,521,360	172	1,812,647	319	5,601,707	1	15,883	9	84,831
1977	606	5,376,275	168	1,840,429	314	5,976,499	3	127,383	9	93,349
1978	562	5,295,933	167	1,921,007	311	6,657,992	5	334,659	9	93,349
1979	552	5,287,628	164	1,956,531	337	7,596,608	11	749,121	8	83,413

SOURCES: U.S. Maritime Administration, U.S. Merchant Marine Data Sheets and Division of Trade Studies and Statistics, August 1980. *Seatrade U.S. Yearbook 1980*, 2nd edition, Colchester, England: Seatrade Publications Ltd.

Table 2-4 U.S. Fleet Age and Size Analysis as of July 1, 1979

Deep-Sea Fleet

Tonnage Ranges	0–4 Years No.	0–4 Years GRT	5–9 Years No.	5–9 Years GRT	10–14 Years No.	10–14 Years GRT	15–19 Years No.	15–19 Years GRT	20–24 Years No.	20–24 Years GRT	25+ Years No.	25+ Years GRT	Total No.	Total GRT
100– 999	913	185,073	971	181,248	793	155,290	152	36,776	163	37,059	945	226,845	3,937	822,291
1,000– 9,999	34	83,131	33	60,915	27	122,447	38	299,099	10	22,836	220	1,430,881	362	2,019,309
10,000–19,999	29	459,864	17	281,667	58	795,646	68	852,890	33	573,379	185	2,607,471	390	5,570,917
20,000–49,999	21	717,718	72	2,187,862	14	340,698	19	533,085	21	495,579	5	130,126	152	4,405,068
50,000–99,999	20	1,501,160	5	288,608	—	—	1	62,434	—	—	—	—	26	1,852,202
100,000 +	7	901,385	2	207,807	—	—	—	—	—	—	—	—	9	1,109,192
Total	1,024	3,848,331	1,100	3,208,107	892	1,414,081	278	1,784,284	227	1,128,853	1,355	4,395,323	4,876	15,778,979

Lake Fleet

Tonnage Ranges	0–4 Years No.	0–4 Years GRT	5–9 Years No.	5–9 Years GRT	10–14 Years No.	10–14 Years GRT	15–19 Years No.	15–19 Years GRT	20–24 Years No.	20–24 Years GRT	25+ Years No.	25+ Years GRT	Total No.	Total GRT
100– 999	4	2,198	3	374	1	402	1	296	3	1,012	24		36	13,388
1,000– 9,999	1	4,263	2	11,218	—	—	1	2,813	—	—	114		118	821,235
10,000–19,999	4	49,812	3	37,402	—	—	2	27,370	5	71,577	33		47	592,722
20,000–49,999	7	238,676	4	97,220	—	—	—	—	—	—	—		11	335,896
Total	16	294,949	12	146,214	1	402	4	30,479	8	72,589	171		212	1,763,241

SOURCE: *Seatrade U.S. Yearbook 1980*, 2nd edition, Colchester, England: Seatrade Publications Ltd., page 13.

Table 2–5   Age of U.S. Privately Owned Fleet (in years as of July 1, 1979)

Tonnage	Total No.	0–4	5–9	10–14	15–19	20–24	25 plus
10,000–19,999	390	29	17	58	68	33	185
20,000–49,999	152	21	72	14	19	21	5
50,000–99,999	26	20	5	—	1	—	—
100,000–Over	9	7	2	—	—	—	—
Total	577	77	96	72	88	54	190
% of Total	—	15.1	17.0	11.1	16.8	8.8	81.2
Cumulative %	—	15.1	32.1	43.2	60.0	68.8	100.0

SOURCE: *Seatrade U.S. Yearbook 1980*, Colchester, England: Seatrade Publications Ltd., page 13.

Table 2–6   Participation of U.S.-Flag Vessels in U.S. Foreign Trade—1977

	Percent Total Tons	Percent Foreign Trade
U.S. Liner	30.2	30.7
U.S. Nonliner	2.0	2.8
U.S. Tanker	3.3	3.5

SOURCE: Computed from statistics of the Division of Trade and Statistics, Maritime Administration, U.S. Department of Commerce.

Table 2-7 Foreign-Flag Ships Owned by U.S. Companies or Foreign Affiliates of U.S. Companies Incorporated under U.S. Laws (as of December 31, 1977*)

Country of Registry	Total			Tankers			Cargo Vessels			Bulk and Ore Carriers		
	No.	GRT	DWT	No.	GRT	DWT	No.	GRT	DWT	No.	GRT	DWT
Liberia	385	22,401,085	46,023,079	285	19,711,638	40,756,871	13	51,108	80,031	87	2,638,339	5,186,177
United Kingdom	100	3,793,202	7,204,037	58	3,509,793	6,821,811	34	113,037	120,671	8	170,372	261,555
Panama	88	3,244,979	6,306,420	64	3,081,907	6,092,115	17	70,760	61,904	7	92,312	152,401
France	11	1,302,883	2,603,874	11	1,302,883	2,603,874	—	—	—	—	—	—
Germany	8	681,655	1,360,782	8	681,655	1,360,782	—	—	—	—	—	—
Spain	6	670,408	1,301,108	6	670,408	1,301,108	—	—	—	—	—	—
Netherlands	7	565,909	1,109,825	7	565,909	1,109,825	—	—	—	—	—	—
Norway	10	248,517	451,417	10	248,517	451,517	—	—	—	—	—	—
Belgium	7	206,028	353,802	4	94,715	159,645	—	—	—	3	111,313	194,157
Italy	3	149,421	285,054	3	149,421	295,054	—	—	—	—	—	—
Argentina	12	192,168	300,695	7	118,470	180,857	—	—	—	5	73,698	119,838
Denmark	6	91,523	156,550	6	91,523	156,550	—	—	—	—	—	—
Australia	4	113,820	190,773	2	32,469	51,558	—	—	—	2	81,351	139,215
British Colonies	6	78,819	141,141	1	59,267	112,834	5	19,552	28,307	—	—	—
Canada	11	71,881	102,879	11	71,881	102,879	—	—	—	—	—	—
Honduras	13	82,842	83,361	—	—	—	13	82,842	83,361	—	—	—
South Africa	1	18,258	31,102	1	18,258	31,102	—	—	—	—	—	—
Finland	2	4,003	6,288	2	4,003	6,288	—	—	—	—	—	—
Cyprus	1	1,599	2,686	—	—	—	1	1,599	2,686	—	—	—
Greece	6	41,879	56,777	2	25,681	42,285	3	12,127	8,448	1	4,071	6,044
Total	687	33,960,879	68,071,650	488	30,438,398	61,626,855	86	351,025	385,408	113	3,171,456	6,059,387

SOURCE: "Foreign Flag Merchant Ships Owned by U.S. Parent Companies," Maritime Administration, U.S. Department of Commerce, 1978.

* Most recent listing produced.

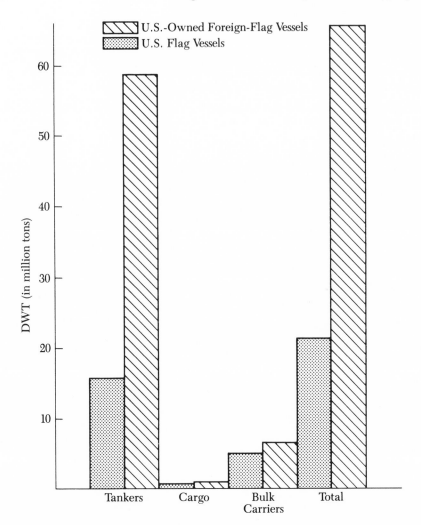

Figure 2-1   U.S.-Owned Merchant Ship Tonnage. *(Source: "Foreign Flag Merchant Ships Owned by U.S. Parent Companies," Maritime Administration, U.S. Department of Commerce, 1978.)*

Table 2–8 U.S. Shipbuilding Output 1952–1977

Year	GRT	Year	GRT
1952	397,017	1966	191,914
1953	600,043	1967	208,841
1954	568,450	1968	367,617
1955	100,180	1969	463,682
1956	126,379	1970	374,907
1957	306,231	1971	489,876
1958	553,339	1972	481,747
1959	769,362	1973	964,165
1960	378,725	1974	733,422
1961	402,169	1975	475,521
1962	397,519	1976	814,530
1963	428,567	1977	1,012,354
1964	249,826	1978	1,033,142
1965	218,345	1979	1,385,312

SOURCE: *Seatrade U.S. Yearbook 1980*, Colchester, England: Seatrade Publications, Ltd., page 21.

Table 2–9   Distribution of U.S. Oceangoing Shipboard Jobs (July 1, 1981)

	Cargo Ships	Tankers	Pass./ Cargo	Total	June 1981	July 1 1980
Total, Private and Government Accounts	12,074	9,899	618	22,591	22,991	22,969
Licensed	3,694	2,863	103	6,660	6,780	6,744
Unlicensed	8,380	7,036	515	15,931	16,211	16,225
Private Account Total	9,771	8,517	618	18,906	19,306	19,814
Licensed	3,074	2,518	103	5,695	5,815	5,953
Unlicensed	6,697	5,999	515	13,211	13,491	13,861
Subsidized Ships	5,110	497	388	5,995	6,061	6,502
Licensed	1,593	171	80	1,844	1,862	1,981
Unlicensed	3,517	326	308	4,151	4,199	4,521
Nonsubsidized Ships	4,661	8,020	230	12,911	13,245	13,312
Licensed	1,481	2,347	23	3,851	3,953	3,972
Unlicensed	3,180	5,673	207	9,060	9,292	9,340
Government Account Total	2,303	1,382	0	3,685	3,685	3,155
Licensed	620	345	0	965	965	791
Unlicensed	1,683	1,037	0	2,720	2,720	2,364
MSC Civil Service Ships	2,303	1,258	0	3,561	3,561	3,062
Licensed	620	301	0	921	921	758
Unlicensed	1,683	957	0	2,640	2,640	2,304
Navy Contract Tankers*	0	124	0	124	124	93
Licensed	0	44	0	44	44	33
Unlicensed	0	80	0	80	80	60

Officer Trainees as of July 1, 1981:†	Federal Aid	Non-Federal Aid	Total
State Maritime Academies	1,874	921	2,795
U.S. Merchant Marine Academy	847	0	847
Total	2,721	921	3,642

SOURCE: U.S. Merchant Marine Data Sheet, U.S. Department of Commerce, Maritime Administration, July 1, 1981.

Note: Estimates are based on established active jobs for licensed and unlicensed personnel aboard oceangoing ships of 1,000 gross tons and over, privately owned and operated; government-owned ships under BBC and GAA, supplemented by MSC employment totals for ships with Civil Service crews; and contract-operated tankers.

* Operated by commercial tanker companies.
† Officer trainee figures are estimated.

Table 2–10 Employment of U.S.-Flag Oceangoing Merchant Fleet as of July 1, 1981: Vessels of 1,000 Gross Tons and Over by Ownership, Status, and Area of Employment (tonnage in thousands)

											Vessel Type				
	Total			Combination Pass. and Cargo			Freighters			Tankers		
Status and Area of Employment	No.	GRT	DWT	No.	GRT	DWT	No.	GRT	DWT	No.	GRT	DWT
Total, Active and Inactive Vessels	859	16,044	24,235	63	682	425	488	6,343	7,506	308	9,019	16,304
Active Vessels	536	12,067	19,017	10	123	84	262	4,262	4,766	264	7,682	14,167
Foreign Trade	199	3,990	5,159	4	45	37	173	3,094	3,424	22	851	1,698
Nearby Foreign	12	184	327	—	—	—	6	34	45	6	150	282
Great Lakes-Seaway Foreign	2	24	29	—	—	—	2	24	29	—	—	—
Overseas Foreign	185	3,782	4,803	4	45	37	165	3,036	3,350	16	701	1,416
Foreign to Foreign	23	1,049	1,155	—	—	—	12	197	190	11	852	965
Domestic Trade	242	5,689	10,465	1	20	8	38	555	633	203	5,114	9,824
Coastwise	115	1,879	3,191	—	—	—	10	138	183	105	1,741	3,008
Intercoastal	60	1,832	3,661	—	—	—	1	14	25	59	1,818	3,636
Noncontiguous	67	1,978	3,613	1	20	8	27	403	425	39	1,555	3,180
Other U.S. Agency Operations	72	1,339	2,238	5	58	39	39	416	519	28	865	1,680
M.S.C. Charter	55	1,196	2,089	—	—	—	29	345	430	26	851	1,659
B.B. Charter & Other Custody	17	143	149	5	58	39	10	71	89	2	14	21

Table 2–10 (continued)

Status and Area of Employment	Total			Combination Pass. and Cargo			Vessel Type Freighters			Tankers		
	No.	GRT	DWT	No.	GRT	DWT	No.	GRT	DWT	No.	GRT	DWT
Inactive Vessels	323	3,977	5,218	53	559	341	226	2,081	2,740	44	1,337	2,137
Temporarily Inactive	30	751	1,238	—	—	—	16	302	401	14	449	837
Laid-Up (Privately Owned)	23	838	1,153	2	30	13	7	81	98	14	727	1,042
Laid-Up (Privately Owned/NDRF)	6	64	66	—	—	—	6	64	66	—	—	—
Laid-Up (MarAd Owned/Other Than NDRF)	10	107	128	1	16	10	8	80	100	1	11	18
Pend. Disp., BB & GAA, etc.	10	107	128	1	16	10	8	80	100	1	11	18
National Defense Reserve Fleet	254	2,217	2,633	50	513	318	189	1,554	2,075	15	150	240
Merchant types	167	1,385	1,878	—	—	—	167	1,385	1,878	—	—	—
Military types	87	832	755	50	513	318	22	169	197	15	150	240

SOURCE: U.S. Merchant Marine Data Sheets, Maritime Administration, Office of Trade Studies and Statistics, Division of Statistics, July 1981.

Note: Figures exclude vessels operating exclusively on the Great Lakes and inland waterways, and those owned by the United States Army and Navy, and special types such as cable ships, tugs, etc.

Table 2–11   U.S. Fleet Size, 1952–1979

Year	No.	GRT	Year	No.	GRT
1952	4,876	27,244,778	1966	3,332	20,797,435
1953	4,800	27,236,876	1967	3,303	20,332,626
1954	4,756	27,344,018	1968	3,232	19,668,421
1955	4,537	26,422,683	1969	3,146	19,550,394
1956	4,432	26,145,642	1970	2,983	18,463,207
1957	4,374	25,910,865	1971	3,327	16,265,669
1958	4,301	25,589,596	1972	3,687	15,024,148
1959	4,196	25,287,972	1973	4,063	14,912,432
1960	4,059	24,837,069	1974	4,086	14,429,076
1961	3,936	24,238,022	1975	4,346	14,586,616
1962	3,749	23,272,856	1976	4,616	14,908,445
1963	3,706	23,132,781	1977	4,740	15,299,681
1964	3,537	22,430,249	1978	4,746	16,187,636
1965	3,416	21,527,349	1979	5,088	17,542,220

SOURCE: *Seatrade U.S. Yearbook 1980*. Colchester, England: Seatrade Publications Ltd., page 17.

2.8.   U.S. Waterborne Trade

U.S. foreign oceanborne trade has tripled in the last 20 years, while domestic oceanborne trade has increased by only 30 percent. This latter fact is due largely to the vast increase in domestic road, rail, and pipeline capacity. This historic change may be expected to shift again as escalating energy costs make coastal water transport increasingly attractive to domestic trade.

In U.S. foreign trade, liquid and dry bulk imports increased most over the last 25 years. Dry bulk imports (mainly coal, phosphate, grain, and so forth) similarly increased more than fourfold. General cargo exports, and even more imports, had a much smaller incline.

The foreign origin and destination of U.S. international oceanborne trade presented in Table 2-12 shows that Asia accounts for only 20.2 percent of U.S. trade by weight; yet, as discussed later, that continent accounts for well over 43 percent of the value of U.S. international trade.

Table 2–12   Comparison of Foreign Origin/Destination of Waterborne U.S. International Trade—1978

World Area	Percentage of Cargo Handled by World Region (Weight Basis)	
	Imports	*Exports*
Western Hemisphere	21.1	21.4
Canada	4.3	10.0
20 Latin American Reps.	10.2	10.4
Other W. Hemisphere	6.6	1.0
Western Europe	5.2	27.7
EEC	3.7	21.9
Other W. Europe	1.5	5.8
Communist Europe	37.5	10.3
Asia	20.2	36.2
Japan	1.7	21.3
Near East	13.4	3.5
Other Asia	5.1	11.4
Australia/Oceania	0.8	0.9
Africa	15.2	3.6

SOURCE: Foreign Trade Statistics 1978, No. FT 155 and FT 455, Bureau of Census, Department of Commerce.

2.8.1. Imports

The United States imports a wide variety of general cargo commodities (Table 2-13). From 1967 to 1977 the value of waterborne general cargo imports entering the United States, measured in constant dollars, grew at an annual rate of 7.9 percent, while personal income grew by only 4.3 percent per annum (see Figure 2-2). The wide fluctuation in value of imports between 1971 and 1976 was due to major economic shifts and cyclic events: the expansion of the U.S. economy from 1971 to 1973; the devaluation of the dollar in 1973, combined with the increase in oil prices and the recession in 1974–75; and, finally, the economic recovery in 1975–77, together with gradual improvement in terms of trade relative to our non-OPEC trading partners.

In 1980 the Bureau of Economic Analysis of the Department of Commerce forecast an annual rate of growth in personal income (in

Table 2–13   Percentage of U.S. Foreign Waterborne Commerce* by Commodity Group (weight basis), 1977

	Imports	*Exports*
Farm products	6.4	3.3
Forest products	1.8	.1
Food and kindred products	8.1	18.2
Tobacco products	—	.1
Basic textiles	1.1	.6
Apparel, finished textile	.6	—
Lumber and wood products	9.6	27.2
Furniture and fixtures	.4	.1
Pulp, paper, printed matter	4.0	6.1
Chemicals and chemical products	15.8	24.7
Rubber and miscellaneous plastic products	.9	.3
Leather	.7	.1
Stone, clay, concrete	5.5	.9
Primary metal products	29.6	2.5
Fabricated metal products	2.7	.7
Machinery (nonelectrical)	2.5	2.8
Machinery (electrical)	1.8	.7
Transport equipment	4.9	1.6
Waste and scrap	.9	8.1
Fish and marine	.9	.1
Other	1.8	1.8

SOURCE: Department of the Army, Corps of Engineers, *Waterborne Commerce of the United States, Calendar Year 1977*.

* Excluding petroleum, coal, coke, metallic ores, non-metallic minerals, petroleum products, grains, and sugar.

Figure 2-2   Change in Value of Waterborne General Cargo Imports, Personal Income, and Relative Prices, 1967–1978. *(Sources: Compiled from Bureau of Economic Analysis data for personal income; Bureau of Census data for imports and PPI; Department of Commerce data.)*

constant dollars) of 3.8 percent from 1980 to 1985, 3.3 percent from 1985 to 1990, and 3.2 percent from 1990 to 2000. During the 1967–1977 period, the value of general cargo imports grew at a rate equal to 1.7 times the rate of growth in personal income. It is assumed that the value of imports will continue to grow faster than personal income because of continuing adjustment in relative prices and an increase in the trade component of the economy. However, the difference between the two growth rates is expected to decrease. The expected growth rates in value of imports for the three periods mentioned above are expected to be 6.0, 5.0, and 3.8 percent,

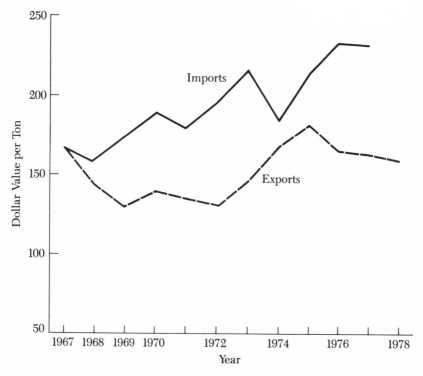

Figure 2-3 Change in Value per Ton of Imports and Exports (in constant dollars). Dollar value is per short ton of U.S. general cargo imports and exports, discounted by Producer Price Index. *(Source: U.S. Department of Commerce, Bureau of Census, Foreign Trade Statistics 1978, FT 155 and FT 455.)*

respectively. (These represent import/income growth ratios of 1.6, 1.5, and 1.2.)

The growth in general cargo import tonnage has been slower than the growth in import value because of the increase in relative prices of imports and a change in the commodity mix. The value per ton of general cargo import increased from 1967 to 1977 at an average of 3.5 percent per year (Figure 2-3); this occurred during a period of decline in the effective exchange rate of the U.S. dollar. This decline is expected to continue through 1990 but at a slower rate. The increase in proportion of high value commodities imported will further increase the cost per ton of import. Because of the uncertainty regarding the rate of increase in value per ton for general cargo imports, a high and a low forecast have been prepared. The former assumes that the per-ton value will increase by 2.5 percent per annum through 1985, then 1.5 percent through 1990, and finally by

Table 2–14   **Forecast of Growth Rates of U.S. Income and U.S. Waterborne General Cargo Import Variables, 1980–2000 (percent)**

	1980–1985	*1985–1990*	*1990–2000*
Personal income (BEA*)	3.8	3.3	3.2
Value	6.0	5.0	3.8
Value per ton: High	2.5	1.5	0.5
Low	1.0	0.5	0.0
Tonnage: High	5.0	4.5	3.8
Low	3.5	3.5	3.3
MarAd†	4.2	2.6	4.7

* Bureau of Economic Analysis.

† Department of Commerce, Office of Policy and Plans, Division of Economic and Operational Analysis, Maritime Administration, *A Long-Term Forecast of U.S. Waterborne Foreign Trade*, November 1977.

0.5 percent through the end of the forecast period. The low forecast assumes that these rates will be 1 percent, 0.5 percent, and 0 percent, respectively. The resulting forecasts of general cargo import tonnage growth rates are shown in Table 2-14.

2.8.2. Exports

The total volume of waterborne general cargo exports from the U.S. increased at a rate of 5.5 percent per annum from 1965 to 1974. The rapid growth in value of general cargo exports between 1972 and 1974 was due to the combination of expanding economic activity abroad and the devaluation of U.S. currency in 1973, which improved the competitive position of U.S. exports. This growth continued through 1974 for general cargo with the deterioration in U.S. terms-of-trade resulting from the quadrupling of oil prices. After 1974 the growth of exports slowed considerably because of the slow rate of economic growth abroad relative to the United States and a reduction in price competitiveness due to the appreciation of the dollar in 1974–75.

The importance of the effects of changes in relative prices on foreign demand for U.S. products makes it extremely difficult to forecast export volume. Changes in relative prices depend on differences in inflation rates and adjustment in exchange rates. In recent years the rapid increase in the cost of petroleum has eroded U.S. terms-of-trade and placed downward pressure on the dollar but, at the same time, a high rate of inflation relative to our trading partners has increased the relative price of U.S. exports. Also, the rate of increase in U.S. industrial productivity has been dropping, thereby reducing U.S. export competitiveness. At the same time, the rate of increase in unit labor costs has not slowed comparably. In the long term, the growth in U.S. general cargo exports will be largely determined by the growth of the economies of the developed and developing nations.

Recent research performed by the Federal Reserve Bank of New York on U.S. export performance indicates that only half of the increase in nonagricultural exports in 1978 could be attributed to the improvement of U.S. price competitiveness that began in 1976. The other half was attributable to cyclical factors, primarily the recovery in economic growth (and investment) of our major trading partners.

A comparison between the growth in foreign gross domestic product (GDP) and imports shows a strong interrelation (see Figure 2-4). Also important is the ratio of investment in capital goods to GNP. Since a large part of U.S. general cargo exports is machinery and equipment, which represent capital investment, the level of investment by our major trading partners is an important determinant of growth in demand for general cargo exports. With some of our major trading partners, the ratio of investment to GNP has been declining, but in Japan and the OPEC countries this figure has been increasing. With increasing economic growth in the less developed nations, it is expected that their investment levels will increase.

Since there is little basis on which to make projections of growth rates in GDP, the ratio of investment to GNP of our major trading partners, and the change in each partner's share of our exports, the projected value of general cargo exports has been based on the assumption that exports will grow at approximately the same rate as imports. Because the total value of imports and exports closely track each other for most countries, a continuing disparity between value of imports and exports would represent a long-term gain or loss in national wealth. Although shifts in terms-of-trade normally prevent this (see Figure 2-5), this relationship is less tight for general cargo.

Since general cargo exports represent a fairly wide mix of commodities, it is not surprising that, when taken in the aggregate, their value in current dollars per ton has risen in proportion to the producer price index (PPI) even though certain commodities may have risen faster or slower than this index (see Figure 2-6). The value per ton of export, discounted by the consumer price index (CPI), is expected to remain relatively constant over the next twenty years as it has over the last ten years, and any fluctuation in exchange rates and relative prices will affect the import values. A major shift in the export commodity mix for general cargo could cause a change

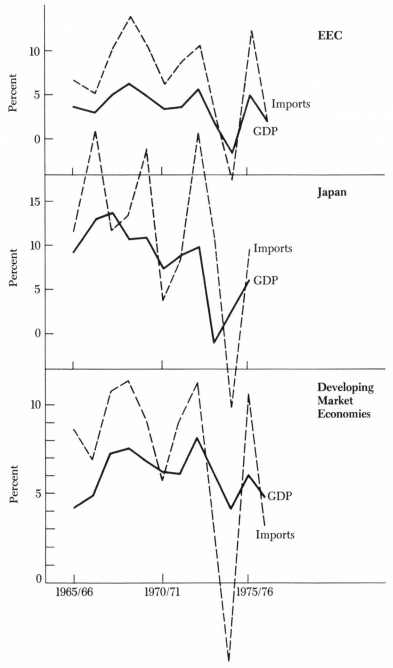

Figure 2-4 Annual Growth Rates of Gross Domestic Product (GDP) and Imports at Constant Prices—EEC, Japan, and Developing Market Economies. *(Source: U.N. Annual Report on National Accounts Statistics, 1978.)*

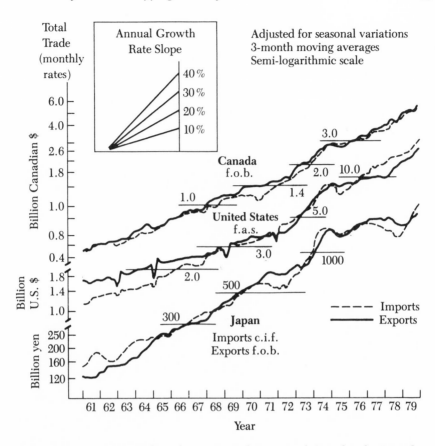

Figure 2-5 Growth in Value of Imports and Exports of Canada, the United States, and Japan, 1960–1979.

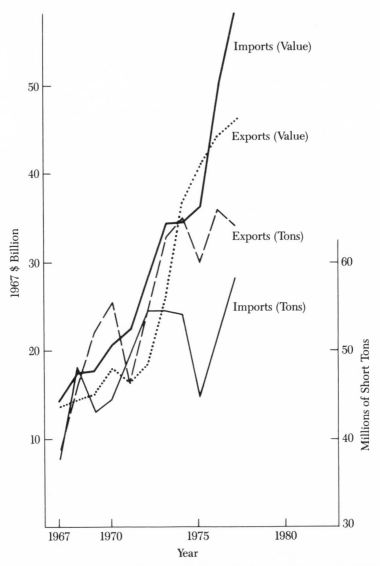

Figure 2-6   Value of U.S. Waterborne General Cargo Imports and Exports 1967–1977. *(Source: Department of Commerce, Maritime Administration, Division of Trade Studies and Statistics, U.S. Waterborne General Cargo Imports and Exports.)*

Table 2–15   Forecast of Growth Rate of U.S. Waterborne General Cargo, Export Tonnage (percent)

	1980–1985	*1985–1990*	*1990–2000*
Masonville Report*	6.0	5.0	3.8
MarAd†	5.7	4.6	5.1

* Based on econometric model in Masonville Marine Terminal Study—Maryland Port Authority, 1981.
† Department of Commerce, Maritime Administration, Office of Policy and Plans, Division of Economic and Operational Analysis, *A Long-Term Forecast of U.S. Waterborne Foreign Trade*, November 1977.

in the value per ton but such a shift is not expected to occur; therefore, a constant value is used to translate the value forecast to a tonnage forecast. Table 2-15 shows the resulting export tonnage growth rates compared with MarAd's growth rates as derived from its U.S. trade forecast.*

2.9.   Comments on U.S. International Trade

The value of U.S. international trade increased by a factor of 2.5 in current prices during the period from 1969 to 1979, as shown in Table 2-16. More importantly, imports and exports as a fraction of U.S. gross domestic product (GDP) increased by 125 percent and 88 percent, respectively. In other words, international trade participation in the GDP more than doubled during this ten-year period

Table 2–16   Relative Size of U.S. International Trade and Its Importance to the U.S. Economy, 1969 and 1979

	U.S. $ billions	
	1969	*1979*
U.S. GDP (current prices)	931.1	2343.5
Total U.S. imports	36.0	206.3
Total U.S. exports	38.0	181.8
Imports as a percentage of U.S. GDP	3.9	8.8
Exports as a percentage of U.S. GDP	4.1	7.7

SOURCES: U.S. Bureau of the Census, Foreign Trade Statistics FT 155 and FT 455; Federal Maritime Commission, "East Asian Trade Study," August 1980; International Monetary Fund, *International Financial Statistics Yearbook*, 1980.

---

* U.S. Department of Commerce, Maritime Administration, *A Long-Term Forecast of U.S. Waterborne Foreign Trade*, November 1977.

and continues to increase as the United States becomes more dependent on foreign trade. The volume of U.S. foreign trade increased similarly from 521 million short tons to over 800 million short tons during that period. The volume of domestic waterborne trade, on the other hand, increased by only about 12 percent with coastwise, lakewise, and local trade declining, while internal (inland water) trade increased significantly.

In summary then, U.S. international trade has an increasing impact on the U.S. economy. More than ever before, shipping policies are therefore required that assure effective terms of shipping of U.S. trade.

Chapter 3

U.S. SHIPPING REGULATION AND GOVERNMENT AID

Most maritime nations regard marine transportation as an area of particular national interest and, accordingly, have formulated specific policies and concomitant regulations toward shipping consistent with their national objectives, method of government, and economic requirements. Generally these policies and regulations can be categorized according to the following goals:

- To meet government transportation requirements in a cost-effective manner;
- To handle a substantial portion of the foreign trade of the country and thereby affect the balance of payments in transportation revenues;
- To effect shipping with particular reference to differential rates in inbound and outbound cargo;
- To maintain the quality of shipping and to generate employment opportunities;
- To provide a market for national shipbuilding sufficient to maintain an economic base;
- To provide ocean transportation properly integrated with domestic services; and
- To encourage technological development in the shipping industry.

Policies toward shipping are usually implemented by regulations and various forms of government aid. The general types of aid employed to realize these policy goals are shown in Table 3-1, and a summary of the major U.S. programs is presented in Table 3-2. In many countries government ownership of national fleets is increasing, particularly in developing countries and countries with planned or centralized economies. (Table 3-3 contains a list of state-owned fleets.)

37

**Table 3–1   Types of Direct or Indirect Government Aid to Shipping and
            Shipbuilding**

Operating subsidies
Construction subsidies
Government construction or ship acquisition loans at low interest
Government operating loans at low interest
Interest subsidies
Credit guarantees (with or without collateral)
Accelerated depreciation
Tax-deferred sinking or reserve funds
Duty-free imports of materials and/or supplies for ship construction
Duty-free imports of materials and/or supplies for ship operation
Tax benefits to operating personnel
Cargo preference (rate and/or carriage)
Cabotage restrictions
Restrictive use laws specifying operations of national flag vessels in domestic and/
   or foreign trade
Exclusive use of domestic and/or government-owned shipping in carriage of
   government-owned or government-controlled cargoes.

In the past, it was unusual for direct operating subsidies to play
an important part in the finances of shipping operations. The major
exception was American-flag shipping where the high wages and
other differential costs made operations without some form of subsidy
virtually impossible. This has changed in recent years as a result of
the large increase in bunkering costs. Italy, France, Spain, Australia,
and Korea, among others, now provide various types of direct payments to private and semiprivate companies engaged in international
shipping. Subsidized items include labor, maintenance, and supply
costs.

In the United States, construction subsidies are much more widely
used. Generally their purpose is to compensate for cost differentials
between American shipbuilders and those of a low-cost shipbuilder
nation. As in most countries, an American owner is not restricted
in the choice of a country for vessel construction. Such subsidies are
more significant to shipyards than to owners.

A number of indirect methods are employed by governments to
assist their shipping and shipbuilding industries. They range from
tax benefits to cargo preference laws, and even to differential pricing
of exports carried in national fleet ships. Countries granting indirect
operating subsidies include the United States, United Kingdom,
Mexico, Norway, Japan, Greece, Italy, Germany, France, Sweden,
and the Republic of China. Many other countries provide indirect
subsidies of varying degrees to their shipping industry.

Financing and protection from competition are given special em-

Table 3-2   Summary of Major Government Programs

Program	Body of Enforcement or Regulation	Recipients	Approximate Annual Cost (1974)	Major Purpose or Requirements
Construction Differential Subsidy (CDS) (Title V)	Maritime Subsidy Board—MarAd*	All U.S. citizen owned U.S.-flag vessels in the foreign commerce of the U.S.	$199 million	Up to 50% of cost for competitive bidding contracts, 35% for negotiated contracts
Operating Differential Subsidy (ODS) (Title VI)	Maritime Subsidy Board—MarAd	U.S.-flag vessels operating on essential foreign trade routes (liners); since 1970 also bulk carriers	$258 million	Cost parity payments covering differential cost of crew (repair and maintenance until 1975) etc.
Mortgage Guarantee (Title XI)	Division of Ship Financing Guarantees—MarAd	All U.S.-built vessels (ocean and inland)	Up to 87.5% of actual costs (75% for subsidized); $7 billion 25-year financing program limit (1975)	U.S. construction for U.S.-flag vessel operation
Construction Loan Guarantee	Division of Ship Financing Guarantees—MarAd	All U.S.-built vessels receiving Title XI		U.S. construction for U.S.-flag vessel operation
Cargo Preference	PL-480, Dept. of Agriculture; AID, Dept. of State; Other government cargoes, various departments such as Defense	All U.S.-flag vessels (including subsidized)	$400 million	Government-owned and/or financed cargo

Table 3–2 (continued)

Program	Body of Enforcement or Regulation	Recipients	Approximate Annual Cost (1974)	Major Purpose or Requirements
Capital Construction Fund (tax exempt)	Internal Revenue Service	All U.S. citizen owners who are qualified operators		No withdrawal except for purposes of ship replacement
Ship Exchange Program	Office of Domestic Shipping—MarAd	All U.S. citizen owners who are qualified operators	$24 million	U.S.-built vessels or U.S.-flag vessels may be exchanged for others in NDRF†
Ship Trade-In Program	Office of Domestic Shipping—MarAd	All U.S. citizen owners who are qualified operators	$6 million	Subsidized operators trade in replacement vessel upon delivery of new subsidized ship
Investment Tax Credit	Internal Revenue Service	All U.S. citizen owners who are qualified operators		Investment in new or used ships
Research and Development	Admin. for Commercial Development—MarAd	All U.S. maritime industry; most programs now based on cost sharing	$32 million	
Cabotage	Jones Act; MarAd	U.S.-flag vessels without subsidy		Restriction of vessels to domestic routes
War Risk Insurance (Title XII)	MarAd (expired 1975)	All vessels in U.S. trade		

Source: U.S. Maritime Administration.

* Federal Maritime Administration.
† National Defense Reserve Fleet.

Table 3–3 Selected Countries with Government-Owned Shipping Fleets

Argentina	Libya
Brazil	Malaysia
Chile	Mexico
Colombia	New Zealand
France	Nigeria
Ghana	Pakistan
India	Peru
Indonesia	Spain
Iran	Taiwan
Ireland	Thailand
Israel	Turkey
Italy	Uruguay
Kuwait	Venezuela

SOURCE: Records of the Federal Maritime Commission, 1980.

phasis by many countries when formulating their respective maritime support programs. For example, special taxation policies are adopted by nearly all nations. These are necessary if a country wishes to maintain its own merchant marine since a ship operation can easily be conducted from almost any location. In the absence of strict controls on foreign investment, special taxation policies, or cargo preference rules, the bulk of a country's merchant marine will gravitate to an organization exploiting tax-free countries (such as Liberia and Panama) for a base of operation. Tax benefits generally occur in the form of: (1) depreciation through escalation (write-offs); (2) direct tax reduction by allowing nontaxable reserve funds; (3) elimination of income tax on earnings; and, (4) reduction of duty on material imports used by the maritime industry. Special or accelerated depreciation is the most popular method of indirect government aid.

3.1. The Role of the Federal Government in U.S. Maritime Transportation

The objectives of U.S. maritime transportation policy have remained relatively constant over 200 years, although priority or emphasis has changed quite often. The major policy objective traditionally has been to assure a provision of marine transportation that will both fairly serve the needs of the public and provide an adequate defense and emergency capability. Providing shipping capability needed for national defense, development of commerce, and protection of American economic interests from noncompetitive market influences continue to be the primary objectives of U.S. ocean shipping policy.

Two other important policy objectives deserve mention. One is a broad maritime policy objective of providing capability to "show the flag" around the world. The other implicitly established, and equally important, objective is to achieve maritime goals with maximum efficiency and minimum waste.

The development of an internationally competitive American merchant marine has long been regarded as a critical factor in the realization of U.S. maritime objectives. Both the language and legislative history of the Merchant Marine Act of 1936[1] indicate that this legislation was intended to help develop an American merchant fleet that would be competitive with foreign-flag fleets. The Act's authorization of operating subsidies aims to reach this goal and has been the primary tool of Congress in its efforts to help American shippers reach parity with foreign competitors.[2]

The goal of providing shipping for national defense or the national security, as discussed before, is to provide the shipping capability required to move military cargo and to move imports needed for the support of essential sectors of the national economy during periods of emergency.

The second basic objective of marine transport—providing shipping for the development of commerce—is difficult to define in quantitative terms. While this objective is related to the economic component of the national security objective, it is in fact separate insofar as it is concerned with the import and export shipping required to support the development and growth of the economy. This commercial development objective, most frequently defined in terms of economic benefits, is often satisfied by the ability to influence freight rates and, consequently, trade participation and balance of payment. Basic economic objectives include:

- Assurance of fair and reasonable freight rates for U.S. imports and exports. (Without representation in the conferences, associations of liner operators which serve its foreign trade, the U.S. could be vulnerable to rate discrimination. However, the potential availability of significant numbers of National Defense Reserve Fleet (NDRF) ships could be used to counteract unilateral and unfair rate increases.)
- Significant contribution to U.S. balance of payments.
- Employment for U.S. citizens and merchant seamen; the latter reinforce U.S. maritime mobilization capability in time of war.
- Promotion of U.S. foreign trade.

Providing the nation with adequate and efficient port facilities is an essential element in meeting national defense and economic objectives through foreign trade. As merchant ships are only one segment of a complex transportation system, ports and related facilities must be developed to optimize overall system performance. Therefore, a further objective is the development of a phased and balanced U.S. port capability and the establishment of compatible ocean transportation system components with their multimodal feeders.

Specific quantitative objectives have not been established in this area. The general objective of assuring provision of essential shipping services to facilitate the flow of U.S. foreign and domestic commerce is obviously affected by technological advancements in the shipping industry and by changing national shipping requirements. Emphasis has been placed on developing ports and related facilities to take advantage of integrated intermodal transportation systems. This provides for the efficient movement of needed raw material imports.

While the objectives of foreign and domestic shipping have remained consistent for a long time, the objectives of inland water transportation have been less well defined. In fact, inland water transportation has for a long time been given little official attention. It is only recently that new inland water transport policies have been introduced that reflect the prevailing pressures on government regarding energy conservation and river pollution.

The programs currently in operation by the federal government to achieve its maritime objectives include:

Direct Financial Aid Programs
- Construction Differential Subsidy (CDS)
- Operation Differential Subsidy (ODS)
- Mortgage loan guarantees
- Construction financing

Indirect Financial Aid Programs
- Cargo preference
- Investment tax credit
- Tax-free capital construction fund
- Ship exchange and trade-in programs

Other Programs
- National Defense Reserve Fleet (NDRF)
- Port development assistance
- Research and development funding

Regulatory Programs
- Common carrier freight rates in domestic shipping
- Vessel safety requirements
- Environmental concerns in ports and inland waterways

Table 3–4   Components and Proposals of U.S. Government Aid Programs

Financial Assistance	Cargo and Revenue Assistance	Administrative Assistance	Incentive Assistance
Per diem subsidy	Cargo sharing agreements	Closed conferences	ODS (based on record)
Construction Differential Subsidy (CDS)	Closed conferences	Standardized design	Profit sharing
Capital shipyard loans	Other pooling	Shippers councils	
Construction Capital Fund (CCF)	Defense	Advisory committee	Low bid cargo sharing and preference contracts
Depreciation rules	Cargo preference		
Investment tax credit	Shipping pools		
Tax rebate	U.S. mail		
Operation Differential Subsidy (ODS)	Domestic and foreign trading		
Mortgage guarantee	Coastwise trading		
Construction loans	Relaxation of essential trade routes		
Elimination of excess profit recapture			

SOURCE: Extracted from Shipping Act of 1916, Merchant Marine Act of 1936, and Merchant Marine Act of 1970.

Government aid programs and proposed programs organized by type and area are shown in Table 3-4.

Economically, the largest policy and program variable available to the government is the income tax policy. (Taxation issues and regulatory programs are considered in detail in Chapter 4 of this volume.)

An important factor influencing future maritime transportation and resulting policy is the rapid growth of maritime nationalism by countries in the Persian Gulf, Africa, South America, and South/South East Asia. It is significant that the communist and Third World or developing countries are the major proponents of maritime nationalism.

3.1.1. Legislative Background of U.S. Maritime Policy

U.S. maritime policy has evolved over a long period of time and the nature of this evolutionary process has been characterized by responses to the problems raised by the implementation of prior policies.[3] Maritime legislation currently in force is a patchwork of congressional reactions to political exigencies and pressures exerted by special interest groups rather than a coordinated program inspired by a consistent commitment to the development and support of the merchant marine.

The first American maritime policy legislation was enacted in 1789. It introduced preferential tariffs which exacted a higher duty upon imports carried by foreign bottoms than by U.S. bottoms. The need to maintain U.S.-flag shipping moved the government to provide aid in the form of ocean mail contracts. This form of financial aid was supplemented and expanded by laws enacted by the Congress in May, 1864, and in March, 1891. Despite these aids, ship ownership remained a prohibitive financial risk. As a result, the United States had virtually no merchant marine at the outbreak of World War I. The United States was consequently unable either to provide the shipping service necessary to maintain its economy or to meet its military needs at the time.

This situation led to the passage of the Shipping Act of 1916,[4] which authorized the organization of the Emergency Fleet Corporation to carry out a shipbuilding and ownership program to support the war effort. By early 1920, the Emergency Fleet Corporation had built or acquired over 1,750 merchant ships. The Act enunciated, for the first time, the primary objective of the U.S. maritime policy and also stated the corresponding policies supporting those objectives.

The Merchant Marine Act of 1936[5] and subsequent amendments incorporated secondary objectives. One such objective was to exert economic muscle by the significant participation of U.S.-flag vessels in major foreign trade routes in order to prevent the imposition of rates discriminating against U.S. trade by foreign shipping interests.

The Shipping Act of 1916[6] created the United States Shipping Board, charged with the duty of identifying unfair practices in the maritime industry and declaring such practices illegal. Section 204(a) of the Merchant Marine Act of 1936[7] then replaced the United States Shipping Board with the United States Maritime Commission. Congress did not intend the Shipping Act of 1916 to establish a new administrative independence for maritime regulation; Section 33 of the Act[8] stated that its action should neither be construed as affecting the power or jurisdiction of the Interstate Commerce Commission (ICC) nor as applying to interstate commerce. The apparent thrust of this section was retention of the autonomy of the ICC and recognition that jurisdictional or policy conflicts should be resolved in favor of the ICC. Thus, through legislative enactment, the ICC's jurisdiction over coastwise and intercoastal shipping was preserved.

The end of World War I brought an end to the need for a government-owned merchant fleet. The Merchant Marine Act of 1920[9] was enacted to dispose the fleet acquired persuant to the Act of 1916. Congress declared in Section 1 of the 1920 Act:[10]

> *That it is necessary for the national defense and for the proper growth of its foreign and domestic commerce that the United States shall have a merchant marine of the best equipped and most suitable types of vessels sufficient to carry the greater portion of its commerce and serve as a naval or military auxiliary in time of war or national emergency, ultimately to be owned and operated privately by citizens of the United States; and it is hereby declared to be the policy of the United States to do whatever may be necessary to develop and encourage the maintenance of such a merchant marine, and, insofar as may not be inconsistent with the express provisions of this Act, the United States Shipping Board shall, in the disposition of vessels and shipping property as hereinafter provided, in the making of rules and regulations, and in the administration of the shipping laws keep always in view this purpose and object as the primary end to be obtained.*

This policy was reaffirmed by both the Merchant Marine Act of 1928[11] (which contained additional provisions for ocean mail contracts), and Section 1 of the Merchant Marine Act of 1936.[12]

The Merchant Marine Act of 1970,[13] presented as a rededication by Congress of its commitment to the American merchant marine, was in fact prompted by alarm over reaction to U.S. military posture in Vietnam. This alarm was triggered by the refusal, in protest, of a foreign crew to transport materials to support U.S. efforts in Vietnam. The language of the Act did, however, reaffirm the objectives promoted by its legislative predecessors. Its passage evinced congressional recognition of the increasing importance of foreign trade and offshore developments and the significant role to be played by the U.S.-flag merchant marine in the economic growth and security of this country. The Act increased support for all types of vessels in the essential U.S. foreign trade and thereby qualified foreign-going bulk carriers and other nonliner vessels for Construction Differential Subsidy (CDS) and (under some conditions) Operating Differential

Subsidy (ODS). It also expanded the merchant shipbuilding program with a plan for the construction of 300 new vessels over a ten-year period.

The various maritime initiatives made by Congress, however, have not amounted to a successful program because government, business, and labor for years have pursued their individual interests at the expense of promoting and perpetuating a sound maritime policy. This has led to a gradual reduction in the size and capacity of the U.S.-flag fleet, with consequent decrease in business opportunities and lessening of U.S. influence in military, political, and economic spheres. As long as tunnel-vision lobbying and administrative responses continue as the *modus operandi* for American maritime policymaking, American shipping and shipbuilding will continue to stagnate. Because U.S. shipping and shipbuilding are essential factors in U.S. defense and economic strategy, this depressed state represents a profound threat to America's ability to meet the heightened economic, political, and military challenges currently confronting the nation. The United States must contend with these challenges in the future.

3.2. Regulation of Aids to U.S. Shipping

3.2.1. Bureaucratic Structure

Maritime regulation includes economic regulation and safety or service regulation. Economic regulation of domestic trade is largely performed by the Interstate Commerce Commission (ICC) and Federal Trade Commission (FTC); foreign and offshore domestic trade is regulated by the Federal Maritime Commission (FMC). Safety and service regulation is a function of the United States Coast Guard (USCG) in the Department of Transportation (DOT), although Coast Guard jurisdiction in inland waterways is rather restricted. The FTC and ICC provide some safety and service regulation, as do the Departments of Health and Human Services, Interior, Agriculture, Defense, Commerce, Treasury, and State.

The U.S. Maritime Administration (MarAd) is the federal agency responsible for allocating all forms of government aid and service to the U.S. merchant marine. It provides financial assistance for construction and operation of vessels in the essential U.S. foreign trade, and its subsidy board determines subsidy eligibility.

MarAd promotes and undertakes maritime research and development. In addition, it supports the development of domestic and

inland water transportation and the U.S. fishing industry; operates
the U.S. Merchant Marine Academy at Kings Point, New York;
controls issuance of mortgage guarantees and war risk insurance
coverage; supports state and civilian nautical schools; administers the
National Defense Reserve Fleet (NDRF) and the associated Ship
Trade-In and Exchange Programs; and supports the general commercial development of the U.S. merchant marine. In carrying out
these functions, MarAd administers the following major programs:
Construction Differential Subsidy (CDS), Operating Differential
Subsidy (ODS), Federal Mortgage and Loan Insurance Program, and
the Capital Construction Fund. The PL-480 Cargo Preference Pro-
gram generally comes under the jurisdiction of the Department of
Agriculture.

The Environmental Protection Agency (EPA), pursuant to the
authority of the National Environmental Policy Act (NEPA) of 1969,[14]
reviews the planning and implementation of many aspects of inland
waterway construction and maintenance for compliance with environmental requirements. As a result, the Army Corps of Engineers
must tailor its navigational channel and inland water project planning
approach to meet EPA requirements. Additional regulations affecting
waterway projects administered by the EPA are the Federal Water
Pollution Control Act Amendments of 1972[15] and the Marine Protection, Research, and Sanctuaries Act of 1972.[16] These statutes
modify the method and degree of dredging operations conducted for
inland water construction and maintenance of navigation improvement projects. The Coast Guard is responsible for regulation and
inspection of marine environmental pollution under both the Port
and Tanker Safety Act of 1978[17] (discussed in detail in Chapter 4)
and the Federal Water Pollution Control Act Amendments of 1972.[18]

The regulation of ports and coastal channels largely overlaps. The
Corps of Engineers regulates the type and location of port construction from the point of view of navigable channels, and prepares
pertinent environmental impact statements. The Coast Guard performs all controls and inspections that relate to operations, life, and
property safety. The Captains of the ports, usually Coast Guard
officers, are responsible for all matters of safety and security of the
ports. The new National Environmental Policy Act (NEPA) requirements are administered by the Coast Guard, which is responsible
for implementing all aspects of the NEPA of 1969,[19] the 1973 Convention on the Prevention of Pollution from Ships, the Federal Water
Pollution Control Act Amendments of 1972,[20] the Marine Protection,
Research, and Sanctuaries Act of 1972,[21] and other federal laws and
regulations for marine environments.

3.2.2. Agency Structure—International Shipping

The Federal Maritime Commission (FMC) authorizes the setting of international sea freight rates and conference policies and regulates against the imposition of illegal rebates and discriminations by carriers. It also investigates complaints of seagoing violations of the Shipping Act of 1916. Similarly, the Commission investigates privileges afforded and burdens imposed by foreign governments upon U.S.-flag vessels engaged in foreign trade. Additionally, it approves rates in foreign commerce, though this function is severely restricted by the need for multinational cooperation.

Common carriers, contract carriers, private carriers, and freight forwarders must register with the FMC and obtain certificates; tramp shipping is outside the jurisdiction of the FMC. Private and contract carriers, while filing to obtain certificates through the FMC, need not file tariffs and are essentially unregulated. Only common carriers and freight forwarders are required to file tariffs. These are scrutinized by the FMC, which frequently disallows rate changes. Because changes in conditions of the contract of carriage (bill of lading) can in fact represent rate changes (increasing the number of days of free storage from three to four if a rate decrease occurs), the contracts made by common carriers are also subject to regulation by the FMC.

The Bureau of Customs handles the registry of vessels, issues certificates of admeasurement (the basis for computing tonnage tax), collects duties on imported merchandise, and enforces the coastwise laws. Customs officers also prepare reports that supply the basic data for statistical reports on commerce and navigation which the Secretary of Commerce submits to Congress.

The USCG is the law enforcement agency of the government on the water[22] and, pursuant to Executive Order, has been assigned responsibility for the protection and security of vessels, harbors, and waterfront facilities. In general terms the Coast Guard regulations state as their functions:

- Maritime law enforcement;
- Saving and protecting life and property;
- Safeguarding navigation on the high seas and navigable waters in the United States; and
- Preparedness for military operations.

These responsibilities are delegated to the District Commander in each of the several Coast Guard Districts in the United States.

The Federal Communications Commission (FCC) has jurisdiction over radio channels and equipment on board vessels, with certain exemptions for government-owned and -operated radio facilities. The Coast and Geodetic Survey provides information for navigation safety.

3.3.   Federal Financial Aid—Regulatory Background and Programs

This section summarizes the most significant laws, regulations and financial aid programs affecting U.S. maritime shipping according to three areas of impact: (1) shipbuilding and operation, (2) taxation, and (3) rate regulation. U.S. government entities with authority in one or more of these areas include the Department of the Treasury, the Maritime Administration, the Federal Maritime Commission, the U.S. Coast Guard, and the Army Corps of Engineers.

The U.S. merchant marine has received government support for the last 100 years (largely through mail contracts), but has enjoyed direct subsidy only since the passage of the Merchant Marine Act in 1936.[23] New ship mortgage insurance was introduced by the Ship Mortgage Act of 1920,[24] but again, the concept of construction loan and direct construction and operation subsidy did not arrive until 1936. There have been numerous amendments since then. However, the basic policy as stated in the Merchant Marine Act of 1936 continues as the basis for maritime policy.[25]

Fostering Development and Maintenance of Merchant Marine

It is necessary for the national defense and development of its foreign and domestic commerce that the United States shall have a merchant marine

(a) sufficient to carry its domestic waterborne commerce and a substantial portion of the waterborne export and import foreign commerce of the United States and to provide shipping service essential for maintaining the flow of such domestic and foreign waterborne commerce at all times, (b) capable of serving as a naval and military auxiliary in time of war or national emergency, (c) owned and operated under the United States flag by citizens of the United States, insofar as may be practicable, (d) composed of the best-equipped, safest, and most suitable types of vessels, constructed in the United States and manned with a trained and efficient citizen personnel, and (e) supplemented by efficient facilities for ship building and ship repair. It is declared to be the policy of the United States to foster the development and encourage the maintenance of such a merchant marine.

Congress realized that liner service on essential trade routes, though obviously important, was only one element in foreign trade. Therefore, in the Merchant Marine Act (MMA) of 1970, the direct subsidy program was extended to include support for liquid and dry bulk carriers operating in the foreign commerce of the United States.[26] The interpretation of foreign commerce was subsequently liberalized to include foreign voyages.

3.3.1. Programs Administered by the Maritime Administration (MarAd)

Direct government financial aid to U.S. shipping is administered through two MarAd subsidy programs, the Construction Differential Subsidy and the Operating Differential Subsidy, as well as through the Title XI Federal Ship Mortgage and Loan Insurance Program. Legislation establishing operating and construction subsidies was originally provided in the Merchant Marine Act of 1936, and ship mortgage insurance was first introduced in the Ship Mortgage Act of 1920. These three aid programs are outlined below.

3.3.1.1. MMA Title V Construction Differential Subsidy (CDS)

The basic policy of CDS is described in Section 501(a) of the MMA:[27]

> *Any proposed ship purchaser who is a citizen of the United States or any shipyard of the United States may make application to the Secretary of Commerce for a construction differential subsidy to aid in the construction of a new vessel to be used in the foreign commerce of the United States. No such application shall be approved by the Secretary of Commerce unless he determines that (1) the plans and specifications call for a new vessel which will meet the requirements of the foreign commerce of the United States, will aid in the promotion and development of such commerce, and be suitable for use by the United States for national defense or military purposes in time of war or national emergency; (2) if the applicant is the proposed ship purchaser, the applicant possesses the ability, experience, financial resources, and other qualifications necessary for the operation and maintenance of the proposed new vessel, and (3) the granting of the aid applied for is reasonably calculated to carry out effectively the purposes and policy of this chapter.*

The basis of the CDS subsidy is cost parity. The CDS subsidy calculations are based on either negotiated shipbuilding contracts or the difference between U.S. competitive bids and the lowest cost foreign bid for an equivalent vessel submitted by a qualified foreign builder. The former procedure, which allows ship purchases and shipbuilders to negotiate merchant shipbuilding contracts, was initiated in the Merchant Marine Act of 1970 with a recommended

CDS ceiling of 45 percent, to decline at 2 percent per annum to 35 percent in 1976, at which time the negotiated contract procedure was to cease. In 1976 Congress extended the procedure to June 30, 1979,[28] and the recommended CDS ceiling was raised to 50 percent, the legal limit under MMA of 1970. MarAd retained the authority to ensure that the CDS and negotiated price properly reflect current market conditions. Congress has not provided for a reextension of the negotiated contract procedure.

Under the competitive bidding procedure, the Maritime Administration, after approving a CDS subsidy request, solicits bids from U.S. shipbuilders for construction of the vessel and generally awards the contract to the low bidder. The competitive bidding procedure also has a 50 percent CDS subsidy ceiling. This procedure predates the negotiated price method enacted in the MMA of 1970, but was not as popular during the 1970s until the declining ceiling of the negotiated price method rendered its use uneconomical. On January 9, 1976, the Maritime Subsidy Board (MSB) gave formal approval to operators receiving CDS subsidies to solicit competitive bids for ships to be built with CDS funds. The ceiling for this purpose was 50 percent.

As the competitive bidding procedure favors more efficient shipping yards, use of this procedure entails lower construction costs, which reduce the required direct governmental subsidy. But because of this intrinsic preference for cost and operational efficiency, the competitive bidding procedure foreclosed profitable existence through successful bidding for many less efficient shipbuilding yards. The return to a competitive bidding procedure will thus likely be accompanied by the shutdown of many such yards. Consequently Congressmen from the districts where less efficient yards are located will predictably exert strong pressure to reextend the negotiated contract procedure so that yards can return to viability.

The 1970 Merchant Marine Act (MMA) modified the construction differential subsidy to restrict subsidy payments to a declining fixed percentage of costs and assumed a phase-out of Title V by 1980;[29] however, recent legislation has raised the subsidy ceilings and it is unclear that the original goal of a 1980 phase-out will be met. Since 1970 all new ships constructed for service in the essential foreign U.S. trade qualify for CDS.

3.3.1.2. MMA Title VI Operating Differential Subsidy (ODS)

The operating differential subsidy is also based on the cost parity principle. It was restricted, like CDS, to liners serving essential foreign trade routes, a restriction lifted by the 1970 Act. The basic policy is stated in Section 601(a) of the MMA:[30]

> *The Secretary of Commerce is authorized and directed to consider the application of any citizen of the United States for financial aid in the operation of a vessel or vessels, which are to be used in an essential service in the foreign commerce of the United States or in such service and in cruises authorized under Section 613 of this title (46 U.S.C. 1183). . . . No such application shall be approved by the Secretary of Commerce unless he determines that (1) the operation of such vessel or vessels in an essential service* is required to meet foreign-flag competition and to promote the foreign commerce of the United States *. . . and that such vessel or vessels were built in the United States, or have been documented under the laws of the United States not later than February 1, 1928, or actually ordered and under construction for the account of citizens of the United States prior to such date; (2) the applicant owns, or leases or can and will build or purchase, or lease, a vessel or vessels of the size, type, speed, and number, and with the proper equipment required to enable him to operate in an essential service, in such manner as may be* necessary to meet competitive conditions, *and to promote foreign commerce: (3) the applicant possesses the ability, experience, financial resources, and other qualifications necessary to enable him to* conduct the proposed operations of the vessel or vessels as to meet competitive conditions and to promote foreign commerce; *(4) the granting of the aid applied for is necessary to place the proposed operations of the vessel or vessels on a parity with those of foreign competitors, and is reasonably calculated to carry out effectively the purposes and policy of this chapter.* (Emphasis added.)

The ODS program, unlike the CDS program, requires that the subsidy be necessary "to meet foreign-flag competition" as well as "to promote the foreign commerce of the United States." Only U.S.-built and crewed ships are eligible. The objective of the subsidy is to establish operating cost parity between U.S.- and foreign-flag operators. Included in the operating costs are: wages for officers and crews; maintenance and repair; and insurance, both hull and machinery as well as protection and indemnity.

In an attempt to reduce the ODS, the Maritime Subsidy Board began, in late 1975, to eliminate maintenance and repair costs from the list of subsidizable items.

The expansion of the coverage of ODS to bulk carriers was accomplished by the MMA of 1970, but the Act failed to specify how these subsidies should be calculated. Instead, the Act gave MarAd discretion to provide whatever subsidy was needed to establish parity in operating costs between a U.S.-flag, U.S.-built vessel in an essential bulk-carrying service and a similar vessel under foreign registry.

Because the ODS attempts to maintain parity between U.S. operating expenses and foreign operating costs, the costs of unilateral U.S. wage increases were passed on to the government. Maritime operators thus had little incentive for taking a tough bargaining position. In 1971 the Maritime Administration began using calculation of "subsidizable wage costs" which were linked to a wage index for other industries rather than to maritime wage increases; however, constraints were placed of ±10 percent on the deviation of the actual wage costs from the "subsidizable wage cost."

The operating differential subsidy is contracted for up to 20 years for bulk carriers. The applicant must not only demonstrate financial capability to meet the long-term commitment, but must also maintain certain minimums of working capital and net worth to distribute dividends according to a conservative dividend policy.

Contractors for ODS funds may not participate in domestic trade unless the contractor was involved in domestic trade since 1935 and limits his activity to the 1935 level. Also, contractors who are not already involved in a specific trade with U.S.-flag vessels cannot enter that trade if there are other U.S.-flag operator(s) involved and their service is considered adequate.

3.3.1.3. MMA *Title XI Federal Ship Mortgage and Loan Insurance Program*

Perhaps the most successful of all government activities connected with the merchant marine is the Title XI Federal Ship Mortgage Insurance Program. The United States government insures commercial loans and mortgages to finance a fixed proportion (up to 87.5 percent for nonsubsidized vessels and 75 percent for subsidized vessels) of the "actual cost" of construction, reconstruction, or reconditioning of U.S.-built merchant and inland water vessels, oceangoing tugs and barges, and some other types of vessels. This insurance is authorized and defined by Title XI of the Merchant Marine Act of 1936 as currently amended,[31] and general guidelines for its implementation are published in the Code of Federal Regulations.[32] The program is administered by the Secretary of Commerce acting through the Assistant Secretary for Maritime Affairs (Head of the Maritime Administration). It is expected, though, that MarAd will be transferred to the Department of Transportation before the end of 1981, with a consequent change of responsibility for the program to the Secretary of Transportation.

Title XI mortgage insurance covers both interest and unpaid balance. It extends over the economic life of a vessel (up to 25 years), while most foreign countries offer vessel financing for a maximum duration of only seven years. Because this guarantee extends for up to 25 years, debt financing can be spread out over the life of the ship. The vessel can then be leased on a long-term basis, market conditions permitting. The lease may be used as collateral for the additional 12.5 to 25 percent construction cost. Together, the long-term lease and government guarantee minimize the equity financing required while ensuring a steady income for the vessel owner.

The statutory limit on total principal and interest which may be insured under the Title XI program is now $7 billion, the ceiling having been raised in several steps from the $1 billion figure in the 1970 Merchant Marine Act to $7 billion in 1975.[33]

3.3.2. Cargo Preference Acts

A number of Preference Acts and Public Laws authorize or direct government agencies to ship preferentially and at negotiated non-competitive terms on U.S.-flag vessels. Cargoes so covered are foreign-aid and food-for-peace cargoes, military assistance cargoes, household articles of federal employees (including military personnel), and all types of cargoes owned by or shipped for or on behalf of the federal government. A high portion of U.S. general cargo vessels are dependent on preference cargo for their continuing operation.

Some components of preference cargoes, such as agricultural goods, are usually shipped 50 percent in U.S. bottoms, provided shipping capacity is available at "reasonable" rates. The freight rates allowed U.S. operators under preference laws are usually such as to allow fair and reasonable profits to the marginal operators offering shipping capacity.

The history of cargo preference dates to the beginning of the century and includes:

- 1904: Provision that American military cargo be shipped on American vessels;
- 1935: Federal law requiring that cargoes obtained through government loans be shipped on American vessels;[34]
- Merchant Marine Act (MMA) of 1936: Created certain classes of preference cargo—U.S. mail[35] (Section 405, since repealed) and federal employees required to travel on U.S. ships (Section 901a);[36] and
- 1954: Federal law requiring 50 percent of relief and aid cargoes to be carried in U.S.-flag vessels.[37]

In addition, Sections 506[38] and 605(a)[39] of the 1936 MMA provided for reductions in subsidies for American ships carrying domestic cargo protected from foreign competition.

The question of subsidies combined with carriage of preference cargo has been widely disputed. The MSB proposed a rule requiring subsidized lines to carry at least 50 percent nonpreference cargo. For vessels earning less than 50 percent of freight revenues from nonpreference cargo, the rule proposed a schedule of proportional reduction in subsidies. This rule was upheld in the 1975 case of *States Marine International, Inc. v. Peterson.*[40] The court found that vessels carrying preference cargo were eligible both for CDS and ODS and that the Board, acting for the Secretary of Commerce, had discretionary authority to limit ODS. The central findings of the Court in *States Marine* are presented below, providing a summary of present thinking regarding the maritime subsidy programs.

> *The Merchant Marine Act was intended to help develop an American merchant fleet that would be competitive with foreign flag fleets. It established an operating differential subsidy which was intended to be paid in order to meet foreign competition, and was not intended to compensate shippers which had no actual or potential competition from foreign lines. The Act does not prohibit the carriage of preference cargo by subsidized carriers, nor does it preclude the payment of any operating differential subsidies to vessels carrying preference cargo.*
>
> *Under Section 204 of the Act authorizing the Secretary of Commerce to adopt all necessary rules and regulations to carry out the powers, duties, and functions vested in him by the Act, the Secretary, and through him the Maritime Subsidy Board, has broad discretionary authority to deal with the ever-changing technological and economic conditions of the commercial shipping industry as long as its actions are reasonable and consistent with the Act.*
>
> *In view of the provision in all operating differential subsidy contracts that failure to comply with any rule or regulation by the Maritime Administration relating to operation of subsidized vessels would constitute an event of default under the contract, each contract was subject to any reasonable interpretation of the Merchant Marine Act by the Maritime Administration and any rule or regulation, applied prospectively, implementing such implementation. Hearings, which were conducted by the Maritime Subsidy Board in connection with rulemaking proceedings to consider relationship between operating differential subsidy and preference cargo, which were extensive, and in which all interested parties presented evidence and briefs in support of their respective positions, constituted a "proper hearing" within section 606 of the Merchant Marine Act providing for board review and readjustment of future operating differential subsidy payments.*
>
> *Long-standing administrative interpretation of foreign-flag competition requirements of the Merchant Marine Act and absence of af-*

firmative action by Congress to change that interpretation did not preclude the Maritime Subsidy Board from changing its policy through adoption of a proposed rule requiring subsidized shipping lines to carry at least 50% non-preference cargo and providing for a proportional reduction in subsidies for vessels earning less than 50% of freight revenues through non-preference cargo, in view of the factual situation and relevant statutes.

A vessel built with a construction differential subsidy may engage in carriage of preference cargo without abatement of subsidy. Congress, in enacting the Merchant Marine Act, did not intend to relate payment of construction differential subsidy to the vessel's actual involvement in foreign competition, nor require a rebate of the subsidy when a recipient ship hauls preference cargo.

3.3.3.   Selected Defense and Domestic Shipping Regulatory Programs

The Jones Act and acts affecting the use of the National Defense Reserve Fleet were enacted by Congress to provide indirect financial support to some segments of the U.S. shipping industry.

3.3.3.1.   National Defense Reserve Fleet (NDRF)

The NDRF was created by the Merchant Ship Sales Act of 1946,[41] whereby vessels owned by the government[42] were to be retained and maintained for the national defense. Other provisions of the Act enabled the government to reduce the huge ship inventory accumulated during World War II through sales to private citizens. The government has, in the past, depended upon the NDRF to satisfy projected ship requirements for such emergencies as might arise. Since Congress has not altered the language of Section 11(a) since 1950, the policy of maintaining a reserve fleet to fill deficiencies in shipping capacity in times of emergency continues. Congress reaffirmed its expressed view of using the NDRF to help upgrade the U.S. merchant marine by the Exchange Act of 1960[43] (extended to 1970), whereby Congress made ships in the NDRF available for operation by U.S. citizens, and the Vessel Trade-In Act.

Since 1946 the federal government has spent a total of $145 million for annual upkeep expenditures of the NDRF, in addition to the cost of establishing the anchorages and facilities. During the 1952 Korean conflict, 541 inactive reserve and 335 chartered-reserve ships, or almost 900 vessels, were provided by logistics support. During the 1956–57 Suez crisis the NDRF augmented the commercial fleet by 230 vessels and was largely effective in mitigating serious rate increases. Fewer ships were withdrawn at other times, as during the

Table 3–5   National Defense Reserve Fleet, 1945–1978

Fiscal Year	No. Ships	Fiscal Year	No. Ships
1945	5	1962	1,862
1946	1,421	1963	1,819
1947	1,204	1964	1,739
1948	1,675	1965	1,594
1949	1,934	1966	1,327
1950	2,277	1967	1,152
1951	1,767	1968	1,062
1952	1,853	1969	1,017
1953	1,932	1970	1,027
1954	2,067	1971	860
1955	2,068	1972	673
1956	2,061	1973	541
1957	1,889	1974	487
1958	2,074	1975	419
1959	2,060	1976	348
1960	2,000	1977	333
1961	1,923	1978	306

SOURCE: Maritime Administration Report, 1979.

Table 3–6   National Defense Reserve Fleet, September 30, 1978

Fleet	Retention*	Scrap Candidates	Special Programs
James River, Va.	85	15	40
Beaumont, Tex.	39	2	7
Suisun Bay, Calif.	87	7	24
Total	211	24	71

SOURCE: Maritime Administration Report, 1979.

* Vessels maintained for emergency activation under the fleet preservation program. Excludes one ship sold but not delivered, three Ready Reserve Fleet Ships, and three moored at Suisun Bay, Calif., on behalf of the U.S. District, Northern District of California.

Berlin crisis. The fleet also served as an effective storage facility for grain and other agricultural bulk commodities between 1958 and 1963. A total of 58 ships were traded in and 54 vessels transferred out under the Exchange Act,[44] while 108 vessels were traded in under the Trade-In Program. The effectiveness of the NDRF can be measured by comparing the cost of the results achieved with the estimated cost of satisfying the different requirements posed without the existence of the NDRF. The Trade-In Program, Exchange Program, and Reactivation Program loss amounted to about $162 million, while the total cost of the NDRF program to 1968 was nearly $14 million. The number of ships in the NDRF is shown in Table 3-5 for the period 1945–1978, while Table 3-6 shows the deposition of the NDRF in September 1978.

3.3.3.2.   Cabotage Laws—The Jones Act

Cabotage laws are laws designed to reserve to a nation's own ships the coastwise trade between a nation's ports. The chief cabotage law of the United States, known as the Jones Act,[45] provides that merchandise transported between points in the United States must be transported in vessels built in the United States, documented under the laws of the United States,[46] and owned by citizens of the United States.[47] If not so transported, the merchandise is subject to forfeiture. Nevertheless, vessels in domestic operations are not eligible for CDS or ODS. For the most part, the cabotage laws consider ports in U.S. territories and possessions to be U.S. ports.

Two provisions are designed to alleviate burdens placed on shipping as a result of the development of new technologies. Empty LASH and Seabee barges, containers, and equipment other than propulsion equipment for use with such barges or containers may be transported between U.S. points in nonqualified vessels. In addition, one nonqualified barge, belonging to the same company or consortium as the "mother ship," may transfer cargo to another nonqualified barge for further movement in U.S. foreign commerce as long as the country of the "mother ship" registry permits reciprocal privileges in its waters to barges registered in the United States.[48] In 1973 the Secretary of the Treasury reported to Congress no developments in reciprocity under the law,[49] and no further developments since the 1973 report have occurred.

Other exemptions from the coastwise laws exist and are potentially lucrative, although they cannot be applied generally. Such exemptions have been awarded for economic or operational considerations. Exemptions have also been awarded to prevent subterfuges of the cabotage laws, or when compelled by emergency. Because there are no criteria for granting these exemptions, it is difficult to predict under what circumstances future exemptions will be made. An attempt to obtain an exemption for the tanker *Sansinema* in 1970, under emergency legislation dating back to the Korean conflict, met with such an uproar that the exemption was withdrawn six days after it was announced.[50]

A vessel may lose its entitlement to engage in the coastwise trade if it is sold foreign, placed under foreign registry, rebuilt anywhere other than the United States, or if its major components are built anywhere other than in the United States.[51]

In 1978 Congress amended the Intercoastal Shipping Act of 1933.[52] In so doing, it altered the authority of the FMC over domestic offshore trade. It was the intention of Congress that changes effected by the amendments would significantly reduce the waste of agency resources and the several-year delays that characterized FMC regulation of proposed rate changes in domestic offshore trades.[53] Because FMC intervention in this area has consistently been economically detrimental to both carriers and shippers, Congress hoped that streamlining the Commission's review procedure, in addition to other changes effected by the amendments, would enable the FMC to be more supportive of the domestic offshore trades.

Prior to the passage of this legislation, the FMC, whether acting on its own initiative or in response to a complaint, was empowered to suspend rate changes made by carriers for a period of four months, pending a hearing to review the justification of the change. FMC review often took many years.[54] Yet rarely were rate changes filed with the Commission later determined to be unjustified.[55] Many suspensions therefore constituted unfair deprivations. Additionally, in order to vindicate their changed rates, carriers were subjected to high litigation costs while the agency made large expenditures of its time and resources to review ultimately meritless complaints.[56]

A carrier's rate increases are immune from suspension if the rate change does not exceed 5 percent per year.[57] However, to better safeguard the interests of shippers and the public in general, the amendments authorize the FMC to extend the maximum suspension period from four months to 180 days where the Commission suspects that an unexempted portion of a rate change (a greater than 5 percent change) or rate changes not filed pursuant to FMC procedures are unreasonable.[58]

Although the remedies provided by Section 22[59] of the original legislation are not precluded, the new legislation provides a specific formula for computing refunds for justified complaints. The authorized refund is now equal to the amount of the change determined to be unjustified, plus interest, based upon the prime rate during the period to which the refund applies.[60] Finally, the FMC is now required to employ an expedited rate review procedure that must be completed within 180 days.[61]

3.4. Taxation of American-Flag Shipping

U.S. shipping firms are subject to income tax on all of their income, regardless of source; however, credits are given for taxes paid by foreign subsidiaries if dividends are repatriated. There are also significant incentives available to the maritime industry provided through the tax laws. U.S. tax policy with regard to shipping is twofold and is designed to (1) encourage construction and operation of a large and modern merchant navy and (2) restrict evasion of taxation by incorporating shipping companies abroad.

The Merchant Marine Act (MMA) of 1970 authorized U.S. ship operators to establish "capital construction funds," the use of which permits indefinite deferral of taxes on much of the shipowner's earnings.[62] In addition to this special financial assistance, U.S. ship operators may take advantage of the depreciation and investment credit provisions, both of which have recently been made more attractive.

The U.S. operator also has the general incentive of special corporate forms available to American enterprises engaged in business abroad, which further reduces his tax burden. By contrast, the American corporation that incorporates a subsidiary abroad for the purpose of operating a vessel from a tax-haven such as Liberia, is, since 1975, subject to the stringent Sub-part F of the MMA—"attribution of income"[63] taxation—and excluded from the above-mentioned incentives. This new stringency is designed to reduce the appeal of operating under a foreign flag. Despite the variety of credits and incentives available to the maritime industry, these have generally failed to overcome the perceived tax advantage of foreign-flag vessels.

3.4.1. Depreciation Charges and Vessel Lifetimes

Depreciation charges for vessels are based on their normal useful life, considered to be 25 years. Three methods of computing depreciation charges are used widely by U.S. industries: straight line, double declining balance, and sum of the year's digits. The latter two methods permit greater depreciation charges during the early life of an asset, thus reducing taxable incomes in those years. U.S.-flag carriers can use any of the three methods, but subsidized ships are restricted to the straight-line method. In recent years Congress has enacted legislation permitting taxpayers to base depreciation charges on a useful vessel life ranging from 14.4 to 21.6 years; presumably the lower-bound figure would be chosen by the taxpayer.

3.4.2. The Capital Construction Fund (CCF)

Any citizen of the United States who owns or leases one or more "eligible vessels" may enter into an agreement with the Secretary of Commerce to establish a capital construction fund. The class of persons eligible ("any citizen of the U.S.") expands pre-1970 MMA requirements, which limited eligibility to subsidized operators. The class of eligible vessels has also been extended to cover any vessel (a) constructed in the United States, and, if reconstructed, reconstructed in the United States; (b) documented under the laws of the United States; and (c) operated in the foreign or domestic commerce of the United States or in the fisheries of the United States.[64]

How does the fund benefit the taxpayer? In general, rather than paying tax on ordinary income and on capital gains, the taxpayer deposits a portion of his income in the fund. Such deposits are then not taxable and may be used to reinvest in new ships and equipment. The tax on the deposits need not be paid until the deposits are withdrawn from the fund and used for a "nonqualified purpose."

How does the fund operate? Prior to 1970 subsidized operators (who were the only persons eligible) were required to deposit each year:

- Depreciation charges on their subsidized vessels;
- Proceeds from the sale, or indemnities for the loss, of subsidized vehicles; and
- Such other portions of their earnings as MarAd discerned to be necessary to build up an adequate replacement fund.

The deposit of depreciation charges has no effect on the operator's tax liability, since these charges are fully deductible from the operator's net income for income tax purposes. Accordingly, they are known as tax-paid deposits. Deposits of capital gains and free earnings, on the other hand, reduce the operator's immediate tax liability. Accordingly, these are called tax-deferred deposits because tax on them has only been postponed. The 1970 legislation required deposits to be segregated into three accounts:

- A capital account, into which are paid: depreciation charges, that part of the proceeds of a vessel's sale constituting gain, and interest on fund assets;
- A capital gain account, consisting of the tax-deferred deposits of long-term (six months or more) capital gains; and
- An ordinary income account, consisting of tax-deferred deposits of ordinary income, and short-term capital gains.[65]

Prior to 1970, subsidized operators were required to deposit annually all depreciation charges on their vessels. However, legislation introduced in the mid-1970s and regulations issued pursuant thereto on February 10, 1976, made a significant change in the rules governing the nature of deposits: a minimum annual deposit of depreciation charges was no longer required. As a result, there is no longer any way of deciding what fraction of deposits represents depreciation charges and what portion free earnings. Thus, if a shipowner has free earnings of $8 million and vessel depreciation of $3 million and he makes a deposit of $5 million, he may decide whether this is a deposit of $5 million free earnings or of $3 million depreciation charges and $2 million free earnings. Since only the deposit of free earnings defers tax liability, it is clear that shipowners will choose the former. The effect of this is to increase greatly the burden of the program on the Treasury.

Although deposits of capital gains and free earnings escape tax initially, they will eventually be recovered. When a withdrawal is made from the fund in order to acquire, construct, or reconstruct a qualified vessel (the definition of which is almost identical to that of "eligible vessel" above, except that it excludes ships used in the coastwise trade), the withdrawal will be treated, first, as made out of the capital account and, second, as made out of the ordinary income account. To the extent that withdrawal is made out of the tax-deferred capital gain account, the taxpayer's basis in the vessel will be reduced $.50 on the dollar. To the extent that it is made out of the tax-deferred income account, the basis will be reduced dollar for dollar. The effect is that in subsequent years the taxpayer's depreciation deduction will be reduced and, consequently, his taxable income increased. However, the operator can avoid paying tax on the earnings of the new vessel simply by depositing those earnings in the same reserve fund. Withdrawals for other purposes (called nonqualified withdrawals) are penalized by requiring the owner of the fund to include the tax-deferred portion of the withdrawn sum in his taxable income in the year of withdrawal.

3.4.3. Investment Tax Credit

Investment tax credits are available to U.S. corporations, including those in the maritime industry. Taxpayers purchasing certain kinds of depreciable equipment are granted a credit against their liability equal to a specified percentage of their investment. The current credit allowed is 10 percent.[66] One type of investment tax credit applies specifically to the U.S. shipping industry.[67] When funds are withdrawn from a capital construction fund for the construction of a vessel, the tax basis of the vessel is reduced by the amount of tax-free funds withdrawn. This reduces the amount of depreciation claimable for the vessel. A reduced investment tax credit (5 percent), however, may be claimed for such funds withdrawn from the capital construction funds.

The provision of investment tax credit for construction of vessels financed by the Capital Construction Fund (CCF) remains in doubt.

The Treasury and Department of Commerce are currently involved in litigation concerning this issue. They tentatively agree on a reduced tax credit of 5 percent, with shipowners maintaining the right to continue their suit. The House of Representatives is considering an amendment to the Merchant Marine Act of 1970 to specifically include the 10 percent tax credit.

3.4.4. Taxation of Special Corporations

The tax code provides reduced taxation for several types of special corporations. The most important of these is the Domestic International Sales Corporation (DISC). The DISC provisions defer tax liability on 50 percent of the DISC's income and tax the other 50 percent directly to the shareholders, whether distributed or not.[68] One of its chief advantages is that the DISC can make loans of its tax-deferred profits to its parent corporation. Because DISC operates as an incentive for large foreign sales, its availability gives multinational firms a competitive advantage over domestic competitors.

3.4.5. Taxation of U.S.-Controlled Foreign-Flag Shipping

To understand the tax treatment of U.S.-owned foreign-flag shipping, it is necessary to refer to the background and principles underlying the tax jurisdiction asserted by the United States and its tax treatment of citizens and foreign business carried on in the United States. In general, the United States taxes its citizens, resident individuals, and domestic corporations on their worldwide income. Corporations organized under foreign law and nonresident aliens are taxed only on income arising in the United States or effectively connected with a trade or business carried on therein.

The Internal Revenue Code provides rules for determining the source of various types of income.[69] Particularly Section 863(b) of the Code[70] and Regulation §1.863–4[71] describe the portion of the income earned by a foreign-flag vessel engaged in international commerce that is subject to tax by the United States. Generally, according to the Code formula, a ship making a transatlantic voyage from a European port to a U.S. port will have derived approximately 10 to 12 percent of its income from U.S. source income.

The U.S. tax code makes provision for avoiding the problems of double taxation and international tax commodity. If the income of foreign vessels was taxed by every nation in which the vessel docked, not only would the expense be great but there would also be a risk of international tax retaliation. To eliminate this double taxation problem, the U.S. tax code provides a unilateral exemption.[72] The Code excludes from the gross income of a foreign corporation or a nonresident alien individual those earnings derived from the operation of ships documented under the laws of a foreign country which grants an equivalent exemption to U.S. citizens and corporations. When this exclusion applies, shipping earnings are protected from U.S. taxation of U.S.-source income[73] and income effectively connected with the conduct of a trade or business in the United States.[74] For the exemption to apply, the foreign country must exempt from taxation the income, derived from U.S. ships, of *both* U.S. citizens and corporations.[75] Both incorporation and documentation must be in the same exempting country.[76]

To further the latter policy, the United States and 21 other nations have entered into tax conventions that contain provisions similar to the equivalency exemption. Also, the 1963 Draft Convention of the Organization of Economic Cooperation and Development (OECD), of which the United States is a member, contains a paragraph providing an equivalent exemption for shipping income derived by enterprises organized in participating member nations.

Before 1962 all income earned by controlled foreign corporations from sources outside the United States (except foreign personal holding companies) was not taxed by the IRS until it was distributed to the shareholders of the corporation in the form of dividends. However, an apparent growing use of controlled foreign corporations as tax shelters by United States persons moved Congress to add Sub-part F to the Code.[77] Under Sub-part F, a United States shareholder who owns 10% or more of the voting power of a controlled foreign corporation is taxed upon his proportionate share of certain of the corporation's current income (known as Sub-part F income) even though it is not distributed. While it is uncertain whether charter hire constitutes Sub-part F income (proposed regulation §1.543–12 would include charters[78]), the question is largely academic as charter operation income is excluded from foreign base company income.[79]

Under additional rules of Sub-part F, vessels which call at U.S. ports in the course of foreign commerce are excluded from the definition of investments in U.S. property so that the vessel's earnings are protected against the constructive dividend treatment[80] that may result from such characterization. The Tax Reduction Act of 1975[81] and the Tax Reform Act of 1976[82] brought vessel charter income under the "Sub-part F income" classification, except to the extent that undistributed profits are reinvested in vessels and vessel services.

Since 1962 certain types of income, even if not distributed to shareholders, must be included in the income of U.S. shareholders.[83]

Two such categories of income are income derived from insurance or reinsurance of U.S. risks[84] and that derived from foreign-based company income.[85] However, a major relief provision allows income to be excluded unless either the creation of the corporation, or the transaction through which the income is obtained, has a significant purpose of income or profits.

The Code discourages simple sheltering of the profits from existing foreign operations by providing an incentive for an aggressive, increasing exports policy.[86]

In order to encourage the repatriation of dividends, a U.S. corporation may take a credit against taxes paid to any foreign country on income or profit.[87] An indirect credit is applicable to the taxes paid by a foreign subsidiary which had paid a dividend to its U.S. parent; this credit provides an incentive for remitting all after-tax earnings of a foreign subsidiary.[88]

3.4.6. Foreign Incorporation and Tax Law

Because countries such as Liberia and Panama levy no income taxes on international operations, significant tax advantage can be obtained by incorporating shipping firms and registering vessels in those countries. Other foreign corporations are subject to U.S. tax only on income from sources within the United States and on income which is effectively connected with the conduct of business in the United States. But a U.S. corporation is subject to tax on all income, whether derived from sources inside or outside the United States. However, as previously mentioned, foreign shipping revenues are exempted from U.S. taxation by the "equivalent exemption."[89]

Current tax law recognizes the gain that may result from a corporate reorganization to which a foreign company is a party unless an IRS ruling[90] is obtained stating that tax avoidance is not the purpose of the reorganization. This reduces the incentive for transferring assets to foreign corporations because the paper gains from such transactions will be taxed as ordinary income. Similarly, stock or security transfers to foreign corporations are subject to taxation.[91]

3.5. Rate Regulation of U.S. Shipping

No nation has jurisdiction to impose comprehensive regulation on the ocean shipping industry because the seas are open to navigation by all. Apparently the only important examples of a nation regulating foreign commerce between its ports and those of other nations are the United States and Australia.[92] As a result, the ocean shipping industry is largely self-regulated through organizations of carriers in each trade route, called "conferences," which set rates and may influence the number of sailings over a given route. Since these agreements would be likely to conflict with the policy of the American antitrust laws, Congress, in the Shipping Act of 1916, extended antitrust immunity to such agreements if they were filed with and approved by the predecessor of the Federal Maritime Commission.[93] Now FMC approval is required.

The 1916 Shipping Act curbed other practices of the carriers that were considered too anticompetitive and were used to discourage carriers competing with the conferences. First, the Act outlawed offering deferred rebates by which a shipper would get a reduced rate on his shipments only after shipping most or all of his goods by a carrier for a certain period of time.[94] Second, the Act outlawed the use of "fighting ships"—ships that undercut the competing rates solely for the purpose of driving a competitor out of business.[95] Third, carriers were forbidden to retaliate against shippers by refusing space when it was available or to employ other discriminatory methods.[96] Fourth, carriers were not allowed to make any unfair or unjust discriminatory contract with a shipper based on the volume of freight offered.[97] In addition, the Act requires that the conference agreement permit freedom of entry into and exit from the conference for carriers.[98]

The status of "dual-rate" contracts was left somewhat unsettled. By this contract a shipper gets a lower rate if he promises all of his cargo or a fixed percentage to a carrier or conference of carriers. After the Supreme Court decided that dual contracts violated the Shipping Act,[99] Congress authorized those in existence to remain while they studied the problem. It ultimately added a provision permitting dual-rate contracts with certain restrictions and subject to the approval of the FMC.[100] Most of the restrictions operate to protect the shipper; for example, the dual rate contract must be available to all shippers on equal terms, the differential may not be more than 15 percent, the shipper must be released from his obligation to ship by conference member when space is not available, and either party may cancel on 90 days notice.

In approving a dual-rate contract, the FMC may order a modification. In one case, the FMC ordered a conference to establish five separate dual-rate contracts corresponding to the three outbound and two inbound trades served by the conference. The conference had sought to bind the shipper to use of conference carriers on all five trades with one contract. The FMC order was upheld because the conference had not shown that the proposed restraint on trade was required by a serious transportation need, necessary to secure

important public benefits or in furtherance of a valid regulatory
purpose of the Shipping Act.[101]

The types of agreements between carriers subject to approval by
the FMC are enumerated in Section 15 of the Shipping Act.[102] The
catchall provision suggests the type of agreement with which Congress was concerned; it covers agreements "in any manner providing
for an exclusive, preferential, or cooperative working arrangement."
The Supreme Court has held that the FMC does not have jurisdiction
to approve a merger agreement because such an agreement is not
an ongoing arrangement imposing continuing responsibilities on the
parties.[103] Similarly, a lower federal court has held that FMC jurisdiction over an agreement which is in substance a merger is not
obtained by adding supplementary agreements of an ongoing nature
(that is, agreements not to compete) over which the FMC might
have jurisdiction.[104] However, the case was stayed until appeals were
taken from the FMC's finding that the implementation of the rate
agreement was not covered by a prior agreement approved by the
FMC. The FMC approval of a merger probably was sought to insulate
the merger from the effect of the antitrust laws.

The antitrust exemption granted by the Shipping Act may be
limited, but FMC approval is necessary for any agreement to qualify
for the exemption. If a rate agreement is challenged by a shipper
or the FMC or the Department of Justice, a court may consider a
suit for damages under the antitrust law because "the implementation
of rate-making agreements which have not been approved by the
Federal Maritime Commission is subject to the antitrust laws."[105]
The conferences are required to be self-policing. However, in at
least one case, a proposed agreement by conference carriers was
deemed potentially unfair to the accused carrier. The agreement was
approved only after amended provisions were proposed.[106]

Generally agreements will be approved when the transportation
benefits under the agreement outweigh antitrust considerations and
other considerations, such as discrimination between ports.[107] For
example, the FMC approved an agreement between a port and
several carriers for preferential use of new container terminal facilities but disapproved a restriction requiring all container traffic from
a certain area to pass through one port.[108] In another case, the FMC
conditioned approval of indirect port calls to Portland (accomplished
by shipping containers overland from Seattle), provided any carrier
offering indirect service made a direct call to Portland on alternate
sailings.[109]

Carriers may not charge a rate unjustly discriminatory between
shippers or ports, and the FMC may modify a charge to correct such
discrimination.[110] Moreover, every carrier and conference of carriers

in foreign commerce must file with the FMC a schedule of rates and charges, and rates actually charged must be in accordance therewith. Initial charges and increases are not effective until 30 days after filing the same with the FMC, which may reject a schedule not filed in conformity with its regulations. Rates improperly filed may be rejected; if so, their use is unlawful.

The FMC may, after a hearing, disapprove a rate found to be so unreasonably high or low as to be detrimental to the commerce of the United States.[111] Under these rudimentary rate powers, the FMC found rate structures on some commodities moving between the United States and the United Kingdom to be unreasonably high and thus a detriment to the commerce of the United States. The Commission consequently ordered that new rates be filed and justified for those commodities.[112] In contrast, tariffs may not be rejected on any basis except the technical grounds involved in the statute. Environmental impact is not one of those grounds.[113]

The FMC has approved overland common point (OCP) rates[114] charged by ocean carriers operating to and from Pacific ports to compete with Gulf and Atlantic ports for traffic originating east of the Rockies. These rates involve either absorption by the ocean carrier of part of the overland transportation cost or negotiation of a lower transportation charge on a through bill of lading than the overland carrier charges as a local rate from the port. Such rate setting (including absorption) was found to be routine rate making which the conference may engage in without further approval of the FMC.[115]

The FMC sanctions the establishment of through routes and rates entered into by the ocean carriers with other carriers, provided the port-to-port portion of the rate to be collected by the ocean carrier is set out in the tariff, along with the names of all participating carriers not subject to FMC regulation and the service to be performed.[116] This rule is no longer required.

3.5.1. Ocean Shipping Act of 1978 (Controlled Carrier Act)

In 1978 Congress passed the Ocean Shipping Act[117] (Ocean Act). The Act amends the Shipping Act by significantly expanding the FMC's authority to regulate rates set by controlled carriers[118] operating as "cross-traders"[119] in the U.S. oceanborne foreign trade. Cross traders are shipping operators serving trade between third countries on a primary trade route in addition to or instead of serving the foreign trade of their own country.

Section 3 of the Ocean Act prohibits controlled carriers from maintaining rates and charges in tariffs filed with the FMC below a level regarded by the Commission as being "just and reasonable."[120] The burden of proof is on the controlled carrier "to demonstrate that its rates, charges, classifications, rules, or regulations are just and reasonable."[121] Factors the Commission may consider in its rate review include the relationship between a rate and a reasonable return for the carrier,[122] rates charged by other carriers in the same trade,[123] a rate deemed necessary to assure the movement of a particular cargo in the trade,[124] and maintaining the levels and quality of service at affected ports.[125] When it believes that new rates filed with it are unjust and unreasonable, the FMC is empowered by the Ocean Act to require a controlled carrier to show cause why the rates should not be disapproved.[126] The Commission may issue an order to show cause why it should not suspend already effective rates.[127] A suspension may not exceed 180 days.[128]

The FMC must transmit all disapproval and suspension orders to the President. When the President finds that such orders conflict with national security or foreign policy objectives, and specifies the reasons for the conflict in a report, he may request the FMC to stay the effectiveness of an order.[129] The President's request for a stay must be given immediate approval.[130]

The Ocean Act exempts from its requirements controlled carriers from countries accorded national or most-favored nation status.[131] Countries subscribing to Note 1 to Annex A of the Code of Liberalization of Current Invisible Operations,[132] adopted by the Council of the Organization for Economic Cooperation and Development, are exempt.[133] Rates issued pursuant to approved conference agreements,[134] rates of a controlled carrier not engaged in cross-trading but, rather, engaged in transporting goods between the state of its ownership and the United States,[135] and trades served exclusively by controlled carriers[136] are also exempt from the Ocean Act.

Although all nonexempt controlled carriers are subject to the "just and reasonable" rate requirement of the Act, Congress primarily targeted this legislation at carriers controlled by the Soviet Union[137] as a reaction to these carriers' exploitation of the protection conferred by the United States to independent operators in the liner trades.[138]

U.S. law prohibits strong tying devices, such as deferred rebates, which enable a member of a closed conference to set rates competitive with those set by independents, while at the same time ensuring the loyalty of shippers to conference member lines.[139] Consequently, in the United States, nonconference lines or independents offering lower rates have operated freely and competitively alongside conference lines in U.S. foreign trades.[140]

Before the passage of the Ocean Act, the Soviet Union exploited this protection and impaired the competitive viability of American independents, vis-à-vis Soviet competition, by offering shippers rate reductions substantially (as much as 60 percent) below rates quoted by American operators.[141] If this competitive superiority had been achieved within a framework of equivalent competitive conditions, Congress would have tried to improve the ability of U.S. operators to compete with carriers controlled by the U.S.S.R. But the conditions were not equivalent, and remain disparate.

Carriers controlled by the Soviet Union, like those controlled by many other states, are not required by the investment community to earn profits to ensure their survival.[142] The U.S.S.R.'s more limited objective of maximizing hard currency is realized if the costs incurred in hard currency units are covered, notwithstanding costs incurred in soft currencies.[143] Moreover, the Soviet Union does not have the high operating costs of its free world competitors. The Soviets, for example, do not depreciate their vessels, and their insurance is carried by the State.[144] Fuel in Russian ports is cheap (estimated by one source to be one quarter of Western world prices) and ships take enough for round trips. These competitive advantages enabled Soviet carriers to offer rate reductions, and consequently to achieve a dramatically increased penetration into U.S. foreign-liner trades during the last decade.[145]

Thus the Ocean Act is necessary to preserve conditions of competitive equality which help ensure that competition in the liner trades is not only free but also fair. In this way it helps safeguard the economic viability of the U.S. merchant marine as it works to avert the threat to our national security posed by increasing U.S. dependence upon Soviet carriage of our exports and imports.

3.5.2. *Joint Rates for Goods in Foreign Commerce*

The Interstate Commerce Commission (ICC) has made feeble and inconsistent attempts to establish a uniform policy for accepting tariffs relating to joint rates for the transportation of goods between points in the United States and foreign countries.

In 1969, and apparently as a result of congressional prodding, the ICC took the position that it has authority to accept tariffs covering a joint rate established by ICC-regulated carriers in conjunction with ocean carriers, subject to the jurisdiction of the FMC.[146] In 1970 comprehensive regulations governing the filing of these joint rates were established by the ICC in the *International Joint Rates and Through Rates* case.[147] About six weeks later the ICC stayed the effectiveness of the order.[148] Nevertheless, by special permission, tariffs continued to be accepted on a case-by-case basis. In 1972 the ICC reconsidered the prior case. The ICC decided five to three (three Commissioners not participating) not to promulgate a general rule but, rather, to reopen the proceeding for reconsideration of the entire period.[149] As of 1979 there has been no reconsideration leading to the promulgation of a general rule.

A vigorous dissent criticized the majority for its indecision and failure to offer any guidance for those desiring to file joint international rates, despite assurances that procedures to facilitate this traffic would be established. The dissent suggests, in a footnote,[150] that action was postponed on the Trade Simplification Act of 1969[151] as a result of the ICC's earlier decision to implement joint rates. The net result did not preclude the filing of international joint rates; the majority even offered equivocal support (but no guidance) for those persons desiring to file joint rates by noting that they are not precluded from following the earlier, suspended regulations.[152]

It appears, however, that special permission to file each tariff must be sought and thus the information to be included in the tariff will be the subject of case-by-case review until the ICC feels it has acquired the experience necessary to again promulgate a general rule. The basic position of the ICC with such review has been to reject applications for joint rates which will affect the competitive status quo. This is a self-defeating policy since the main objective of developing joint rates is to encourage the intermodal coordination and operational efficiencies that result in a more competitive posture.

3.5.3. Export-Import Rates and Interstate Shipment

The ICC accepts tariffs that provide for transportation between a port and an interior point of exported or imported goods at a rate different from that charged for the same transportation of domestic goods. Whether goods are being imported or exported is a difference justifying a different rate;[153] a different rate is therefore not unreasonably discriminatory.[154] Both rates must be just and reasonable[155] and meet all other conditions imposed on ICC-regulated rates. For example, the rates may not unjustly discriminate between ports.[156] Notwithstanding this requirement, an Administrative Law Judge of the FMC found that the Gulf-Europe "Minibridge" rates (for containers shipped by rail from Gulf ports to Charleston, S.C. and then by ship to Europe) do not violate the Shipping Act of 1916 by depriving Gulf ports of traffic naturally tributary to them. In addition, a higher rate may not be charged for a shorter distance than for a longer distance without ICC approval.[157]

A common carrier regulated by the ICC is not required to establish through routes from interior points of the United States to foreign countries in conjunction with an ocean carrier operating between the United States and foreign ports. However, if the domestic carrier establishes a through rate from a port with one ocean carrier, the ICC may order the domestic carrier to make similar arrangements with all other ocean carriers operating from the U.S. port.[158]

3.6 Restrictive Regulations

3.6.1. Import Quota System

President Eisenhower introduced the Oil Import Quota System of 1959[159] which asserted his authority to increase restrictions on imports threatening to impair the national security. As amended, the regulations set fees for licenses to import petroleum and petroleum products. The purpose of requiring license fees was to create favorable long-term conditions for increased domestic production of petroleum and for expanding the capacity of domestic refineries and petrochemical plants.

The present fee schedule is sufficient to finance full remission of the difference between U.S. and foreign costs of tanker construction and operations. Such rebates permit U.S. tankers built and operating without subsidy to serve in this trade. This allows exchangeable use of U.S. tankers in both the domestic and foreign trade of the United States.

To encourage carriage in U.S. tankers, license fees on imported petroleum and petroleum products so carried could be remitted. An alternative plan to increase carriage in U.S. tankers might provide for rebates of license fees on all imported crude petroleum and petroleum products transported in U.S.-built and operated ships, with simultaneous suspension of Construction Differential Subsidy (CDS) payments on tankers.

3.6.2. Trade Route Restrictions

Although the Merchant Marine Act[160] of 1936 reduces restrictions on subsidized liner operators, operating subsidy requirements stipulate essential trade route and service frequency, as well as basic schedules needed for servicing a particular route. The Act imposes detailed government supervision of the operator's performance and audit of costs, in addition to a variety of other restrictions on ship repair and other service-related management decisions.

Government requirements regarding essential trade routes and specific service quality in terms of routing, frequency, schedule, and ship type must be eliminated if U.S. operators are to realize a profit. Operators should be permitted to decide to reschedule, reroute, or change level or quality of service within a general concept of trade without government approval. This does not imply that a liner operator may unilaterally give up a route without government (MarAd) approval, but he should have the same freedom in berth service terms that his foreign competitor enjoys.

3.7. U.S. Shipping under Flags of Convenience

Legislation introduced in the House of Representatives by Representative Murphy in January of 1977 would have required at least 20 percent of all imported oil to be carried by U.S.-flag vessels in 1977, 25 percent in 1978, and 30 percent thereafter. A similar measure was passed by Congress and vetoed by President Ford in 1974. The 1977 Murphy bill was eventually amended to require that by 1982 no less than 15 percent of imported oil be aboard U.S.-flag vessels. This amendment agreed with a proposal for such legislation by President Carter.

This cargo preference legislation revived the debate over ships that fly a "flag of convenience." Such ships fly the flag of the state in which they are registered, but are owned by nationals—individual or corporate—of another state. Of tankers privately owned by Americans, there are currently more than twice as many foreign-flag tankers as there are U.S.-flag tankers. U.S. foreign-flag tonnage is over five times that of U.S.-flag tanker tonnage.

Representative Murphy's bill is not the first occasion Congress has had to consider this issue. Repeated hearings on the flags-of-convenience issue for the past 25 years have exposed these vessels as tax evasive and a factor in the displacement of American seamen and shipbuilders.

Flag-of-convenience shipping has strong support in the maritime industry, however. The Federation of American Controlled Shipping (FACS) and the American Petroleum Institute (API), both of which include major oil companies in their membership, are among its proponents. FACS includes all the large independent tanker operators save two. Its members control 297 ships, with a cargo-carrying capacity of 30.6 million tons. Members of the API own and operate about two thirds of all the privately owned U.S.-flag tankers.

The owners of these vessels claim that because international shipping is one of the most competitive industries in the world, it is impossible to operate U.S.-flag vessels, pay American wage scales, adhere to American construction and repair costs and yet remain competitive. Data presented by FACS suggest that manning costs account for 16 to 23 percent of the operating cost and 7 to 12 percent of the total cost of a tanker for one year.

Both sides have some merit, but political influence appears to agree with those favoring flags-of-convenience shipping. On October 19, 1977, the House of Representatives defeated a bill requiring that by 1982, no less than 9.5 percent of all oil shipped to the United States be carried by U.S.-flag vessels built and registered in the United States.

3.7.1.   The Future of Flag-of-Convenience Vessels

Flags of convenience (FOC), or open registry of vessels, has been used by many owners, particularly owners domiciled in developed countries, for the tax, regulatory, and cost advantages to be attained. Currently 31 percent of world tonnage, or 214 million DWT, fly FOC and the proportion is rapidly increasing. FOC ships, which consist largely of bulk carriers (87 percent), and in fact primarily tankers, generated gross earnings of over $15 billion in 1979. The actual earnings and, more importantly, profits obtained from these operations are difficult to ascertain since nations that operate open registries have laws limiting requirements regarding disclosure of ownership, earnings, and profits, as well as operating information. These laws also permit large flexibility of manning, insurance, classification, and operating procedures. Liberia controls about 73.7 percent of FOC tonnage, followed by Panama with 16.2 percent, Singapore 6 percent, Cyprus 1.6 percent, Bermuda 1.4 percent, Hong Kong 1 percent, and the Bahamas 0.1 percent. It is interesting to note that Central American FOC registry (Panama, Honduras, and so forth), which comprised a significant proportion of FOC tonnage just a few years ago, has been greatly reduced from 28 percent in 1970. The reasons are the terms and security offered by new FOC countries such as Singapore and Hong Kong, which offer not only the traditional tax and disclosure advantages, but also provide excellent support for ship financing and related services.

The ownership of FOC vessels is mainly in the United States, Hong Kong, Japan, Greece, and West Germany. In fact, 35 major companies own 55 percent or 128 million DWT of the FOC fleet; 22 of these companies are owned by or affiliated with major oil companies. Independent of ownership, many of the FOC-registered vessels are operated by one-ship companies most of which are wholly owned subsidiaries of companies registered in FOC nations or, more often, other more traditional tax havens such as Monaco, Bermuda, and the Bahamas. Many of the ships are under long-term charter to the "parent" company or some affiliate, although "vessel-swapping" to disguise the relationship often takes place among such parents.

Most FOC ships are manned (200,000 seamen) by nationals of South Asia and the Orient. Governments operating open registries usually treat earnings from foreign shipping as income earned abroad and therefore not liable for either corporate or individual local taxation. Similarly, home governments generally do not tax shipping earnings that are not repatriated. As earnings are usually transferred to the tax haven, these tax savings become a vital cash-flow contribution to the parent. To benefit the original parent registered in a high-tax country, transfer pricing is used. This is the practice of making sales between subsidiaries and parent companies in order to minimize profits in countries of high taxation and maximize them in areas where rates are low.

There has always been a question regarding the reliability and safety of operations of FOC fleets. It is often claimed that the FOC fleet safety record is worse than the average because of lower quality standards with respect to both crew and vessels. Considering Lloyds' casualty figures between 1974–1978 (five years), it is noted that vessels registered to Liberia and Panama have a larger-than-average casualty record, with an average of 1.1 percent of registered tonnage lost in this five-year period, compared to a world average of 0.7 percent. The record of far eastern FOC, such as Singapore and Hong Kong, is close to the world average.

The United Nations Conference on Trade and Development (UNC-TAD) has investigated the role of FOCs for many years, and the recent UNCTAD V (1979) meeting on the Law of the Seas in Manila advocated the phasing out of FOC shipping by 1991. A 43-nation working group met in Geneva in January 1980 on whether to request or require governments to abolish FOC.

The major arguments opposing continued open registry are based on safety records, working conditions aboard, tax evasion, and control of shipping. The contention is that FOC is really not a registry, as jurisdiction is exercised by neither the FOC country, the country of the beneficial owners, nor by the country of origin of the crew. Notwithstanding some of the above claims, the major arguments favoring the phasing out of FOC are economic and rest on a desire for better redistribution of world wealth in terms of shipping revenues.

It is claimed that phasing out of FOC shipping would contribute more to the implementation of the "New Economic Order," which calls for an increasing and equitable participation of developing countries in world shipping. While registration fees in FOC countries are small and make a negligible 0.2 percent contribution to their GNP, there is major potential for income based on shipping revenues, particularly if ownership and registry are required to be codomiciled.

3.8. Effectiveness of U.S. Shipping Regulation and Government Aid

U.S. maritime policy is largely expressed in terms of government regulation of and aid to shipping. It has failed to accomplish its primary objective of assuring a strong, viable U.S.-flag shipping industry, largely because the regulation and aid proffered appear not to provide sufficient incentives on the one hand and are restrictive on the other. The approach also lacks the flexibility needed to deal with continuously changing conditions and opportunities. The changing world economic and political environment in which U.S. trade and shipping operate require a revaluation of the premises and structure of U.S. shipping regulation and government aid as the expression of U.S. shipping policy.

Endnotes

1. 46 U.S.C. §§1101 et seq. (1976).
2. 46 U.S.C. §1151(a)(1976) provides that the payment of subsidies to help construct American vessels for foreign commerce may be granted only to aid in the promotion and development of foreign commerce. 46 U.S.C. §1173(b)(1976) provides the formula for determining the amount of subsidy which may be awarded and states that the payment shall be made in such a way as to equalize the costs of American vessels and ships of foreign registry which are substantial competitors with their American counterparts. 46 U.S.C. §1174(1976) provides for additional subsidies to offset the effect of governmental aid paid to foreign competitors.
3. See generally: G. Gilmore & C. Black, *The Law of Admiralty*, Ch. XI (2d ed. 1975).
4. 39 Stat. 728 (codified at 46 U.S.C. §§801 to 842 (1976).
5. 46 U.S.C. §§1101 et seq. (1976).
6. 46 U.S.C. §§801 et seq. (1976).
7. 46 U.S.C. §1114(a)(1976).
8. 46 U.S.C. §832 (1976).

9. 46 U.S.C. §861 et seq. and 911 et seq. (1976).

10. 41 Stat. 988 (codified at 46 U.S.C. §861 (1976)).

11. Ch. 675, 45 Stat. 689 (codified at 46 U.S.C. §§891 et seq. (1976)).

12. 46 U.S.C. §1101 (1976).

13. Pub. L. No. 91-469, 84 Stat. 1018.

14. 42 U.S.C. §§4321, 4331–4335, 4341–4347 (1976 and Supp. II 1978).

15. Pub. L. No. 92-500, 86 Stat. 816.

16. 16 U.S.C. §§1431–1434 (1976 and Supp. II 1978); 33 U.S.C. §§1401, 1402, 1411–1421, 1441–1444 (1976 and Supp. II 1978).

17. 33 §§1221–1232 (1976 and Supp. II 1978); 46 U.S.C. §§214, 391(a) (1976 and Supp. II 1978).

18. Pub. L. No. 92-500, 86 Stat. 816.

19. 42 U.S.C. §§4321 et. seq. (1976).

20. Pub. L. No. 92-500, 86 Stat. 816.

21. 16 U.S.C. §§1431–1434 (1976 and Supp. II 1978); 33 U.S.C. §§1401, 1402, 1411–1421, 1441–1444 (1976 and Supp. II 1978).

22. 14 U.S.C. §2 (1976).

23. 46 U.S.C. §§1101 et. seq. (1976).

24. Ch. 250, §30, 41 Stat. 1000.

25. 46 U.S.C. §1101 (1976).

26. Pub. L. No. 91-469 §14, 84 Stat. 1023.

27. 46 U.S.C. §1151(a)(1976).

28. Negotiated Shipbuilding Contracting Act of 1976, Pub. L. No. 94-372, 90 Stat. 1042 (codified at 46 U.S.C. §1152(a) and (b) (1976)).

29. Pub. L. No. 91-469 §7, 84 Stat. 1019.

30. 46 U.S.C. §1171(a)(1976).

31. 46 U.S.C. §§1271 to 1280 (1976).

32. Obligation Guarantees, 46 C.F.R. §§298.1–298.43 (1979).

33. Pub. L. No. 94-127, 89 Stat. 680.

34. 46 U.S.C. §1241-1 (1976 and Supp. II 1978).

35. 46 U.S.C. §1145 (repealed 1960).

36. 46 U.S.C. §1241(a)(1976).

37. 46 U.S.C. §1241(b)(1976).

38. 46 U.S.C. §1156 (1976).

39. 46 U.S.C. §1175(a)(1976).

40. 518 F. 2d 1070 (D.C. Cir. 1975), *cert. denied,* 424 U.S. 912 (1976).

41. 50 U.S.C. §1744 (1976).

42. And contracted for before September 2, 1945, under the provisions of the Merchant Marine Act of 1936.

43. Pub. L. No. 86-575, 74 Stat. 312.

44. *Ibid.*

45. Merchant Marine Act of 1920, Ch. 250, 41 Stat. 988 (codified in scattered sections of 46 U.S.C.).

46. For the purposes of the coastwise trade documented under the laws of the United States, refer to enrollment within the meaning of Chap. 12, 46 U.S.C. §251 et seq. (1976).

47. Citizenship of a corporation is defined at 46 U.S.C. §802 (1976). American subsidiaries of foreign corporations meeting statutory criteria may operate vessels in the coastwide trade, 46 U.S.C. §883-1 (1976).

48. The Secretary of Treasury is given discretionary authority to suspend the application of the Jones Act with respect to the vessels of any country granting reciprocal privileges. This was designed to meet three problems: first, to provide assurance of reciprocal treatment for American vessels before suspension of the effect of the Jones Act; second, to surmount a difficulty that if reciprocal privileges were granted to any nation to whom the United States owed most-favored nation (MFN) obligations, the privileges would have to be granted to all other nations to which MFN obligations were owed; third, to prevent the intended effect from being dissipated by granting reciprocal privileges for operations in the waters of a flag of convenience (based on a vessel's registry) and not in the waters at the foreign end of a trade route. S. Rep. No. 417, 92nd Cong., 1st Sess., [1971] reprinted in U.S. CODE CONG. & AD. NEWS 1750. The Senate Committee report offers an example of the operations necessitating the legislation, *Id.* at 1751–52.
49. 119 Cong. Rec. 5092 (1973).
50. Lowry III, *Jones Act*, 40 I.C.C. Prac. J. 779, 779 n. 2, 790–92 (1973).
51. 46 U.S.C. §883 (Supp. II 1978).
52. 46 U.S.C. §§843–848 (1978 and Supp. II 1978), amended by Pub. L. No. 95-475, 92 Stat. 1494.
53. S. Rep. No. 1240, 95th Cong., 2nd Sess., reprinted in [1978] *U.S. Code Cong. & Ad. News* 3331, 3334.
54. *Id.* at 3334.
55. *Id.* at 3335–6.
56. *Ibid.*
57. Pub. L. No. 95-475, 92 Stat. 1494 (codified at 46 U.S.C. §§845(c)(1)(B)).
58. Pub. L. No. 95-475, 92 Stat. 1495 (codified at 46 U.S.C. §845(b)).
59. 46 U.S.C. §821 (1976).
60. Pub. L. No. 95-475, 92 Stat. 1496 (codified at 46 U.S.C. §85(c)(2).
61. Pub. L. No. 95-475, 92 Stat. 1495 (codified at 46 U.S.C. §5845(b)).
62. Pub. L. No. 91-469 §21, 84 Stat. 1022 (codified at 46 U.S.C. §1177).
63. I.R.C. §951–964.
64. 46 U.S.C. §1160 (1976).
65. Pub. L. No. 91-469 §21 (codified at 46 U.S.C. §1177(e)(1976)).
66. I.R.C. §46(a)(2)(B).
67. I.R.C. §46(g).
68. I.R.C. §§991–997.
69. I.R.C. §§861–864.
70. I.R.C. §863(b).
71. 26 C.F.R. §863–4 (1980).
72. I.R.C. §§872(b), 883(a).
73. I.R.C. §881.
74. I.R.C. §882.
75. 26 C.F.R. §1.883-1(a)(2)(1980).
76. Rev. Rul. 73-350, 1973-2 C.B. 251.
77. I.R.C. §§951–964.
78. Proposed Income Tax. Reg. §1.543-12.
79. I.R.C. §954(b).
80. I.R.C. §§951(a)(1)(B), 956(a), (b).
81. Pub. L. No. 94-12, 89 Stat. 26 (codified in scattered sections of 26 U.S.C.).

82. 26 U.S.C. §§1 et seq. (1976 and Supp. II 1978).
83. I.R.C. §951.
84. I.R.C. §953.
85. I.R.C. §951.
86. I.R.C. §§991–994.
87. I.R.C. §901.
88. I.R.C. §902.
89. I.R.C. §883(a)(1).
90. The ruling must be obtained pursuant to I.R.C. §367(a), (b).
91. I.R.C. §367(a).
92. Maritime Transport Committee of the Organization for Economic Cooperation and Development, *Developments & Problems of Seaborne Container Transport* (1971).
93. 46 U.S.C. §814 (1976).
94. 46 U.S.C. §12 (1976).
95. *Ibid.*
96. *Ibid.*
97. 46 U.S.C. §812 (1976).
98. 46 U.S.C. §814 (1976). One comment on this aspect of the law follows: "The United States trades tend to attract access world capacity because foreign conferences generally restrict entry and regulate intraconference service competition, and because of the demonstrated ability of United States trade conferences to maintain profitable rates at low levels of utilization." (footnotes omitted) Note, Rate Regulation in Ocean Shipping, 78 *Harv. L. Rev.* 635, 652–53 (1965).
99. *Federal Maritime Bd. v. Isbrandtsen Co., Inc.*, 356 U.S. 481 (1958).
100. 46 U.S.C. §813(a) (1976). Existing contracts were legalized during the study period by Act of Aug. 12, 1958, Pub. L. No. 85-626, 72 Stat. 574 (codified at 46 U.S.C. §812).
101. *Latin American/Pacific Coast Steamship Conf. v. FMC*, 465 F. 2d 542, 545 (D.C. Cir.); *cert. denied*, 409 U.S. 967 (1972), quoting from *FMC v. Aktiebolaget Sevneka Amerika Linien (Swedish American Line)*, 390 U.S. 238, 243 (1968), quoting from the Federal Maritime Commissioner.
102. 46 U.S.C. §814 (1976) provides that agreements in seven categories must be filed with the FMC:
     Fixing or regulating transportation rates or fares;
     Giving or receiving special rates, accommodations, or other special privileges or advantages;
     Controlling, regulating, preventing, or destroying competition;
     Pooling or apportion earnings, losses, or traffic;
     Allotting ports or restricting or otherwise regulating the number and character of sailings between ports;
     Limiting or regulating in any way the volume or character of freight or passenger traffic to be carried; or in any manner
     Providing for an exclusive, preferential, or cooperative working arrangement.
103. *FMC v. Seatrain Lines, Inc.*, 411 U.S. 726 (1973). Antitrust exemptions by implications are not favored, so the Supreme Court was unwilling to grant antitrust exemption to mergers without explicit statutory language giving the FMC authority to approve mergers.

104. *American Mail Line, Ltd. v. FMC*, 503 F. 2d 157 (D.C. Cir. 1974). *cert. denied*, 419 U.S. 1070 (1974); see 43 Geo. Wash. L. Rev. 635 (1975).

105. *Carnation Co. v. Pacific Westbound Conf.*, 383 U.S. 213, 216 (1966).

106. *States Marine Lines, Inc. v. FMC*, 376 F. 2d 230 (D.C. Cir. 1967).

107. Only four reasons for disapproval of an agreement are permitted under 46 U.S.C. §814 (1976). Agreements will be disapproved which contain provisions which are: unjustly discriminatory, detrimental to the commerce of the United States, contrary to the public interest, or violative of the Shipping Act of 1916.

108. *In re Agreements Nos. T-2108 and T-2108—A Between the City of Los Angeles and Japan Line Ltd.; Kawasaki Kisen Kaisha, Ltd.; Mitsui O.S.K. Lines, Ltd.; and Yamashita-Shinnihon Steamship Co., Ltd.*, 12 F.M.C. 110 (1968).

109. *Intermodal Service to Portland*, FMC Docket 70–19, summarized in 41 ICC Prac. J. 485-86 (1974).

110. 46 U.S.C. §816 (1976).

111. 46 U.S.C. §817(b)(5)(1976).

112. *Investigation of Ocean Rate Structures in the Trade between the United States North Atlantic Ports and Ports in the United Kingdom and Eire*, 12 FMC 34 (1968), *aff'd sub nom. American Export—Isbrandtsen Lines v. FMC*, 417 F. 2d 749 (D.C. Cir. 1969).

113. *Pennsylvania v. FMC*, 392 F. Supp. 795 (D.D.C. 1975). Since rejection could only be on technical grounds, and since (a)gencies are exempted from compliance with NEPA when compliance would give rise to agency violation of statutory obligations," *Id.* at 802, the court refused to order the FMC to reject the tariff.

114. Generally, overland rates are outbound ocean rates, while OCP rates are inbound ocean rates, although there is no substantial difference in their nature or purpose and the distinction is not always observed. *Investigation of Overland and OCP Rates and Absorptions*, 12 F.M.C. 184, 188 (1969), *aff'd sub nom. Port of New York Auth. v. FMC*, 429 F. 2d 663 (5th Cir. 1970), *cert. denied*, 401 U.S. 909 (1971).

115. *Ibid.*

116. 46 C.F.R. §536.8 (1979).

117. 46 U.S.C. §§801, 817, 842 (Supp. II 1978).

118. A controlled carrier is a state-owned carrier.

119. Cross-traders are carriers which operate in a specific trade and do not fly the flag of exporting or importing nations in that trade.

120. 46 U.S.C. §817(c)(1)(Supp. II 1978).

121. *Ibid.*

122. 46 U.S.C. §817(2)(i)(Supp. II 1978).

123. 46 U.S.C. §817(2)(ii)(Supp. II 1978).

124. 46 U.S.C. §817(2)(iii)(Supp. II 1978).

125. 46 U.S.C. §817(2)(iv)(Supp. II 1978).

126. 46 U.S.C. §817(4)(Supp. II 1978).

127. *Ibid.*

128. *Ibid.*

129. 46 U.S.C. §817(5)(Supp. II 1978).

130. *Ibid.*

131. 46 U.S.C. §817(6)(i)(Supp. II 1978).

132. Although the United States does not subscribe to the full text of this note, the 20 countries which have subscribed have pledged that their shipping policies would be based on the principle of "free and fair" competition, therefore pledging to avoid the kinds of unfair competitive practices at which the Ocean Act is aimed, S. Rep. No. 1260, 95th Cong., 2nd Sess., reprinted in [1978] *U.S. Code Cong. & Ad. News* 3536.
133. 46 U.S.C. §817(6)(ii)(Supp. II 1978).
134. 46 U.S.C. §817(6)(iii)(Supp. II 1978).
135. 46 U.S.C. §817(6)(iv)(Supp. II 1978).
136. 46 U.S.C. §817(6)(v)(Supp. II 1978).
137. S. Rep. No. 1260, 95th Cong., 2d Sess. 12, reprinted in [1978] *U.S. Code Cong. & Ad. News* 3536, 3545.
138. *Id.* at 3538.
139. *Ibid.*
140. *Ibid.*
141. *Id.* at 3542.
142. *Id.* at 3538.
143. *Ibid.*
144. *Id.* at 3547.
145. *Id.* at 3545.
146. *In re Tariffs Containing Joint Rates and Through Routes for the Transportation of Property between Points in the United States and Points in Foreign Countries* (hereinafter *International Joint Rates and Through Route*), 341 I.C.C. 246 at 249 (1972)(dissent).
147. 377 I.C.C. 625 (1970).
148. 35 Fed. Reg. 16,722 (1970), cited in *International Joint Rate and Through Routes*, 341 I.C.C. 246, 250 n. 5 (1972).
149. *International Joint Rates and Through Routes*, 341 I.C.C. 246 (1970).
150. *Id.* at 254 n. 11.
151. Cited in the first *International Joint Rates and Through Routes*. 337 ICC 625, at 633 (1970) as H.R. 14489, 91st Cong. 1st Sess. (1969). Also indexed by the Congressional Record as the Trade Simplification Act of 1969 and probably identical to S. 3142 which is printed with a section-by-section analysis at 115 Cong. Rec. 34241–44.
152. Key provisions of the earlier regulations were that the tariff could be filed by any common carrier, whether regulated by the ICC or not, or by a conference of ocean carriers, but not by freight forwarders or common carriers not owning vessels. The tariff was required to show the participating carriers and the division due the ICC carrier. The tariff could cover transportation from any U.S. point to any foreign point.
153. *Pittsburgh Plate Glass Co. v. Pittsburgh, Cin., Chic. Louis Ry. Co.*, 13 I.C.C. 87, 100 (1908): (T)he transportation of import traffic from the port of entry to an interior destination in completion of a through movement from a point in a foreign country is not like service to that involved in the transportation of domestic traffic originating at such port, even where the transportation in all other respects is performed under like conditions.
154. *Id; Texas & P. Ry Co. v. ICC*, 162 U.S. 197 (1896); *National Gypsum Co. v. United States*, 353 F. Supp. 941, 947–48 (W.D.N.Y. 1973). *In Texas & Pac. Railway* the Texas and Pacific published a lower rate for transportation

from New Orleans to California of traffic imported from Europe than for carriage of identical domestic traffic between the same points. The lower rate was justified as necessary to avoid the loss of the European traffic altogether to competition which would transport it to the California coast by water. The Supreme Court upheld the discrimination as justified. The viability of the principle established by *Texas & Pacific Railway* has repeatedly been confirmed. (Numerous additional citations are applicable to this issue.)

155. *Pittsburgh Plate Glass Co. v. Pittsburgh, Cin, Chic. & St. Louis Ry. Co.*, 13 I.C.C. 87 (1908).

156. See: *Canaveral Port Auth. v. Ahnapee & W. Ry. Co.*, 337 I.C.C. 671 (1970).

157. See: *Application of Domestic v. Import or Export Rates*, 339 I.C.C. 9 (1970).

158. 49 U.S.C. §6(12)(1976). There is no comparable provision distributing imports equally where more than one railroad serves a port.

159. Amended by Presidential Proclamation on April 19, 1973 and June 21, 1973.

160. 46 U.S.C. §1101 et seq. (1976).

Appendix 3A

THE FUNCTIONS OF THE FEDERAL MARITIME COMMISSION

The Federal Maritime Commission (FMC) is responsible for regulating the ocean commerce of the United States. Generally, the duties of the FMC are to regulate the rates charged for shipping in domestic commerce, to license ocean freight forwarders, to permit shipping companies to form rate setting conferences that would otherwise be in violation of antitrust statutes, to review rates filed by common carriers and to ensure that carriers adhere to the rates on file, and to investigate charges of discriminating practices in ocean shipping.[1]

> *Charges of discriminatory treatment (by terminal operators, for-warders, etc.) are investigated and resolved by administrative pro-ceedings conducted by FMC staff. Formal complaint proceedings, in-vestigations, and other administrative proceedings usually include a prehearing conference, a formal hearing before an administrative law judge, the judge's decision, oral argument before the commissioners and a final report.*
>
> *The Commission's decisions may be appealed to the U.S. Court of Appeals.*

The role of the FMC in liner shipping is to balance the interests of the shipping companies which provide liner services and shippers, the American importers and exporters who use those services. To do this, the FMC grants antitrust immunity to carriers where it decides that such restraints on competition will operate in the public interest, and it tries to prevent undue discrimination among shippers, carriers, and ports.[2]

---

[1] Federal Regulatory Directory (1980–81), p. 508.

[2] L. Kanuk, Statement before the House Merchant Marine and Fisheries Com-mittee, April 2, 1981.

The FMC derives its authority to regulate liner conferences from the Shipping Act of 1916.[3] Section 15 of the Shipping Act grants to the FMC its most important power, the power to approve anticompetitive agreements between common carriers by water. Any anticompetitive agreements between common carriers, including those affecting rates, accommodations, competition, pooling, sailings, cargo movement, or working arrangements must be filed with and approved by the FMC.

Each agreement is evaluated individually. According to the FMC, "(t)he current case-by-case approach . . . recognizes the complexity of U.S. international trading patterns which extend from our several coasts to virtually every nation on the globe."[4]

The proponents of the agreement must show that the proposed agreement is neither "unjustly discriminatory (nor) unfair as between carriers, shippers, exporters, importers, or ports, or between exporters from the United States and their foreign competitors, (nor) to operate to the detriment of the commerce of the United States, (nor) to be contrary to the public interest."[5] Once approved, a section 15 agreement is exempt from the antitrust laws of the United States.

A carrier may not act on an agreement that has not been approved by the FMC. If it does so, it may be fined up to $1,000 per day.

Apart from economic considerations, there are certain standards that agreements must meet in order to merit FMC approval. For example, the FMC may approve only those conference agreements that allow open membership. That is, the agreement must provide for reasonable and equal terms and conditions for admission and readmission to the conference of any qualified carrier in the trade. It must also provide that any member may withdraw from membership upon a reasonable notice without penalty.

The Commission enforces conference agreements, in part, by disapproving any agreement that does not adequately provide for self-policing of obligations under the agreement. As a result, every conference agreement contains a list of prohibited malpractices. A malpractice is generally any action by a member of the conference that violates the terms of the conference agreement or of the requirements imposed on conferences and carriers by the regulatory authorities and which may result in that member gaining an undue advantage over other members, or may give an undue advantage to particular shippers as compared with other shippers.

The FMC has responsibility for accepting or rejecting tariff (rate) filings of domestic offshore carriers (carriers that move goods between the U.S. mainland and other states, possessions, and territories of the United States) and common carriers engaged in foreign commerce.[6]

---

[3] Shipping Act, 1916 §§14–20, 22–33, 46 U.S.C. §§812–819, 821–832.

[4] L. Kanuk, Statement before the House Merchant Marine and Fisheries Committee, April 2, 1981, p. 7.

[5] Shipping Act, 1916, Sec. 15, 46 U.S.C. §814 (1976).

[6] Federal Regulatory Directory (1980–81), p. 508.

The Shipping Act[7] provides that every common carrier by water in interstate commerce must charge just and reasonable rates. The maximum rates charged must be filed with the FMC. The carriers may not charge rates that exceed those filed with the FMC unless they obtain FMC approval to do so. If the FMC finds that any rate filed with it is unjust or unreasonable, it may prescribe a just and reasonable maximum rate.

Every common carrier by water operating in the foreign trade, and every conference of such carriers, must file its rates with the FMC. The tariffs are kept open to the public and must contain the following:

- The places between which freight is carried;
- The classification of freight in force;
- Other services and charges rendered;
- Any rules and regulations affecting rates; and,
- Examples of rate documents.

A conference may charge only those rates published in the tariffs.

If a carrier wants to raise its rates or institute the new rate, effective immediately, it must file the new tariff with the FMC and publish notice of the change at least 30 days before the new rate becomes effective. After a hearing, the FMC will approve a rate unless it is so unreasonably high or low that it would be detrimental to the commerce of the United States. The FMC may, upon a showing of good cause, allow a rate to become effective in less than 30 days. A hearing is not necessary if a non-state-controlled carrier chooses to decrease its rates, in which case the new rate is effective immediately upon publication and filing.

The FMC is also responsible for enforcing laws regulating conference activity in the United States. Several of these laws regulate the way in which a common carrier, operating between a United States port and a foreign port, may compete for business. For example, it may not use fighting ships—vessels used by a carrier in a particular trade to undercut the freight rates charged by its competitors. It is also prohibited from unfairly discriminating against a shipper who has given business to a competitor. Particularly, the carrier may not refuse to carry the shipper's cargo if the carrier, in fact, has room for it. It is illegal for the carrier to make a contract that is unfair or unjustly discriminates between customers based on the volume of freight offered.

Dual-rate contracts are permitted. A carrier may apply to the FMC for the right to use dual-rate contracts. Under such contracts, the full rate is charged to shippers who do not give the carrier all or a specified part of their business. A lower rate is charged to shippers who give the carrier the requisite share of their business.

The Commission, after notice and a hearing, will permit the carrier this right as long as the contract will not be detrimental to the commerce of

---

[7] 46 U.S.C. §817 (1976).

the United States or contrary to the public interest or unjustly discriminatory or unfair between shippers. The law specifies, in some detail, what type of provisions must be in a dual-rate contract.

The Commission has the authority to investigate, on a complaint or upon its own initiative, any violation by a carrier of these shipping act provisions. If the FMC finds that a foreign carrier has violated this law, or that it has combined with other carriers to break this law and to exclude American carriers, the FMC may suspend the tariff and notify the Commissioner of Customs. The Commissioner of Customs can deny the right of entry to U.S. ports to the ships of the violating carrier until the violation ceases. If an American carrier violates one of these provisions, it may be subject to a fine.

Another FMC responsibility is to enforce laws prohibiting discriminatory behavior by carriers. The thrust of these laws is that carriers must charge the same rates to all shippers. It is illegal for a carrier to use any means to transport goods at less than the established rate. It is also illegal for the carrier to give preference to any person, locality, or destination.

A carrier operating in foreign commerce may not discriminate between shipper or ports. It is also prohibited from charging a rate that is unjustly prejudicial to U.S. exporters, compared to their foreign competitors. If the FMC finds that an unjustly discriminatory or prejudicial rate has been charged, it may suspend the tariff.

Some other responsibilities of the FMC include the duty to issue licenses to individuals, partnerships, corporations, and associations engaged in the ocean freight-forwarding business. It also issues certificates of financial responsibility to shipowners and operators to guarantee payments for judgments against shipowners and operators in case of injury or death, and to ensure that passengers receive refunds if a voyage is cancelled.

Finally, the FMC requires proof of financial responsibility from owners and operators of vessels that may be liable to the United States for the costs of removing oil and other hazardous materials from the navigable waters of the United States, adjoining shorelines, and waters of the contiguous zone.[8]

Laws administered by the FMC include:[9]

> Shipping Act, 1916 *(39 Stat. 728, 46 U.S.C. 801). Signed by the president Sept. 7, 1916. Required that shippers file tariffs (rates) with the FMC, established guidelines for maintaining competition among shippers, for the filing of tariffs, and for the reporting of agreements among common carriers.*
>
> Intercoastal Shipping Act, 1933 *(49 Stat. 1425, 46 U.S.C. 843). Signed by the president March 3, 1933. Delegated to the FMC duties related to regulation and control of rates, fares, charges, classifica-*

---

[8] Federal Regulatory Directory (1980–81), p. 509.
[9] *Id.* at p. 511.

tions, tariffs and practices of common carriers in domestic offshore trade (movement of cargo by ship between the U.S. mainland and possessions, states or territories of the United States).

Federal Water Pollution Control Act Amendments of 1972 *(86 Stat. 815, 33 U.S.C. 1254). Vetoed by the president Oct. 17, 1972; veto overridden Oct. 18. Authorized the FMC to demand that each vessel that carries oil or other hazardous material maintain a fund to cover cost of cleaning up a spill of oil or other material in navigable waters of the United States.*

Clean Water Act of 1977 *(91 Stat. 1566, 33 U.S.C. 1251). Signed by the president Dec. 27, 1977. Raised liability limit on oil spill cleanup costs.*

Merchant Marine Act *(41 Stat. 988, 46 U.S.C. 13). Signed by the president June 5, 1920. Empowered the commission to make rules and regulations to reduce the effect on American shippers of unfavorable rules made by foreign countries. It also gave the commission power to adopt rules and regulations, make reports and recommendations to Congress, subpoena witnesses, administer oaths, take evidence and require the production of books, papers and documents.*

Public Law 89-777 *(80 Stat. 1356, 46 U.S.C. 362). Signed by the president Nov. 6, 1966. Authorized the FMC to require evidence of adequate financial resources from owners or operators of vessels with accommodations for 50 or more passengers that take on passengers at U.S. ports to cover judgments for personal injury or death and to repay passengers if the voyage fails to take place.*

Public Law 90-298 *(82 Stat. 111, 46 U.S.C. 817). Signed by the president April 29, 1968. Gave the FMC power to allow carriers to refund or waive a portion of freight charges if the tariff rate included a clerical or administrative error.*

Public Law 91-416 *(86 Stat. 653, 46 U.S.C. 814). Signed by the president Aug. 29, 1972. Amended the Shipping Act, 1916, and the Intercoastal Shipping Act, 1933, by changing some criminal penalties to civil penalties and imposed a civil penalty for violation of a commission rule, order or regulation.*

Trans-Alaska Pipeline Authorization Act *(87 Stat. 584, 43 U.S.C.). Signed by the president Nov. 16, 1973. Imposed liabilities for oil spills associated with the Alaska pipeline.*

Appendix 3B

SHIPPING ACT OF 1981

Senator Slade Gorton (R, Washington) introduced S.1593[1] in September 1981 to revise the Shipping Act of 1916 by simplifying the regulation of liner shipping and strengthening the Liner Conference System. The primary objective of the bill is to improve the viability of liner shipping in U.S. foreign trade by granting complete antitrust immunity to liner conference activities consistent with international shipping practice. The bill addresses issues of rate setting or tariffs; intermodal agreements; the extent of time provided for action on agreements; methods and standards for approval of agreements; continuing surveillance of agreements; cause and authority for rejection of agreements; regulation of freight-forwarders prohibited acts; and, finally, intergovernmental maritime agreements.

The main concern of this bill is to assure equity in the enforcement of antitrust laws, which have been more effective against domestic than foreign carriers. Antitrust laws also impede carriers in other ways. They do not permit intra- and intermodal rationalization of services or the most rational use of capacity. The bill, for example, would greatly liberate opportunities for intermodal carriage. This bill, S.1593, covers similar issues as bill HR.25 filed in the House of Representatives.

One potential problem exists with the automatic extension of antitrust immunity between or among liner operators performing services of common carriers or to shipper council agreements—this immunity eliminates a major incentive for the filing of agreements for approval by the FMC. As noted by the chairman of the FMC,[2] the act limits this immunity to "agreements between or among common carriers to prevent, control, or reduce competition among themselves" (Section 4(a)(6)). This stipulation may make conference agreements vulnerable to the antitrust laws, as such agreements are by their very nature anticompetitive.

---

[1] Coauthors of S.1593 with Sen. Gorton were Ted Stevens (R, Alaska), Robert W. Kasten (R, Wisconsin), and Daniel K. Inovye (D, Hawaii).

[2] Statement of Chairman Alan Green, Jr. before Senate Commerce Committee, Subcommittee on the Merchant Marine, September 21, 1981.

The act also improves upon the tariff filing requirements of intermodal traffic, an important issue especially for liner operators in the U.S. trade, who are increasingly engaged in containerized intermodal through traffic. The act clarifies the authority of the FMC to approve intermodal agreements among ocean carriers. Under the act, conferences would be permitted to offer intermodal service and quote through rates. Other parts of the act resolve issues of standards and processing of agreements, such as time limits for action on agreements filed for approval with the FMC.

The act does much to clarify and streamline the regulation of common carriers in U.S. commerce.

S.1593

Be it enacted by the Senate and the House of Representatives of the United States of America in Congress assembled; That this Act may be cited as the Shipping Act of 1981.

Sec. 2. DECLARATION OF POLICY

The objectives of United States regulation of international liner shipping are:

(1) to develop and maintain an efficient ocean transportation system through commercial means, with a minimum government involvement, in order to serve the needs of United States foreign commerce;

(2) to foster reliable and responsible service by ocean common carriers and conferences;

(3) to assure ocean transportation rates and practices for United States exporters and importers that are internationally competitive, and which are not unjustly discriminatory;

(4) to harmonize United States shipping practices with those of its major trading partners;

(5) to permit cooperation among carriers and rationalization of services; and

(6) to facilitate efficient and timely regulation by a single Federal agency of the various aspects of international liner shipping responsive to the growth of ocean commerce and international developments affecting that commerce.

Sec. 3. DEFINITIONS

As used in this Act—

(1) "agreement" means understandings, arrangements and associations, written or oral, and any modification or cancellation thereof;

(2) "antitrust laws" means the Act of July 2, 1890 (ch. 647, 26 Stat. 209), as amended; the Act of October 15, 1914, (ch. 323, 38 Stat. 730), as amended; the Federal Trade Commission Act (38 Stat. 717), as amended;

sections 73 and 84 of the Act of August 27, 1894 (28 Stat. 570), as amended; the Act of June 19, 1936 (ch. 592, 49 Stat. 1526), as amended; the Antitrust Civil Process Act (76 Stat. 548), as amended; and amendments and Acts supplementary thereto;

(3) "bulk cargo" means—

(A) cargo that is loaded and carried in bulk without mark or count; and

(B) cargo commonly termed "neo-bulk," such as forest products in an unfinished or semifinished state, which requires specialized handling and is moved in lot sizes which range from being too large for containers up to, and including, shipload lot sizes;

(4) "Commission" means the Federal Maritime Commission;

(5) "common carrier" means a person, whether or not actually operating a vessel, who holds himself out to engage in transportation by water for hire as a public employment and undertakes to carry for shippers indifferently;

(6) "conference" means an association of ocean common carriers which provides ocean transportation on a particular route or routes and which operates within the framework of an agreement establishing rates and any other conditions of service;

(7) "controlled carrier" means any ocean common carrier that is, or whose operating assets are, directly or indirectly owned or controlled by the government under whose registry the vessels of such carrier operate. Ownership or control by a government shall be deemed to exist with respect to any carrier if—

(A) a majority portion of the interest in the carrier is owned or controlled in any manner by that government, by any agency thereof, or by any public or private person controlled by that government; or

(B) that government has the right to appoint or disapprove the appointment of a majority of the directors, the chief operating officer or the chief executive officer of the carrier;

(8) "deferred rebate" means a return, by an ocean common carrier, of any portion of the freight money to any shipper as a consideration for that shipper giving all, or any portion, of his shipments to that or any other ocean common carrier, or for any other purpose, the payment of which is deferred beyond the completion of the service for which it is paid, and is made only if, during both the period for which computed and the period of deferment, the shipper has complied with the terms of the rebate agreement or arrangement;

(9) "fighting ship" means a vessel used in a particular trade by an ocean common carrier or group of such carriers for the purpose of excluding, preventing, or reducing competition by driving another ocean common carrier out of such trade;

(10) "loyalty contract" means a contract with an ocean common carrier or conference by which a contract shipper obtains lower rates by committing all or a fixed portion of its cargo to such carrier or conference;

(11) "non-vessel-operating common carrier" means a common carrier by

water that does not operate the vessels by which the ocean transportation service is provided. A non-vessel-operating common carrier is a shipper in his relationship with ocean common carriers;

(12) "ocean common carrier" means a vessel-operating common carrier, except ferry boats and ocean tramps, engaged in the transportation by water of passengers or cargo between the United States and a foreign country, whether in the import or export trade;

(13) "other person subject to this Act" means any person engaged in the business of consolidating, freight forwarding, or furnishing wharfage, dock, warehouse, or other terminal facilities in connection with an ocean common carrier;

(14) "ocean freight forwarder" means a person in the United States who—

(A) dispatches shipments via ocean common carriers; and

(B) processes the documentation or performs related activities incident to such shipments;

(15) "person" includes individuals, corporations, partnerships, and associations, existing under or authorized by the laws of the United States, or of any State, Territory, District, or possession thereof, or of any foreign country;

(16) "rates" means charges, classifications, rules, or regulations that have a direct impact on a shipper's ocean transportation costs;

(17) "shipper" means an owner or person for whose account the ocean transportation of cargo is provided or the person to whom delivery is to be made;

(18) "shipper's council" means an association of shippers or their agents, other than ocean freight forwarders, and non-vessel-operating common carriers;

(19) "surcharge" means any temporary change in rates that is necessary to cover a sudden or extraordinary change incurred by an ocean common carrier or conference with respect to its costs or revenues;

(20) "tariff" means any schedule of rates pertaining to ocean transportation, including any supplement, amendment or reissue;

(21) "through transportation" means transportation by two or more carriers at least one of which is an ocean common carrier, between a United States point or port and a foreign point or port;

(23) "United States" means the several States, the District of Columbia, the Commonwealth of Puerto Rico, the Commonwealth of the Northern Marianas, and all other United States territories and possessions.

Sec. 4. AUTHORIZED ACTIVITIES

(a) *Conference Activities.* Ocean common carriers or other persons subject to this Act may agree to—

(1) discuss, fix, regulate, and agree upon rates, surcharges, accommodations and other conditions of services;

(2) pool or apportion earnings, losses, or traffic;

(3) allot ports or restrict or otherwise regulate the number and character of sailings between ports;

(4) limit or regulate the volume or character of cargo or passenger traffic to be carried;

(5) engage in exclusive, preferential, or cooperative working arrangements;

(6) enter into other agreements to control, regulate, or prevent competition among themselves; and

(7) limit, in the case of conferences, membership.

(b) *Intermodal Activities.* Ocean common carriers or other persons subject to this Act may agree with each other or with any combination of air carriers, rail carriers, motor carriers, or other common carriers by water to—

(1) establish through transportation routes for the movement of cargo; and

(2) establish through intermodal rates, or concur in tariffs.

(c) *Shippers' Council Activities.* Shippers who are members of a shippers' council organized or existing under the laws of the United States may—

(1) mutually consult and exchange information or views regarding general rate levels, rules, practices, or services;

(2) agree upon common positions; and

(3) consult and negotiate with any ocean common carrier or conference regarding general rate levels, rules, practices, or services.

Sec. 5. AGREEMENTS

(a) *In General.* No concerted activity authorized by section 4 shall be permitted under this Act except pursuant to an agreement that has become effective under section 6.

(b) *Filing Requirements.* A true copy of every agreement entered into with respect to any activity described in section 4 shall be filed with the Commission. In the case of oral agreements, complete memoranda specifying in detail the substance of such agreements shall be filed. Within ten working days of receipt, the Commission shall transmit a notice of filing to the Federal Register for publication.

(c) *Conference Agreements.* Every conference must—

(1) provide that any limitation on membership is based on commercially reasonable criteria;

(2) permit any member to withdraw from membership upon reasonable notice without penalty;

(3) engage the services of an independent neutral body to police fully the obligations of the conference and its members;

(4) provide the right of independent action—

(A) in any agreement between carriers not members of the same con-

ference, for each carrier, and, in any agreement between conferences serving different trades that would otherwise be naturally
competitive, for each conference; or

(B) in any intermodal agreement, for air carriers, rail carriers, motor
carriers, or common carriers by water not subject to this Act to
establish their portion of through intermodal rates or to establish
rules and regulations that apply exclusively to the services performed by such carriers.

(5) provide for a consultation process designed to insure—

(A) commercial resolution of disputes;

(B) cooperation in preventing malpractice;

(C) procedures for promptly and fairly considering shippers' requests
and complaints; and

(D) regular and orderly communication and exchange of information
with shippers and shippers' councils in their trade.

(d) *Shippers' Council Agreements.* Every shippers' council must—

(1) limit membership to those shippers that have a direct financial
interest in the export or import of the commodities covered by the
agreement;

(2) provide that membership is voluntary;

(3) provide that the members have the right to act independently with
any carrier or conference;

(4) provide for a consultation process designed to insure—

(A) commercial resolution of disputes;

(B) cooperation in preventing malpractice;

(C) regular and orderly communication and exchange of information
with conferences in their trade.

Sec. 6.   ACTION ON AGREEMENTS

(a) *Rejection by the Commission.*   Any agreement that does not conform
to the requirements of section 5 shall be rejected by the Commission.

(b) *Standards.*   The Commission shall by order, after notice and hearing,
disapprove or modify any agreement that it finds—

(1) to be unjustly discriminatory or unfair as between carriers, shippers,
exporters, importers, or ports, or between exporters from the United
States and their foreign competitors; or

(2) to operate to the detriment of the commerce of the United States.
The Commission shall approve all other agreements.

(c) *Burden of Proof.*   The burden of proof in any proceeding under this
section shall be on the party opposing the agreement.

(d) *Duration of Effectiveness.*   Agreements that are approved shall remain in effect until withdrawn, cancelled, or modified. The Commission
shall not on its own motion limit the duration of an agreement's effectiveness.

(e) *Final Decision-Time.*   The Commission shall issue a final decision on
any agreement within 180 days after filing with the Commission. For good

cause the Commission may extend the time period once for not more than 90 days.

(f) *Delay*. If a final decision is not issued within the 180 day period referred to in subsection (b), or by the end of the extension period, the agreement shall go into effect as filed. If the Commission determines that it is unable to issue a final order within such period or extension due to willful delays directly attributable to either a proponent or a complaintant, the Commission may disapprove the agreement, or permit it to become effective, solely on the basis of such delay.

(g) *Compliance with Subpoena or Discovery*. In any proceeding under this section, the Commission may disapprove any agreement for failure of a proponent of the agreement to comply with any subpoena or discovery order lawfully issued by the Commission.

Sec. 7. LOYALTY CONTRACTS

(a) *Contract Requirements*. Any conference or ocean common carrier engaged in foreign commerce may utilize loyalty contracts, if each such contract meets the following requirements:

(1) The contract is available to all shippers on equal terms and conditions.

(2) The contract shipper is permitted prompt release from the contract with respect to any shipment or shipments for which the contracting carrier or conference of carriers cannot provide space requested on reasonable notice by the shipper.

(3) The contract provides that whenever a rate for the carriage of goods under the contract becomes effective, insofar as it is under the control of the carrier or conference, the rate—

(A) may not be increased on less than 90 days' notice, except upon agreement of the applicable shipper; and

(B) may be increased on not less than 30 days' notice if the increase is to a level no higher than that from which the particular rate was reduced within 180 days immediately preceding the filing of the increase, or if the increase is a surcharge.

(4) The contract covers only those goods of the contract shipper as to the shipment of which it has the legal right at the time of shipment to select the carrier. It shall be deemed a breach of the contract if, before the time of shipment and with the intent to avoid its obligation under the contract, the contract shipper divests itself, or with the same intent permits itself to be divested of the legal right to select the carrier and the shipment is carried by a carrier which is not a party to the contract. In any dispute under this paragraph the burden of proof shall be on the contract shipper.

(5) The contract shipper is not required to divert shipments of goods from natural routings not served by the carrier or conference where direct carriage is available.

(6) The damages recoverable for breach by either party are limited to

actual damages to be determined after breach in accordance with the principles of contract law. The contract may specify, however, that in the case of a breach by a contract shipper the damages may be an amount not exceeding the freight charges computed at the contract rate on the particular shipment, less the cost of handling.

(7) The contract shipper is permitted to terminate at some time without penalty upon 90 days' notice.

(8) The carrier or conference is permitted on 90 days' notice to terminate the contract rate system in whole or with respect to any commodity without penalty.

(9) The contract provides for a spread or series of spreads, to be commercially determined, between tariff rates and rates charged contract shippers that shall not exceed an aggregate of 15 per centum.

(10) The contract excludes bulk cargo.

(b) *Treatment of Contract Not in Conformity.* The utilization of a loyalty contract that is not in conformity with one or more of the requirements set forth in subsection (a) shall be treated as a violation of this Act.

Sec. 8. EXEMPTION FROM ANTITRUST LAWS

(a) The antitrust laws shall not apply to:

(1) any agreement or activity described in section 4;

(2) any loyalty contract that conforms with the requirements of section 7, or any activity pursuant to that loyalty contract;

(3) any agreement or activity that relates solely to transportation services between foreign countries;

(4) any agreements or activity that relates to shippers' councils operating exclusively outside the United States; and

(5) any agreement or activity to provide or furnish wharfage, dock, warehouse, or other terminal facilities exclusively outside the United States.

(b) This Act shall not be construed to extend antitrust immunity to air carriers, rail carriers, motor carriers, or common carriers by water not subject to this Act.

Sec. 9. TARIFFS

(a) *In General.*

(1) Except with regard to bulk cargo, every ocean common carrier shall file with the Commission, and keep open to public inspection, tariffs showing all its rates between all points on its own route and on any through transportation route which has been established. Such tariffs shall plainly indicate the places between which cargo will be carried, list each classification of cargo in use, state separately each additional charge, privilege, or facility under the control of the carrier or conference and any rules or regulations that in any way change,

affect, or determine any part or the aggregate of such rates or charges, and include sample copies of any loyalty contract, bill of lading, contract of affreightment, or other documents evidencing the transportation agreement.

(2) Copies of such tariffs shall be made available to any person and a reasonable charge may be assessed for them.

(b) *Initial Rates and Rate Changes.* No initial rates or increases in existing rates shall become effective earlier than 30 days after filing with the Commission. Any change in the rates that results in a described cost to the shipper may become effective upon publication and filing with the Commission. The Commission, for good cause, may allow rate increases or surcharges to become effective in less than 30 days.

(c) *Refund of Charges.* The Commission may permit an ocean common carrier or conference to refund a portion of freight charges collected from a shipper or waive the collection of a portion of the charges from a shipper where it appears that there is an error in a tariff of a clerical or administrative nature due to inadvertence in failing to file a new tariff and that such refund will not result in discrimination among shippers, ports, or carriers. The application for refund must be filed with the Commission within 180 days from the date of shipment.

Sec. 10. CONTROLLED CARRIERS

(a) *Controlled Carrier Rates.* No controlled carrier subject to this section shall maintain rates in its tariffs filed with the Commission that are below a level that is just and reasonable. The Commission may, at any time after notice and hearing, disapprove any rate which the controlled carrier has failed to demonstrate to be just and reasonable. In any proceeding under this subsection, the burden of proof shall be on the controlled carrier to demonstrate that its rate is just and reasonable. Rates filed by a controlled carrier that have been rejected, suspended, or disapproved by the Commission are void, and their use is unlawful.

(b) *Rate Standards.* For the purpose of this section, in determining whether rates by a controlled carrier are just and reasonable, the Commission may take into account appropriate factors including, but not limited to, whether—

(1) the rates which have been filed are below a level which is fully compensatory to the controlled carrier based upon that Carrier's actual costs or upon its constructive costs, which are hereby defined as the costs of another carrier, other than a controlled carrier, operating similar vessels and equipment in the same or a similar trade;

(2) the rates are the same as or similar to those filed or assessed by other carriers in the same trade;

(3) the rates are required to assure movement of particular cargo in the trade; or

(4) the rates are required to maintain acceptable continuity, level, or quality of common carrier service to or from affected ports.

(c) *Effective Date of Rates.* The rates of controlled carriers shall not, without special permission of the Commission, become effective sooner than the thirtieth day after the date of filing with the Commission. After the date of the enactment of this section, each controlled carrier shall, upon the request of the Commission, file, within 20 days of request, with respect to its existing or proposed rates, a statement of justification that sufficiently details the controlled carrier's need and purpose for such rates, upon which the Commission may reasonably base its determination of the lawfulness thereof.

(d) *Disapproval of Rates.* Whenever the Commission is of the opinion that the rates, filed by a controlled carrier may be unjust and unreasonable, the Commission may issue an order to the controlled carrier to show cause why such rates should not be disapproved. Pending a determination as to their lawfulness in such a proceeding, the Commission may suspend such rates at any time before their effective date. In the case of rates that have already become effective, the Commission may, upon the issuance of an order to show cause, suspend such rates on not less than 60 days' notice to the controlled carrier. No period of suspension under this subsection may be greater than 180 days. Whenever the Commission has suspended any rate under this subsection, the affected carrier may file new rates to take effect immediately during the suspension period in lieu of the suspended rates; except that the Commission may reject such new rates if it is of the opinion that they are unjust and unreasonable.

(e) *Presidential Review.* Concurrently with the publication thereof, the Commission shall transmit to the President any order of suspension or final order of disapproval of rates of a controlled carrier subject to this section. Within ten days after the receipt or the effective date of such Commission order, whichever is later, the President may request the Commission in writing to stay the effect of the Commission's order if he finds that such stay is required for reasons of national defense or foreign policy which reasons shall be specified in the report. Notwithstanding any other provision of law, the Commission shall immediately grant such request by the issuance of an order in which the President's request shall be described. During any such stay, the President shall, whenever practicable, attempt to resolve the matter in controversy by negotiation with representatives of the applicable foreign governments.

(f) *Exceptions.* The provisions of this section shall not apply to—

(1) any controlled carrier of a state whose vessels are entitled by a treaty of the United States to receive national or most-favored-nation treatment;

(2) any controlled carrier of a state which, on the effective date of this section, has subscribed to the statement of shipping policy contained in note 1 to annex A of the Code of Liberalization of Current Invisible

Operations, adopted by the Council of the Organization for Economic Cooperation and Development;

(3) rates of any controlled carrier in any particular trade which are covered by an agreement effective under section 6, other than an agreement in which all of the members are controlled carriers not otherwise excluded from the provisions of this subsection;

(4) rates governing the transportation of cargo by a controlled carrier between the country by whose government it is owned or controlled, as defined herein and the United States;

(5) a trade served exclusively by controlled carriers; or

(6) any controlled carrier registered in a state which, on the effective date of this Act, is among those designated a beneficiary developing country for purposes of the generalized system of preferences, provided for in title V of the Trade Act of 1974 (88 Stat. 2066, 19 U.S.C. 2461 et seq.), and set forth in general headnote 2(g) of the Tariff Schedules of the United States Annotated (1978), and which has vessels registered within its jurisdiction that are privately owned and not operated by a controlled carrier.

Sec. 11. OCEAN FREIGHT FORWARDERS AND NON-VESSEL-OPERATING COMMON CARRIERS

(a) *Bonding Requirement.* No person may act as an ocean freight forwarder or non-vessel-operating common carrier unless that person has furnished a bond approved by the Commission of no less than $150,000 that is issued by a surety company found acceptable by the United States Department of the Treasury.

(b) *Exception.* A person whose primary business is the sale of merchandise may forward shipments of such merchandise for his own account without a bond.

(c) *Compensation of Forwarders by Carriers.*

(1) An ocean common carrier shall compensate an ocean freight forwarder in connection with any cargo shipment dispatched on behalf of others only when the ocean freight forwarder has certified in writing that it has performed the following services:

(A) engaged, reserved, or contracted directly with the carrier or its agent for space aboard a vessel or confirmed the availability of such space; and

(B) prepared and processed the ocean bill of lading, the dock receipt, or other similar documents with respect to such cargo.

(2) An ocean common carrier shall not pay compensation for services described in paragraph (1) more than once on the same cargo shipment.

(3) An ocean common carrier shall not pay compensation as provided in this subsection to its agents or any other ocean common carrier or its agents.

(4) No compensation shall be paid to an ocean freight forwarder except in accordance with the tariff provisions contained in section 9(a); and no such forwarder is entitled to receive compensation from a common carrier with respect to any shipment in which the forwarder has a direct or indirect beneficial interest.

Sec. 12.   PROHIBITED ACTS

(a) *By Ocean Common Carriers.*   No ocean carrier may—
  (1) rebate, refund, or remit in any manner, or by any device, any portion of its rates except in accordance with a tariff that is on file with the Commission;
  (2) extend or deny to any person any privilege, concession, equipment or facility, except in accordance with such tariffs;
  (3) allow any person to obtain transportation by water for cargo or any service in connection therewith at less than the applicable rates by any means;
  (4) charge rates which are determined to be so unreasonably high or low as to be detrimental to the commerce of the United States;
  (5) charge rates which are unduly prejudicial to United States exporters or compared with their foreign competitors;
  (6) continue to impose any surcharge after the increase in costs or loss of revenues that were the subject of the surcharge have been recovered;
  (7) retaliate against any shipper by refusing, or threatening to refuse, space accommodations when such are available, or resort to other discriminatory or unfair methods, because such shipper has patronized any other carrier or has filed a complaint charging unfair treatment, or for any other reason;
  (8) make any unfair or unjustly discriminatory contract with any shipper based on the volume of freight offered, or unfairly treat or unjustly discriminate against any shipper in the matter of—
  (A) rates,
  (B) cargo space accommodations or other facilities, due regard being had for the proper loading of the vessel and the available tonnage;
  (C) the loading and landing of freight in proper condition, or
  (D) the adjustment and settlement of claims;
  (9) use any fighting ship or engage in any practices designed to reduce or eliminate the participation of non-conference carriers;
  (10) offer or pay any deferred rebates; or
  (11) demand, charge, or collect any rate or charge which is determined by the Commission to be unjustly discriminatory between shippers or ports.

(b) *By Shippers, Ocean Freight Forwarders or Non-Vessel-Operating Common Carrier.*   No shipper, ocean freight forwarder, or non-vessel-operating common carrier may obtain or attempt to obtain transportation from an ocean common carrier at rates that are less than those specified in such carriers' tariffs on file with the Commission.

(c) *By Other Persons.* It shall be unlawful for any ocean common carrier, shipper, or other person subject to this Act—

(1) To operate under any agreement described in section 4 that has not become effective under section 6, has been rejected, suspended, or disapproved, or to operate except in accordance with any modification made by the Commission to the agreement; or

(2) knowingly to disclose, offer, solicit, or receive any information concerning the nature, kind, quantity, destination, consignee, or routing of any property tendered or delivered to an ocean common carrier or other person subject to this Act without the consent by such shipper and consignee if that information—

(A) may be used to the detriment or prejudice of such shipper or consignee;

(B) may improperly disclose its business transactions to a competitor; or

(C) may be used to the detriment or prejudice of any carrier. Nothing in paragraph (2) shall be construed to prevent providing such information, in response to any legal process, to the Government of the United States or any State, or to any independent neutral body operating within the scope of its authority to fulfill the policing obligations of the parties to an agreement approved under this Act.

Sec. 13. COMPLAINTS, INVESTIGATIONS, AND REPARATIONS

(a) *Filing of Complaints.* Any ocean common carrier, shipper, or other person subject to this Act may file with the Commission a sworn complaint alleging a violation of this Act and may seek reparation for any injury caused to the complainant by that violation.

(b) *Satisfaction or Investigation of Complaints.* The Commission shall furnish a copy of a complaint filed pursuant to subsection (a) of this section to the person named therein, who shall, within a reasonable time specified by the Commission, satisfy the complaint or answer it in writing. If the complaint is not satisfied, the Commission shall investigate it in such manner and by such means, and make such order as it deems proper.

(c) *Commission Investigations.* The Commission shall enter a written report of every investigation made under this Act in which a hearing was held, which states its conclusions, decisons, findings of fact, and order. A copy of such report shall be furnished to all parties. The Commission shall publish such reports for public information and such authorized publications shall be competent evidence of such reports in all courts of the United States, and of each of the States, territories, districts, and possessions thereof.

(d) *Reparations.* After notice and hearing of any complaint filed pursuant to subsection (a) of this section within one year, the Commission may when appropriate direct the payment of reparations to the complaintant for actual injury caused by a violation of this Act.

Sec. 14.   SUBPOENAS AND DISCOVERY

(a) *In General.*   In investigations and adjudicatory proceedings under this Act—

(1) depositions, written interrogatories, and discovery procedures may be utilized by any party under rules and regulations issued by the Commission, which rules and regulations, to the extent practicable, shall be in conformity with the rules applicable in civil proceedings in the district courts of the United States; and

(2) the Commission may by subpoena compel the attendance of witnesses and the production of books, papers, documents, and other evidence.

(b) *Witness Fees.*   Witnesses shall, unless otherwise prohibited by law, be entitled to the same fees and mileage as in the courts of the United States.

(c) *Suspension of Tariffs.*   After notice and opportunity for hearing, the Commission may suspend any or all tariffs of any ocean common carrier, or the right of a conference member to utilize conference tariffs, if the carrier or conference fails to supply information authorized to be obtained under subsection (a). Any suspension ordered pursuant to this subsection shall be immediately submitted to the President who may disapprove it if he finds such disapproval is required for national defense or foreign policy reasons.

(d) *Civil Penalty.*   Any ocean common carrier who accepts or handles cargo for carriage under tariffs which have been suspended pursuant to this section shall be subject to a civil penalty of not more than $50,000 for each shipment.

(e) *Assistance of Secretary of State in Obtaining Information.*   If, in defense of its failure to comply with a subpoena or discovery order issued under this section, an ocean common carrier alleges that documents or information located in a foreign country cannot be produced because of the laws of that country, the Commission shall immediately notify the Secretary of State of such failure to comply and of the allegation relating to foreign laws. Upon receiving such notification, the Secretary of State shall promptly consult with the government of the nation within which the documents or information are alleged to be located for the purpose of assisting the Commission in obtaining the documents or information sought.

Sec. 15.   PENALTIES

(a) *Assessment of Penalty.*   If the Commission finds, after notice and opportunity for hearing, that any shipper, shippers' council, ocean common carrier, conference, ocean freight forwarder, or other person subject to this Act has violated any provision of this Act, or any regulation issued thereunder, such person is liable to the United States for a civil penalty. The amount of the civil penalty, unless otherwise provided in this Act, may not exceed $5,000 for each violation unless the violation was willfully and knowingly committed, in which case the amount of the civil penalty may not exceed $25,000 for each violation. Each day of a continuous violation shall constitute a separate offense. The amount of each civil penalty shall be assessed by the Commission, by written notice. In determining the amount of such penalty, the Commission shall take into account the nature, circumstances, extent, and gravity of the violation committed and, with respect to the violator, the degree of culpability, any history of prior offenses, ability to pay, and such other matters as justice may require.

(b) *Tariff Suspension for Rebating.*
  (1) For any violation of Section 12(a)(1), (2), and (3), the Commission may suspend any or all tariffs of any ocean common carriers, or the member's right to use conference tariffs, for a period not to exceed 12 months. Any suspension ordered pursuant to this subsection shall be immediately submitted to the President who may disapprove it if he finds such disapproval is required for national defense or foreign policy reasons.
  (2) Any ocean common carrier who accepts or handles cargo for carriage under tariffs which have been suspended pursuant to this subsection shall be subject to a civil penalty of not more than $50,000 for each shipment.

(c) *Review of Civil Penalty.* Any person against whom a civil penalty is assessed under subsection (a) of this section may obtain review thereof under chapter 158 of title 28, United States Code.

(d) *Action Upon Failure to Pay Assessment.* If any person fails to pay an assessment of a civil penalty after it has become final and an unappealable order, or after the appropriate court has entered final judgement in favor of the Commission, the Commission shall refer the matter to the Attorney General of the United States, who shall recover the amount assessed in any appropriate district court of the United States. In such action, the validity and appropriateness of the final order imposing the civil penalty shall not be subject to review.

(e) *Compromise or Other Action by Commission.* The Commission may compromise, modify, or remit, with or without conditions, any civil penalty which is subject to assessment under this section.

(f) *Limitations.*
  (1) No fine or other punishment shall be assessed on any person for criminal conspiracy after August 29, 1972, to violate any provision of this Act or to defraud the Commission by concealment of any such violation.

(2) Any formal proceeding to assess any penalty under this section shall be commenced within five years from the date when the violation occurred.

Sec. 16. COMMISSION ORDERS

(a) *In General.* Orders of the Commission relating to any violation of this Act or to any regulation issued thereunder shall be made only after opportunity for hearing and upon complaint or on its own motion. Each order of the Commission shall continue in force for the period of time specified in the order, or until suspended, modified, or set aside by the Commission or a court of competent jurisdiction.

(b) *Reversal or Suspension of Orders.* The Commission may reverse, suspend, or modify any order made by it, and upon application of any party to a proceeding may grant a rehearing of the same or any matter determined therein. No rehearing shall, except by special order of the Commission, operate as a stay of such order.

(c) *Enforcement of Nonreparation Orders.* In case of violation of any order of the Commission or for failure to comply with a Commission subpoena, the Commission, or any party injured by such violation, or the Attorney General may seek enforcement by any United States district court having jurisdiction over the parties. If after hearing, the court determines that the order was properly made and duly ordered, it shall enforce the order by an appropriate injunction or other process, mandatory or otherwise.

(d) *Enforcement of Reparation Orders.*

(1) In case of violation of any order of the Commission for the payment of reparation, the person to whom such award was made may seek enforcement of such order in any United States district court having jurisdiction of the parties.

(2) In any United States district court the findings and order of the Commission shall be prima facie evidence of the facts therein stated, and the petitioner shall not be liable for costs, nor for the costs of any subsequent stage of the proceedings, unless they accrue upon his appeal. A petitioner in a United States district court who prevails shall be allowed a reasonable attorney's fee to be assessed and collected as part of the costs of the suit.

(3) All parties in whose favor the Commission has made an award of reparation by a single order may be joined as plaintiffs, and all other parties in such order may be joined as defendants, in a single suit in any district in which any one such plaintiff could maintain a suit against any one such defendant. Service of process against such defendant not found in that district may be made in any district in which is located any office of, or point to call on a regular route operated by, such defendant. Judgement may be entered in favor of any plaintiff against the defendant liable to that plaintiff.

(e) *Statute of Limitations.* Any action seeking enforcement of a Commission order shall be filed within one year from the date of the order.

(f) *Representation in Court.* Attorneys employed by the Commission shall, if the Commission so directs, appear for and represent the Commission in any case before a court of the United States or a State of the United States.

Sec. 17. EXEMPTIONS

The Commission, upon application or on its own motion, may by order or rule exempt for the future any specified activity or class of agreements between ocean common carriers or other persons subject to this Act from any requirement of this Act, if it finds that such exemption will not substantially impair effective regulation by the Commission, be unjustly discriminatory, or be detrimental to commerce. The Commission may attach conditions to any such exemption and may, by order, revoke any such exemption. No order or rule of exemption or revocation of exemption shall be issued unless opportunity for hearing has been afforded interested persons.

Sec. 18. REGULATIONS

The Commission shall make such rules and regulations as may be necessary to carry out the provisions of this Act.

Sec. 19. REPEALS AND CONFORMING AMENDMENTS

(a) *Repeals.* The laws specified in the following table are repealed:

Shipping Act, 1916:

14a	46 U.S.C. 813
14b	46 U.S.C. 813a
18(b)	46 U.S.C. 817(b)
18(c)	46 U.S.C. 817(c)
26	46 U.S.C. 825
43	46 U.S.C. 841a

Merchant Marine Act, 1920:

20	46 U.S.C. 812

Merchant Marine Act, 1936:

212(c)	46 U.S.C. 1122(e)
214	46 U.S.C. 1124

(b) *Conforming Amendments.*

The Shipping Act, 1916, is amended by redesignating section 3, and all references thereto, as section 4 and inserting the following new section after section 2:

"*Sec. 3.* Commencing with the date of enactment of this section, the provisions of sections 4, 15, 16, 17, 18, 20, 21, 22, 23, 24, 25, 27, 29, 30, 31, 32, 33, 34, 35, and 44 of this Act shall be deemed to apply only to commerce related to transportation by water of passengers or property on the high seas or the Great Lakes on regular routes from port to port between one State, Territory, District, or possession of the United States and any other State, Territory, District, or possession of the United States or between places in the same Territory, District, or possession."

(c) *Effect on Certain Agreements and Contracts.*   All agreements, contracts, and modifications previously approved by the Commission will continue in force and effect as it approved under the provisions of this Act, and all new agreements, contracts, and all modifications to existing, pending, or new contracts or agreements shall be considered under the provisions of this Act.

Chapter 4

EVALUATION OF ECONOMIC AND REGULATORY ASPECTS OF U.S. MARITIME POLICY

U.S. maritime policy is largely expressed in terms of operational and economic regulation. Recently the cost-benefit calculus of economic regulation in general has been the target of searching reappraisal. Regulation of maritime transport must also inevitably withstand such scrutiny if it is to remain intact. While it is generally assumed that regulation assures fairly priced maritime transport to users, it is certainly wasteful when it forces service on uneconomic routes or encourages the use of uneconomic transport to service a route.

Considerable doubts exist regarding the role and effectiveness of federal regulation of and aid to the U.S. maritime transportation. The dismal cost-benefit figures associated with U.S. maritime regulation substantiate such doubts. For example, in 1978 about $500 million was spent in direct subsidies and about $200 million in indirect subsidies of the U.S. foreign-going merchant marine during that year. The subsidy cost was then nearly $1.00 per dollar of foreign exchange earned and nearly $0.42 per dollar of revenue. There are many types of regulation that have been questioned with regard to both content and method.

Safety regulation particularly warrants reevaluation. Although it is generally conceded that U.S. vessels are built and operated in accordance with higher standards of safety than foreign vessels, numerous studies have shown the safety record of U.S. vessels to be no more distinguished than the records of vessels emanating from other Western maritime nations.

The most important criticism of current maritime regulation is probably the lack of federal transportation policy coordination and long-range planning, with resulting failure to develop effective, desirable, and achievable comprehensive goals and objectives. This problem might be attributed to an excessively decentralized administrative and legislative structure. Currently 32 federal agencies and 12 congressional committees are responsible for transportation policy and programs, more than half of which have responsibilities in maritime transportation. This bureaucratic and administrative fragmentation follows from a maritime policy that is more the creature of special interest and exigency than the product of concern for the long-range welfare of the industry. Still, despite the demonstrated failings of U.S. maritime regulation, there is strong resistance to change.

The problems that result from this lack of planning and coordination are revealed particularly in the intermodal area. Because the federal government lacks regulation supporting intermodal coordination of rates and services, carriers are severely handicapped when trying to develop joint rates and services. The prohibition of the Interstate Commerce Commission (ICC) against joint rates that affect competition virtually guarantees that the U.S. maritime industry will continue struggling to compete against its foreign counterparts, who typically enjoy the advantage of being able to furnish joint rates and services. In recognition of this problem, several proposals designed to integrate modal regulation have been introduced into Congress.

In contrast to the disappointing performance of maritime regulation related to ocean transport, the inland water improvement program conducted by the Army Corps of Engineers has succeeded in stimulating the growth of inland transportation in recent years. However, this program has generated its own controversy. The railroads have complained that the use of public funds by Congress to maintain inland waterways discriminates against them because they alone must bear the financial burden of laying tracks, in addition to paying municipalities for rights of way, and because it thereby provides an undue advantage to inland water shipping. The needs of domestic shipping, on the other hand, are met effectively by the cabotage laws, which restrict this service to unsubsidized U.S.-flag and U.S.-built vessels. Federal expenditure for domestic and coastal water transport is relatively small and consists largely of costs for providing navigational channels and aids.

4.1. Economic Objectives of the Maritime Subsidies Program

The purported economic objectives of maritime subsidies include improved balance of payments, higher employment, increased productivity and capacity in the shipbuilding and ship operating industries, and assurance of nondiscriminatory freight rates. The resources allocated to meet these objectives must be subjected to opportunity cost analysis.

The argument for improving balance of payments is based on the fact that revenues of the U.S. merchant marine are either in the form of foreign exchange or in U.S. currency; without the U.S. fleet, all payments for shipping services would be paid for in foreign exchange. This position assumes that any contribution to positive balance of payments is welcome, regardless of its resource allocation efficiency. However, available resources, including subsidies, could be more productively employed either in export producing or import-substituting industries.

The objectives of maintaining both employment and productive capacity in the shipbuilding and ship operating industries are, respectively, to maintain present levels of employment and to avoid the future costs in time, capital, and training of labor necessary to expand the U.S. mechant marine, should the need arise. But the employment objective insufficiently accounts for the economy's ability to absorb this labor force into more productive activities in other industries. While the employment objective may apply to less skilled workers, its application to welders, engineers, and other skilled workers is questionable.

The objective of anticipating start-up costs in the future assumes that the world market will not be able or willing to supply the construction capacity and, in many cases, the secondhand tonnage needed to meet an increase in demand. But with present overtonnage of bulk carriage capacity, the overcapacity in the worldwide ship-building capability, and the resulting low cost of new bulk carriers, expanding the domestic fleet is not expected to be a problem in the near future.

The objective of assuring nondiscriminatory freight rates assumes that both conferences and tramp operators will price their services more competitively. But the manner in which a noncompetitive situation would arise and the means for sustaining this condition over periods of time have not been clearly conceived. Given the large carrying capacity of dry bulk carriers and the downward effect on rates of rather small increments of overcapacity, the prospects for rate-sustained discrimination appear unlikely.

In addition to specific economic objectives, the national security objective has been part of merchant marine legislation since passage of the Merchant Marine Act (MMA) of 1920.[1] This objective should be reanalyzed. It is based upon the assumption that the U.S. merchant marine is inherently more reliable than foreign shipping—that is, a domestic fleet, as well as a shipbuilding and ship repair industry, will ensure a steady flow of commerce during peacetime and an adequate flow of military cargo during wartime. But a basically competitive, profit-oriented market with completely mobile capital and equipment requires closer examination and fewer nationalistic assumptions when evaluating reliability.

In determining the fleet size required to meet the national security objective, it would be necessary to postulate the size, location, and duration of potential conflicts, the importance of cargo transport for a successful outcome, and the likelihood that foreign shipping would not be available. The fact that the United States was able to maintain a relatively smooth flow of ocean trade throughout the Vietnam conflict and the oil embargo, despite substantial reliance upon foreign vessels, points to a need to reconsider the essential fleet requirements.

Looking ahead, it is also necessary to examine the trend toward the development of national fleets and its effects on the availability of competitive U.S. commercial shipping under foreign-flag registry. This examination should extend to U.S.-controlled shipping to determine the probability that its services should be conscripted during time of national emergency.[2] It is necessary to review the level of trade, particularly in raw materials, which the United States will require, and the mix of private, public, national, and multinational entities involved in the production, marketing, and shipment of both imports and exports.

Most important for effective implementation of the national security objective is the involvement of the U.S. Department of Defense (DOD) in both the definition of requirements and their implications. At present, subsidies are planned and financed through the Department of Commerce (DOC). It costs the DOD nothing to voice support for the continued growth in these subsidies. Despite this fact, former Defense Secretary McNamara took issue with the proposal for a high shipbuilding program for the merchant marine. Without a clear definition of national security requirements and a concomitant allocation of resources and funds from the DOD, this objective will remain more jargon than judgement.

4.2.   Cost Framework of Maritime Programs

The costs of the various components of the maritime subsidy program can be computed in some cases and estimated in others. Operating Differential Subsidy (ODS), Construction Differential Subsidy (CDS), Title XI mortgage guarantee, cargo preference laws, and the Capital Construction Fund (CCF) are major components. The costs of these programs may be viewed as transfer payments, made to the shipyards in the case of CDS, and to the maritime unions, insurance companies, and repair yards in the case of ODS—all with the goal of maintaining a U.S.-built and -crewed merchant marine. In fact, much of the government aid proffered to help maintain a competitive U.S. Merchant Marine really ends up sheltering U.S. marine auxiliary and support industries.

The costs of shipping preference cargo are higher than competitive costs for tramp and liner-type shipments. Tramp shipment cargoes, if shipped in U.S.-flag vessels, which cost about twice as much to build and somewhat more to operate as foreign vessels, pay a higher than world rate. With liner shipments or cargoes shipped under open rates, the higher costs of U.S. liner operations can be passed on directly in determining conference rates. For preference cargo, shipped under conference rates, there is no primary savings associated with shipping in foreign vessels operating under the same conference rates. However, the influence of large shipments of preference cargo can cause the U.S. members of the conference to push for oligopolistic pricing toward these captive cargoes where they do not significantly depress demand from nonpreference sources.

For Defense Department shipments between 1952 and 1972, the cost of using U.S. vessels exclusively was estimated to be $3.8 billion, or 42 percent of the total commercial payments by the Military Sealift Command. This figure may be conservative since the costs, particularly during the Vietnam buildup, included not only the liner conferences' oligopolistic price, but also the monopolistic price of U.S.-flag vessels serving a war zone. These cargo preference figures exclude operating subsidies paid to subsidized liners carrying preference cargo.

The total of direct and indirect costs of all federal programs is estimated at between $600 to $900 million per year now. At this time it is difficult to determine the value of the economic benefits derived from these expenditures. The percentage of U.S. trade carried by U.S.-flag vessels is diminishing. It is apparent that, notwithstanding massive expenditures of direct and indirect aid and some discriminatory regulation in favor of shipping by U.S.-flag vessels, the objectives of maintaining a large and viable merchant marine in foreign trade has not been accomplished.

Two statements from *American Shipper* (September 1976), referring to the effectiveness of the Merchant Marine Act (MMA) of 1970 on the U.S. bulk carrier fleet, summarize the present situation:

> *The Merchant Marine Subcommittee . . . acknowledged that the 1970 revisions of the Merchant Marine Act, which extended several maritime aid programs, including subsidies, had failed to produce the expected surge in American ship construction.*

MarAd reports . . . that bulk vessels are being built at a faster rate than any other type of ship everywhere except the U.S. The world bulk fleet increased by 563 ships in 1973, while the number of U.S. flag bulk carriers dropped from 30 to 19 in the same year. The 1970 revisions of the Merchant Marine Act extended operating and construction differential subsidies to the nonliner fleet—mostly dry bulk carriers—but only two ore/bulk/oil (OBO) carriers, the Ultrasea and the Ultramar, have been built as a result of the 1970 Act.

4.2.1. Capital Construction Fund

The cost to the government of the Capital Construction Fund Program is technically the present value of the costs resulting from deferred collection of taxes. Total Capital Construction deposits amounted to about $650 million in 1970. They continue to increase. Assuming a mix of capital gains and corporate earnings of about 1:3, this amounts to about $275 million in tax receivables, collection on which has been deferred. An additional $100 million was estimated to have been deferred in the period between 1936 and 1947, thus increasing total tax deferrals to approximately $375 million.

The cost of the Operating Subsidy Program (OSP), excluding administrative costs, totalled $5.2 billion from 1936 to 1978 (Table 4-1). The amounts for 1976–78 were $386.4, $343.9, and $303.2 million, respectively. It is difficult to project cost levels in the 1980s because of the large number of proposals pending which would drastically change the method, allocation, and amount of subsidy funding of the maritime industry.

As of September 30, 1979, eight operators in the liner trades and 12 operators in the bulk trades were receiving ODS subsidies. Included in this program were 165 liners and 21 bulk carriers. These figures do not include Soviet grain ODS contracts effective as of September 30, 1978.

4.2.2. CDS Program

The cost of the Construction Subsidies Program was $2.9 billion from 1936 to 1978 (Table 4-1). In the years 1976 through 1978, the costs were $233.8, $203.5, and $148.4 million, respectively. The generally low level in recent years reflects the general recession in shipbuilding activity worldwide as well as a serious decline in the United States. Of the 20 ships delivered by U.S. shipyards in fiscal year 1978, four were subsidized. Of the liquid and dry bulk carriers, one crude oil tanker was subsidized, while four crude oil tankers, one LNG, and two bulk carriers were not (Table 4-2). Worldwide ship deliveries are listed in Table 4-3.

Table 4-1 Maritime Subsidy Outlays, 1936–1978

Fiscal Year	CDS	Reconstruction Subsidy	Total	ODS	Total ODS and CDS
1936–1955	$ 248,320,942*	$ 3,286,888	$ 251,607,830	$ 341,109,987	$ 592,717,817
1956–1960	129,806,005	34,881,409	164,687,414	644,115,146	808,802,560
1961	100,145,654	1,215,432	101,361,086	150,142,575	251,503,661
1962	134,552,647	4,160,591	138,713,238	181,918,756	320,631,994
1963	89,235,895	4,181,314	93,417,209	220,676,685	314,093,894
1964	76,608,323	1,665,087	78,273,410	203,036,844	281,310,254
1965	86,096,872	38,138	86,135,010	213,334,409	299,459,419
1966	69,446,510	2,571,566	72,018,076	186,628,357	258,646,433
1967	80,155,452	932,144	81,087,566	175,631,860	256,719,426
1968	95,989,586	96,707	96,086,293	200,129,670	296,215,963
1969	93,952,849	57,329	94,010,178	194,702,569	288,712,747
1970	73,528,904	21,723,343	95,252,247	205,731,711	300,983,958
1971	107,637,353	27,450,968	135,088,321	268,021,097	403,109,418
1972	111,950,403	29,748,076	141,698,479	235,666,821	377,365,300
1973	168,183,937	17,384,604	185,568,541	226,710,926	412,279,467
1974	185,060,501	13,844,951	198,905,452	257,919,080	456,824,532
1975	237,895,092	1,900,571	239,795,663	243,152,340	482,948,003
1976†	233,826,424	9,886,024	243,712,448	386,433,994	630,146,442
1977	203,479,571	15,052,072	218,531,643	343,875,521	562,407,164
1978	148,690,842	7,318,705	156,009,547	303,193,575	459,203,122
Total	$2,674,563,762	$197,395,889	$2,871,959,651	$5,182,131,923	$8,054,091,574

SOURCE: Compiled from *Annual Reports, 1965–1979* Maritime Administration, U.S. Department of Commerce.
* Includes $131.5 million CDS adjustments covering the World War II period, $105.8 million equivalent to CDS allowances which were made in connection with the Mariner Ship Construction program, and $10.8 million for CDS in fiscal years 1954 to 1955.
† Includes totals for FY 1976 and the transition quarter ending September 30, 1976.

Table 4-2   New Ships Delivered from U.S. Shipyards during FY 1978

Owner	Builder	Type	No. of Vessels
Subsidized			
Gulf Oil Corp.	Bethlehem (Sparrows Point, Md.)	Crude oil tanker	1
El Paso Southern Tanker Co.	Newport News Shipbuilding and Dry Dock (Va.)	LNG carrier	1
Wilmington Trust Co. (Summit II, Inc.)	General Dynamics (Quincy, Mass.)	LNG carrier	1
Wilmington Trust Co. (Summit III, Inc.)	General Dynamics (Quincy, Mass.)	LNG carrieer	2
Total Subsidized Deliveries			4
Nonsubsidized			
SOHIO Subsidiaries	Avondale Shipyards (La.)	Crude oil tankers	4
Manufacturers Hanover Trust Co. (Shipmor Associates)	National Steel and Shipbuilding (Cal.)	Crude oil tankers	3
General Electric Credit Corp. (Shell Oil Co.)	National Steel and Shipbuilding (Cal.)	Crude oil tankers	1
Patriot I Shipping Corp.	General Dynamics (Quincy, Mass.)	LNG carrier	1
SOHIO Subsidiary	Sun Ship (Del)	Crude oil tanker	1
Standard Oil Co. of Calif.	FMC (Cal.)	Product tanker	1
Cleveland Tankers, Inc.	Levingston Shipbuilding (Tex.)	Product tanker	1
Matson Navigation Co.	Bath Iron Works (Me.)	Containership	1
Bethlehem Steel Corp.	Bay Shipbuilding	Bulk carrier	1
American Steamship Co.	Bay Shipbuilding	Bulk carrier	1
CF Industries	Avondale/Peterson Builders	Tug/barge	1
Total Nonsubsidized Deliveries			16
Total New Ships Delivered FY 1978			20

SOURCE: *U.S. Shipbuilders Council Report,* 1979, p. 18.

Table 4–3 Worldwide Ship Deliveries—Calendar Year 1977 (tonnage in thousands)

Country of Construction	Total, All Types		Comb. Passenger and Cargo		Freighters		Bulk Carriers		Tankers	
	No.	DWT	No.	DWT	No.	DWT	No.	DWT	No.	DWT
United States	17	1,621.8	—	—	2	37.0	—	—	15	1,584.8
Brazil	21	544.5	1	2.5	12	99.5	9	445.0	—	—
Denmark	32	1,211.6	1	0.7	20	165.4	5	243.8	6	799.9
France	27	1,555.7	—	—	15	197.5	—	—	11	1,357.5
Germany, East	30	387.1	—	—	26	298.0	4	89.1	—	—
Germany, West	89	2,248.0	—	—	66	702.2	9	586.3	14	959.8
Italy	19	1,094.1	—	—	5	64.0	5	520.9	9	509.2
Japan	670	19,744.4	—	—	287	3,453.7	320	10,507.4	63	5,783.3
Korea, South	39	1,173.8	—	—	23	307.9	12	273.8	4	592.1
Netherlands	41	275.4	1	1.7	38	195.4	—	—	3	80.0
Norway	49	752.8	—	—	25	170.1	4	188.6	19	392.4
Poland	30	659.6	—	—	18	215.4	6	237.6	6	206.6
Spain	60	3,227.7	—	—	37	367.0	8	157.3	15	2,703.4
Sweden	32	4,002.4	—	—	3	15.1	6	628.5	23	3,358.8
United Kingdom	48	2,466.9	—	—	24	350.1	13	549.2	11	1,567.6
U.S.S.R.	31	395.5	—	—	21	134.1	6	41.2	4	220.2
Yugoslavia	13	682.3	—	—	3	45.4	8	575.6	2	61.3
All others	116	2,933.8	1	1.9	59	415.9	35	1,173.7	21	1.342.3
Total	1,364	44,977.7	4	6.8	684	7,233.7	450	16,218.0	226	21,519.2

4.2.3. Title XI Mortgage Guarantees

The total amount of shipbuilding mortgages covered under Title XI in June, 1978, amounted to 257 deep draft vessels (tankers, general cargo, LNG, bulk/oil) with a total value of $3.7 billion, with an additional 75 vessels valued at $3.6 billion in pending applications. A summary of Title XI financing is shown in Table 4-4.

4.3. Impact of Government Programs

Howard Casey, then Deputy Assistant, Secretary for Maritime Affairs, stated while addressing the Third Flag Lines Seminar in New York in 1976 that "measured against long-term goals of the 1970 Merchant Marine Act, U.S. shipping results and shipbuilding potentials are now disappointing."[3]

In 1977 U.S.-flag carriers transported 35 million tons, 4.5 percent of the 775 million tons of waterborne cargo that moved in U.S. trade. In 1976 the comparable percentage was 4.8 percent and the average percentage, since the passage of the Merchant Marine Act of 1970 through 1977, was merely 5.3 percent.

These averages are far below comparable levels of participation by merchant fleets of other nations which typically lift from 30 percent to 70 percent of their foreign trade tonnage. For example, for years the Soviet Union's fleet has carried 50 percent of its foreign trade shipments. Also impressive are the percentages of the following fleets: People's Republic of China, 70 percent; Greece, 45 percent; Japan, 39 percent; Norway and Spain, 37 percent; United Kingdom, 34 percent; and West Germany and France, approximately 30 percent.

Secretary Casey noted that "the comparatively low level of U.S.-flag carriage is due to the lack of a modern bulk carrier fleet." (Table 2-2 and Table 4-5). In fact, as of September, 1978, only 15 bulk carriers were being operated in the American fleet. Contrasted with the small size of the U.S.-registered bulk carrier fleet is the excess of 45 million DWT of world shipping. Of the 24 new vessels on which CDS was being paid as of September, 1978, not one was a bulk carrier.

In 1977 approximately 438.6 million tons of tanker cargo moved in U.S. foreign trade. Of this amount, only 14.6 million tons, or 3.3 percent, were carried by American flag vessels. Turning to tramp and other nonliner cargoes, which totalled 289 million tons last year, U.S.-flag vessels accounted for only 5.7 million tons, a dismal 2.0 percent (Table 4-6).

Secretary Casey cited 1974 and 1975 statistics to support his contention that "the only respectable level of U.S. foreign trade carriage

Table 4–4 Federal Ship Financing Guarantees* (Title XI) Program Summary—Principal Liability on September 30, 1978

	Contracts In Force		Applications Pending	
Vessel Types	*Vessels Covered*	*Principal Amount†*	*Vessels Covered*	*Principal Amount†*
Deepdraft Transport Vessels				
Tankers	63	$1,141,749,229	7	$ 369,352,000
Cargo	163	945,652,292	31	706,076,525
LNGs	16	1,395,446,400	21	2,318,710,750
Bulk/OBOs	15	221,791,934	16	219,490,750
Total, Transport Vessels	257	$3,704,639,855	75	$3,613,630,025
Industrial and Service Vessels				
Drill Rigs/Ships	50	695,787,998	11	177,261,240
Tugs/Barges/Drill Services	2,082	1,134,978,017	350	706,126,367
Miscellaneous	6	80,812,866	9	115,074,760
Total, Industrial/Service Vessels	2,138	$1,911,578,881	370	$ 998,462,367
Total Vessels	2,395	$5,616,218,736	445	$4,612,092,392
Shipboard Lighters	1,732	$ 62,767,990	0	
Total, Vessels and Lighters	4,127	$5,678,986,726	445	$4,612,092,392

SOURCE: U.S. Department of Commerce, Maritime Administration, *Annual Report*, 1979.
* Statutory limit $9.925 billion.
† Rounded to the nearest dollar.

Table 4–5 Employment of U.S.-Flag Oceangoing Fleet*—September 30, 1978

Status and Area of Employment	Total		Combination Pass./Cargo		Freighters		Tankers	
	No.	DWT (000)	No.	DWT (000)	No.	DWT (000)	No.	DWT (000)
Active Vessels	554	17,649	9	75	284	4,969	261	12,605
Foreign Trade	247	7,960	4	37	185	3,522	58	4,401
Nearby Foreign†	43	2,791	0	0	1	25	42	2,766
Great Lakes–Seaway Foreign	4	65	0	0	4	65	0	0
Overseas Foreign	200	5,104	4	37	180	3,432	16	1,635
Foreign to Foreign	19	524	0	0	15	270	4	254
Domestic Trade	221	7,721	0	0	46	685	175	7,036
Coastwide	124	3,539	0	0	6	111	118	3,428
Intercoastal	16	517	0	0	0	0	16	517
Noncontiguous	81	3,665	0	0	40	574	41	3,091
Other U.S. Agency Operations	67	1,444	5	38	38	492	24	914
MSC Charter	45	1,232	0	0	23	339	22	893
Bareboat Charter & Other Custody	22	212	5	38	15	153	2	21
Inactive Vessels	287	3,604	53	327	206	2,436	28	841
Temporary Inactive	21	462	0	0	15	259	6	203
Laid-Up (privately owned)	30	745	2	13	18	258	10	474
National Defense Reserve Fleet (NDRF)‡	227	2,283	50	304	165	1,815	12	164
Laid-Up (MarAd-owned) Pending Disposition**	9	114	1	10	8	104	0	0
Total, Active and Inactive	841	21,253	62	402	490	7,405	289	13,446

SOURCE: U.S. Department of Commerce, Maritime Administration, U.S. Merchant Marine Data Sheet, Nov. 1978, p. 3.

* Excludes vessels operating exclusively on the inland waterways and Great Lakes, those owned by the U.S. Army and Navy, and special types such as tugs, cable ships, and so forth.

† Nearby foreign trade includes Canada, Mexico, Central America, West Indies, and north coast of South America.

‡ Includes three vessels of Pacific Far East Line, Inc., berthed by NDRF.

** Other than vessels in the National Defense Reserve Fleet.

Table 4–6 U.S. Oceanborne Foreign Trade/Commercial Cargo Carried

	Tonnage (in millions)									
	1968	1969	1970	1971	1972	1973	1974	1975	1976	1977
Total tons	418.6	427.5	473.2	457.4	513.6	631.6	628.9	615.6	698.8	775.3
U.S.-flag tons	25.0	19.8	25.2	24.4	23.8	39.9	40.9	31.4	33.8	34.8
U.S. percent of total	6.0	4.6	5.3	5.3	4.6	6.3	6.5	5.1	4.8	4.5
Liner total tons	46.1	41.9	50.4	44.2	44.6	51.3	51.4	44.3	49.8	47.8
Liner U.S.-flag tons	11.1	9.7	11.8	10.1	9.8	13.2	15.4	13.6	15.4	14.4
Liner U.S. percent	24.0	23.1	23.5	22.9	21.9	25.8	29.8	30.7	30.9	30.2
Nonliner total tons	209.5	212.1	240.7	220.7	242.6	281.9	282.7	275.3	289.6	289.0
Nonliner U.S.-flag tons	6.4	4.6	5.4	4.8	3.8	4.5	5.0	3.8	4.9	5.7
Nonliner U.S. percent	3.0	2.2	2.2	2.1	1.6	1.6	1.8	1.4	1.7	2.0
Tanker total tons	163.1	173.5	182.1	192.5	226.4	298.4	294.8	296.0	359.4	438.6
Tanker U.S.-flag tons	7.5	5.5	8.0	9.5	10.2	22.2	20.5	14.0	13.6	14.6
Tanker U.S. percent	4.6	3.2	4.4	4.9	4.5	7.4	7.0	4.7	3.8	3.3

Table 4–6 (continued)

| | Dollar Value (in billions) | | | | | | | | | |
	1968	1969	1970	1971	1972	1973	1974	1975	1976	1977
Total value	41.1	41.9	49.7	50.4	60.5	84.0	124.2	127.5	148.4	171.2
U.S.-flag value	8.5	8.1	10.3	9.9	11.1	15.9	22.0	22.4	26.4	28.0
U.S. percent of total	20.7	19.1	20.7	19.6	18.4	18.9	17.7	17.5	17.8	16.4
Liner total value	25.8	27.2	33.5	32.4	37.4	49.6	63.4	64.0	75.8	82.3
Liner U.S.-flag value	7.8	7.5	9.7	9.2	10.3	14.4	19.4	20.0	23.9	25.2
Liner U.S. percent	29.0	27.6	28.8	28.4	27.7	29.1	30.6	31.2	31.6	30.7
Nonliner total value	10.8	11.1	12.2	13.2	17.4	25.2	34.7	36.6	38.2	42.7
Nonliner U.S.-flag value	.5	.4	.4	.4	.4	.7	.8	1.0	1.1	1.2
Nonliner U.S. percent	4.5	3.6	3.3	3.1	2.4	2.5	2.3	2.8	2.8	2.8
Tanker total value	3.4	3.6	4.0	4.9	5.7	9.2	26.0	26.9	34.4	46.2
Tanker U.S.-flag value	.2	.2	.2	.3	.4	.8	1.8	1.4	1.4	1.6
Tanker U.S. percent	6.6	5.6	5.6	5.5	6.2	9.1	6.9	5.1	4.2	3.5

SOURCE: U.S. Department of Commerce, Maritime Administration, Division of Trade Studies and Statistics, Nov. 1978.

Note: Cargo includes government-sponsored cargo; excludes Department of Defense cargo and U.S./Canada translakes cargo.

achieved by any segment of the American flag fleet has been in liner operations." This statement is confirmed by more recent statistics. In 1976 and 1977 U.S.-flag liner companies accounted for 15.4 and 14.4 million tons respectively, which was equated to 30 percent of U.S. liner cargo shipments that moved in foreign trade during those years. This percentage is a significant improvement over the years 1966–1973, when U.S.-flag liner carriage averaged less than 24 percent of the tonnage moved.

To summarize, government programs have become increasingly expensive to the taxpayer and as a function of public expenditure. While the terms of many of these programs have been liberalized to benefit U.S.-flag bulk shipping (in addition to other segments of the maritime industry), their success in expanding the fleet of U.S.-flag services, particularly in bulk shipping, has been primarily marginal at best.

4.4. Shortcomings of Current Government Programs

Of the major programs aimed at achieving the objectives of U.S. maritime policy (Table 3-1), only cargo preference, mortgage guarantee, construction loan guarantee, investment tax credit, ship exchange, and cabotage laws applied to bulk shipping until 1970. The Merchant Marine Act of 1970 authorized the construction and operating differential subsidy (ODS) to be applied to U.S.-built, U.S.-flag bulk vessels in the foreign trade of the United States.[4] Yet even this liberalization of the law has done little to improve incentives for the investment in and operation of U.S.-flag bulk carriers or other type carriers.

Lack of improvement can be attributed to the fact that the disadvantages, managerial burdens, complications, costs, and disincentives associated with these programs and policies have rendered well-intentioned programs, both counterproductive and ultimately prohibitive to investment and fleet expansion. Consequently, U.S. maritime programs and policies have neither promoted the growth of the U.S. merchant marine, nor succeeded in helping it achieve significant participation in international trade, particularly in the bulk trades.

At one time the consequences of such failure might not be significant: This is not true today. Much of the foreign-flag fleet capacity used in U.S. trade consists largely of tankers and bulk carriers registered under flags of convenience yet U.S. owned. For many years the fleet has been considered available to serve the purpose of the U.S. government in times of emergency. Recently, however, some doubts have been expressed regarding this assumption based on increasing nationalism and independence in international affairs of countries that traditionally have offered registry to vessels under flags of convenience.

Under existing legislation the interests of the U.S. government often clash with those of both shippers and operators. Existing programs are inflexible and often frustrate the U.S. maritime industry's ability to respond effectively to changes in the conditions and terms of world shipping. A review of several areas in which implementation of programs is slow, unwieldy, and encumbering follows.

Many intermediate management decisions of operators are subjected to lengthy government reviews. For example, liner operators must obtain Maritime Administration (MarAd) approval for changes in schedule or routing when serving "essential trade routes." Moreover, federal auditors and cost accountants in the offices of each subsidized operator are charged with a continuous review of operators' crews, maintenance, and repairs, as well as other subsidizable costs. Complying with documentation requirements for subsidy claims is cumbersome.

Routes and schedules remain inflexible. Operators are required to serve assigned routes long after some or all such service becomes unprofitable or non-essential, while approvals to serve new profitable routes are fraught with delays. A typical example is the rapidly developing trade with countries in the Persian Gulf. U.S. liner operators lost major opportunities as a result of delay in providing increased service to the area on a timely basis, and the current unsettled situation in the area makes prediction of future developments there impossible.

The unavailability (until recent years) of large U.S.-built marine diesels, and the interpretation of the 'Built American' subsection of the MMA to mean that not only the whole ship but each major subsection thereof must be made in the United States, has resulted in new U.S. ships being equipped with fuel-inefficient steam turbine plants. This has been the case even in recent years of skyrocketing fuel prices.

Present policies have raised the costs of American flag operation; existing legislation has neither provided the incentives necessary for expansion nor promoted efficient operation of U.S. international shipping. Under the present system, operational savings accrue in large measures to the benefit of the government, rather than to the operator, and are certain to increase capital costs. Thus any attempt to decrease operating cost, if successful, is less important to a subsidized operator than the problem of financing new construction, terminals, and operations in general. Consequently most subsidized operators have resisted or lagged behind in the adoption of labor-saving and other cost-reducing measures; basic economizing, such as reducing crew size and negotiating favorable contracts, has been resisted. It is not surprising, therefore, that both subsidy and cargo preference costs have continued to rise.

4.5. Problems Affecting Specific Programs

To be eligible for MMA Title XI assistance, the shipowner must meet certain requirements. His net worth and working capital must cover the difference between the capitalizable cost of the vessel and the amount of the mortgage guarantee. In addition, the owner must obtain MarAd consent to perform major financial transfers, such as withdrawal of capital, payment of dividends, significant increase in employee compensation, transfer of funds to stockholders other than dividends, increase in indebtedness, or the transfer of control of vessels.

The Construction Differential Subsidy (CDS), as currently implemented, has several disadvantages. First, the vessel must be involved in U.S. commerce and cannot participate in domestic trades, except with MarAd approval and with a proportional refund of CDS funds. Second, the vessel must be constructed with U.S. materials, insofar as practical, thus limiting access to foreign technology and equipment.[5] Third, there is the inevitable delay and paperwork involved in dealing with the government. Finally, perhaps the most serious impediments are the requirements in Section 804(a) of the MMA of 1936, the "grandfather clause"[6] stating that:

> (e)xcept as provided in subsections (b) and (c) of this section, it shall be unlawful for any contractor receiving an operating-differential subsidy under Title VI or for any charterer of vessels under Title VII of this Act, or any holding company, subsidiary, affiliate, or associate of such contractor or such charterer, or any officer, director, agent or executive thereof, directly or indirectly, to own, charter, act as an agent or broker for, or operate any foreign flag vessel which competes with any American flag service determined by the Secretary of Commerce to be essential as provided in Section 211 of this Act . . . .

Section 804(b) states that the Secretary of Commerce may waive this provision for a specific contractor and for a specific limit of time.[7] Section 804(c) states that the provisions do not apply to a contractor who has filed with the Secretary of Commerce a list of foreign-flag vessels which he "directly or indirectly owned, chartered, or acted as an agent or broker for or operated on April 15, 1970."[8] The contractor is permitted to continue owning, operating, and/or chartering these vessels until April 1990 if they are engaged in the carriage of dry or liquid bulk cargoes.

The principal disadvantage of the Operating Differential Subsidy (ODS) is the governmental interference in management which accompanies it. Other disadvantages also associated with this subsidy program include the required maintenance of specialized levels of operating funds and net worth,[9] limits on distribution of dividends, and a prohibition on domestic trade (except with written permission of the Maritime Subsidy Board). A recipient is required to perform all, except emergency, repairs in the United States or Puerto Rico. Furthermore, U.S. subsidized liner operators are restricted in their competition with other existing U.S.-flag subsidized operators in a given trade.

Recipients of ODS are also subject to excess profit recapture. Operators who make a profit (gross) in excess of 10 percent on the "Capital Employed" in their operation must return ODS funding equal to such excess profits. As a result, operators tend to limit their profit so they do not exceed the 10 percent level, with a resulting increase in operating cost attributable to extravagant expenditures made in order to avoid recapture.

The requirement that a subsidized vessel be replaced at the end of its statutory life (usually by an "equivalent" vessel) introduces major constraints on operations. Frequently it is advisable to replace a vessel well before or after expiration of the statutory vessel life.

Furthermore, both CDS and ODS restrict the flexibility of the owner in disposing of his ship. If the owner wishes to sell the vessel during its statutory life, which is 25 years for dry bulk carriers, he must sell it to an operator who will maintain its U.S.-flag status. The ODS will be transferred with the ship only if the new owner meets MarAd subsidy requirements. In the ODS contract, the applicant agrees to own or lease vessels, of a number or type, to remain competitive in the trade. The owner can therefore be required to replace the vessel at the end of its statutory life, regardless of the condition of the vessel. If MarAd makes such a request and the owner refuses, he can lose his ODS funds.

Moreover, good business practice often requires replacement with a different type or size of vessel, or no vessel at all. Although the MMA of 1970 was supposed to open subsidy and other government aid programs to U.S.-flag bulk shipping, it has had little effect in developing the bulk shipping fleet. The existing preference laws still benefit older tonnage, much of which is acquired at rock-bottom prices through the Ship Exchange and Trade-in Program. It is difficult for an owner to justify investment in new bulk tonnage, even with CDS, when he can obtain adequate, yet inefficient tonnage through the above programs at a fraction of the capital cost and without the various statutory requirements imposed on a recipient of CDS, and he may trade in his vessel when he wishes. The total cost of owning such an exchange vessel is small compared to the cost of depreciating a new subsidized vessel.

In fairness, the problems of the U.S. maritime industry should not be attributed exclusively to maritime policies and programs. Other factors have contributed to the current situation. The current global surplus of bulk carriers, the lead time necessary for ship construction, and taxation disadvantages of American flag ownership have played important roles. The high energy cost of running U.S.-flag vessels, which, unlike their foreign counterparts, are not diesel fueled, should not be discounted. Nevertheless, the current programs have fostered artificial cost parity, inhibited productivity, and to some extent, have hindered effective operations management. The competitive posture of the U.S. merchant marine has suffered as a result.

4.6. Future or Pending Policy Issues and Suggested Policy Changes

Over 90 percent of all U.S. foreign trade is carried by ocean transportation. This is expected to increase as trade with neighboring Canada and Mexico diminishes in importance. Although U.S. foreign trade is expected to double in volume between 1980 and 1990, the share of U.S. foreign trade carried by U.S.-flag vessels is dropping. The ability to control discriminatory factors against U.S. foreign trade and to compete effectively in the world market is thus seriously eroding.

The current technological revolution in shipbuilding, shipping, and oceanology provides an opportunity for the United States to regain maritime leadership. Possibly U.S.-flag operations may compete worldwide without subsidy, with results that would include enhanced U.S. leadership in foreign trade, improvements in the balance of payments, and greater employment opportunities in maritime transportation. In addition, employment opportunities would flow from private involvement, American ingenuity, and the commitment of the United States to free enterprise, labor, and industry.

This can be accomplished if the current emphasis of government aid in combination with governmental regulation of management, which generally has been ineffective, is discontinued. It must be replaced with an efficient system of subsidies and preferences geared to creating sound commercial operations that must eventually be able to stand unaided and thus entail decreasing reliance on federal funding and control. A system of dispensing aid based on performance, as well as need, can serve this purpose and the public interest because:

- The recipient of aid is motivated by self-interest to produce more and to cut costs, resulting in higher profits and increased returns on his capital investment.
- Production is the manifestation of the capability to produce. It is the measure of the public benefit.

The United States should adopt a *national* maritime policy and program and enact supporting legislation if its merchant marine is to be revitalized. An adequate merchant fleet should consist of every kind of advanced ship needed, not only to carry a meaningful part of U.S. foreign commerce, but also to satisfy emergency transportation requirements as needed for the economic health and military posture of the nation.

In addition, a unified effort is required to coordinate efficiently all federal maritime activities and to implement policies of the Merchant Marine Resources, Engineering, and Development Acts, with full participation by private and local interests. A vigorous, meaningful, and well-coordinated research and development effort for all maritime transportation aspects is also required.

American maritime regulation and policy should encourage new investments, improved management, and more responsive operation in U.S. maritime transportation. Various changes in policy and regulation could be adopted that might improve U.S. maritime transportation. These include: liberalization of tax clauses relating to reserve funds and capital investments (including terminal construction, containers, wheelbody, dockside equipment, finance, etc.); extension of international agreements on trade liberalization; documentary simplification and reduction in inspection and formality requirements for cargoes and vessels in international trade; and repeal of counterincentive measures.

The following sections present policies that might be considered as part of an overall federal maritime policy. These proposals are not necessarily complementary nor consistent, but are offered as approaches to be considered.

4.6.1. Integrated Foreign and Domestic Inland Water Transportation

Inland water transportation is cost effective and energy efficient, but it is not fully utilized because of the large split in federal regulatory and policy responsibilities.

Policy Statement. Technological developments allow foreign oceangoing vessels or component parts thereof, such as barges discharged from barge-carrying ships or integrated barge tows, to enter domestic inland waterways and provide direct delivery at an inland point. Currently, only U.S.-flag vessels may provide inland service, with some exceptions. Because barges are interchanged and often form part of an international pool, this policy may interfere with efficient, integrated operations. This is particularly relevant to tin, lead, zinc, and other minerals customarily shipped on liner (common carrier) shipping.

Possible Policy Change. One proposed change is to relax present policy to permit vessels of any registry to ply U.S. inland waterways, as long as their inland destinations are used only for discharge of import cargoes and their inland origins are used only for the loading of export cargoes. This could be done by designating certain inland water ports as foreign trade ports.

4.6.2. Use of Domestic Vessels in Foreign Trade and Vice Versa

Policy Statement. Changing demands make it advisable that U.S.-flag bulk carriers be used interchangeably in domestic and international trade. As domestic fleet vessels are all built without the benefit of CDS, they have a distinct disadvantage when used interchangeably in foreign trade. The domestic market for the employment for such ships has deteriorated in recent years due to several economic factors. Yet in the future the domestic market may offer better opportunities than foreign trade for some types of ships.

In view of their higher construction and interest costs, these vessels cannot compete with subsidized U.S. vessels or foreign-flag vessels for U.S. foreign commerce. These vessels are, therefore, primarily consigned to the carriage of government-impelled cargoes. When such cargoes are not available, the vessels are usually laid up. During the winter of 1972 about 12 percent of U.S.-flag tonnage was in lay-up because of lack of cargoes. Of this, approximately 80 percent was independently owned; the remainder was owned by the major oil companies.

Possible Policy Change. A possible policy change is to consider some form of governmental aid to domestic fleet and similar vessels built without CDS funds, under Section 603(b) of the Merchant Marine Act.[10] This would include a subsidy applicable to vessel depreciation costs and the interest expenses for vessels constructed, or substantially reconstructed, recently. Only the most competitive U.S.-flag tonnage providing essential services should be considered. This restriction could preclude extending the employment of obsolete tonnage beyond its economic life.

4.6.3. International Shipping

The following are potential future policy issues affecting U.S.-flag international bulk shipping:

4.6.3.1. Flat Rate ODS and CDS

Policy Statement. Operating Differential Subsidies (ODS) are designed to assure parity of U.S. operating costs with lower foreign costs for crew wages, liability insurance, and other specific items on particular trade routes. As a result, subsidized U.S. operators have insufficient motives for resisting exorbitant wage and other cost increases because the government absorbs much of the increases through higher ODS payments.

Similarly, the present system of granting Construction Differential Subsidies (CDS) as a percentage of total costs allows the ship owners to pass on many "custom" design features. This works against the design for least cost consistent with the requirements of the intended service.

Potential Policy Change. A possible change would be to establish fixed levels of ODS subsidies for a five-year period. Increased costs above the levels indicated by the GNY deflator would be borne by the operators. Similarly, the Maritime Subsidy Board could set fixed amounts of CDS (in dollars rather than percentages) for representative sizes of the principal types of ships.

This policy change was implemented in a decision by the Maritime Subsidy Board on April 21, 1976, which awarded to American Export Lines a "lump sum" operating subsidy for North Atlantic operations. The Board felt that the AEL case was a good opportunity to experiment with the less than full subsidy award.

4.6.3.2. Reduction of Shipbuilding Cost through Increased Direct Support

Policy Statement. Under the present program, the shipbuilding community obtains direct subsidy payments. As the cost to the subsidized owner is independent of actual U.S. shipbuilding costs, he has no incentive to increase his demand. Also, the shipbuilder is subject to a fixed percentage subsidy, which is a counterincentive.

Potential Policy Changes. Changes in regard to this issue might include:

- Offering a fixed dollar subsidy independent of price of ship or price to owner;
- Improving tax credit provision for shipbuilders with large new-facility investment;
- Providing tax credit to the supplier industry;
- Requiring conformity of U.S. contract provisions and specifications to accepted foreign standards and, as a result, better

comparative cost analysis; and
• Subsidizing interest rates for shipyard facility investments.

4.6.3.3. Substitution of Tax and Credit Incentives for ODS and CDS

Policy Statement. Government support of the U.S. merchant marine is now by direct subsidies. Aid by indirect subsidies, on the other hand, in the form of tax and credit incentives, might achieve the same general objectives and provide a more stable basis by eliminating present dependence on annual legislative appropriations for subsidies.

Potential Policy Changes. A possible change would be to substitute indirect supports for ODS and CDS and to extend these indirect supports equally to all U.S.-flag foreign shipping operations rather than to "qualified" operators only. Some viable approaches would include:

• Subsidizing interest rates on ship mortgages and shipyard investment, as well as accelerated depreciation of ship investments;
• Changing ship tax depreciation and permission for reinvestment of ship sales proceeds with deferred tax liability;
• Eliminating ODS, CDS, and preference cargo terms; and
• Retaining other MMA provisions,[11] including the Jones Act[12] and Title XI.[13]

4.6.3.4. Creation of Maritime International Sales Corporations (MISC) with Tax and Credit Incentives

Policy Statement. To attract U.S. companies with foreign-flag operations, provisions for the deferment of taxes on undistributed profits earned through the sale of U.S.-flag shipping services in foreign trade could be used. Shipping companies would be allowed to set up U.S. corporate subsidiaries for new ships to be built in U.S. yards and employed in foreign trade. The net income of such subsidiaries would be similar in concept to the Domestic International Sales Corporation (DISC) authorized by the 92nd Congress (see Section 3.4. on taxation). To make U.S.-flag operations preferable, gradual suspension of tax deferral privileges of foreign-flag operators may be advisable.

Potential Policy Changes. Possible changes resulting from a revised policy on tax deferment and credit incentives would (1) permit reinvestment of income from the sale of ship services, with tax liability deferred; and (2) suspend tax deferral privileges on foreign shipping income by U.S.-owned foreign-flag shipping companies.

4.6.3.5. Restrictions for Bulk Carriers

Policy Statement. Section 804(c) of the Merchant Marine Act of 1936[14] permits an operator with foreign-flag vessel affiliations to participate in the ODS programs without immediately divesting its foreign-flag interests acquired before April 15, 1970, so long as these foreign-flag holdings are divested by April 15, 1990. This provision was designed to freeze the foreign-flag operations of operators who desired to build U.S.-flag vessels for subsidized operations. To qualify, such operators were required by Section 804(d)[15] to file, within 90 days after enactment of the Act, with the Secretary of Commerce, a list of the foreign-flag ships that they or related persons owned, chartered, acted as agent or broker for, or operated on April 15, 1970.

Conversely, Section 805(a) of the Merchant Marine Act of 1936[16] provides that it is unlawful, without the written permission of the Secretary of Commerce, to award or pay any subsidy under Title VI[17] or to charter any vessel under Title VII[18] to any person who either directly or indirectly owns or operates a U.S.-flag vessel engaged in the U.S. domestic or coastwise service. The section further provides that the Secretary shall give a hearing to any person having an interest in an application and that the Secretary may not grant the application if he finds that it will result in unfair competition to any person operating exclusively in the domestic, coastwise, or intercoastal service.

Section 808 of the Merchant Marine Act of 1936[19] provides that it shall be unlawful for any persons receiving an operating differential subsidy (ODS) under Title VI[20] or for any charterer under Title VII[21] to discriminate in any manner to give preference directly or indirectly to cargo in which the contractor or charterer has a direct or indirect ownership, purchase, or vending interest. This provision was designed to prevent subsidized operators of liner vessels from discriminating in favor of cargoes in which they might have a proprietary interest. Since subsidized liners are common carriers committed to serving the public by transporting American exports and imports, it would be inequitable to allow operators to discriminate in favor of their own cargoes or the cargoes of a related entity. Interpreted literally, this section would apply to a proprietary bulk operator who receives subsidy under Title VI[22] or to charterers of bulk vessels under Title VII.[23] The provisions of this section should apply to the concept of common carriage but not to proprietary bulk operations.

Proposed Policy Changes. Section 804(c)[24] of the 1936 Act could be amended to exempt from its provisions ownership, charter, acting as agent or broker for, or operation of foreign-flag bulk cargo-carrying vessels by contractors receiving an ODS contract or Title VII charter involving only U.S.-flag bulk-carrying vessels.

Section 805(a)[25] could be amended to provide that a waiver would be automatically granted by the Secretary without a hearing when the only domestic operations of an applicant for ODS under Title VI or chartering of vessels under Title VII is in the bulk trades and the application is for the operation of U.S.-flag bulk cargo-carrying vessels. To ensure that subsidy funds or assets acquired specifically for subsidized operations would not be used to permit an operator to compete unfairly in the domestic trade, the provision of this act making it unlawful to divert such funds or properties from a foreign trade operation into a domestic trade could be retained, even with respect to bulk carriers.

It should be noted that Section 506 of the Act[26] requires the payback of these funds if a vessel built with the aid of such funds is used in the domestic trade, and that Section 605(a)[27] provides that no ODS shall be paid with respect to voyages on which a vessel is engaged in the coastwise or intercoastal trades. Both of these provisions should be retained in order to protect the interest of operators engaged exclusively in the domestic trade.

Section 808[28] could be amended to exclude bulk vessels from its coverage. Section 4.8 discusses additional proposals contained in pending legislation affecting bulk shipping.

4.6.3.6. Double Subsidy

Policy Statement. Under existing laws, subsidized operators handling contracts under Title VI of the Merchant Marine Act,[29] as amended, may, under certain conditions, carry preference and military cargoes.

Proposed Policy Change. Preference and other government-owned or controlled cargoes could be offered only to nonsubsidized U.S.-flag operators at fair and reasonable negotiated rates. Liner operations normally carry four different categories of cargo preference cargoes:

- P.L.-480 cargoes
- Export-Import Bank cargoes
- AID cargoes
- Defense Department shipments

If Title VI carriers are selected to carry such cargoes, the government should pay no more than the established conference rates, or require the operators to repay, or reduce the subsidy proportionally.

4.6.3.7. ODS to Nonliner Operators

Policy Statement. Section 603(b) of the Merchant Marine Act of 1970 authorizes the Secretary of Commerce to pay sums in lieu of the ODS, determined under procedures applicable to liner vessels or vessels engaged in an essential bulk cargo-carrying service as described in Section 211(b).[30] Pursuant to this authority, the Secretary of Commerce may pay sums necessary "to make the cost of operating such vessel competitive with the cost of operating similar vessels under the registry of a foreign country."[31]

The present law stipulates ODS as a cost-parity aid, based on comparative cost of a U.S. and foreign-flag operator serving the identical trade. Cost parity has not provided significant incentives. U.S. operators maintain that such cost-parity payments may be insufficient under depressed market conditions to permit U.S.-flag vessels to operate at a reasonable profit. Unlike the situation prevailing for liner operators, bulk carriers are exposed to a truly competitive marketplace. While ODS, based on cost parity, may not assure a U.S.-flag operator a reasonable return, it offers him the same opportunity as his foreign competitor.

Possible Policy Change. Section 603(b)[32] could be amended to permit the Secretary of Commerce to pay, with respect to any vessel in an essential bulk cargo-carrying service, a variable ODS providing the incentives necessary for efficient U.S. operators to increase their participation in U.S. bulk trades.

Considerations may also be given to link subsidy or government aid to revenue instead of cost, or payment of a fixed amount of subsidy per dollar of revenue earned from carriage of commercial and nonpreference cargo.

4.6.3.8. Binding Arbitration between Shipping Companies and Seagoing Unions

Policy Statement. Repeated large wage increases have been a major factor in the decline of the U.S. Merchant Marine—both the fleet and its personnel. The government policy of noninterference has had little influence on assorted responsibility or in restricting such increases, which it ultimately has responsibility for paying.

Possible Policy Changes. Formal arbitration procedures could be established so that labor and management segments of the shipping community would be required to agree to settle all disputes through binding arbitration.

4.6.4. Shipbuilding

The major government policy issues concerning the U.S. shipbuilding industry are the size and form of subsidization required to improve industry efficiency and productivity to desired levels.

4.6.4.1. Shipbuilding Subsidies

Problem Statement. The shipbuilding industry is less than effective and productive because of obsolete facilities, traditional management, and rigid labor practices. In addition, it suffers from widely fluctuating market conditions. A restructured shipbuilding subsidy program and a more effective naval ship procurement program, planned for a longer-range series order ship-procurement policy, should introduce the required incentive and cash flow to permit this industry to improve its production and management procedures and to reduce gradually the gap between the U.S. and foreign costs. Labor cost differentials are continuously converging. Some foreign shipbuilding labor rates will have as great a competitive advantage as they did in the past.

An incentive structure must be built into shipbuilding subsidy allocation within existing legislation to encourage improved productivity, management, and material procurement approaches in this industry. This would result in the elimination of federal cost-parity subsidies within a few years. The goals of such a program would be to enhance the shipbuilding capability and productivity in this country and to return the active U.S.-flag merchant marine to a viable size while concurrently assuring more uniform shipbuilding levels.

Proposed Policy Changes. Protective policies by the federal government and the parcelling out of limited ship orders throughout the country must be reduced. The shipbuilding industry has the lowest ratio of capital investment to sales of any major industry in the United States. Various tax incentives for capital investment, increased cash flow, and higher productivity appear feasible and may result in substantial overall increases in sales and actual tax revenue.

U.S. shipyards, under current procurement and subsidy policies, are forced to produce ships custom designed by outside consultants and engineering groups unfamiliar with ship production procedures in the procuring yard and potential design/production savings. Shipyards should be encouraged to offer their own designs.

Construction differential subsidies should be limited to a fixed percentage of costs, as presently enacted, but individual shipbuilding terms should be negotiated. No particular defense features should be included (mandatory or voluntarily) in construction contracts and no extras should be subsidizable. On the other hand, shipbuilding aid in the form of construction and mortgage loan guarantees and other applicable aid should be provided for all types of vessels, excluding inland water craft.

The U.S. government has subscribed to practically all international agreements on maritime safety and maritime construction, inspection, and operational standards. However, many of the construction operations and inspection standards and regulations, as applied to the U.S. maritime industry and in particular to ship design or construction, go well beyond these agreements. The result is a construction and operating cost detriment to the U.S. maritime transportation industry. There is no proof that many of these standards or requirements improve the safety or quality of the U.S. merchant ships, as compared to ships built and operated by foreign nations that adhere to the modern international standards and rules of major classification societies.

The Department of Transportation, Coast Guard, U.S. Health Service, and other federal agencies should reevaluate their requirements, in light of modern, scientific, and technological knowledge, to permit use of the most effective materials, methods, and operating procedures and thereby to assist the industry's potential competitiveness.

4.6.4.2. CDS Differentials

Policy Statement. Section 502(b) of the Merchant Marine Act of 1936,[33] as amended, provides that construction differentials subsidy shall not exceed the difference between the domestic cost and the foreign construction cost. This is interpreted as the difference in ship price paid to the domestic or foreign shipbuilder. Under this view, "interest" cost is not a "construction" cost and consequently is not a factor to be considered in measuring comparative construction costs under Section 502(b).

Possible Policy Changes. Amendment of Section 607[34] would permit the repatriation of foreign-flag income, on a tax-deferred basis, for the purpose of establishing a capital construction fund.

4.6.4.3. Alternative CDS and Shipbuilding Aid

Policy Statement. Currently CDS is paid on the basis of cost differential between a U.S. and foreign yard for the same vessel.

The 1970 Act has reduced the maximum percentage of CDS payable from 55 percent in 1970 to 35 percent in 1976, yet all U.S.-flag vessels must be U.S. built. This was enacted to assure continued viability of U.S. shipbuilding.

Possible Policy Changes. To ensure greater incentives, the U.S. building requirements for U.S.-flag vessels could be relaxed, and for every new contract, bids could be obtained from both U.S. and foreign yards. The invitations for bids should specifically state that permission normally will be given for foreign construction when the difference between the responsible low domestic and foreign bids exceeds the permissible percentage of subsidy. Yards will be expected to "bid in" with their own detailed designs, within established specification limits.

If a contract is awarded to a foreign bidder, no construction subsidy will be paid. The operator can purchase the ship at the foreign bid price, and will deal directly with the foreign shipyard in the purchase. A foreign-built ship so purchased would be eligible for registry under U.S. flag with all the normal U.S.-flag privileges now enjoyed by a ship operating in the foreign trade.

4.7. MarAd and Shipbuilders' Council Policy Recommendations

In a recent report to the Federal Maritime Administration (MarAd),[35] major revisions to the Merchant Marine Act relating to bulk carriers were recommended. These included:

- Unrestricted subsidized foreign-to-foreign operations of U.S. bulk fleet, including chartering to foreign interests;
- U.S. owners of foreign-flag vessels to operate U.S.-flag, U.S.-built bulk carriers with advantage of subsidies, but without necessity of disposing of foreign holdings;
- Opportune sale of U.S.-flag, U.S.-built bulk carriers on open world market with proceeds deposited in Capital Construction Funds for later U.S. ship construction;
- Subsidized vessels to engage in domestic trades;
- Removal of ceiling on construction differential subsidy (CDS) and CDS determined by lowest foreign market price;
- Computations of operating differential subsidy (ODS) on basis of lowest foreign cost;
- Elimination of vessel replacement requirement as part of ODS contracts; and
- Tax inducement to shippers.

Another set of policies was suggested by the president of the Shipbuilders Council of America speaking before the House Merchant Marine Subcommittee in November 1975. He suggested a goal of increasing the percentage of U.S. trade carried in U.S.-built and operated ships. To increase the size of the U.S. fleet, he made several policy recommendations to facilitate shipbuilding. These included:

- Extension of option of negotiated contracting between shipbuilder and ship purchaser (accomplished in August 1976);
- Adoption of improved escalation clause in shipbuilding contracts to offset pernicious inflation;
- Restatement of CDS percentage guidelines to enable flexibility in relation to ever-changing world shipbuilding conditions (increased to 50 percent in August 1976);
- Application of investment tax credit to qualified withdrawals from Capital Construction Funds (currently provided for);
- Adoption of appropriate manpower training programs as recommended by Seapower Subcommittee of Committee on Armed Services, as well as by Commerce and Navy Departments, to provide constant reservoir of skilled workers for shipbuilding/ ship repairing;
- Acceleration in placement of commitments against ODS merchant ship replacement program;
- Clarification of "grandfather clause" in 1970 Act[36] which inhibits acquisition of U.S.-built ships by U.S. owners of foreign-flag vessels; and
- Authority for proceeds from sales of U.S.-owned foreign-flag vessels to be deposited in Capital Construction Funds as basis for replacement with U.S.-built ships.

4.8.   Pending Legislation of Concern to the U.S. Merchant Marine

The Omnibus Bill of 1980 and the Maritime Bulk Trade Act of 1979 represent recent legislative efforts directed at the needs of the U.S merchant marine. While the Omnibus Bill covers many aspects of Maritime transportation, including liner conferences and cargo sharing, subsidization, and diesel conversion, the Bulk Trade Act focuses on increasing the U.S. share of its bulk trade shipping. Each bill is described in more detail in the following sections.

4.8.1. Omnibus Maritime Regulatory Reform, Revitalization, and Reorganization Act of 1980

The Omnibus Bill of 1980[37] is the result of a redraft by the House of the Senate bill and considers certain aspects of the proposals of the Carter Administration and the National Maritime Council (NMC). The key points and their purposes in the House redraft bill are:

- *Modified closed conference*—To provide a full range of actions while restricting membership, for the purpose of keeping rates and capacity in liner shipping under reasonable control.
- *Shippers Council*—To provide a greater voice to and better communications by the users of shipping.
- *Antitrust immunity for intermodal agreements*—To protect users and operators of intermodal transportation from legal actions or constraints, and to assure full benefits derived from freely competitive intermodalism.
- *Retention of 15 percent dual-rate spread*—To assure flexibility in rate setting; the 15 percent spread is lower than the 18 percent proposed by the Senate and the NMC.
- *Repeal of the Shipping Act of 1916*[38]—To relieve the cause of overtonnage and high freight rates of the open cartel conference system.
- *Responsive bilateralism*—To accept the reality that usefulness of the "open sea" concept is past, and that workable bilateral or multilateral agreements provide a workable basis for the planning and operation of international shipping.
- *U.S. carriage goal of 50 percent*—To increase U.S.-flag shipping participation higher than the recent United Nations Conference on Trade and Development (UNCTAD) cargo-sharing proposal; while implemented on only a small number of trade routes, it would be difficult and expensive to introduce and control.
- *Per diem ODS as option of ODS/CDS*—To permit vessels to move among trades without dedicating vessels to particular services, a flexible subsidy is proposed for both bulk and liner operators; this could both stimulate ship construction and revitalize ship operations by providing a means for more efficiency in U.S. international shipping.
- *Foreign-built vessels eligible for ODS*—To allow U.S.-owned, foreign-built vessels to apply for ODS when CDS is not available and a similar vessel is built in a U.S. shipyard with CDS within five years.
- *Subsidized vessels in foreign cross-trades*—To assure greater operational flexibility to U.S. operators; coupled with per diem ODS, it would also reduce government expenditure.

- *Ownership by U.S. subsidized operators in foreign-flag vessels*—To provide greater attractiveness to U.S. owners of foreign-flag shipping to engage in U.S.-flag shipping; tax and balance of payment benefits are expected.
- *"Buy American" constraints*—To satisfy the "Buy American" restriction, a proposal stating that a vessel containing 50 percent of U.S. value is considered appropriate.
- *Diesel conversion program*—To encourage conversion to more fuel-efficient machinery; the proposal is not specific regarding government assistance in such conversion.
- *Undersecretary of Commerce for Maritime Affairs*—A proposal to unite the FMC and MarAd under one administration.

4.8.2. The Maritime Bulk Trade Act of 1979

Bulk trade is essential to the welfare of the United States as bulk imports are relied upon to provide raw materials for American industrial production. By providing an outlet for American production, bulk exports provide a major source of employment, in addition to being an important factor in the U.S. balance of payments. Despite the significance of the bulk trades, the United States carries a dismally low percentage of the cargo comprising its bulk trades.

The Maritime Bulk Trade Act of 1979 (H.R. 5113)[39] was introduced into Congress in August of 1979 to help remedy this situation. The bill's major goal is to increase bulk carriage participation of both the U.S. merchant marine and the merchant marine of countries with which the United States has entered into bilateral trade agreements. The bill expects that increased bulk carriage participation will not only be economically beneficial to the United States and its bilateral partners but also promises to ensure the availability of a merchant fleet for U.S. bulk trades, regardless of economic instability or pressures.

To realize these objectives, the bill makes a variety of proposals. Section 2(a)(8) gives specific content to Section 101 of the MMA of 1936[40] by defining the phrase "a substantial portion of the waterborne export and import foreign commerce of the United States" to represent not less than 40 percent of such commerce. Section 2(b)(1) imposes a 10-year deadline for reaching a 40 percent participation.

Section 4 of this Act[41] directs the Secretary of State to negotiate bilateral agreements ("Governing International Maritime Agreements") with each of its trading partners whose trade with the United States exceeds 5 percent of the total tonnage or value of U.S. foreign trade. The Secretary is also authorized to negotiate bilateral agreements with countries whose trade with the United States constitutes less than 5 percent by tonnage or value of total U.S. bulk trade, at the request of such nation.

H.R. 5113 would also make it unlawful for nonnational-flag ships not documented under the laws of a bilateral trading partner to engage in the transportation of bulk commodities. As of February 1980, no action had been taken on this bill.

The "Merchant Marine Act Bulk Shipping Amendments of 1979"[42] was also introduced to Congress in August of 1979. If enacted, this bill would amend Title IV of the Merchant Marine Act of 1936.[43] The objective of this bill is to stimulate U.S. shipyard construction of bulk-carrying vessels for domestic and foreign trade.

The bill would make several important changes in existing direct subsidies programs. First, it would lift present restrictions on subsidy-receiving vessels that prevent them from engaging in foreign trade. Second, it would modify the current subsidy system by requiring computation of a combined per diem rate for CDS and ODS subsidies. As proposed, the payment of these subsidies would be made in a combined monthly payment, based on the number of days the eligible vessel engaged in foreign trade during the relevant period.

Section 3 of the bill[44] would require all vessels receiving CDS subsidies to be documented under the laws of the United States for a period of at least 10 years or longer if the United States is owed any principal or interest, on account, of the purchase price of the vessel. Since the present minimum documentation period under Section 503 of the Merchant Marine Act of 1926[45] is 25 years, this proposal would reduce this period. However, the section further provides that:

> *Unless the vessel has been documented under the laws of the United States for a period of twenty-five years, the net proceeds of sale if transferred to another nationality shall be deposited in the owner's Capital Construction Fund and committed within a period of two years in the construction of a qualified replacement vessel or vessels.*

Section 4(b) of the proposed amendments[46] would restrict the right of contractors receiving an operating subsidy under Title VI of the Merchant Marine Act,[47] or any charterer receiving ODS under Title VII,[48] or any affiliated party of such contractor or charterer, to operate any foreign-flag vessel that competes with any American-flag service determined by the Secretary of Commerce to be essential, except where special circumstances and good cause are demonstrated to the Secretary. However, all other exceptions currently in force under Section 804 of the MMA of 1936[49] would be stricken. Thus the current exemptions pertaining to foreign-flag vessels engaged in carriage of liquid or dry cargoes in bulk would no longer be available.

As of February 1980, no action had been taken on this bill.

4.9. Environmental and Safety Legislation—
The Port and Tanker Safety Act of 1978[50]

In late 1976 the back-to-back *Argo Merchant* and *Sansienena* disasters alerted the American public to the great danger posed to its marine environments from maritime transport of hazardous cargoes such as oil.[51] This recognition was coupled with public concern that an increasing dependence upon imported oil, and the increasing level of maritime vessel traffic resulting from such dependence, significantly escalated the risk of environmental catastrophe.[52] The 95th Congress shared this concern,[53] and in 1978 it passed the Port and Tanker Safety Act (hereinafter Tanker Safety Act).[54]

The purpose of this legislation is to reduce the risk to life and property and prevent cargo loss and damage to the marine environments of the United States by attempting to prevent the occurrence of operational and traumatic spills caused by faulty vessel design, collisions, groundings, and so forth.[55]

The Tank Vessel Act of 1936[56] and the Port and Waterways Safety Act of 1972[57] were in force at the time of passage of the Tanker Safety Act, and the previous legislation, taken as a whole, reflects the same objectives as the new Act. However, in the wake of the *Argo Merchant*, the *Sansienena*, and other spills of a less catastrophic scale occurring in late 1976 and early 1977, Congress determined that the previous legislation was neither sufficiently comprehensive nor rigorous to effect their respective espoused objectives of improving vessel safety and protecting the marine environment.[58] The Tanker Safety Act of 1978 amended both the Tank Vessel Act of 1936 and the Ports and Waterways Safety Act of 1972 in order to remedy this situation.

The 1978 Tanker Safety Act amends the 1972 Ports and Waterways Safety Act to provide for a congressional policy on the general issues of navigation and vessel safety and protection of the marine environment.[59] It authorizes the Secretary of Transportation (the Department in which the Coast Guard operates) to establish, operate, and maintain vessel traffic services, including reporting and operating requirements, surveillance and communications systems, routing systems, and fairways. Several purposes fall within the purview of this mandate: to control and supervise vessel traffic;[60] to direct specific activities of vessels in emergency situations;[61] to designate needed port access routes for vessels proceeding to or from ports or places subject to the jurisdiction of the United States;[62] to consider certain criteria in carrying out vessel traffic service supervision;[63] and to take necessary action to prevent damage to or destruction of structures or shore areas adjacent to the navigable waters of the United States and to protect such waters and the resources therein.[64]

It similarly stipulates a requirement for federally licensed pilots to be used in certain situations where individual states have failed to act.[65] Finally, it requires the investigation of incidents and accidents on structures subject to the act.[66]

The new Act also prohibits the entry to ports of the United States of vessels deficient in specific categories, and authorizes the Secretary of Transportation to waive certain prohibitions once he is satisfied that the deficient conditions have been corrected.[67] In addition, this new legislation encourages the President to enter into negotiations with neighboring nations to establish compatible vessel standards and vessel traffic services in boundary areas.[68] Consequently, the Secretary of Transportation is further authorized to implement international agreements on vessel traffic services[69] and to issue necessary implementing regulations. He is also directed to establish certain consultation procedures in arriving at those regulations.[70]

Civil and criminal penalties are authorized for violations of the Act or implementing regulations. Provision for *in rem*[71] liability of vessels and the denial of entry or withholding of customs clearance for certain vessels not in compliance with the Act or regulations are included. The Act establishes eligibility requirements for the issuance of federal licenses for the pilotage of certain vessels not covered by requirements of recognized state pilotage laws.[72]

The Tanker Safety Act of 1978 amends the Tanker Vessel Act of 1936 by providing for a congressional statement of policy on the carriage by vessels of certain hazardous cargoes and the standards applicable to such vessels.[73] It grants regulatory authority to the Secretary of Transportation to issue appropriate regulations for the design, construction, alteration, repair, maintenance, operation, equipping, personnel qualification, or manning of such vessels.[74] It requires the Secretary to prescribe, as a minimum, particular construction and equipment standards, and requires the installation of certain construction features for vessels engaged in U.S. coastwise trade.[75] The Act establishes a system for monitoring compliance with appropriate regulations by requiring certificates of inspection with appropriate endorsement for U.S. vessels, and certificates of compliance for foreign vessels operating in U.S. waters.[76] Under the Act foreign certificates issued pursuant to international agreements are recognized as a basis for such certificates of compliance.[77]

The Act prescribes personnel and manning standards for vessels of the United States, including training, license qualifications, health and physical fitness criteria, periodic retraining, and recognition of experience, completed training, and performance testing in the determination of licenses and certificates.[78] Certification of crew members for specific qualifications in the handling of oil or hazardous materials are prescribed.[79] The Act prohibits the violation of regulations or the refusal to permit authorized officers to board a vessel to enforce applicable provisions of law,[80] and provides for civil *in rem* liability, denial of entry, and the withholding of customs clearance in appropriate circumstances.[81] It establishes a national inspection program to ensure that any vessel subject to the provisions of the Tank Vessel Act is in compliance with that Act or the regulations thereunder.[82] The Secretary of Transportation is furthermore directed to establish a marine safety information system, through which necessary data may be obtained as to the identification, ownership, and operational history of any tank vessel.[83] This is important because of the many incidents of oil spillage which are not effectively traced to particular ships. The transfer of oil or hazardous materials in a port or place subject to the jurisdiction of the United States is prohibited under the Act if the cargo has been previously transferred from another vessel in the navigable waters of the United States, unless such earlier transfer was conducted in accordance with appropriate regulations issued by the Secretary of Transportation and unless both the vessels involved in the earlier transfer had onboard certificates of inspection of compliance as required, or as would have been required, for a transfer in a port or place subject to the jurisdiction of the United States.[84] This is to prevent the indiscriminate commingling of potentially hazardous or objectionable cargoes. The Act authorizes the Secretary of Transportation to issue appropriate regulations regarding transfers: it prohibits the transfer of cargo in a port or place subject to the jurisdiction of the United States if the vessel has previously discharged tank washings at sea in violation of law, in preparation for loading cargo,[85] and directs the Secretary to submit an annual report on the administration of the Act.[86]

Finally, the Act includes a savings clause for regulations previously issued under applicable law.[87]

4.10.   International Legal Issues in the Use of the Coastal Zone

Two fundamental questions pervade international law in regard to jurisdictional conflicts: What is the scope of a state's jurisdiction over foreign parties? and What is the governing source of law (assuming a proper exercise of jurisdiction)?

In the area of the "law of the sea," these questions take the following form: How many miles from its shore does a coastal state enjoy enforcement jurisdiction? For purposes of this discussion, the question is even more refined: To what extent may the United States exercise, in accordance with international law, civil and/or criminal enforcement jurisdiction over foreign citizens and/or vessels for violations of vessel traffic rules issued pursuant to the Port and Tanker Safety Act of 1978?

U.S. courts have consistently adhered to the customary[88] rule of international law that, "within its territorial sea, a state may exercise any jurisdiction and do any act which it may lawfully do upon its own land territory."[89] It follows that such power includes the right to regulate navigation and vessel traffic within its territorial waters. Phillip Jessup, an international law scholar from the United States, analogized a foreign vessel's duty to obey a coastal state's traffic restrictions when traversing that state's territorial sea to the duty of a tourist to observe vehicle traffic laws when visiting a foreign country.[90] Consistent with this position is a long-standing American interpretation of international law, namely, that the right to impose conditions of entry upon foreign vessels desirous of docking at United States ports, or to deny a right to enter ports to ships not complying with such conditions, is an example of the sovereignty over its territorial sea accorded to a state by international law.[91]

This claim of right to regulate entry into American ports is embodied in both Section 9 of the Ports and Waterways Safety Act of 1972, which makes entry into U.S. ports conditional upon compliance with that section,[92] and Section 13(e) of the Act, which authorizes the Secretary of Transportation to close off entry, not just to American ports, but to any waters subject to the jurisdiction of the United States.[93]

The right to condition or deny entry does not operate to require vessels to procure express permission from a coastal state to dock or traverse a territorial sea. In 1812 the Supreme Court, in *Schooner Exchange v. McFadden*,[94] announced a still-valid rule of international law, i.e., that although the right to regulate entry includes the right to close off a port: "(i)f there be no prohibition, the ports of a friendly nation are considered as open to the public ships of all powers with whom it is at peace. . . ."[95]

In fact, an indiscriminate, arbitrary closing of a coastal state's port to a foreign vessel would transgress customary international law: "(i)n case of vessels not in military service, the ports of a state are open to their visit without any prior notification, except where the state has expressly provided otherwise."[96]

4.10.1. Enforcement Measures with Regard to Foreign Vessels

The Port and Tanker Safety Act of 1978[97] amended the Ports and Waterways Safety Act of 1972 as follows:

Section 13 of the Ports and Waterways Safety Act of 1972[98] offers the Secretary of Transportation a variety of enforcement options against foreign parties and vessels found to violate the vessel traffic regulations promulgated pursuant to the Act.

Section 13(a)(1) authorizes civil penalties of up to $25,000 against persons who, after notice and opportunity for a hearing, are found by the Secretary to have violated a vessel traffic regulation.[99]

Section 13(a) provides that, "(e)ach day of a continuing violation shall constitute a separate violation."[100]

Section 13(c) provides further for *in rem* liability against vessels which commit violations of the Act or regulations issued thereunder: "(a)ny vessel subject to the provisions of this Act, . . . shall be liable *in rem* for any *civil* penalty assessed pursuant to subsection (a) and may be proceeded against in the United States district court for any district in which such vessel may be found."[101] (emphasis added).

Section 13(b)(1) authorizes criminal penalties: "(a)ny person who willfully and knowingly violates this Act or any regulation issued hereunder shall be fined not more than $50,000 for each violation or imprisoned for not more than five years, or both."[102]

Section 13(a)(3) authorizes imposition of criminal penalties against any person who defaults on payment of a civil penalty after it has become final.[103]

The District Courts of the United States are empowered by Section 13(d)[104] to issue injunctions to restrain violations of the Ports and Waterways Safety Act of 1972. Thus, the Secretary of Transportation may petition the District Court for an injunction against foreign vessels not complying with vessel traffic regulations.

Section 13(e) empowers the Secretary of Transportation to deny a foreign vessel the right to enter any waters including territorial waters subject to the jurisdiction of the United States, where a vessel fails to comply with regulations issued pursuant to the Act.[105]

4.10.2. Innocent Passage

A major exception to a coastal state's right to bar entry into its territorial waters has traditionally been accorded to foreign vessels engaged in innocent passage.[106] Article 14(a) of the 1958 Geneva Convention on the Territorial Sea and the Contiguous Zone (hereinafter Territorial Sea Convention) defines passage as "navigation through the territorial sea for the purpose either of traversing that sea without entering internal waters, or of proceeding to internal waters, or of making for the high seas from internal waters."[107] Article 14(3) of the Convention[108] qualifies this by adding that "passage includes stopping and anchoring, but only insofar as the same are incidental to ordinary navigation or are rendered necessary by *force majeure* or by distress." Article 14(1) of the Convention codified this historic entitlement: "ships of all states, whether coastal or not, shall enjoy the right of innocent passage through the territorial sea."[109]

However, the right to innocent passage does not include an immunity from navigational and vessel traffic regulation. Article 17 states that "(f)oreign ships exercising the right of innocent passage shall comply with the laws and regulations enacted by the coastal state . . . ."[110] Compliance with the laws of the coastal state is, in fact, essential to the determination that the passage of the foreign vessel is "innocent." According to Article 14(4), "(p)assage is innocent so long as it is not *prejudicial* to the peace, good order, or security of the coastal State . . ."[111] (emphasis added).

4.10.2.1. The U.N. Third Conference on the Law of the Sea (1975)

Although the above-mentioned legally codified Articles are important contributions to the achievement of uniformity in the Law of the Sea, their generality limits their usefulness in resolving the jurisdictional disputes which impelled their ratification. The Territorial Sea Convention did not formulate objective criteria to apply when analyzing "prejudice" as contained in Article 14(4). Yet such criteria are essential to achieve uniform determinations and necessary to avert the subjectivity, arbitrariness, and unpredictability in applications of the Article that have resulted in the absence of agreed-upon standards.

In 1975 the United Nations Third Conference on the Law of the Sea tried to remedy this. The Informal Single Negotiating Text of the Conference (hereinafter Negotiating Text)[112] lists specific acts deemed to be prejudicial to coastal state interests.[113] The Negotiating Text contains other clarifications of the Territorial Sea Convention which, if adopted, would provide a more explicit basis in international law for the enforcement of the Tanker Safety Act (and similar vessel safety and traffic regulation).

In order to help settle the issue concerning what type of regulation does not unreasonably burden innocent passage, the Negotiating Text states, in part, that

> (t)he coastal state may make laws and regulations, in conformity with the provisions of the present Convention and other rules of international law relating to innocent passage through the territorial sea, in respect of . . . the safety of navigation and the navigation and the regulation of marine traffic, including the designation of sealanes and the establishment of traffic separation schemes . . . .[114]

The Negotiating Text includes additional provisions to ensure that the coastal state's rights to regulate in certain subject areas are established as principles of international law. *Articles 19 and 20 of the Negotiating Text provide that tankers and ships carrying nuclear or inherently dangerous, noxious substances may be required to confine their passage to sealanes or follow traffic separation schemes designated by the coastal state.*[115]

To reduce the risk of placing unreasonable regulatory burdens upon passage, and as a safeguard to what could become a reckless application of the objective criteria furnished in Article 16(2), Article 23 of the Negotiating Text[116] proposes imposing liability upon a coastal state for an improper obstruction of innocent passage.[117]

4.10.2.2. Enforcement Jurisdiction Over Vessels Engaged in Innocent Passage

Although according to international law a coastal state can fully regulate throughout its territorial sea, proper regard for the right of innocent passage requires that a coastal state refrain from exercising jurisdiction in some instances.

Article 26(1), which applies to ships purportedly engaged in innocent passage, states that "(t)he coastal State should not stop or divert a foreign ship passing through the territorial sea for the purpose of exercising civil jurisdiction in relation to a person on board the ship."[118]

This provision should not be read as a prohibition. Such a literal interpretation would entail relinquishing a fundamental incident of sovereignty—the right to assert civil jurisdiction over a person within the territorial sea. That the Convention intended such a divestiture is inconceivable.

How then should Article 26(1) be read? Professor George Smith explains that "should not" in Article 26(1) was intended as a mere exhortation rather than as a mandatory command for the coastal state to refrain from exercising its civil jurisdiction.[119]

Professor Smith's explanation seems sensible: An exhortation regarding the exercise of civil jurisdiction would implicitly urge coastal states to exercise civil jurisdiction over persons on board foreign vessels engaged in innocent passage only to the extent necessary to safeguard legitimate national interests so as not unnecessarily to encumber the right to innocent passage. Logic aside, Professors McDougal and Burke point out that, in fact, the general attitude of states at the Territorial Sea Convention in 1958 was that "their civil jurisdiction did most assuredly extend to those ships which passed in their territorial seas."[120] Such an attitude was consistent with the customary law exercised at the time of the Convention that, "in the absence of treaty provisions to the contrary, a foreign merchant vessel has no legal rights to protest against *any* exercise of jurisdiction whatsoever on it by the local sovereign."

Thus, as applied to the United States, neither Article 20(1) specifically, nor the right to innocent passage generally, proscribe the United States' exercise of civil enforcement jurisdiction over foreign vessels pursuant to the Tanker Safety Act.

Article 25(1) of the Negotiating Text limits criminal enforcement jurisdiction: "(t)he criminal jurisdiction of the coastal State *should not* be exercised on board a foreign ship passing through the territorial sea to arrest any person or to conduct any investigation in connection with any crime . . ."[121] (emphasis added).

This Article might be read literally as a partial preemption of the criminal jurisdiction authorized by the Ports and Waterways Safety Act. But this would be nonsensical. A person charged with violating a law having an impact on the coastal state could not be regarded as engaged in innocent passage as defined by Article 16;[122] as such conduct would be inherently prejudicial to the peace and good order of the coastal state, immunity conferred by Article 25(1) would therefore be forfeited. This Article should also be read as merely an exhortation to coastal states to refrain from exercising criminal jurisdiction against a person who commits a crime on board which does not affect the coastal state; a parallel Article in the Negotiating Text confirms this interpretation. A coastal State criminal jurisdiction *should not* be exercised as foreign ships pass through the territorial sea either to assess or conduct investigations into crimes committed on board the ship unless: the consequence of the crime disturbs the country's peace or the territorial sea's good order; the ship's captain or consular officer of the country whose flag the ship flies requests assistance; or the coastal state interference is necessary to suppress illicit narcotic trade and psychotropic substances.[123]

In conclusion, the Territorial Sea Convention urges coastal states to refrain from exercising civil and/or criminal jurisdiction on foreign vessels engaged in innocent passage in certain situations. But none of the suggested self-restraints conflict with or bar the exercise of civil or criminal enforcement jurisdiction exercised pursuant to the Ports and Waterways Safety Act for violation of vessel traffic rules authorized by the Act.

4.10.3. *International Conflict Regarding Proper Width of Territorial Sea*

In the early 20th century, international law clearly limited a coastal state's claim to sovereignty over the sea to the distance of three miles from its shore.[124] But the three-mile territorial limit has virtually found universal rejection in recent years, with a corresponding diminution of the customary status accorded the three-mile limit.[125]

The only real surviving international relevance of the three-mile rule is to delineate a state's minimum rightful claim to sovereignty over coastal waters. International law does not presently dictate any specific width of territorial waters over which a coastal State is sovereign.[126] But the question of how far beyond three miles from shore a coastal state may retain jurisdiction is unsettled.

The 1958 Territorial Sea and Contiguous Zone Convention went far toward resolving international conflicts involving a coastal state's authority to exercise civil and criminal jurisdiction over a foreign-flag vessel that were engendered and inflamed by the demise of the three-mile rule. Because the Convention formulated definitions of critical terms and sought important agreements concerning rights of coastal states and foreign-flag vessels, its ratification resolved many issues that had previously frustrated the attainment of uniformity in the Law of the Sea. However, as no agreement was reached on the maximum width of the territorial zone, the Convention's contribution is substantially relegated to the theoretical realm. The Law of the Sea is unequipped to resolve disputes involving the legality of extensive assertions of civil and/or criminal jurisdiction, exercised pursuant to purported sovereignty over the area of the sea involved, by coastal states over foreign-flag vessels.

4.10.4. Coastal State Regulation Outside the Territorial Sea

International law generally prohibits a state from interfering with the exercise of freedom of navigation by ships sailing on the high seas.[127] However, customary international law accepts the concept of the legitimacy of coastal state action on the high seas in a contiguous zone beyond the territorial sea. Acceptance occurs when such action is necessary to protect generally recognized special interests of a coastal state, unless a coastal state's regulation and assertion of jurisdiction over the coastal zone operates in disregard of the reasonable interests of other states.[128]

Article 24 of the Territorial Sea Convention codified the customary international law concept of the contiguous zone as follows:[129]

> 1. *In a zone of the high seas contiguous to its territorial sea, the coastal state may exercise the control necessary to:*
>   a. *Prevent infringement of its customs, fiscal, immigration, or sanitary regulations within its territory or territorial sea;*
>   b. *Punish infringement of the above regulations committed within its territory or territorial sea.*
> 2. *The contiguous zone may not extend beyond twelve miles from the baseline from which the breadth of the territorial sea is measured.*

Because 1(a) of Article 24 does not expressly provide for vessel traffic regulation, it might be inferred that the Convention intended to limit a coastal state's right to regulate in the area beyond its territorial sea, designated as a contiguous zone, to those classes of regulation specified in 1(a). However, this is unlikely because at the time of Article 24's ratification, many countries already claimed sovereignty over waters extending as far as 12 miles from their shore.[130]

Thus, to read Article 24 so narrowly would repudiate the evolving customary practice rather than codify that practice. Furthermore, it is doubtful that the signatories to the Convention intended to have recognition of a coastal state's right to fully regulate a coastal area within a 12-mile radius depend upon whether or not a coastal state claimed as its territorial sea an area coextensive with the contiguous zone as demarcated by Article 24(2). This would invite circumvention, as Article 24 could be easily bypassed by simply asserting a larger territorial claim.

The real import of Article 24 seems to be twofold. First, it employs the contiguous zone concept as an adjustment mechanism specifically to recognize claims of jurisdiction beyond the territorial sea by countries with less extensive territorial claims in order to equalize regulatory and enforcement rights among coastal states. Second, the designation of 12 miles from shore as the outer boundary to the contiguous zone preserves the historic right of free passage on the high seas by outlawing unreasonable assertions of jurisdiction.

Not all coastal states have ratified the Territorial Sea and Contiguous Zone Convention. Canada and Norway are among the nonsignatories, but since most coastal states have ratified the Convention (including the Soviet Union), it is the authoritative source of international law on the rules it codifies. It is virtually certain that the United States would be acting in accordance with international law when exercising civil and/or criminal jurisdiction over individuals and vessels charged with violating the vessel traffic regulations issued pursuant to the Ports and Waterways Safety Act at least up to 12 miles from its shore.

Whether the United States can enforce the 1972 Ports and Waterways Safety Act in areas of the high seas more than 12 miles from its shore is not certain. In light of current practice, it would probably be consistent with international law. The Informal Negotiating Text, which emerged from the 1974 Law of the Sea Conference, proposed a standard width for coastal zones. The Text provides that a state may choose to establish a 12-mile territorial sea, a 24-mile contiguous zone, and a 200-mile economic zone. Thus, the Informal Negotiating Text would permit vessel traffic regulation up to 36 miles from shore.

In its present unratified form, the Informal Negotiating Text is not international law. But it indicates the direction of customary practice and furnishes support for the position that the civil and criminal enforcement jurisdiction of the 1972 Ports and Waterways

Safety Act could be, in accordance with international law, extended beyond 12 miles from the shoreline of the United States.

4.11. Conclusions

U.S. maritime policy has major economic and regulatory impacts on American shipping. Current government programs have recently come under increasing scrutiny. After failure of passage of the proposed "Omnibus" bill in 1980, new and more realistic proposals for a changed maritime policy were placed before Congress at the end of 1981. These proposals deal mainly with deregulatory issues and in particular with the elimination of many constraints under which American shipping operates. We have discussed many aspects of U.S. maritime policy and its impact, including the effects of potential changes in the policy. The decisions are difficult ones because the environment in which American international shipping operates today is not only far more complex than ever before, but also continually changing.

Endnotes

1. 46 U.S.C. §§861 et seq. (1976).
2. See: Department of Defense, Sealift Procurement and National Security Study (1972).
3. U.S. Maritime Objectives Continue to be Elusive, No. 49 Shipping World (Dec. 2, 1976).
4. Pub. L. No. 91–469, 514, 84 Stat. 1023.
5. This provision has been partially waived in the case of slow speed diesels made with foreign components.
6. 46 U.S.C. §1222(a) (1976).
7. 46 U.S.C. §1222(b) (1976).
8. 46 U.S.C. §1222(c) (1976).
9. Typically working capital equal to 50 percent of the average annual voyage expenses for each subsidized ship and net worth equal to 25 percent of the owner's actual cost for each subsidized ship.
10. 46 U.S.C. §1173(b) (1976).
11. Pub. L. No. 91–469, 84 Stat. 1018.
12. Merchant Marine Act of 1920, Ch. 250, 41 Stat. 988 (codified in scattered sections of 46 U.S.C.).
13. 46 U.S.C. §§1271–1280 (1976) and Supp. II 1978).
14. 46 U.S.C. §1222(c) (1976).
15. 46 U.S.C. §1222(d) (1976).
16. 46 U.S.C. §1223(a) (1976).
17. 46 U.S.C. §§1171–1183(a) (1976).
18. 46 U.S.C. §§1191–1206 (1976).

19. 46 U.S.C. §1226 (1976).

20. 46 U.S.C. §§1171–1183(a) (1976).

21. 46 U.S.C. §§1191–1206 (1976).

22. 46 U.S.C. §§1171–1183(a) (1976).

23. 46 U.S.C. §§1191–1206 (1976).

24. 46 U.S.C. §1222(c) (1976).

25. 46 U.S.C. §1223(a) (1976).

26. 46 U.S.C. §1156 (1976).

27. 46 U.S.C. §1175(a) (1976).

28. 46 U.S.C. §1226 (1976).

29. 46 U.S.C. §§1171–1183(a) (1976).

30. 46 U.S.C. §1121(b) (1976).

31. 46 U.S.C. §1173(b) (1976).

32. *Id*.

33. 46 U.S.C. §1152(b) (1976).

34. 46 U.S.C. §1177 (1976).

35. See *American Shipper* (September 1976) for discussion of the final report on the "National Assessment and Planning Conference on U.S. Flag Bulk Shipping," July 12–14, 1976.

36. 46 U.S.C. §1222(a) (1976).

37. H.R. 4769, 96th Cong., 1st Sess. (1979).

38. 46 U.S.C. §§801 et seq. (1976).

39. H.R. 5113, 96th Cong., 1st Sess. (1979).

40. 46 U.S.C. §1101 (1976).

41. H.R. 5113, 96th Cong., 1st Sess. (1979).

42. H.R. 5145, 96th Cong., 1st Sess. (1979).

43. 46 U.S.C. §1411.

44. H.R. 5145, 96th Cong., 1st Sess. (1979).

45. 46 U.S.C. §1153.

46. H.R. 5145, 96th Cong., 1st Sess. (1979).

47. 46 U.S.C. §§1171–1183(a) (1976).

48. 46 U.S.C. §§1191–1206 (1976).

49. 46 U.S.C. §1222 (1976).

50. Pub. L. No. 95-474, 92 Stat. 1471 (codified at 33 U.S.C. §§1221–1232, 46 U.S.C. §§214, 391a (Supp. II 1978)).

51. H.R. Rep. No. 1384, 95th Cong., 2nd Sess. 6, *reprinted in* [1978] *U.S. Code Cong. & Ad News,* 3270, 3274–3275.

52. *Ibid*.

53. *Id*. at 3277.

54. 33 U.S.C. §§1221–1232 (Supp. II 1978).

55. 33 U.S.C. §1221 (Supp. II 1978).

56. 46 U.S.C. §391(a) (1976).

57. 33 U.S.C. §§1221–1227 (1976).

58. H.R. Rep. No. 1384, 95th Cong. 6, 2nd Sess., *reprinted in* [1978] *U.S. Code Cong. & Ad News* 3270, 3274–3275.

59. 33 U.S.C. §1221 (Supp. II 1978).

60. 33 U.S.C. §1223 (Supp. II 1978).

61. 33 U.S.C. §1223(b)(3) (Supp. II 1978).

62. 33 U.S.C. §1223(c) (Supp. II 1978).

63. 33 U.S.C. §1224 (Supp. II 1978).
64. 33 U.S.C. §1225 (Supp. II 1978).
65. 33 U.S.C. §1226 (Supp. II 1978).
66. 33 U.S.C. §1227 (Supp. II 1978).
67. 33 U.S.C. §1228 (Supp. II 1978).
68. 33 U.S.C. §1230 (Supp. II 1978).
69. 33 U.S.C. §1223(c)(5)(D) (Supp. II 1978).
70. 33 U.S.C. §1231 (Supp. II 1978).
71. *"In rem"* refers to seizure of the vessel for the purpose of selling and applying resulting proceeds to satisfy liabilities and penalties incurred by the vessel's owner.
72. 33 U.S.C. §1232 (Supp. II 1978).
73. 46 U.S.C. §214 (Supp. II 1978).
74. 46 U.S.C. §391a (1) (Supp. II 1978).
75. 46 U.S.C. §391a (6) (Supp. II 1978).
76. 46 U.S.C. §391a (7) (Supp. II 1978).
77. 46 U.S.C. §391a (8) (Supp. II 1978).
78. 46 U.S.C. §391a (8)(C) (Supp. II 1978).
79. 46 U.S.C. §391a (11) (Supp. II 1978).
80. 46 U.S.C. §391a (10) (Supp. II 1978).
81. 46 U.S.C. §391a (13) (Supp. II 1978).
82. 46 U.S.C. §391a (14) (Supp. II 1978).
83. 46 U.S.C. §391a (15) (Supp. II 1978).
84. 46 U.S.C. §391a (16) (Supp. II 1978).
85. 46 U.S.C. §391a (17) (Supp. II 1978).
86. 46 U.S.C. §391a (18) (Supp. II 1978).
87. 46 U.S.C. §391a (19) (Supp. II 1978).
88. "The territorial sea is that belt of the sea adjacent to the coast of a state beyond its land territory and its internal waters over which the sovereignty of the state extends." In S. Swartztrauber, *The Three-Mile Limit of Territorial Seas* 3, (1972) (hereinafter cited as Swartztrauber).
89. P. Jessup, The Law of Territorial Waters and Maritime Jurisdiction, 49 (1927) (hereinafter cited as Jessup).
90. Jessup at 137.
91. Lowe, "The Right of Entry into Maritime Ports in International Law," 14 *San Diego L.R.* 597, 613 (1976–77) (hereinafter cited as Lowe).
92. 33 U.S.C. §1228 (Supp. II 1978).
93. 33 U.S.C. §1232(e) (Supp. II 1978).
94. 11 U.S. (7 Cranch) 116 (1812).
95. *Id.* at 141. This rule applies with equal force to merchant ships, Lowe at 621.
96. Restatement, Second, Foreign Relations Law of the United States §50, Comment a (1965).
97. Port and Tanker Safety Act of 1978, Pub. L. No. 95–474, §6(c), 92 Stat. 1493.
98. 3 U.S.C. §1232 (Supp. II 1978).
99. 33 U.S.C. §1232(a)(1) (Supp. II 1978).
100. *Id.*
101. 33 U.S.C. §1232(c) (Supp. II 1978).
102. 33 U.S.C. §1232(b)(1) (Supp. II 1978).
103. 33 U.S.C. §1232(a)(3) (Supp. II 1978).

104. 33 U.S.C. §1232(d) (Supp. II 1978).
105. 33 U.S.C. §1232(e) (Supp. II 1978).
106. Jessup at 120.
107. 516 U.N.T.S. 205, 5 U.S.T. 1606, T.I.A.S. No. 5639, *in force* Sept. 10, 1964.
108. *Id.*
109. *Id.*
110. *Id.*
111. *Id.*
112. *Reprinted* in International Legal Materials 14, 682 (1975).
113. Negotiating Text, part II, Article 16(2), *reprinted* in International Legal Materials 14 at 714 (1975). These acts are: threats or uses of force *against the territorial integrity or political independence of the coastal States or in any other manner* violative of the United Nations Charter (emphasis added); any weapons exercise or practice; acts designed to collect information which would prejudice the defense or the security of a coastal state or disseminate propaganda with the same intent or purpose; the launching, landing, or taking on board of any aircraft of any military device; acts of embarkation or disembarkation of any commodities, currencies, or people which would be violative of coastal State sanitary regulations, customs or fiscal integrity; acts of willful pollution; research or survey activities of any kind; acts that would interfere with coastal communication networks or other facilities or installations; and, finally, any other activity *not* having a direct bearing on passage.

Article 16(3) provides that if *prior authorization* is given by a coastal State for passage of a vessel, or if *force majeure* distress necessitates passage under certain conditions, or if samaritan assistance is being given to persons, ships, or aircraft, the restrictions do not apply. The coastal state is to be notified promptly when circumstances of this nature arise.
114. Negotiating Text, Part II, Article 18(1), *reprinted* 14 International Legal Materials at 715 (1975).
115. Negotiating Text, Part II, Articles 19 and 20, *reprinted* 14 International Legal Materials at 716 (1975).
116. Negotiating Text, Part II, Article 23, *reprinted* 14 International Legal Materials at 717 (1975).
117. This should be distinguished from imposition of liability upon the coastal state for damage to the vessel and cargo suffered as a result of compliance with *reasonable* vessel traffic regulations.
118. Negotiating Text, Part II, Article 26(1), *reprinted* International Legal Materials at 717 (1975).
119. J. R. Smith, "The Politics of Lawmaking: Problems in International Maritime Regulation—Innocent Passage v. Free Transit," *Pitt L. Rev.* 487, 516 (1976).
120. M. McDougal and W. Burke, "The Public Order of the Oceans," 272–274 (1952).
121. Negotiating Text, Part II, Article 25(1), *reprinted* 14 International Legal Materials at 717 (1975).
122. Negotiating Text, Part II, Article 16, *reprinted* 14 International Legal Materials 714–715 (1975).
123. Negotiating Text, Part II, Article 25, *reprinted* 14 International Legal Materials 717 (1975).
124. Swartztrauber at 115.

125. Josef L. Kunz, "The Changing Law of Nations," 339–340, cited in Swartztrauber at 250.
126. Kelsen and Tucker, "Principles of International Law," 324–325, cited in Swartztrauber at 249.
127. Jessup at 75–76.
128. *Id.* at 99.
129. 516 U.N.T.S. 205, 5 U.S.T. 1606, T.I.A.S. No. 5639, in force September 10, 1964.
130. See: Bilder, "The Canadian Arctic Waters Pollution Prevention Act: New Stresses on the Law of the Sea," 69 *Michigan L. R.* 1, 14 (1970–71).

Appendix 4A

SUMMARY OF DIRECT AND INDIRECT SUBSIDIES OF MAJOR MARITIME NATIONS

ARGENTINA

Direct Subsidies

Operating Subsidy:

a. Art. 13, Law 20, 447 (5/22/73) provides for subsidies to state fleets when required by national interest to cover deficits.

b. 25 percent operating subsidy to river fleet.

Construction Subsidy:

a. Construction subsidy for companies owned/controlled by Argentine citizens authorized for cost differential between domestic and Western European costs.

b. Includes modernization and conversion.

c. None granted in recent years as no foreign-going ships built.

Indirect Subsidies

Tax Benefits:

a. ELMA (nationally owned line) exempt from all taxes.

b. Income Tax Act establishes promotional regulations for private ship enterprises.

Loans and Interest on Loans:

a. National Fund for the Merchant Marine supplies loans up to 90 percent of total cost; repayable in 15 years.

Note: This summary is compiled from *Maritime Subsidies*, U.S. Maritime Administration, 1978, and information and interviews of embassy staff of major maritime nations.

b. Interest rated on promotional basis determined by Ministry of Public Works and Services.

Cargo Preference and Cabotage:

a. 1973 Merchant Marine Law enforces Argentine right to carry 50 percent of their waterborne trade. Government will not recognize international agreements to the contrary and will deny port facilities to nonagreeing nations.

b. Equal access agreement with U.S. bilateral agreements with Chile and USSR for equal division of carriage.

Government Ownership: 48 percent of merchant fleet, including ELMA, major oil company, and river fleets.

AUSTRALIA

Direct Subsidies

Operating Subsidy:

a. Direct assistance to Tasmanian shippers.

b. No operating subsidy as of 7/1/76.

Construction Subsidy:

a. Sliding scale bounty will be phased down from 35 percent maximum to 25 percent maximum by 1/1/81. Bounty applies to vessels 150–92,000 DWT.

b. Ships imported only if Australian yards do not submit bids, or if Australian price, minus bounty, exceeds overseas price.

c. Except in special circumstances, importation of used vessels prohibited.

Indirect Subsidies

Tax Benefits:

a. No special tax benefits.

b. Depreciation:

20 years on cargo vessels; 16 years on bulk carriers, tankers, RoRo, and container ships. Choice of straight line or reducing balance method.

Profits from vessels sold for more than depreciated value tax exempt if offset against replacement vessel or other depreciable ships or items.

c. 20 percent investment allowance on plants for domestic use ordered between 7/1/81–6/30/83, and installed for use by 6/30/84.

Customs:

a. 20 percent duty on imported vessels below bounty range.

b. Occasionally machinery unavailable may be imported duty-free.

Loans and Interest on Loans: None.

Cargo Preference and Cabotage: Cabotage

Government Ownership:

a. Government-owned Australian Nat'l. Line has 7 vessels as of 6/30/76, plus 2 container/RoRo vessels and 4 120/140,000 DWT bulk carriers on order.

b. Cockatoo Island Dockyard in Sidney; mostly for naval use.

c. Various state-owned vessels and yards.

BELGIUM

Direct Subsidies

Operating Subsidy: None.

Construction Subsidy: 8 percent of contract price in 8 equal annual payments. (This figure may be outdated).

Indirect Subsidies

Tax Benefits:

a. Depreciation for new ships, modernization, repairs: first year 20 percent, second year 15 percent, each additional year 10 percent.

b. Value-added tax (VAT) exemptions for:

Deliveries and imports of seagoing and inland waterway vessels (no yachts).

Services for seagoing and inland waterway vessels (no yachts).

Building and supply material delivered or imported to owners of above vessels.

Customs: Exemption of construction, repair, and maintenance material for seagoing vessels and tugs, and some inland waterway vessels.

Loans and Interest on Loans:

a. 1948 Act gives credit for shipowners building ships in Belgium or elsewhere, or purchasing ships abroad, at 5 percent for up to 10 years, and to 70 percent of value of ship. Interest subsidies averaged $3,116,532 in 1971, and $4,861,000 in 1975.

b. Ship export credits for up to 70 percent cost of ship, maximum 7 years, at least 8 percent interest.

c. Government insurance at credit risks up to 7 years, .65–5.65 percent premiums.

Cargo Preference and Cabotage: None.

Comments: Shipbuilding research grants in 1975 = $667,820.

BRAZIL

Direct Subsidies

Operating Subsidy: None to private shipping. Operating losses of Lloyd Brasileiro (government owned) covered by government.

Construction Subsidy:

a. Decree 60679 (5/3/67) established Merchant Marine Refinancing Fund which pays the difference between Brazilian and average Western European cost of new construction and repair.

b. Government benefits to aid shipyard development since 1958.

Indirect Subsidies

Tax Benefits:

a. Decree 4622 (1965) exempts shipbuilding materials from import and consumption tax. Similar exemption for services and supplies for shipbuilding.

b. 1975 law extends to 1980 the exemption of shipbuilding material from import duties and manufactured goods taxes.

c. 20 percent on imported and coastwise freight is earmarked for ship purchase, construction, and modernization.

Loans and Interest on Loans:

a. Government credits to Brazilian lines cover up to 85 percent of ship's cost; interest 6 percent; repayment in 15 years.

Cargo Preference and Cabotage:

a. Cabotage

b. Decree 666 (7/2/69)—All imports/exports receiving government financial assistance must be carried on national-flag ships. Exceptions:

Reciprocal equal carriage agreements with other countries;

No Brazilian-flag vessel available;

Superintendency of merchant marine will designate carrier when trading with nation not served by ships of both nations.

c. Government monopoly on petroleum transport.

d. Except where there are special agreements, paper imports to be carried in Brazilian ships.

e. Coffee exported to United States; 50 percent Brazilian ships, 40 percent U.S. ships, 10 percent third-flag ships (as of 6/1/71). However, as of 3/22/73, this was replaced by 40–40–20 for the U.S. East and Gulf coasts.

f. Only foreign shipping companies belonging to a shipping conference to which Brazil belongs can operate from Brazil.

g. Since 1967 cargo quotas call for Brazil-Partner-third-flag quota ratio of 40–40–20; 50–50 with Argentina, Mexico, Chile.

h. Special access and pooling agreements with three U.S. lines.

Government Ownership: 80 percent of tonnage, including Lloyd Brasileiro and tanker fleet.

CANADA

Direct Subsidies

Operating Subsidy:

a. None to foreign trade.

b. Coastal and inland service to communities unservable on commercial basis receive subsidies when required by public convenience and necessity, or where such service will promote new trade.

Construction Subsidy—1975 Program:

a. Subsidy of 14 percent of approved cost of Canadian-built vessels. Subsidy reduced 1 percent/year starting 1976 until diminished to 8 percent.

b. 3 percent incentive grant on vessels to yards investing equal amount on modernization of facilities.

c. Export Development Corporation to help finance $475 million in sales of new vessels for export.

Indirect Subsidies

Tax Benefits:

a. Tax on proceeds from book profits on sales of vessels are remitted if proceeds used to build new approved vessels.

b. Depreciation:

First user of Canadian-built ship: 33⅓% per annum straight line.

All other ships: 15 percent per annum, diminishing balance basis.

c. Tax relief when insurance proceeds used for replacement.

Customs:

a. No duty on material imported for export vessels.

Loans and Interest on Loans—Export Credits:

a. Up to 5 percent/year of insurance on bank-provided export credits.

b. Export credits up to 70 percent cost. Repayment up to 7 years. Interest at least 8 percent except for special aid programs.

Cargo Preference and Cabotage:

a. Much of coastal trade in eastern region and Great Lakes reserved for Canadian vessels.

b. British Commonwealth vessels in Canadian coastal trade at time of exclusion may still operate when there are no Canadian vessels available.

c. Foreign-built vessels can be registered tax and duty free, but then can only engage in international trade.

Government Ownership:

a. Canadian Nat'l. Railway ferries, and 6 other ferries on charter to private operators.

b. Government purchases only from Canadian yards.

Comments: 50 percent research grants to industry.

CHILE

Direct Subsidies

Operating Subsidy:
a. Deficits of national line met by treasury.
b. None to private lines.
Construction Subsidy: None.

Indirect Subsidies

Tax Benefits:
a. 20 percent of profits placed in tax exempt reserve fund. Can be withdrawn to purchase new tonnage.
b. Equipment of domestic shipbuilding enterprises can be revalued annually to reduce taxable income.
c. Exemption of up to 50 percent of income tax is allowed if proceeds used to renew fleet (1956–66); in practice it was 20 percent.
Loans and Interest on Loans: None.
Cargo Preference and Cabotage:
a. Half of cargo going between Chile and countries served by Chilean lines to go on Chilean ships. Foreign shipping lines can carry this cargo if they have a cargo pool with a Chilean line.
b. Foreign vessels allowed in coastal trade only when Chilean vessel unavailable.
c. Equal portion agreements with Argentina and Brazil. CSAV has pooling agreements with 2 U.S. companies.
Government Ownership:
a. EME is a government owned company engaged largely in coastal trade.
b. Government owns 25–30 percent of CSAV.
Comments: Chilean line can convert foreign currency at a 20 percent advantage over market rate.

CHINA (TAIWAN)

Direct Subsidies

Operating Subsidy: None.
Construction Subsidy: Granted in special cases. One third of expenses resulting from construction in Taiwan instead of abroad.

Indirect Subsidies

Tax Benefits:
a. Income taxes do not apply for 4–5 years for national-flag ships.

b. Depreciation 12–15 percent on tankers, 15–20 percent on cargo ships.
Customs: No duty on items imported for shipbuilding.
Loans and Interest on Loans:
a. Loans for 80 percent of cost given at 7.5 percent.
Cargo Preference and Cabotage:
a. No legislation. Mutually agreed that 50 percent of trade with Japan go in national bottoms.
b. Preference to national companies for certain bulk goods.
Government Ownership:
a. One government-owned yard with 100,000 ton capacity.
b. 2 government-owned fleets with 700,000 ton total.

COLUMBIA

Indirect Subsidies

Tax Benefits:
Flota mercante Grancolombiana, the Colombian flag merchant fleet, is exempt from income and capital tax.
Cargo Preference and Cabotage:
a. 50 percent of general cargo, bulk, liquid, and refrigerator cargo is reserved for Colombian-flag vessels, except where conflicting with previous governmental obligations.
b. Reciprocity with registered Latin-American shipowners.
c. Cabotage
d. 50-50 sharing agreement with Argentina, Uruguay.

CYPRUS

Direct Subsidies: None.

Indirect Subsidies

Tax Benefits:
No corporate taxes or personal taxes on dividends on proceeds from shipping for period 1963–1983.
Loans and Interest on Loans: None.
Cargo Preference and Cabotage: None.

DENMARK

Direct Subsidies: None.

Indirect Subsidies

Tax Benefits:
a. All vessels at least 20 GRT exempt from VAT.
b. 30 percent write-off possible before delivery, no more than 15 percent per year, vessels over 32,500 DWT
Loans and Interest on Loans:
a. Loans available to Danish owners of domestic and foreign vessels, and foreign owners of Danish vessels, up to 50 percent value of vessel (more with security), through Ship Credit Fund.
b. Loans and guarantees to operators of small coasters for construction and conversion. Mortgages to 70 percent cost, 15-year period, equal installments.
c. Ships built at Danish yards follow OCED terms: 70 percent maximum credit; maximum repayment 7 years from delivery, interest at least 8 percent per annum.
Government Ownership: Ferries, Greenland trade vessels.
Comments:
a. Licenses required for ship imports.
b. $480,000/year to shipbuilding research.

EGYPT

Indirect Subsidies

Cargo Preference and Cabotage:
a. All cargo on business of the UAR, its public institutions, organizations, and their affiliates must be arranged and supervised by the Egyptian Company for Maritime Transport.
Government Ownership:
Government owns Egyptian Navigation Co. and Petroleum Organization of Egypt.

ENGLAND

Direct Subsidies

Operating Subsidy: None in foreign trade. Aid given to domestic essential service to sparsely settled areas.
Construction Subsidy: None.

Indirect Subsidies

Tax Benefits:

a. Refund of indirect taxes to shipbuilders and building suppliers. Rate of relief is 2% of the value of the vessels under building contract.

b. Ships of at least 15 tons exempt from value-added tax (VAT).

Loans and Interest on Loans:

a. Million loaned to Cunard at 4½ percent for *Queen Elizabeth*.

b. Guaranteed loans for ships constructed for export.

c. Guaranteed loans for ships and offshore installations constructed for UK owners.

Cargo Preference and Cabotage: None.

Customs: Exemptions for some imported shipbuilding materials.

Government ownership:

a. Interest in BP (tankers).

b. Interest in some nationalized shipowning bodies.

c. Proposed 1975 bill to nationalize major shipbuilding industries.

Comments: Cost escalation insurance. Private and government research grants available.

FINLAND

Direct Subsidies: None

Indirect Subsidies

Tax Benefits:

a. 30 percent/year book value depreciation; extra depreciation not exceeding 60 percent (1969–73) of taxable income of firm.

b. Depreciation begins on signing of contract for Finnish-built vessels.

c. Note: New Tax laws in preparation as of 1976.

Customs: Customs duty and turnover tax exemption for materials used in vessels over 10 meters.

Loans and Interest on Loans:

a. State Guarantee Board guarantees loans for acquisition of new and less than 10 year-old used ships.

Cargo Preference and Cabotage: Cabotage

Government Ownership:

a. Small interest in Finlines, Ltd.

b. Ownership of nonmerchant vessels—icebreakers and survey vessels.

c. Controlling interest in the largest shipbuilder, Valmet, Oy.

FRANCE

Direct Subsidies

Operating Subsidy:

a. General and mail carriage subsidy to semipublic lines.

b. Operating subsidy to compensate for differences between France and other countries.

c. $222 million available to merchant fleet 1974–79.

Construction Subsidy:

a. Lump sum subsidies abolished 1976.

b. Modernization grants up to $22 million total available 1976–80, paying 2–15 percent of contract price. Passenger vessels and long-range tanker excluded.

Indirect Subsidies

Tax Benefit:

a. No VAT on ship sales, domestic or foreign.

b. Choice of reducing or straight line depreciation schemes.

Customs: Ship construction and repair materials duty free.

Loans and Interest on Loans:

a. Ship export credits through private banks supported by official institutions. Under OECD agreement, duration must be less than 12 yrs., total less than 70% percent of cost, and interest greater than 8 percent.

Cargo Preference and Cabotage:

a. Two thirds imported crude oil must be in French bottoms; exemptions allowed.

b. Cabotage

c. Trade to present and ex-colonies sometimes restricted to French and colonial ships.

d. Government can restrict freedom of French owners to charter their own and foreign vessels.

Government Ownership:

a. Principal shareholder in largest shipping company, Compagnie Generale Maritime.

b. 17 percent ownership in company promoting French shipping industry.

Comments: Shipping lines partially reimbursed for personnel accident and illness costs.

GERMANY

Direct Subsidies

Operating Subsidy: None.
Construction Subsidy:
a. Through Ministry of Transportation: Up to 16 percent of construction cost. 1976 total = $65 million. Must be repaid in full if vessel sold within 6 years. Refund reduced 20 percent for each consecutive active year. For large tankers, up to 15 percent construction subsidy. Must be repaid if vessel sold within 12 years.
b. Through Ministry of Economics: subsidies to shipyards.

Indirect Subsidies

Tax Benefits:
a. Book profit on sale of vessel can be transferred to a reserve fund to be used to replace vessel.
b. For vessels built between 1965 and 1970 an additional depreciation, up to 30 percent/year, is allowed.
c. Depreciation period: 14 years dry cargo, 12 years tankers, refrigerator, container, LASH vessels.
d. VAT exemption on new seagoing vessels.
Customs: Imported shipbuilding material duty-free.
Loans and Interest on Loans:
a. Limited loans for fleet modernization from the returns to the European Recovery Program Fund and capital market. Up to 70 percent cost, 8 percent interest, 12-year period.
b. Reduction of interest rates up to 2 percent on vessels built for export. For 1976–79 program, funds cover only 60 percent of the total supportable volume, and also extend to domestic orders. Optimal insurance of export credits to 90 percent.
c. Credit for port expansion: 6.5 percent over 10–12 years.
Cargo Preference and Cabotage:
a. Foreign ship can be used in domestic trade only if German ships unavailable, or available at substantially less favorable rates.
Government Ownership: 75 percent of one large shipyard.

GREECE

Direct Subsidies

Construction Subsidy: None.
Operating Subsidy: None.

Indirect Subsidies

Tax Benefits:
a. No income tax on earnings of Greek-flag ships.
b. "Net tonnage tax" due instead as shown in chart:

Category 1 Vessels (Over 500 GRT)		*Category 2 Vessels (Up to 500 GRT)*
Ship Age	*Tax per ton*	Up to $76.66 on 1st 100 GRT then
0–10	$ .00	$1.17/ton additional to 500 GRT
10–20	.20	
20–25	.30	
over 25	.40	

Exemptions:	*Exemptions:*
Vessels less than 10 years old	Vessels less than 12 years old, built and registered in Greece
Vessels less than 12 years old, built and registered in Greece	
Vessels less than 30 years old, transferred to Greek flag and in foreign commerce; 5-year exemption	Vessels less than 30 years old, transferred to Greek flag and in foreign commerce; 5 year exemption
Vessels less than 20 years old with improvements made	
	For cargo, tanker and bulk ships 10–20 years old when Greek registered, 50 percent tax exemption first 5 years, two-thirds exemption over 10 years, if repairs or improvements double original purchase price. For vessels over 20 years old, if replaced by Greek-registered vessel of at least two-thirds tonnage, 10–15 years old, and 50 percent Greek-built, registered vessels are not taxed until 12 years old; other vessels until 10 years.

c. No income tax on foreign-flag ships owned by companies operating in Greece.

Loans and Interest on Loans:
a. Government guarantees shipbuilding loans for Greek-flag vessels for up to 80 percent of construction costs. Interest 7.5 percent.
b. Bank of Greece subsidizes difference between 7.5 percent and foreign lending rate. Will guarantee 2 percent profit spread.
c. Loans available:
   • Conversions—7 years at 7.5 percent per annum.
   • Construction of Mediterranean cargo vessels to 300 GRT, coastal cargo vessels, and passenger vessels—7.8 percent per annum, 12½ years with 2½-year grace.

• Repairs: 80 percent financed at 9.5 percent per annum.

d. Credit for purchase of vessels:

Foreign-flag vessels:

• Ships less than 12 years old—government authorizes local banks to issue letters of guarantee up to 50 percent, payable in 4 years.

• Coastal cargo, passenger, ferry vessels less than 8 years old—80 percent guarantee to vessels worth up to $1 million; above that requires special approval of currency committee.

Greek-flag vessels: (less than 15 years old)—local loans to 50 percent value of vessel or $100,000 maximum; repayable in 3 years, 1-year grace.

e. Loans for Working Capital: short term, 13 percent per annum interest.

Cargo Preference and Cabotage: Cabotage.

Comments:

a. Depreciation inapplicable because of lack of income tax.

b. Bilateral shipping agreement with USSR.

c. Special home banking privileges to Greek seamen abroad. Transfer tax exemption on real estate to Greek seamen abroad at least 3 yrs.

HONG KONG (Not listed in 1976 source)

Direct Subsidies: None.

Indirect Subsidies: None.

INDIA

Direct Subsidies

Operating Subsidy: None.

Construction Subsidy: Subsidies to government-owned yard of 5 percent of international value of the vessel. Starting 1976, to be reduced 1 percent every 2 years.

Indirect Subsidies

Tax Benefits:

a. Development rebate of 40 percent for vessels ordered before 12/31/73 and delivered until 12/31/76.

b. Variable rates of depreciation depending on class of vessel and period.

Loans and Interest on Loans:

a. Loans are made to national shipping company at 4.5 percent, which is much lower than the usual rate.

b. Loans cover 95 percent of new Indian-built vessels, 90 percent of foreign vessels, and 75 percent of used foreign vessels.

Cargo Preference and Cabotage:
a. Plans for all oil to be carried in Indian bottoms.
b. Government accounts carried in national flag vessels.
c. Mutual trade agreements with various nations for equality of carriage.
d. Cabotage.
e. Export-Import bank cargoes carried in U.S. or Indian vessels.

Government Ownership: Extensive. Shipping Corporation of India has 115 vessels (1,767,253 GRT) in 1974; Mogul Line Ltd. has 9 vessels (81,115 GRT) Jayanti Shipping Corp.; many shipyards and docks.

INDONESIA

Direct Subsidies: None.

Indirect Subsidies

Tax Benefits: None.
Loans and Interest on Loans: None.
Cargo Preference and Cabotage:
a. Indonesian freight board has unlimited power to discriminate in favor of national flag. As of 1969, it has not exercised this power.
b. Trans-shipments are required to be in national-flag bottoms unless unavailable, and to use only Indonesian trans-shipment ports.
c. 40 percent of all cargo between Indonesia and Europe to be on national-flag ships.
d. 4 percent tax on gross revenues of foreign shipping from, not to, Indonesia.
e. 45 percent of European cargoes reserved for Indonesian ships.
f. Trade agreement with USSR allocates bilateral cargoes to either flag.
Government Ownership:
Indonesian National Shipping Co. (PELNI), national interisland fleet, Djakarta Lloyd (largest international line), the oil company PN Pertamina, and the Carya Putra shipyard.

IRAN

Direct Subsidies: No subsidies in Iran.

Comments: Arya Shipping Co., the major company, is a quasi-government company.

IRELAND

Direct Subsidies

Construction Subsidy:
State subsidies for vessels built in Irish yards.

Indirect Subsidies

Tax Benefits:
a. Initial allowance of 60 percent for capital expenditure on new or used vessels.

b. Special allowance of 40 percent instead of the above for new vessels.

c. Independent depreciation for wear and tear.

d. Profits from shipbuilding and repairs, and export sales profits wholly exempt from income and corporate profit taxes for 15 years, plus further 5 years of reducing relief until 4/5/90.

Loans and Interest on Loans:
a. Government investment bank through Shipping Finance Corp., Ltd., extends loans to Irish shipowners, enabling them to offer credit comparable to that offered abroad.

b. Extensive government loans, grants, and share subscriptions in Verolme Cork Dockyard.

Government Ownership:
Government owns Irish Shipping Ltd., P & I Co. (ferries, RoRos, LoLos). Another ferry/RoRo owned jointly with Scandanavian interests.

ISRAEL

Direct Subsidies

Operating Subsidy:
Direct payment for operation of 2 passenger-car ferries, owned 50–50 by government and Zim Lines. Zim Lines 30 percent government owned. Government absorbs from this operation $1 million/year losses.

Construction Subsidy: None.

Indirect Subsidies

Tax Benefits: Tax advantages to shipyards at all stages of operation.

Customs: Customs and indirect exemption for materials required for building by Israel Shipyards, Ltd.

Loans and Interest on Loans[1]:
a. Loans for construction of ships at Israel Shipyard, Ltd.

b. Government will guarantee 80 percent of purchase price, providing

---

[1] Information may be obsolete.

another guarantor for 13½ percent can be found; government has first mortgage.

Cargo Preference and Cabotage:

a. All meats imported must go on Israel-flag ships.

b. Foreign vessels chartered only when domestic vessels unavailable.

Government Ownership:

a. Zim Israel Navigation Co.: owned by Israel Corp. (50 percent), government (30 percent), Histadrut (national labor union—10 percent), and Jewish Agency (10 percent). Zim includes cargo vessels, tankers, bulk carriers and passenger vessels.

b. Government also owns Israel Shipyard Ltd., the only yard with over 1000 GRT capability.

Comments:

a. Government and shipping companies share 50–50 in officer training costs.

b. Ship must be at least 50 percent Israeli owned for Israeli registration.

ITALY

Direct Subsidies

Operating Subsidy: $147 million to FINMARE (government holding company owning Italia, Lloyd Triestino, Adriatica and Tirreria) and private companies operating public interest transport (mail and passenger service to home islands) in 1974.

Construction Subsidy: To offset difference between Italian and foreign yards, 1974–1980 period.

a. $215 million to new ship construction, conversion, and repairs; $20 million for modernization and expansion of shipyards; $6 million for manufacture of marine engines.

b. Scrap-and-Build Law 19 of 1/74: $54 per ton subsidy for replacement vessels of at least 50 percent tonnage of vessel scrapped.

c. Investment Subsidies: 10% for building, conversion, and repair; 6 percent for construction of marine engine factories.

Indirect Subsidies

Tax Benefits:

a. Tax-free replacement reserves on book profits from vessel sales.

b. VAT exemption for vessels and construction materials.

c. Straight line depreciation on accounting life of 10 yrs. for tankers, passengers, and cargo vessels. Accelerated depreciation for 3 yrs. following year of expenditure; max. 40% cost of vessel. Yearly max. 15% cost of vessel.

Customs: No duty on all material imported for construction of ocean-going ships.

Loans:

a. Law 26 of 2/2/74: Ministry of Merchant Marine authorized construction, modernization and repair loans up to 70 percent of cost, at 6–7 percent, repayable 15 yrs., government pays difference between this and actual rate.

b. Law 720 of 12/23/75: 6.5 percent rate for orders after 1/1/76. Loans to 80 percent cost for vessels under 3000 GRT.

c. Follows Organization for Economic Cooperation and Development (OCED)"Understanding on Export Credit for Ships." Maximum credit 80 percent of cost; interest 7½ percent minimum, payable in 8 years.

Cabotage and Cargo Preference:

a. Ships of countries discriminating against Italian flag can be used only with permission.

b. Cabotage.

Government Ownership: Government owns the bulk of the stock of Italian shipping companies.

JAPAN

Direct Subsidies

Operating Subsidy:

a. Subsidies to domestic island/mainland service totaled $4,491,000 in 1975.

Construction Subsidy: None normally, but government has paid three quarters of the cost of a nuclear ship.

Indirect Subsidies

Tax Benefits:

a. Choice of constant ratio method or constant amount method ship-by-ship depreciation.

b. Extra 20 percent depreciation for ships at least 2000 GRT (4/75 to 3/77).

Loans and Interest on Loans:

a. Scrap-and-Build Plan of 1961: Shipowner replacing old domestic trade vessel can receive up to 70 percent loan from Maritime Credit Corp. on condition he share ownership with Credit Corp. Interest 8.9 percent; repayment 7–12 years after 3-year grace period.

b. Through Development Bank of Japan, government makes loans up to 70 percent for container ships (5 percent self-financed, 25 percent private banks), and 60 percent for other ships (20 percent self-financed, 20 percent private banks). Development Bank interest 5.9–6.4 percent, private banks

6.9–7.4 percent. Repayment 10 years after 3-year grace. Subsidies repaid in proportion to shipowner's profits.

c. Other government-supported organizations make loans for construction of replacement fishing, cargo, and passenger vessels.

d. Ship Export Credits: Government-supported Export-Import Bank of Japan and private banks cover up to 60 percent of ship's construction costs (27 percent EXIM, 33 percent private). Then Japanese yards are able to grant deferred payments to foreign buyers on same condition as combined loan—term, 7 years; interest, 3 percent, 30 percent payment upon delivery. EXIM financing meets OECD "Understanding on Export Credit for Ships."

Government Ownership: Small coasters.

Research: $4.9 million annually from Ship Institute of Ministry of Transport. Nuclear Ship Development Agency established 1963.

KOREA

Direct Subsidies

Operating Subsidy:

a. Losses incurred by ships operating in international trade and earning foreign exchange will be made up. Ship receiving this aid may be ordered to operate on given routes.

b. Encouragement of subsidies to businessmen operating or utilizing Korean-flag ships in international trade and earning foreign currency.

Construction Subsidy: When ship receiving operating subsidy is too old, government orders replacement or improvement and bears the loss.

Indirect Subsidies

Tax Benefits and Customs:

a. Shipbuilding materials imported duty-free and without payment of internal taxes.

b. Preferential interest rate for importing raw materials for export production when imported raw materials carried in Korean bottoms.

Loans and Interest on Loans:

a. Loans up to 85 percent of construction cost. Repayment in 15 years; interest 7.5 percent per annum.

b. Shipyard development loans repayable in 10 years, interest 7.5 percent per annum.

c. Loans available for importation, improvement, and repair of ships, and for chartering ships to carry Korean goods. Ships may be used as collateral for importing and chartering ships.

Cargo Preference and Cabotage:

a. Cabotage.

b. Government frequently buys FOB and ships on Korean vessels.

c. Trade agreements with U.S., W. Germany, Japan. Cargo transported under these agreements goes on national lines at slightly lower tariff.

d. Crude oil, iron ore, fertilizer, and grain to be carried only on Korean ships.

e. Korean importers and exporters must use only Korean ships.

Comments: Government maritime transportation organization to encourage international trade.

KUWAIT

Indirect Subsidies

Loans: 2–3 percent low-interest loans to Kuwaiti shipping companies. 1967 total $2.8 million, 1968 total $9.24 million.

Cargo Preference and Cabotage: Crude oil preference to Kuwaiti-flag tankers or those partly Kuwaiti-owned.

Government Ownership: 75 percent of Kuwaiti Shipping Co.

LEBANON (no 1976 update)

Direct Subsidies: None.

Indirect Subsidies

Tax Benefits:
a. No income tax on shipping enterprises.
b. New shipbuilding industries tax exempt for 5 years.
Customs: Shipbuilding materials imported duty-free.
Loans and Interest on Loans: None.
Cargo Preference and Cabotage: Shippers required to pledge not to ship on Israeli vessels or on ships blacklisted because of calls at Israeli ports.

LIBERIA

Direct Subsidies: None.

Indirect Subsidies

Tax Benefits: None.
Loans and Interest on Loans: None.
Cargo Preference and Cabotage: None.
Comments: Through the Liberia Shipping Corporation (1961), Liberia is a partner in two shipping companies.

MALAYSIA

Direct Subsidies: None

Indirect Subsidies

Loans and Interest on Loans: Government guaranteed commercial loans for 5 LNG tankers ordered by Malaysian International Shipping Corp., 1974.

Government Ownership: 51 percent of Malaysian International, 50 percent of shipyard at Johore Bharu.

MEXICO

Direct Subsidies

Operating Subsidy: Up to 50 percent of fuel subsidy.
Construction Subsidy: None.

Indirect Subsidies

Tax Benefits: None.
Loans and Interest on Loans: Guaranteed loans for one shipping company.
Cargo Preference and Cabotage:
a. Cabotage
b. Import licenses approved conditionally on the use of Mexican vessels (only when Mexican carrier requests).
c. PEMEX (oil company) restricted to Mexican-flag vessels when available.
d. Where there are import quotas, importers using Mexican vessels are not charged for transportation against their quotas.
e. 1967 decree gives reductions on cotton export tax accompanied by preferential treatment when Mexican-flag or Mexican-chartered vessels are used.
f. Bilateral carriage agreement with Brazil.
Government Ownership:
a. PEMEX owns largest tanker fleet.
b. Major yards nationalized.
c. 30 percent Transportation Maritima Mexicana government owned.
Comments:
a. 25 percent subsidy of freight to shippers of products to U.S., Guatemala, or Br. Honduras on Mexican-controlled transportation.
b. 2 percent reduction in tax on bee honey if shipped on Mexican ships.
c. 50 percent subsidy of freight for final products (25 percent for intermediate goals) for exports on Mexican ships.
d. Foreign exchange is rationed. Sea transport on Mexican vessels is not included in quota.

NETHERLANDS

Direct Subsidies: None.

Indirect Subsidies

a. Owners of vessels registered in Netherlands can subtract 5 percent/year of investment for 5 years from pre-tax shipping profits. This system might be replaced by a new system of investment premiums.

b. No VAT on vessels, supplies, construction materials, or on imported vessels.

c. Depreciation: one third of investment depreciated in advance of amount determined by linear or reducing method applied to the other two thirds.

Customs: No duties on products imported for oceangoing shipbuilding.

Loans and Interest on Loans:

a. Interest subsidies to shipbuilders to enable them to furnish credits at reduced rates to domestic and foreign customers.

b. Government guaranteed commercial loans in special circumstances for investment.

Government Ownership: Majority shareholder in North Sea ferry service.

Comments: Government finances maritime research program.

NORWAY

Direct Subsidies

Operating Subsidy: None in foreign trade. Aid given to domestic shipping service of sparsely populated outlying districts.

Construction Subsidy: None.

Indirect Subsidies

Tax Benefits:

a. Any business can deposit 20 percent of its annual income in tax deferred funds to be spent in 4 years on depreciable property.

b. Goods delivered to shipbuilding or repair yards not subject to turnover tax (13 percent of selling price).

c. Complex and "unfavorable" depreciation rules.

d. VAT exemption for all vessels.

e. Capital gains from loss or sale of ships must be used within 8 years to finance new ships or write down existing ships. Then tax on such gains is released.

Customs: Refund of import duties paid on commodities incorporated into goods exported.

Loans and Interest on Loans:

a. Permanent provision for granting of loans of up to 20 percent of cost of ship through government-supported mortgage institute. Loans secured by second mortgage on vessels, interest 8 percent.

b. Guaranteed loans to owners of ships and drilling vessels through guarantee institute; limit, $725 million.

c. Guaranteed loans to shipyards obtaining foreign credit; limit, $725 million.

d. $54 million loan guarantee to Kvaener Shipbuilding Co.

Cargo Preference and Cabotage: None.

PAKISTAN

Direct Subsidies

Operating Subsidy: None.

Construction Subsidy: Up to 40 percent of building cost of ships built at Karachi yard (KSEW).

Indirect Subsidies

Tax Benefits and Customs:

a. Fuel oil and lubricants for coastal shipping exempt from customs duty and sales tax.

Loans and Interest on Loans:

a. Foreign loans and credit are arranged by the government.

b. Government finances purchase of ships and is repaid on "pay as you earn" scheme by shipping companies.

Cargo Preference and Cabotage:

a. Cabotage.

b. Portion of shipping conference cargo is reserved for Pakistani ships.

c. One half U.S. and World Bank cargo reserved to national-flag ships.

d. Some berths reserved for coastal vessels.

Government Ownership:

a. Merchant fleet nationalized 1/1/74.

b. Government-owned Karachi Shipyard run on commercial lines, and is semiautomatic.

Comments:

a. Shipping companies granted 30 percent bonus on foreign exchange turned into government for rupees.

b. Official and semiofficial agencies (except U.S. AID) must purchase marine insurance from Pakistan Insurance Co.

PANAMA

Direct Subsidies: None.

Indirect Subsidies

Tax Benefits: No income tax payable on either earnings of ship or crew.
Cargo Preference and Cabotage:
a. Cabotage.
b. Up to $150 permit charged to foreign vessels for use of nongovernment ports or Panamanian navigable waters.
c. Fines to $100,000 for foreign vessels fishing in Panamanian waters without license.

PERU

Direct Subsidies

Operating Subsidy: CPV (Corporacion Peruvana de Vapores) receives subsidy from government revenues derived in part from 4 percent export and import freight tax.
Construction Subsidy: Law of 1/9/62 authorized establishment of government-sponsored naval construction industry supported by export and import tax revenues. Remainder of tax funds go to CPV.

Indirect Subsidies

Tax Benefits: CVS tax exempt.
Loans and Interest on Loans: Industrial Bank of Peru grants government guaranteed credits of at least 80 percent of ship construction cost. Interest not to exceed that charged abroad or in no case above 7 percent per annum.
Cargo Preference and Cabotage:
a. Cabotage.
b. Public bodies use CPV preferentially and also contract through CPV for any transportation that CPV cannot handle.
c. Up to 50 percent exports/imports reserved for Peruvian lines.
d. CPV receives preference in all cargoes.
e. Import-free cargoes must be carried preferentially by Peruvian-flag vessels; foreign vessels chartered by Peruvian companies; foreign vessels associated with Peruvian companies.
f. Peru has 50-50 sharing agreements with India and Argentina.
Government Ownership: CPV and shipyards formerly naval-owned.
Comments:
a. No foreign vessel purchased after 6/12/72 of types built by Peruvian shipyards without the approval of the Naval Industry Commission.
b. All Peruvian vessels to be repaired only in Peruvian yards unless

emergency abroad or lack of Peruvian capacity.

c. Peruvian vessels enjoy 50 percent discount for clearance fees, two thirds for drydock fees, and 40–50 percent for mooring fees.

PHILIPPINES

Direct Subsidies

Operating Subsidy:

a. Presidential Decree 806 (10/3/75) provides direct incentives to domestic vessels and lines.

Construction Subsidy: None.

Indirect Subsidies

Tax Benefits:

a. 10-year exemption of income derived from shipping provided all profits are reinvested.

b. Exporters using Philippine-flag vessels can deduct from their taxes 150 percent of overseas freight expenses and Philippine port charges, plus 200 percent of their shipping costs.

Loans and Interest on Loans:

a. 11-year loans for 100 percent of value of vessel at 3 percent interest, 3-year grace period.

b. Loans to rehabilitate and replace interisland fleet; 12 percent interest plus mortgage on vessels or real estate.

—New Vessels: 20 years repayment, loan to 80 percent value of ship.

—Vessels up to 12 years old: 5 years repayment, loan to 60 percent value.

—Vessels 12–16 years old: 5 years repayment, loan to 40 percent value.

Customs: Shipbuilding material exempt.

Cargo Preference and Cabotage:

a. Presidential Decree 806 (10/3/75): Philippine vessels to carry at least as much as vessels of another state between the two states.

b. Presidential Decree 894 (2/26/76): Government agencies, government-owned organizations, tax-exempt entities, and persons to use Philippine registered vessels.

c. 50 percent of special U.S. imports in Philippine bottoms when available. These imports are agricultural products under Section 402 of U.S. Mutual Security Act and U.S. Public Law 480.

d. Cabotage.

e. Import licenses granted only when cargo is carried on Philippine-flag ship, except when capacity unavailable, which is frequently the case.

Government Ownership: Philippine National Lines (these ships are under charter to private companies with purchase options), and National Shipyard Corp., and one small shipyard.

Comments: Maritime Industry Authority (MARINA) established 1975 to coordinate maritime development and expand and modernize merchant fleet.

PORTUGAL

Direct Subsidies: None.

Indirect Subsidies

Tax Benefits:

a. 25 percent reduction in maritime trades tax for use of ships of countries having signed trade and navigation agreements with Portugal.

Loans and Interest on Loans: Merchant Marine Renewal Fund (est. 1946) grants loans and guarantees to finance renovation, modernization, and new construction to enlarge the merchant fleet. Interest 6.25 percent plus 0.25 percent commission per annum; repayment over 20 equal semesters. Acquisition and construction loans limited to 75 percent cost of vessel, and fixed on a yearly basis by Ministers of Finance and Navy.

Cargo Preference and Cabotage:

a. Cabotage.

b. Cargoes to military or scientific bases must go in Portuguese ships.

c. Bilateral equal carriage agreement with USSR.

Government Ownership:

a. National Navigation Co. and Portuguese Sea Transport Co. nationalized by decree 4/16/75.

SINGAPORE

Indirect Benefits

Tax Benefits:

a. Registered vessels exempt from income taxes on vessel profits.

b. Registered vessels receive 50 percent reduction in registration fee if 25 percent of crew are nationals.

c. Guarantee of no registration fee increase for 20 years.

Loans and Interest on Loans (for Singapore-built vessels):

a. Deferred credit financing through shipyards for vessels over 5000 DWT; interest follows OECD rate.

b. For vessels below 5000 DWT, credit through Development Bank of Singapore, Ltd., 9.5 percent interest per annum. For both categories, loans up to 50 percent of value of vessel available, repayable up to 7 years, after delivery.

c. Additional loans available commercially.

Government Ownership: Neptune Orient Lines, Keppel Shipyard, Jurong Shipyard (partially), Sembawang Shipyard (Pte.) Ltd., (public share participation).

SOUTH AFRICA

Direct Subsidies

Operating Subsidy: None.

Construction Subsidy:

a. 500–6000 GRT: 25 percent contract price, 200–500 GRT: 10 percent contract price.

b. Higher rates in exceptional cases; subsidies to vessels not covered above, under special circumstances.

c. Subsidies for government agency contracts to compensate for difference between local price and overseas price plus duty.

Indirect Subsidies

Tax Benefits:

a. Initial depreciation of 40 percent; 10 percent each succeeding year until total equals cost of ship.

b. Rebates on taxes on imported ships.

Customs: 20 percent customs duty on ships built abroad and registered in South Africa. Rebate if purpose of the ship is approved.

Loans and Interest on Loans: Guaranteed loans and interest subsidy of 2 percent to approved buyers.

Cargo Preference and Cabotage: All goods from UK or Europe must go on ships belonging to members of South and South East African Shipping Conference.

Government Ownership: 37.5 percent of South African Marine Conference (SAFMARINE).

SPAIN

Direct Subsidies

Operating Subsidy:

a. High Seas: Subsidy to two companies for "special" services in interest of state.

b. Coastal: Reimbursement for losses.

Construction Subsidy: In line with OECD, aids eliminated in 1975.

Indirect Subsidies

Tax Benefits: Tax repayments of 12 percent given to shipbuilders.

Customs: Imported material for export ships exempt. Rebates for material for domestic ships.

Loans and Interest on Loans:

a. Private banks and Banco Exterior provide export credits covering 70 percent of contract price for 7 years, 8 percent interest.

b. Private banks lend to domestic owners on same terms as for export credits. Construction Credit Bank participates in such loans for up to 25 percent for building ships over 8,000 GRT.

c. Government credits for shipyard modernization; 1968–71 plan: 70 percent cost, 9 years repayment at 8 percent interest.

Cargo Preference and Cabotage:

a. Cabotage.

b. Imports of petroleum, tobacco, and cotton restricted to Spanish ships.

Government Ownership: Government owns 10 percent of fleet over 100 GRT; has interest in shipyards.

Comments: License required for ship imports.

SWEDEN

Direct Subsidies

Operating Subsidy: Some for domestic trade.

Construction Subsidy: Some for archipelago trade.

Indirect Subsidies

Tax Benefits:

a. Taxable earnings from sale of vessels can be transferred to reserve fund and are not taxable if used to replace vessel.

b. 30 percent of price of vessel can be written off before delivery in period 1976–79.

c. Depreciation: 30 percent per year, or complete write-off in 5 years; depreciation not to exceed price of vessel.

Customs: Imported material for oceangoing shipbuilding exempt.

Loans and Interest on Loans:

a. $2.923 billion in loan guarantees for shipbuilding loans from domestic or foreign credit institutions over 1976–78 period.

b. Swedish Ships' Mortgage Bank has government guaranteed fund supplying credits for construction of Swedish vessels. Interest depends upon current bond market; 15 year period, installments 1/15 per annum.

Government Ownership: 51 percent of largest yard. Another yard completely government owned.

Comments: Loans and grants for shipbuilding research.

TURKEY

Direct Subsidies: None.

Indirect Subsidies

Tax Benefits: None.
Loans and Interest on Loans: 1967—$4 million used for loans to build steel ships under 6000 tons; 6-year payment period; 6 percent interest.
Cargo Preference and Cabotage:
a. Public sector cargoes to be carried in Turkish-flag ships. Maritime Bank encourages exporters to use Turkish ships.
b. 1975 decree: Cabotage unless Turkish vessel unavailable.

VENEZUELA

Direct Subsidies

Operating Subsidy: Deficits of national line (CAVN) are made up. None has failed to show profit since 1955 and as of 1976.
Construction Subsidy: None.

Indirect Subsidies

Tax Benefits: None.
Loans and Interest on Loans: None.
Cargo Preference and Cabotage:
a. Government gives preference to CAVN (national line).
b. Various types of pooling arrangements ensure CAVN share of cargo.
c. Cabotage.
Government Ownership: CAVN is a stock company owned by the government. DIANCA, the national shipyard, is fully government financed.

Appendix 4B

LINER FREIGHT RATES

An important factor that is claimed to affect the U.S. balance of trade is the structure of liner rates for ocean shipments in the foreign trade of the United States. To assess the impact of liner rates on the balance of trade, and therefore the U.S. economy, we must consider rate discrimination in U.S. export trades and other factors.

Studies to this effect were part of hearings sponsored by the Joint Economic Committee beginning in 1963,[1] convened to consider the possibility that U.S. exports suffered from discriminatory shipping rates—specifically that U.S. exporters paid higher rates for outbound freight than did foreign exporters for similar shipments inbound to this country, and that foreign exporters to third-country markets paid lower freights per ton mile than did U.S. exporters for the same commodities. In both cases it was alleged that these freight rate differentials were not explained by real differences in liner costs and that the freight rate differences had a significant impact on the competitiveness of U.S. exports and on the balance of trade.

During those hearings, evidence relevant to the first allegation was presented by the Federal Maritime Commission, to the effect that

The international ocean freight rate structure is weighted against U.S. exports . . . . Government studies reveal that on trade between the U.S. Pacific coast and the Far East, freight rates on American exports exceeded rates on corresponding imports on 80 percent of the sampled items. The same discrimination prevails on 70 percent of the products shipped by American exporters from U.S. Atlantic and Gulf ports to the Far East and 60 percent of the commodities shipped from the Atlantic coast to Western Europe.[2]

To test the impact of these differentials, further studies were undertaken by the Department of Commerce, the results of which were presented

---

[1] U.S. Congress, Joint Economic Committee Hearings, *Discriminatory Ocean Freight Rates and the Balance of Payments*, June 1963–March 1964.

[2] 89th Congress, 1st Session, Senate Report No. 1, *Discriminatory Ocean Freight Rates and the Balance of Payments*, January 6, 1965, p. 3.

during a second round of hearings in 1965 and 1966.[3] Evidence obtained through interviews with liner conference representatives in one study indicated that value-of-service considerations were a major factor in the rate-setting process and that the relative bargaining power of shippers may have an important impact on the structure of rates. Estimates of unit shipping costs for different commodities were developed in a second study, although no attempt was made at the time to compare these costs with rates charged for those commodities on particular routes.[4] The results of this study revealed several important factors in cost variations, including differences in operating costs between U.S.-flag and foreign vessels and in cargo handling costs at individual ports.

Finally, a preliminary attempt was made to estimate the impact of rate differentials on the U.S. balance of trade. A pilot study of three major U.S. trading routes was undertaken to determine the feasibility of a more general study. Data on the quantity and value of sample inbound and outbound freights (mainly manufactured products) were obtained from actual shipping declarations and were matched with appropriate rates in the conference tariffs. A comparison of the overall rate structure confirmed the earlier FMC finding that substantial disparities between inbound vs. outbound rates existed. Furthermore, based on estimates of aggregate supply and demand elasticities for U.S. exports and imports, it was found that removing the differentials would have a significant impact on the U.S. balance of trade on those routes.

While the evidence presented in these hearings encouraged more concern with discriminatory rates on the part of the Federal Maritime Commission, it provided only a first step toward estimating the extent and causes of rate discrimination and its effects on U.S. trade. While fairly substantial inbound vs. outbound disparities on one major route were documented, for instance, it was not determined how common this condition was on other routes. Since those hearings, studies of rates on other routes have indicated that such disparities are fairly common. However, the finding that the U.S. balance of trade on the first route was impaired has not been more generally demonstrated.

Analyzing the nature and impact of rates in every major U.S. trade would be a prohibitively large undertaking. Once the factors which lead to discriminatory pricing are identified in a model of liner behavior, however,

---

[3] U.S. Congress, Joint Economic Committee, Subcommittee on Federal Procurement and Regulation Hearings, *Discriminatory Ocean Freight Rates and the Balance of Payments*, April-June 1965, and June 1966.

[4] A later study compared the unit costs with tariff rates published in the JEC hearings. It was found that the range of rates across commodities exceeded the range of unit costs, implying that differentials were not entirely cost-based. See J. O. Jansson, *Costs and Prices for the Carriage and Port Handling of General Cargo by Sea*, mimeographed I.C.H.C.A., London, October, 1971.

it will be possible to consider the prevalence of those factors in U.S. trades. In this way, the general magnitude of the harm to U.S. trade may be estimated.

Most of the empirical work presented at the JEC hearings or done later has dealt with liner routes to and from the United States. Only fragmentary evidence was presented in the hearings to show that it costs more to ship U.S. exports to third-country markets (in particular, South America, Africa, and India) than it does to ship comparable European and Japanese products to these markets. No estimate of the impact of differentials on U.S. exports to those areas has been made as yet.[5] A major stumbling block in conducting a more thorough study of third-country discrimination has been the lack of information on tariff rates for trades not involving the United States.

Most importantly, the behavior of liner conferences in setting rates is poorly understood. The Department of Commerce study indicated that liner conferences go to some lengths to match rates to the perceived demand for services. However, no systematic study was made of the impact of differential costs, of potential competition (nonconference liner, tramp ship, or other mode), or of the bargaining power of shippers on rate-setting behavior.

More recent work on the nature of conference behavior has thrown more light on the factors which determine the structure of rates.[6] Using different theoretical models of cartel behavior,[7] these studies have assessed the impact of costs and noncost factors in explaining rate variations on sample routes. The results have generally highlighted the importance of unit-value pricing. However, some of the studies also indicate that cost considerations (especially stowage factors) and competitive conditions (extent of tramp competition, imbalances in cargo, and the nature of shipper organizations) are also important determinants of rates.[8]

---

[5] A study has been commissioned by the Department of State on the African trade.

[6] See, for example, S. G. Sturmey, "Economics and Liner Services," *Journal of Transport Economics and Policy*, Vol. 1, No. 2, May 1967; Trevor D. Heaver, "Trans-Pacific Trade, Liner Shipping, and Conference Rates," *The Logistics and Transportation Review*, Vol. 8, No. 2, 1972, and "A Theory of Shipping Conference Pricing and Policies," *Maritime Studies and Management*, Vol. 1, No. 1, July 1973; Esra Bennathan and A. A. Walters, *The Economics of Ocean Freight Rates*, 1969; Ingrid Bryan, "Ocean Liner Freight Rates," *Journal of Transport Economics and Policy*, Vol. 3, No. 2, May 1974; J. W. Devanney III, V. M. Livanos and R. J. Stewart, *Conference Ratemaking and the West Coast of South America*, Massachusetts Institute of Technology Commodity Transportation and Economic Development Laboratory, Report No. MITCTL 72-1, January 1972.

[7] For instance, Sturmey (1967) explains conference actions in terms of deterrence to competition, while Heaver (1973) suggests that conferences act to maximize revenue subject to a minimum profit constraint.

[8] For example, see Bennathan and Walters (1969), Bryan (1974), and Heaver (1972).

The Relationship Between Liner Rates and Costs

Because of the nature of liner costs, the relationship between costs and specific rates is ambiguous. Aside from loading and unloading costs, most liner costs are common to all services and cannot be simply and directly identified with any single cargo or even a single leg of a route. Rather, the costs incurred as a consequence of trade flows in the long run are subtle and complex. Most liner firms are organized into conferences which act to discourage internal and external rate competition. Therefore, conferences may exercise great discretion in allocating those costs by setting rates for individual cargos and routes, especially in the short run. Liner conferences are known to behave as discriminating monopolists, that is, to set prices to reflect the elasticity of demand for transport for each commodity.[9] Unit value is often used as a measure of this elasticity: the higher the unit value of the commodity, the less elastic the demand for its transport with respect to shipping rates is expected to be.

The market power that permits unit-value pricing, and the ambiguity of defining nondiscriminatory rates when average costs of units of service are not easily determined, have led to numerous complaints about discriminatory pricing by liner conferences. In particular, it is believed that the existing structure of liner rates discriminates against U.S. exports.

Ocean Transport Costs

The cost of ocean transportation is complex because it involves a variety of factors, pricing mechanisms, and methods of computation. The recent rapid increases in fuel costs, as well as worldwide inflation, have resulted in a major growth of costs of shipping operations, while simultaneously deflating the market for both new and used ships. Costs of operations of the subsidized liner segment of U.S. shipping, in particular, are affected by direct and indirect operating and construction differential subsidies. These and other factors, in turn, influence labor agreements and costs, use of technology, as well as level and quality of service.

Changes in ship design, construction, and operation designed to meet increasingly stringent environmental and other regulatory (or classification) requirements affect ship investment and operating costs and therefore the cost of goods haulage. Conventional liner operators are increasingly replaced by full containerized liner service which, in turn, results in the reduction of port calls in the trading areas served. Of particular importance is the effect of transport system integration on costs of shipping operations.

Models capable of simulating the costs of ship operations for a variety

---

[9] This is often referred to as "charging what the traffic will bear," or pricing according to the "inverse elasticity rule."

of service types, route characteristics, factor cost scenarios, and ship technologies are available. This permits introduction of the cost effects of transport system integration, physical form change of commodities, terminal interface, government aid, regulation, jurisdiction, safety, environmental protection, and other factors.

Fully automated ships are a technical reality now, and although completely unmanned ships are not expected to sail for some time to come, ships manned by skeleton crews only are envisioned soon. However, automation, including ship routing and loading, may affect fuel and maintenance costs more than manning costs.

Chapter 5

ISSUES IN U.S. INTERNATIONAL AND INLAND SHIPPING POLICYMAKING

U.S. shipping policy, particularly in the international sphere, has been in disarray for many years. In its current state, it is an amalgam of many bills amended over the years to satisfy particular demands or needs. Many of these amendments to the primary maritime act or law were designed to meet the demands of special industry segments or groups within or outside the U.S. maritime industry. The United States is certainly not the only maritime country that provides subsidies, cargo reservation, and other government aids to its maritime industry. But as a foremost "free trade" advocate and as an early supporter of protection for its maritime industry, this country has always borne the burden of conflict inherent in the two positions. This conflict has consequently often been reflected in maritime policymaking.

5.1. The Need for New Policy Approaches

As discussed in Chapter 3, U.S. maritime protection is historically based on the dual premise of the strategic requirement of a strong shipping and shipbuilding industry and the maintenance of cost parity of U.S. operators or shipbuilders working in the high-cost, high living-standard environment of the United States. While there may still be a strategic justification, and in fact an urgent need, for the maintenance of U.S. shipping and shipbuilding capacity, the need for government aid and protection to assure cost parity and to limit competition of low-cost foreign operators or shipyards has long evaporated. In fact, unit labor costs are higher today in many major

191

Western maritime and shipbuilding countries than they are in the United States. Similarly, the old myth of superior U.S. shipbuilding quality as an added justification for protection is being increasingly challenged. Inevitably we must face productivity as the prime issue in the U.S. maritime industry, as we must face it in many other industries where the United States has been a traditional world leader.

An overview of the major problems confronting U.S. shipping policy reveals that (1) it tries to satisfy many interested parties and, as a result, satisfies few, if any; (2) an inordinately large number of administrative and executive agencies of the federal government are involved in its formulation and implementation, or lack thereof; and (3) it has become largely a political issue, making even more difficult the task of addressing the complex issues in economic and strategic terms.

Additional complicating factors arise within the various government agencies that try, by their positions and actions, to satisfy the demands of different constituencies, often with opposing interests. For example, the U.S. Maritime Administration (MarAd) can be said to be concerned primarily with the well being of the U.S. maritime industry, while the concern of the State Department is primarily relations with foreign nations. Maritime industry matters are handled in the White House by the domestic policy staff concerned with public domestic issues, while the Federal Maritime Commission includes in its role the fair treatment of shippers. The Departments of Agriculture, Transportation, Defense, Energy, and the U.S. trade representative have other constituencies. Even within the Department of Commerce, both the Office of International Trade and the Maritime Administration usually have widely diverging interests in regard to maritime policymaking or implementation. It is therefore not surprising that little leadership or uniformity in the approach toward a single maritime policy results.

Maritime regulatory and protective policy is largely unilaterally imposed and based on domestic contingencies. The United States has not attempted to formulate a consistent policy or to assume a strong leadership position in world shipping, despite "inroads into free trade principles and threats to competition by unilateral cargo reservation and predation. Insofar as maritime policy is concerned, the United States basically stands alone, and is isolated from and in conflict with its trading partners."[1] The lack of effective U.S. maritime policy can, in part, be blamed on a similar lack of effective and coordinated U.S. foreign trade policy. In fact, international trade

---

1. R. Bank, "U.S. Shipping Policy—Where is it Heading?" *Seatrade*, November 1980.

policymaking in the U.S. government is nearly as fragmented as maritime policymaking, due to an apparent basic lack of interest by Congress to get involved in trade policy except on a case-by-case basis.

The effect of this lack of focus and direction regarding maritime policy has been devastating—not only in terms of its effect on U.S. shipping companies and shipbuilders, but also on the credibility of the U.S. as an effective trading partner, a proponent of free trade, and a reliable, effective ally. There is an increasing frustration with the lack of a U.S. position not only among our allies, but also among the different U.S. groups with interests in the maritime industry, which events of recent years in the industry illustrate. For example, several old U.S. liner companies have recently gone bankrupt, notwithstanding long-term receipt of subsidies. Similarly, several major shipyards recently have had to shut down or limit their operation to ship repairs. In addition the U.S. dry-bulk carrier fleet, which has the greatest need for expansion, is shrinking in terms of its participation in the carriage of U.S. dry-bulk trade. It must therefore be recognized that whatever maritime policy we may have had, or presume to have, does not work and that a new approach is needed.

A new approach, however, can no longer consist of amendments of outdated bills. Even when the so-called "Omnibus" bill was proposed in 1979—a bill designed to satisfy the largest possible number of interested parties, including liner operators, nonliner operators, unions, shippers, and various maritime associations—it failed to pull these parties together to secure passage and subsequent implementation. Traditional rivalries and a lack of trust appear to be prime factors in preventing cooperation. Yet as a nation in probably its most critical economic and political situation in modern time, we can no longer afford the dangerous vacuum that lack of an effective U.S. shipping policy invites.

In attempting to remedy this situation, some new approaches might consider the following factors:

- The linking of the U.S. shipbuilding and shipping industry under the maritime laws appears inappropriate; in no other segment of the U.S. transport industry are there similar restrictions or linkages betwen operators and builders. This is not to say that some form of government support or even protection is not necessary. But government involvement should be largely economic, not regulatory, and operators and builders should be dealt with as separate groupings with their own distinct interests and problems.
- Restrictions on import and export of ships, particularly for use in international trade, are today difficult to justify. For a limited

time, the government may want to impose import duties, or
various taxes to ease the transition, but it appears important to
limit regulation of ship or flag-of-registry transfer by use of
economic rather than legal barriers.

- Repatriation of U.S.-owned, foreign-registered vessels should
be facilitated by certain import relaxations.
- Export and sale of U.S.-built ships should be encouraged by
providing across-the-board, low-interest loans and some subsidies independent of buyers' nationality or projected use of vessel.
- Government aids should be available to U.S. operators of U.S.-
registered shipping in all foreign trades and services, without
distinction to type of service or method of operation.
- Government regulatory involvement in U.S. shipping should be
minimized, and government aid or supportive programs aimed
at the U.S. shipping industry should be economic in nature and
provide incentives for productivity and revenue improvements,
without government involvements in or constraints on a shipping
management operating decision.

These are just a few considerations that could influence the growth
and effectiveness of the U.S. maritime industry, as well as the U.S.
role in world shipping and trade. Implementation along these lines
might provide the first steps toward formulation of a consistent and
acceptable maritime policy and a reemergence of U.S. leadership
in world shipping.

5.2. The Changing Environment of International
Shipping Policy

Shipping policy—national, regional and international—is usually
composed of a large number of explicitly and implicitly defined rules
and measures pronounced, enacted, or adopted by public government, regional and international agencies, as well as semipublic or
even private organizations. These rules are, in turn, designed to
effect the management, composition, and operation of shipping, as
well as the carriage of goods in line with given, stated, or implicit
objectives. Traditionally shipping has been assumed to be subject
to free market forces operating largely in an international environment and therefore only partially subject to national or regional
policymaking. However, growing nationalism since World War II,
resulting in expanding national fleets and increasing division of world
markets into political or economic spheres of influence, has had a
marked effect on the market environment in which shipping operates. The use of flags of convenience and mobility of ship registration

are under increasing attack by interests claiming that shipping should play a larger role as an arm of more limited national policy.

Shipping policy is therefore now increasingly affected by measures promoting national-flag shipping and foreign (export/import) trade of the nation: in other words, it is increasingly nationalistic, and includes greater government regulatory involvement.

Regulation presents particular problems. Traditionally international shipping, largely privately owned, relied primarily on self-regulation based on bilateral or multilateral agreements among parties in voluntary association, with a minimum of government involvement. These agreements attempted to serve the needs of both shipping operators and shipper.

The need for international cooperation in shipping has long been recognized but is now further emphasized by the increase in specialization and integration of international shipping. Further, technological and operational developments in shipping cause a continuous state of flux which now demands adjustments in policy.

Shipping policy is largely affected by shipping organizations—intergovernmental, private, semiprivate, or governmental—with advisory, policymaking, regulatory, or implementation functions (or combinations thereof). Private shipping organizations are usually established to further economic objectives of their members. Intergovernmental organizations, on the other hand, function to set policy affecting shipping among them. Intergovernmental organizations are usually voluntary or, by public acceptance, subject to international law, yet seldom involve or are joined by all nations; they usually comprise only a limited number of nations and are joined for reasons of national or mutual interest.

Many international shipping organizations are subordinate to other international organizations and consequently have limited competence or jurisdiction. Overlap of activities and regulation among various private and intergovernmental international shipping organizations also occurs. The primary role of international shipping organizations is usually not rate setting, but policy setting, although many determine minimum adequacy or fairness of rates.

5.3. U.N. Role in International Shipping and Trade[2]

The role of United Nations' agencies has become increasingly important in recent years with regard to changes in the international

---

2. Compilation of material from *Handbook of the United Nations*, 1979, and various U.N. publications.

shipping environment. Many United Nations programs have important implications for the shipping industry. For example, in recent
years U.N. economic programs have been aimed largely at assisting
less developed countries (LDCs). The Department of Economic and
Social Affairs has a Resources and Transport Division which, through
its Center for Planning and Projections, provides assistance in trade
negotiations and in the standardization of the design and operation
of transport systems. The U.N. Secretariat sponsors conferences and
publications programs, coordinates work performed by different
U.N. organizations, and provides some support to agencies such as
the U.N. Development Program.

Among the regional economic commissions discussed, the Economic Commission for Europe, for example, in cooperation with the
Council of European Ministers of Transport, has been engaged in
facilitating intermodal transportation and container systems. Various
U.N. special programs and related bodies, such as the International
Law Commission, the U.N. Commission on International Trade Law,
and GATT, are also involved in shipping. The Law Commission, for
example, developed the 1958 Conventions on the Law of the Sea,
which codified the rights and responsibilities of shipping in the various zones of marine jurisdiction.

The U.N. deals with shipping policy questions through regional
commissions such as:

ECE	Economic Commission for Europe
ESCAP	Economic and Social Commission for Asia and Pacific
ECME	Economic Commission for Middle East
ECA	Economic Commission for Africa
ECLA	Economic Commission for Latin America

These commissions are usually concerned with economic cooperation
to facilitate interregional and intraregional trade by developing maintenance of efficient shipping services. In recent years and since the
adoption of the UNCTAD Code of Linear Conference (1974, with
later amendments), the economic commissions have attempted to
improve shipping legislation in member countries and strengthen
control of linear conferences, their operations, and conduct. The
commissions have also tried to intervene in the relations among
governments, conferences, shipping companies, shippers' councils,
and shippers. Their mission is usually interpreted as promoting foreign trade, and among their goals is the transfer of shipping income
to developing countries.

A Committee of Shipping was established by the U.N. Trade and
Development Board in 1965 to be concerned with shipping, seaborne
trade, and port economics of developing countries. The Committee
was ostensibly formed in recognition of the importance of shipping
in the foreign trade and in the balance of payments of developing

countries. The actual functions of the Committee, which meets usually once a year, are rather general. The activities of the Shipping Committee, unlike those of IMCO, do not directly influence the operations of shipping companies but are more policy advisory in nature.

The major convention drawn up by UNCTAD is the Code of Conduct for Liner Conferences, which includes cargo sharing by a formula such as the 40–40–20 recommendation. It also includes such suggestions as:

- Notice of 150 days in case of general freight increases, excluding the imposition of surcharges; and
- Prescribed conciliation procedures in case of disagreements between shippers and shipowners.

If the Code is universally applied, the impact will be rather severe. It may bring about changes in the international distribution of income from shipping, at a substantial increase in the cost of shipping, with net economic effects that are therefore questionable.

5.3.1. United Nations Conference on Trade and Development (UNCTAD)

UNCTAD was established as a continuing organization of the United Nations General Assembly in December 1964, and its primary function was envisioned to be the acceleration of the economic development of less developed countries through revised international trade policies. UNCTAD is involved in economic and technical issues of shipping, port facilities, container systems, and future developments in shipping technology.

Issues relating to terms of trade and economic development are usually highly political, and since UNCTAD has no enforcement powers, the Conference must rely on the support of each of the three major blocks of the world's nations (developed, less developed, and socialist nations). The "Common Measure of Understanding" adopted by the 1964 Conference is the basis of UNCTAD's work in shipping. This includes recognition of the necessity for the liner conference system in order to secure stable rates and regular services, and encouragement of closer cooperation between conferences and shipper groups.

5.3.2. The UNCTAD Code of Conduct for Liner Conferences and Its Effects on Shipping

The proposed and implicit goal of the Code of Conduct for Liner Conferences drawn up by UNCTAD and accepted by the majority of its members is to promote greater participation of developing countries in the operations, ownership, and control of shipping, with particular reference to liner shipping. While it is primarily aimed at increasing shipping operations between developed and developing nations, the primary method proposed—cargo sharing—obviously affects shipping among all trading nations. The implicit objective actually is to strengthen the position of developing nations vis-à-vis developed nations by assuring greater participation of developing nations' shipping in their bilateral trade.

The Code also sets some basis for acceptance and legitimization of conference systems under restricted code of conduct rules whereby conference membership and procedures are defined. Similarly, it establishes the entitlements of shipping to trading shares and legitimizes as well as empowers shippers' councils in their relations with conferences.

The result is that imposition of the Code affects freedom of shipping, particularly liner shipping and conferences, by requiring consultation with shippers' councils and surveillance by appropriate national authorities. Other requirements are that freight rates must be determined by "negotiation and conciliation" between conferences and shippers' councils rather than by rate setting of conferences or individual shipping operators subject to competitive market conditions. It is contended by some that the imposition of the Code will result in less efficient, more expensive shipping services which, in turn, may cause a reduction rather than a furthering of trade between nations subject to such bilateral cargo sharing agreements.

The effect on liner trade is expected to be less severe than on bulk trades, should a similar code be imposed on such trades, or the existing code be extended to cover bulk trades as well. Because trade between nations is usually imbalanced and fluctuating, efficient shipping services usually require multilateral arrangements to assure effective utilization of applied capacity and resulting low cost and efficiency of service. Similarly, it is usually impractical to assign specific cargo to shipping companies according to some agreed-upon rules.

Restrictions on entry and operations of shipping companies serving a route introduce severe constraints on the marketplace, restrict service, and as a result, limit shippers' choice of carrier and service. In fact, the introduction of strict cargo sharing may cause the offering of a minimum of services. Nonconference and third-flag operations and competition would obviously be seriously curtailed or eliminated from providing alternative services on a trade route, which would further decrease shippers' choices. Finally, there is the problem of the effects of additional regulatory intervention by intergovernment agencies, conferences, shippers' councils, and others on shipping. Such added administration and regulation or rule making introduces an inertia into the system which could severely affect the ability of shipping to respond to the needed changes introduced by variation in the market of trading demands. The issues of the growing trend towards cargo sharing, the UNCTAD Liner Code, and the potential for the imposition of similar restrictions in other components of the shipping industry are discussed in more detail in Chapter 6.

5.3.3. U.N. Regulatory and Aid Agencies

Several specialized U.N. financial, modal, or other agencies have programs related to shipping. These include the World Bank and its affiliated agencies, the International Civil Aviation Organization (ICAO), the World Meteorological Organization (WMO), the Food and Agricultural Organization (FAO), the International Telecommunications Union (ITU), Intergovernmental Maritime Consultative Organization (IMCO), the Shipping Committee of the U.N. Conference on Trade and Development (UNCTAD), and the International Labor Organization (ILO). A diagram presenting U.N. agencies involved with shipping is shown in Figure 5–1.

5.3.3.1. Intergovernmental Maritime Consultative Organization (IMCO)

IMCO is the U.N. agency with the widest role in maritime affairs. Its membership of 72 nations includes all major countries registering ships under their flag. Formed in March 1958, its functions involve technical, legal, and facilitation problems. The agency has sponsored conferences leading to the adoption or amendment of four major international conventions; has issued a number of recommended practices to advance the safety and efficiency of sea transport; and has conducted technical studies on a variety of practical ship construction and operating problems.

Initially, the charter for IMCO included the promotion of fair competition in shipping and a provision to encourage cooperation in technical and operational matters. The IMCO charter includes in its aims the "removal of discriminatory action and unnecessary restrictions by governments," yet the agency has seldom attempted to affect economic issues in shipping. IMCO has recently assumed an active role in control of marine pollution and is the chief focus of international efforts toward this objective. It is also taking an increasingly active role in legal issues relating to shipping, particularly those arising from environmental impact.

5.3.3.2. UNCTAD Shipping Committee

In recent years, the role of liner conferences and the impact of their monopolies have come under increasing scrutiny. The Shipping Committee of UNCTAD encourages consultation between confer-

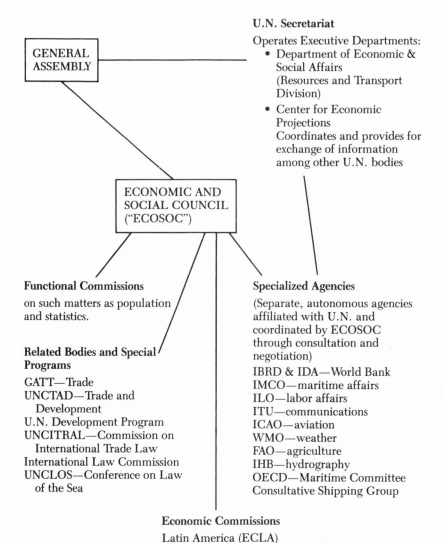

U.N. Secretariat

Operates Executive Departments:
- Department of Economic & Social Affairs (Resources and Transport Division)
- Center for Economic Projections Coordinates and provides for exchange of information among other U.N. bodies

GENERAL ASSEMBLY

ECONOMIC AND SOCIAL COUNCIL ("ECOSOC")

Functional Commissions

on such matters as population and statistics.

Related Bodies and Special Programs

GATT—Trade
UNCTAD—Trade and Development
U.N. Development Program
UNCITRAL—Commission on International Trade Law
International Law Commission
UNCLOS—Conference on Law of the Sea

Specialized Agencies

(Separate, autonomous agencies affiliated with U.N. and coordinated by ECOSOC through consultation and negotiation)

IBRD & IDA—World Bank
IMCO—maritime affairs
ILO—labor affairs
ITU—communications
ICAO—aviation
WMO—weather
FAO—agriculture
IHB—hydrography
OECD—Maritime Committee
Consultative Shipping Group

Economic Commissions

Latin America (ECLA)
Africa (ECA)
Europe (ECE)
Asia and Far East (ECAFE)

Figure 5–1   United Nations Agencies Dealing with Shipping

ences and shippers' councils, and supports economic analysis and discussion of the unique sea transport problems of less developed states. Its economic analysis also includes studies aimed at identifying factors of shipping route and freight rate determination. One of five standing committees of the Conference, the Committee on Shipping is open to all states participating in UNCTAD. There are about 50 members, including all major shipping nations.

The Shipping Committee in 1969 formed the Working Group on Shipping Legislation, which considers economic and commercial aspects of international legislation that affect or may affect shipping. The Committee reviews charter parties, marine insurance, bills of lading, and other issues such as binational agreements.

5.3.3.3. International Labor Office (ILO)

The ILO is among the oldest intergovernmental agencies under the U.N. and is a holdover agency from the League of Nations. The ILO Joint Maritime Commission has developed many conventions and recommendations for a comprehensive Maritime Labor Code, which has been ratified by most maritime nations. This code includes international standardization of working conditions aboard ocean-going ships, provisions of manning, hours of work, pensions, vacation and sick pay. Minimum wage requirements are tied to the social and economic development of the seaman's country.

Like all ILO bodies, the Joint Maritime Commission includes both ship owners and labor representation, together with public members appointed by the ILO. The International Shipping Federation (owners) and the International Federation of Transport Workers (labor) support the work of the ILO. Labor shortages in many European countries, which increasingly cause the employment of mixed crews, add to the pressures for internationally similar treatment of seafaring personnel.

5.4. Functions of Other International Shipping Organizations

There are numerous international, intergovernmental agencies with interest or functions in legal or political issues. The Permanent Council of Arbitration at The Hague and the International Hydrographic Bureau are just two of these. The U.N.-affiliated International Court of Justice and the Permanent Court of Arbitration both restrict their activities to disputes between states requiring interpretation of international law. Regional or economic multinational organizations, such as OECD's Maritime Committee and the thirteen-nation Consultative Shipping Group, are regional groups representing a particular economic interest. The OECD Maritime Committee and the Consultative Shipping Group represent European and Japanese economic positions.

There are also many nongovernmental groups or associations dealing with aspects of shipping, such as the Baltic and International Maritime Conference, the International Tanker Owners' Association (INTERTANKO), and the International Shipping Federation. Others include the International Chamber of Shipping, and the International Chamber of Commerce. In addition there are organizations concerned with operations or more specific technical or managerial aspects. Among these are

5.4.1. International Cargo Handling Coordination Association (ICHCA)

The major function of ICHCA is to consider improvement in cargo handling methods within the transportation industry.

5.4.2. International Association of Ports and Harbors (IAPH)

The function of IAPH is to improve the efficiency of ports and harbors through information exchange and technical assistance.

5.4.3. International Standards Organization (ISO)

The ISO is the association of national standards bodies of 53 countries. Growing use of containers, pallet, or other unitization in shipping has caused the problem of containment standardization to become one of the key issues before the ISO.

5.4.4. Council of European Shipper's Councils

Many international agencies consult, advise, represent, or regulate the shipping industry. Their functions overlap widely and their jurisdiction, if any, is usually quite limited. Among these, for example, is the International Federation of Forwarding Agents Associations (FIATA), a trade association.

5.5. Inland Water Transportation Policy Issues

With over 25,543 miles of navigable inland waterways, over 34 percent of which have depths in excess of 12 feet, the United States, next to the USSR, has the largest network of inland waterways in the world. Much of this network is established and/or maintained at public expenditure, though much of this expenditure serves other water resource development in addition to inland navigation. During the 12-year period 1957–1969, for example, total federal construction expenditures for inland and intracoastal water transportation were $1.6 billion, or about $133 million per year, while expenditures for operation and maintenance in 1969 totalled $79 million. In addition, local (state, municipal, private, and so forth) expenditures generally exceed federal expenditures.

The amount of appropriations for inland and intracoastal waterways (including construction, operation, and maintenance) grew substantially to $411 million in 1973. It should be noted, though, that this is minute compared to public expenditures for other modes such as highways ($23.6 billion in 1973).

Dry and liquid bulk are the principal commodities in inland water transport (IWT). Because of their relative low value they require low-cost transportation, which has for many years been their major attraction to inland waterways. By far the most controversial policy issue concerning IWT is the imposition of user charges. Some argue the question of equity regarding these charges—such as intermodal equity, equity among different transport users, and equity toward taxpayers throughout the nation, many of whom do not benefit from IWT directly. On the other hand, IWT is not unique in benefiting from federally financed waterway facilities; in fact, basically all transport modes benefit from such provisions.

5.5.1. Recommended Policy Changes

Changes of policy in inland water transportation have been under discussion for many years. The Doyle Report, prepared for Congress in 1961, provided several ideas for such changes. The following recommendations in the report related to inland waterways remain pertinent.

5.5.1.1. Bulk Carrier Recommendations

- Redefine bulk commodities so that transportation of such commodities would not be regulated in terms of 1939 technology. The suggested definition of a bulk commodity was one shipped without wrappers, containers, mark, or count and such that delivery of any minimum quantity was adequate because the commodity was fungible.
- End the distinction between towing and freighting authorities, and permit uniform definition.

- Give the operator on a main stream priority on new rights to operate on tributaries; give operators on tributaries priority for new rights on main stream. Because there is some evidence that this result has been reached in some cases without establishment of formal priorities, a problem may not exist in practice.
- Establish a new licensing category of for-hire bulk cargo carriers serving the general public with grandfather rights. Under the report's suggestion, these bulk carriers would be restricted to exempt cargoes in tow or in the vessel, while common carriers would be allowed to carry regulated and exempt cargoes (as they now are under amendments to § 303 (b)).
  —Authorize operations by a bulk carrier over an entire waterway system without point-to-point restrictions.
  —Authorize operations by a bulk carrier on proof of applicant's fitness and ability only, but permit a protestant to prove that authorization would result in excessive competition, in a violation of the national transportation policy, or would be contrary to the public interest.
  —Require filing by the bulk carrier of minimum rates with control based on cost formulas and designed to assure a reasonable return to efficient operators.
- Give such licensed bulk carriers priority in issuance of common carrier certificates for the waterway served.
- Repeal present bulk exemption sections, §§ 303 (b), (c), and (d), along with establishment of new licensing category.

Other areas of concern to inland water transport manifest policy stances, either explicitly or implicitly, and these are noted here briefly.

It appears to be the policy that railroads shall own no other system of transportation. While this has not made it impossible for railroads to operate trucks or water carriers, the railroads have a harder time justifying intermodal ownership.

While it is doubtful that any simple statement can express the ICC and congressional views of competition, there is some evidence that competition is desired to stimulate innovation and improve service but that competition merely designed to destroy competitors is not desired. It sometimes appears that innovation is approved if it does not upset the competitive balance, although this may be an unfair reading of sentiments concerning destructive competition.

5.5.1.2. User Charges for Inland Water Transport

A long-standing debate in the shipping industry concerns whether user charges should be imposed on the nation's waterways. The National Waterway Conference takes the position that waterways operators are entitled to the benefits of free navigation as part of governmental policy dating back to the founding of the country. The Doyle Report, on the other hand, refutes any claim that the government lacks the authority to collect tolls, although repeal of part of the Rivers and Harbors Act of 1882 would be required. With increased federal aid to railroads, it may be that this controversy will either subside or become more insoluble. While user charges have frequently been recommended, it may be that proposals have foundered on the practical problems of attempting to ensure that the person charged has received some service commensurate with the charge and of separating costs of navigation-related services from other services, such as flood control.

Resolution of the user charge issue would be likely to have broad impact. The example of barge transport will serve as illustration here. Barges provide low cost service and this has been said to be part of their inherent advantage. Benefits provided by the public (highways, waterways) do not enter into a determination of cost advantage (such determinations may be obsolete with amendment of § 15a(3)). Because user charge would enter calculation of a barge-service cost, barge service over expensive user-charge waterways might cease being competitive.

5.5.1.3. Regulatory Issues in Inland Water Transport

After the Railroad Revitalization and Regulatory Reform Act (RRRRA) of 1976, there is some question concerning the degree of competitive intermodal rate-making (for example, rail competing with barge) allowable. Through the office of public counsel established by the RRRRA in 1976, Department of Transportation attorneys might be authorized to intervene in ICC proceedings to assert the interests of the national transportation policy.

Questions of costs also remain. Should an attempt be made (especially in the case of barges) to include public costs if inland water rates are to be compared with the rates of any other mode? Should total cost of barge transportation be analyzed, rather than cost to shipper, in planning national transportation policy?

The purpose served by certification is not entirely clear from a review of cases. While certification brings the carrier under rate regulation, it precludes possibly excessive demands on other carriers for through routes and interconnections.

The question also arises as to whether regulation of water carriers is really necessary. Spychalski (as summarized by Blood[3]) argues that

---

3. Blood, Dwight M., *Inland Waterway Policy in the U.S.*, (Washington, D.C.: American Waterway Operators, Inc., 1972).

regulation is not really needed. However, Blood also notes that his premises, though widely accepted, have not been the subject of empirical research. Regulation may promote regular and adequate service without interruptions due to business failures. The Doyle Report took as a given that some regulated transportation was necessary to assure adequate service, and that unregulated transportation should not be allowed to weaken the regulated sector.

The ICC seems to favor increasing size of the barge company through growth or intramodal merger. Similarly, in intermodal mergers, an increased financial base may be a factor of approving the merger, or it may be an indication that the new company would have such an advantage that competition will be destroyed.

The ICC has indicated approval of the idea of carrying truck trailers on barges or other vessels ("fishyback"), but it is not known whether the ICC has been confronted with any specific proposals.

From this outline of pertinent IWT policy issues, the lack of a cohesive national water policy is apparent, as is a concomitant lack of national transport objectives within which IWT policy issues can be evaluated. At this time policy still evolves as a result of specific purposes and projects such as the recent RRRRA (1976).

Inland water transport policy has developed incrementally over the years, usually in response to particular needs. As the industry assumes a larger and increasingly important role in national transportation, IWT policy decisions may have to be more integrated with national transportation policy.

Appendix 5A

INTERNATIONAL SHIPPING ASSOCIATIONS AND ORGANIZATIONS

Association of West European Shipbuilders (AWES), Kingsbury House, 15–17 King Street, St. James's. London SW1Y 6QU, UK. Tel: (01) 839 1314, Telex: c/o 261126, Director: R.D. Brown.

Baltic and International Maritime Conference (BIMCO), 19 Kristianlagade, 2100 Copenhagen, Denmark. Tel: 26 30 00 TA: "Bimcoship, Copenhagen," Telex: 19086, President: G. Warnderink Vinke, Amsterdam, General Manager: W. Møller Sørensen.

Bureau International Des Containers (BIC), 38 Cours Albert 1er, 75008 Paris, France. Tel: 225.82.24, Telex: 650 770, President: J. Martial.

CENSA (Council of European and Japanese National Shipowners' Associations), 30–32 St. Mary Axe, London, EC3A 8ET, UK. Tel: 01-623 3281, Telex: 8951282, Int Sec G, Chairman: B.P. Shaw, Secretary General: I. Ross-Bell.

Central Commission for Navigation of the Rhine, Palais du Rhin, Strasbourg, France. Tel: (88) 32.47.94 and 32.35.84, Chairman: C. Bauwens, Secretary General: R. Doerflinger.

Federation of National Associations of Ship Brokers and Agents, c/o Institute of Chartered Shipbrokers, Baltic Exchange Chambers, 24 St. Mary Axe, London, EC3A 8DE, UK. TA: "Fonasba, London, EC3," Tel: 01-283 1361, Telex: 8812708 Answer back: Broker G.

Inter-Governmental Maritime Consultative Organization (IMCO), 101–104 Piccadilly London, W1V OAE, UK. Tel: 01-499 9040, Telex: 23588, Secretary-General: C.P. Srivastava.

Intergovernmental Oceanographic Commission, Unesco, Place de Fontenoy, 75700 Paris, France. Tel: 577.16.10 Enquiries: ext 60.71, TA:

Note: This appendix is from *Directory of Ship Owners, Shipbuilders, and Marine Engineers* (London: IPC Industrial Press Ltd., 1981).

207

"Unesco, Paris," Telex: 204461 Paris, Chairman: Dr. A. Ayala-Castañares (Mexico), Secretary: M. Ruivo (ext 60-74).

International Association of Classification Societies (IACS), Polski Rejestr Statkow, Waly Plastowskie 24, 80–855 Gdansk, Poland. Tel: 31 72 23, Chairman of Council: H. Cygan.

International Association of Dredging Companies (IADC), Postal address: PO Box 80521, 2508 GM, The Hague, The Netherlands. Tel: 070-54 56 02, Telex: 31102, TA: "Dredging, The Hague," Executive Secretary: Dr. J.G.Th. Linssen, Public Relations Officer: Nic Oosterbaan.

International Association of Independent Tanker Owners (INTERTANKO), PO Box 1452 Vika, Radhusgaten 25, Oslo 1, Norway, Tel: 41 60 80, Telex: 19751 Itank N, Chairman: Sir Yue-Kong Pao, CBE, LLD, JP, General Manager: Tormod Rafgard.

International Association of Lighthouse Authorities—IALA (Association International de Signalisation Maritime—AISM), 43 Avenue du President Wilson, 75116 Paris, France. Tel: 553 83 04 President: J.N. Ballinger, Canadian Coast Guard, Ministry of Transport, Tower A, Ottawa, K1A 0N7, Ontario, Canada. Secretary General: J. Prunieras (Directeur du Service des Phares et Balises, 12 route de Stains, 94380 Bonneuil-Sur-Marne, France).

International Association of Ports and Harbours, Kotohira-Kaikan Building, 2–8 Toranomon 1-Chome, Minato ku, Tokyo 105, Japan. TA: "Iaphe-central, Tokyo," Tel: 03-591 4261, Telex: 2222516. President: Paul Bastard, Ministry of Transport, France, 1st Vice-President: A.S. Mayne, Port of Melbourne Authority, 2nd Vice-President: Anthony Tozzoli, Port Authority of New York and New Jersey, 3rd Vice-President: B.M. Tukur, Nigerian Ports Authority, Honorary Vice-President: Fumio Kohmura, Nagoya Port Authority, Secretary-General: Dr. H. Sato. Business Biennial Conferences and publication of monthly "Ports and Harbours." Membership: about 395, comprising port authorities and affiliated organizations in 73 nations.

International Cargo Handling Co-ordination Association (ICHCA), Abford House, 15 Wilton Road, London, SW1V 1LX, UK. Tel; 01-828 3611, TA: "Icha London SW1," Telex: 261106. President: Jan-Erik Jansson (Finland), Chairman Council and Executive Board: B. Couvert (France), Chairman, Technical Advisory Committee: Bjorn Ljungström (Sweden), Chairman, Policy Committee: R.P. Holubowicz (USA), Secretary General: John G. Warburton.

International Chamber of Commerce, International Headquarters, 38 Cours Albert 1er, 75008 Paris, France. Tel: 261-85-97. TA: "Incomerc, Paris," Telex: 650770. President (1980), Sir Reay Geddes (United Kingdom), Secretary-General: Carl-Henrik Winqwist, Liaison Offices with the United Nations: Bangkok, Geneva, New York, British National Committee, Chairman: Peter Macadam, Director: A.A. Golds. Headquarters: Centre Point, 103 New Oxford Street, London, WCIA 1QB, UK, Tel: 240 5558/60.

International Chamber of Shipping, 30–32 St. Mary Axe, London, EC3A 8ET, UK. Tel: 01-283 2922, TA: "Logboard, London EC3," Telex: 884008, Chairman: H.T. Beazley, Vice-Chairmen: W.H. Brouwer, N. Werring Jr., Secretary General: J.C.S Horrocks.

International Christian Maritime Association, 150 Route de Ferney, 1211 Geneva 20, Switzerland. Correspondence to the General Secretary, c/o St. Michael Paternoster Royal, College Hill, London, EC4R 2RL, UK. Tel: 01-248 5202.

International Council of Marine Industry Associations, Boating Industry House, Vale Road, Oatlands, Weybridge, Surrey, KT13 9NS, UK. Tel: Weybridge 54511, Telex: 885471 Boatin, President: A.A. Hauser (USA), Secretary General: A.L.L. Skinner.

International Federation of Shipmasters' Associations (IFSMA), HQS Wellington, Temple Stairs, Victoria Embankment, London, WC2R 2PN, UK. Tel: 01-240 1695. TA: "Shipmaster London WC2," President: Capt. R. Grønsand, Federation Secretary: Miss M. Reeve Allen.

International Hydrographic Organization, Ave. Pres. J.F. Kennedy, Monte Carlo, Principality of Monaco. Tel: (93) 50 65 87, TA: "Burhydint Monaco," Telex: MCS Carlo 46 98 70, Attn. Inhorg. Directing Committee: President, Rear-Admiral G.S. Ritchie, CB, DSC (Retd) (Great Britain), Directors: Rear-Admiral D.C. Kapoor, AVSM (Retd) (India), Capt. J.E. Ayres (Retd) (USA). The Organization has 47 Member States. Promotes standardization of navigational charts and documents and publishes monthly information on latest charts available from all Member States.

International Labour Organisation, CH-1211, Geneva 22, Switzerland. Tel: 99.61.11, Telex: 22271 Bit CH, Director-General: Francis Blanchard (France).

International Marine Transit Association, PO Box 29307, New Orleans, LA 70189, USA. President: John J. Kelly. Exchanges information and technical data regarding all aspects of waterborne passenger transit operations.

International Maritime Committee (Comite/Maritime International), 17 Borzestraat, B2000 Antwerp, Belguim. TA: "Commarint Antwerp," Tel: (031) 32.24.71, Telex: 31-653, President: Francesco Berlingieri, Hon. Vice-President: Kaj Pineus (Gothenburg), Vice-Presidents: William Birch Reynardson (London), Arthur M. Boal (New York), Andrei K. Joudro (Moscow), Walter Muiier (Basel), Tsunéo Ohtori (Tokyo), Nagendra Singh (New Delhi), Jean Warot (Paris), Secretary-General Executive: Jan Ramberg (Stockholm), Secretary-General Administrative and Treasurer: Henri Voet (Antwerp), Chief Administrative Officer and Headquarters CMI: Henry Voet-Génicot, 17 Borzestraat, B2000 Antwerp (Belgium).

International Maritime Industries Forum, c/o Kleinwort, Benson Ltd, 20 Fenchurch Street, London, EC3P 3DB, UK. Tel: 01-623 8000, Secretary-General: J.G. Davis.

International Maritime Pilots' Association, 20 Peel Street, London W8, UK. Tel: 01-727 1844, President: Capt J.A. Edmondson (UK), Secretary-General: Edgar Eden.

International Passenger Ship Association (IPSA), Suite 631, 17 Battery Place, New York, NY 10004, USA. Tel: (212) 425-7400. Executive Officer: Wm. J. Armstrong, Assistant Executive Officer: R.J. Kwortnik.

International Radio-Medical-Centre, Via Dell'Architettura 41, 00144 Rome, Italy. Tel: 593.331. President: Professor Sante Ciancarelli, Director: Dr. Nino Rizzo.

International Ship Brokers' and Agents' P & I Club Ltd, Registered Head and Claim Office, 15 St. Helen's Place, London, EC3A 6JD, UK. Tel: 01-638 1001, TA: "Isbaclub, London EC3," Telex: 884644 Intlex G. Managers: Isbaclub UK Management Ltd., Chairman and Managing Director: Robert G.D. Butler, Secretary: Paul G.D. Smith.

International Ship Electric Service Association, Halton House, 5th Floor, 20–23 Holborn, London EC1N 2 JD, UK. Tel: 01-405 6506, Telex: 885456 ISES. Secrtary-General: D. Cope.

International Ship Masters Association of the Great Lakes, 1510 Torrison Drive, Manitowoc, Wisconsin 54220, USA. Grand President: H.E. Macdermid, Grand Secretary: Kurth R. Grainger. Tel: 414-682 1592.

International Ship Suppliers Association (The Hague), President: James C. Taylor, c/o R.J. Taylor Co., 3200, Annetta Avenue, Baltimore, Maryland 21213, USA. Secretary General: Peter J.A. Burnyeat, PO Box 23, Harlow, Essex, CM20 1BA, UK. Secretariat: Dr. Norbert Traub, Raboisen 101, 2000 Hamburg 1, W. Germany. Tel: Hamburg 32 40 82 and 33 82 95, Telex: Via 0211 366.

International Shipowners' Association (INSA), Sieroszewskiego Street 7, Gdynia, Poland. Tel: 21-09-74, Telex: 054250. President: Ryszard Karger, Secretary-General: Capt. G.N Fedtchenko.

International Shipping Federation Ltd., 30–32 St. Mary Axe, London EC3A 8ET, UK. Tel: 01-283 2922. TA: "Logboard, London EC3," Telex: 884008, President: Sir Frederic Bolton, MC, Vice Presidents: F. de Azqueta, F. Lorentzen, C.M. Master, Director: J.K. Rice-Oxley, Secretary: M.R. Brownrigg.

International Tanker Nominal Freight Scale Association Ltd., (Worldscale Assoc (London) Ltd.), Price Rupert House, 64 Queen Street, London EC4R 1AD, UK. Tel: 01-248 4747, Telex: 885118 WSCALE, G.

International Tanker Owners Pollution Federation Ltd., Staple Hill, Stonehouse Court, 87–90 Houndsditch, London EC3A 7AX, UK. Tel: 01-621 1255, Telex: 887514, Managing Director: J.N. Archer.

International Tin Research Institute, Fraser Road, Perivale, Greenford,

Middlesex, UB6 7AQ, UK. Tel: 01-997 4254, TA: "Tinsearch, Greenford," Director: D.A. Robins.

International Towing Tank Conference, (1978, 15th International Towing Tank Conference, P250), c/o J.D. van Manen, Netherlands Ship Model Basin, Haagsteeg 2, PO Box 28, 6700 AA Wageningen, The Netherlands. Tel: 08370-19140, Telex: 45148.

International Transport Workers' Federation, 133–135, Great Suffolk Street, London, SE1 1PD, UK. Tel: 01-403 2733, TA: "Intransfe London, SE1," General Secretary: Harold Lewis.

International Union for Inland Navigation, 19 Rue de la Presse, Brussels. President: H. Becker, c/o Lehnkering AG, Postfach 101103, D4100 Duisburg 1, W. Germany.

International Union of Marine Insurance. Stadthausquai 5, 8001 Zurich, Switzerland. Tel: 01-221.12.15, President: Walter Rostock, Munich, General Secretary: Dr. Peter Alther, Zurich.

Lake Carriers' Association, 1411 Rockefeller Building, Cleveland, Ohio 44113, USA. Tel: 216-621-1107, President: Paul E. Trimble, Vice-President: David L. Buchanan, Secretary: John A. Packard.

Latin American Shipowners' Association (Asociacion Americana de Armadores (ALAMAR), Casilla de Correos 767, Montevideo, Uruguay. TA: "Alamar, Montevideo," Telex: 398-866, Tel: 987449 and 983620, Executive Vice-President and Secretary General: Enrique Olsen P., Administration Secretary: Julio C. Amarelle.

Nordic Ships' Officers' Congress, c/o Norwegian Mates Associations, Arbiensgt, 11, Oslo 2, Norway. Tel: 56 62 32, President: Ragnar Groensand, Secretary: Trygve Stoltenberg.

Nordisk Skibsrederforening (Freight, Demurrage and Defence Club), Kristinelundv 22, Oslo 2, Norway. Tel: 565275, TA: "Nordisk," Telex: 16825 north n, President: Halfdan Ditlev-Simonsen Jr., Managing Director: Ole Lund.

Northern Shipowners' Defence Club, Kristinelundv 22, Oslo 2, Norway. Tel: 565275, Telex: 16825 (north n), Chairman: Halfdan Ditlev-Simonsen Jr., Managing Director: Ole Lund.

Oil Companies International Marine Forum, Bank of Bermuda Building, Front Street, Hamilton 5, Bermuda. Tel: Bermuda (809 29) 51422, Telex: Bermuda 3213 CODAN BA. *London Office:* 6th Floor, Portland House, Stag Place, London SW1E 5BH, UK. Tel: 01-828 7696, 01-828 6283, Telex: 24942, TA: "Ocimfor London SW1." Director: C.A. Walder.

Organisation for Economic Co-operation and Development (OECD) Maritime Transport Committee, 2 Rue André Pascal, 75775 Paris, Cedex 16. Tel: 524-82-00, TA: "Developeconomie Paris," Telex: 62160 Paris. Chairman: B. Voss (Sweden), Vice-Chairmen: J.T. Stewart (USA), S. Plytzanopoulos (Greece), R. Stettler (Switzerland), Secretary: R.A.

Humphrey. Council Working Party No. 6 on Shipbuilding. Chairman: Ambassador A. Grübel (Switzerland), Secretary: J. Delelienne.

Pacific Cruise Conference, 311 California Street, San Francisco, California 94104, USA. Tel: (415) 981-5370. General Manager: R.C. Lord.

Permanent International Association of Navigation Congresses, Résidence Palace, Quartier Jordaens, 155 rue de la Loi, B-1040, Brussels, Belgium. Tel: 733.96.70 Ext. 2176 HS. President: Prof. Gustave Willems, Hon. Secretary General of the Ministry of Public Works, Secretary General: H. Vandervelden, Director General of the Office of Navigation.

Transocean Marine Paint Association, Central Office: Mathenesserlaan 300, PO Box 25107, 3001 HC Rotterdam, Netherlands. Tel: 763044, TA: "Transpaint," Telex: 24389, Secretary General: W.G. Van Aalst, UK Member : Croda Paints Ltd, Bankside, Hull. Represented in Australia, Brunei, Cameroon, Canada, Denmark, Egypt, France, Germany, Greece, Indonesia, Iran, Republic of Ireland, Italy, Ivory Coast, Japan, Kenya, Malaysia, Malta, Morocco, Netherlands, New Zealand, Nigeria, Norway, Philippines, Portugal, Senegal, Singapore, South Africa, South Korea, Spain, Sweden, Tunisia, Turkey, United Kingdom, USA, Yugoslavia, Hongkong and Switzerland.

Union International De La Navigation Fluviale (International Union for Inland Navigation), 19 Rue de la Presse, Brussels 1. President: Herr Direktor H. Becker, Sprecher des Vorstandes der Lehnkering AG, Postfach 101103, D 4100 Duisburg 1, W. Germany, Secretary: H. Mullenbach, 1 Place de Lattre, F67000 Strasbourg. Members: National Inland Waterways Organisations of: Belgium, G. Britain, France, W. Germany, Italy, Netherlands, Switzerland, Luxembourg. Functions: to promote the interests of Inland Waterways Carriers before all International Bodies. Publications: Annual and Occasional Reports.

World Association of Travel Agencies, 37 Quai Wilson, 1211 Geneva, Switzerland. Tel: 31.47.60, Telex: 22447, President: Jules Cortell, General Secretary: Herve Choisy.

Chapter 6

POTENTIAL IMPACTS OF CARGO SHARING ON U.S. SHIPPING

Cargo sharing has become an important aspect in liner shipping. Although it is usually associated with the Code of Conduct for Liner Conferences adopted by the United Nations Conference on Trade and Development (UNCTAD) in 1974, and expected to come shortly into force, cargo sharing in a variety of forms has been practiced by many countries, including the United States, for many years. Most existing cargo-sharing agreements are bilateral agreements, involving cargo or revenue sharing; many other types of agreements, such as pooling, space charter, and more, are aimed at increased efficiency or profitability of liner shipping.

Bulk shipping has, until recently, been largely exempt from cargo-sharing arrangements, with the exception of government-to-government shipping agreements such as U.S. grain exports and similar trades that often involve government-owned, financed, or controlled cargoes. However, there is an increasing pressure now to introduce cargo sharing into the bulk shipping trades as well, and rationalization of services under cargo-sharing agreements is expected to be more difficult than in the liner trades.

6.1. Agreements Filed with the Federal Maritime Commission

Section 15 of the Shipping Act[1] requires that all anticompetitive agreements between common carriers by water must be filed with and approved by the Federal Maritime Commission (FMC). A brief summary of the general nature and the most common types of these agreements follows. (Appendix 6A contains suggested language for several of these agreements from the Code of Federal Regulations.[2])

6.1.1. Conference Agreements—An Overview

A conference agreement is the basic document defining the contractual relationship among the members of a conference. It is essentially a compromise among competing member lines. It usually serves the purpose of restricting or eliminating competition between the member lines and of meeting the existing and potential competition from the lines outside the conference.

Most conference agreements are confidential documents. However, the agreements of conferences operating in the ocean trade of the United States must be filed with the FMC. They are considered public documents and so are available for study. The following is a summary of the contents of the U.S. agreements.*

The scope of the conference agreement differs widely among conferences and depends largely upon the competition between member lines and existing and potential competition between conference members and nonconference operators. At a minimum, conference agreements provide for members to charge uniform rates and follow the same rules and regulations for calculating and collecting freight charges on all cargo shipped in vessels owned, controlled, chartered, or managed by the members of the conference in the area of operation covered by the conference agreement. Further, in some conferences the member lines, in a separate agreement, agree to pool their freight earnings, either totally, those deriving from some specific area, or from one or more specified commodities within the overall conference operation, and to share them among members of the pool according to agreed percentages. Conference expenses are borne by members either equally or based on agreed proportions.

A conference agreement may cover all or some of the following matters:

- The sphere of the conference, i.e. the range of ports and activities that come within the purview of the agreement;
- Types of membership, e.g., full (or regular) members and associate members, their rights and obligations, terms and conditions of membership, viz. admission fee, security deposit, faithful performance bond;

---

* Much of this discussion of the form and structure of the conference agreements is taken from or based on the UNCTAD document, *The Liner Conference System* (1970).

- Rules regarding admission, withdrawal, suspension, and expulsion of a member;
- Rules regarding conference meetings and voting procedures;
- Conference secretariat, the officers, and their duties;
- Obligations of member lines in rate matters and in the operation of conference services;
- Practices of member lines prohibited under the conference agreement;
- Self-policing provisions, including investigation of and penalties against malpractices of the member lines;
- Appointment of committees;
- Arbitration of disputes between members; and
- Participation in other agreements.

Any action on the part of a member line that violates the terms of the conference agreement or the requirements imposed on conferences and carriers by the regulatory authorities and which may result in that member gaining an undue advantage over other members, or may give an undue advantage to particular shippers as compared with other shippers, is considered a malpractice. The following are some of the prohibited malpractices:

- Calculating or collecting freight charges in any way except as provided in the conference tariff;
- Paying freight brokerage except as provided in the conference agreement;
- Absorbing at loading or discharging port charges which are properly payable by shippers and/or consignees;
- Granting a free storage;
- Postdating or predating of bills of lading or falsification of shipping documents in any other manner;
- Granting of any other indirect benefits such as free passage to shippers;
- Payment of unsubstantiated claims; and
- Entertainment of clients beyond reasonable limits.

A member line is also responsible for the malpractice of its parent company, agent, subagent, affiliate, subsidiary, or freight broker.

Each member is required to deposit with the conference the amount prescribed as security deposit or faithful performance bond. This is a guarantee of faithful performance and prompt payment of any liquidated damages that may accrue against it, or of any reward or judgment that may be rendered against it.

Under conference agreement self-policing provisions, a member must report to the conference chairman or to the neutral policing authority any suspected violation of the agreement by another member. Continuing investigation of member line activities by an outside neutral body is also required. Full cooperation with the neutral body, including accessibility to confidential records, is mandatory for all members. Subject to required rules of fundamental fairness, a member found to have committed a malpractice may be required to pay a fine or liquidated damages.

Generally each member of the conference has one vote. For voting purposes, members of a joint service in the conference are regarded as one. If a conference covers more than one distinct trading area, voting on area matters may be limited to members actually serving an area. However, all members are entitled to vote on matters of general interest.

The obligations of member lines toward each other are as follows:

- No member line can represent directly or indirectly any carrier in the conference trade other than a carrier who is a party to the conference agreement, and agency arrangements of the member lines must be consistent with this;
- No part of the commission or remuneration due to any agents of member lines can be paid or allowed by such agents, directly or indirectly, to merchants, shippers, consignees of cargo, or any other party;
- Members are obliged to quote, charge, or collect rates, classify cargoes, refund, or remit freight charges strictly in accordance with the conference tariff; and
- A member line can resign from the conference, without penalty, only upon giving due notice.

The headquarters of the conference is usually located in the country or region in which a majority of member lines of the conference are established. Often both the inward and outward conferences between two destinations have their headquarters at the same place. Even though the trades are formally separate, there is a substantial common membership between the two conferences. Both conferences take round-voyage operation into consideration in decisions regarding conference rates and services.

Conferences usually have a titular head, such as a chairman, who presides over conference meetings and acts as a coordinating authority. His duties, power, and influence vary from one conference to another. The main executive officer of the conference is the conference secretary. In practice, however, his powers are usually very limited. Policy issues are decided by the member lines of the conferences and the function of the secretary is to carry out the day-to-day business of the conference on the basis of the guidelines provided by these decisions. He provides the necessary liaison between member lines of the conference and between the conference and the shippers by coordinating and circulating information regarding conference rates and services, and receiving on behalf of conference members complaints and representations from shippers.

All policy decisions of the conference are made at meetings of all members where either a vote is taken or a consensus is informally arrived at and acknowledged. If the exigencies of the situation so require, and a sufficient number of members agree, a decision may be reached without holding a meeting and in such cases all members are contacted by telephone or cable.

Some conferences have only one type of meeting, that is, a meeting of the conference as a whole attended by representatives of the full members. Other conferences have two or more types of meetings of the members. One is a regular conference meeting to consider more or less routine matters, and another, which is usually called a principals' meeting, is, by convention, attended by top executives of member lines mainly to decide policy issues. Matters of overall policy are decided only at principals' meetings.

While conference policy decisions are made in the meetings of the full membership, some conferences have appointed committees to deal with specific matters. Normally the function of these committees is to make recommendations and the decisions are arrived at by the conference membership as a whole. Most of these committees function at the headquarters of the conference, while others, called "local committees," function at other centers. If the sphere of conference operation is wide, separate local committees are appointed to consider matters relating to specific areas. If the conference agreement includes an arrangement to restrict the number of sailings or to pool the cargo and/or freight revenue of different members, then committees are established to look after the working of such arrangements.

Whether or not a conference appoints local committees depends upon the area covered by the conference and the local problems involved. The membership of local committees normally consists of all member lines serving the particular sections of the trade, although membership may be limited and shared among member lines in rotation.

All agreements of conferences operating in the ocean trades of the United States must be filed with the FMC. They are classified as conference agreements or rate agreements. A conference agreement is primarily a price-fixing agreement that usually constitutes the dominant competitive force in the trade, has a formal administrative and business structure, and generally allows its members little or no unilateral or competitive action. A rate agreement usually does not constitute the dominant competitive force in the trade, has less formal administrative and business procedures, and allows its members a greater degree of unilateral competitive action.

6.1.1.1. Pooling Agreements

The Code of Federal Regulations defines a pooling agreement as "[a]n agreement which provides for the division of the cargo carryings or earnings and/or losses among the parties in accordance with a fixed formula."[4] Agreements may take several forms. Some merely control the number of sailings of each pool member, while others actually control the cargo carried or the revenue earned by each member. All pooling agreements result in a limitation of competition among pool participants.

A cargo pool usually controls the carriage of a certain commodity or group of commodities. Under the agreement, each member has the right to carry a specified percentage share of the freight tons of the item(s) concerned carried by all members of the pool. In a revenue pool, each member is entitled to receive a specific percentage of the total freight revenue earned by all the pool members.[5] Generally the revenue paid into the pool is either a fixed percentage of total revenue or the total revenue minus certain expenses.

Pooling agreements filed with the Federal Maritime Commission pursuant to Section 15 of the Shipping Act are all revenue-pooling rather than cargo-pooling agreements.[6] The revenue shares of the pool members are sometimes matched by a corresponding obligation to carry close to the same percentage of cargo as their share of the revenue pool. (This is true of the Chilean and Peruvian agreements, but not of the agreements with Argentina, Brazil, and Japan.)

The Federal Maritime Commission has approved 17 pooling agreements now in effect. These agreements provide for the division of cargo revenue among the parties in accordance with a fixed formula. Seven of them provide for equal access to government-controlled cargo.

All of the agreements cover cargo moved between the United States and another country. In 15 of the agreements, the members include the national flag lines of both of the trading countries operating carriers on the route covered by the agreement. Usually if another national flag line of the two trading countries begins to carry cargo on the route after the agreement is in effect, it may become a member upon application.[7] Six of the agreements either include third-nation flag lines in the original membership or allow that they may become members if they enter the trade covered by the agreement.

Most pooling agreements are between United States lines and the lines of a trading partner. The two Japanese agreements differ from the rest in that they are between Japanese lines that carry cargo between Japan and the United States rather than between Japanese lines and United States lines.

All the agreements follow the same basic pattern. Although style and degree of detail vary a great deal from agreement to agreement, all contain many of the same provisions. For example, each agreement contains a section telling what cargo is covered by the agreement. Agreements generally provide that all the cargo carried by members between certain ports is covered and then proceeds to list the exceptions. Cargoes requiring special stowage or cargo-handling equipment, or cargoes for which there is basically no competition between members, are usually excepted from the pool agreement.[8] Items such as bulk cargoes, liquid cargoes in bulk, government-controlled cargoes, and cargoes such as live animals, luggage, and motor cars belonging to passengers traveling on another ship of the same line are often excepted from the pool.[9]

Each agreement also has a section telling how the total freight revenue will be calculated and what share of it will be given to each party. In return for a share of the revenue pool, each party must agree to a minimum number of sailings, imposed by the agreement. A few agreements also require a minimum number of port calls; others require that the parties provide a certain amount of cargo space per sailing. If a specific amount is not required, then the parties must agree to provide cargo space sufficient to carry all the cargo covered by the agreement. If a party fails to meet a sailing, port call, or cargo requirement, its share of the pool revenue is reduced. Some agreements provide a formula for calculating the loss. Others simply say that the revenue share is reduced in proportion to the deficiency in sailings, port calls, or cargo space.

Agreements abound in administrative detail. Members appoint a Pool Committee, composed of representatives from each member line, to administer the pool. The committees' responsibilities include assessing the movement of cargo and watching the actual performance of each member of the pool. The Pool Committee appoints the Pool Accountant, an independent accounting firm, to take care of the books. The Pool Accountant collects pool data from all members, consolidates them, and computes the balance at the end of the pool period for the purpose of settling accounts.

Any disputes arising between pool members in the interpretation and fulfillment of the agreement are submitted to arbitration, usually at the pool headquarters. Finally, each agreement contains a section providing for the various ways in which the agreement may be cancelled or terminated.

6.1.1.2. Joint Service Agreements

The Code of Federal Regulations defines a joint service agreement as "[a]n agreement which establishes a new and separate line or service to be operated by the parties as a joint venture. The new and separate service fixes its own rates, publishes its own tariffs, issues its own bills of lading, and acts generally as a single carrier."[10]

Parties to a joint service agreement agree to establish and maintain a joint cargo or a joint cargo and passenger service. They cooperate to supply tonnage for the joint service as their owned and chartered vessels are available. Generally the parties do not pool the profits or losses. Instead, the profit or loss accrues to the benefit of the owner or charterer of the vessel.

Usually each party delegates to a separate corporation all management and organizational responsibility of the joint service, such as the booking and solicitation of cargo and passengers, the collection of freight and passenger revenues, and so forth. Dues and expenses of a Conference or pooling agreement membership are prorated among the parties of the joint service according to the number of sailings they have in the respective trade from year to year.

A joint service may become a party to, and may resign or withdraw from, any Section 15 agreements, including agreements to establish a Conference, a pool, a joint service, or any other lawful arrangement. It acts as a single party to these agreements. The joint service agreement sets forth the signature to be used by the joint service in signing these agreements.

Rates charged by the joint service are those set by the Conference of which it is a member. If the joint service operates in a trade without a Conference, or it is not a member of the Conference, the parties may set just and reasonable rates. The rate agreements must be submitted to the FMC for approval.

Although the parties participate in a joint service, their bills of lading, dock receipts, and passenger tickets must show the name of the party for whose account the vessel is operated. All these papers must also be submitted to the FMC for approval.

A joint service may be terminated by mutual consent of the parties or by one of the parties giving the required notice to the other party and to the FMC.

6.1.1.3. Space Charter Agreements

A space charter agreement is an agreement by which common carriers by water agree to charter a certain amount of space on each other's vessels. The agreement sometimes includes a provision that the parties will coordinate their port calls and frequency of sailings.

Under the terms of the agreements, the parties will coordinate certain operational phases of their respective services to fully utilize their containerships operating in the trades covered by the agreements. They agree to charter space on each other's vessels in order to transport their containers on their own and on each other's vessels.

Although the parties charter space from one another for the most part, they do not act jointly. Rather, the parties maintain separate identities. For example, the parties solicit and book containerized cargoes for their own separate accounts; there is no joint solicitation or booking among them. In the same vein, the parties issue their own separate bills of lading. In addition, there is usually no pooling of revenues or sharing of operational expenses between the parties.

6.1.1.4. Sailing Agreements

The Code of Federal Regulations defines a sailing agreement as "an agreement which established a schedule of ports which each carrier will serve and the frequency of each carrier's calls at those ports."[11] Parties to a sailing agreement agree to coordinate their sailing dates in order to avoid conflicting sailing dates and to space the sailings from each port. Each party continues to use its own discretion in the operation of its vessels and operates at its own risk. The parties do not pool or share profits or losses. Rather, the revenues earned by each vessel accrue to its operator.

The parties to a sailing agreement are members of the freight conferences covering their trade. However, if a party ceases to be a member of the Conference, or if they begin to operate on a trade not covered by a Conference, the parties must submit any rate agreements to the FMC for approval.

The parties may advertise their respective services separately. Some agreements permit them to advertise together. Whether advertising separately or together, they must show the full corporate or trade names of the parties in such a way as to reflect clearly their separate identities.

An agreement becomes effective when it is approved by the FMC and, where required, the appropriate government authority in the country of the foreign line. The agreement can be terminated by mutual consent or by written notice by one party to the other and to the FMC.

6.2. UNCTAD Code of Conduct for Liner Conferences

The Code was initiated by the United Nations Conference on Trade and Development (UNCTAD) and adopted in April 1974. At that time, 72 nations voted in its favor. The Code was largely proposed to deal with the increasing discontent of the group of 77 developing nations with the operation and effect of the ocean liner conference system. It had long been contended that conferences exercised undue monopoly power in their trades. This was expressed through limitations on conference membership and the authority of conference over rates and practices. Developing countries felt that they were adversely affected by conferences and that they were constrained in their ability to:

- Develop their own merchant marine, and obtain employment, control, and other operational benefits;
- Increase their international trade by use of shipping in market development; and
- Assist their economy by the earnings or savings of foreign exchange, as well as by setting rates that would make national trade more competitive.

The primary purpose of the Code was to deal with these concerns by entering into a multilateral treaty governing the conduct of ocean shipping conferences which would "take into account the needs and problems of the developing countries with respect to the activities of liner conferences serving their foreign trade." The Code is now expected to become international law sometime in 1981 when, according to Article 49, 24 countries with a combined tonnage of at least 25 percent of world tonnage will have ratified the Convention.[12]

As of mid-1980, 45 countries with 12.1 million GRT of shipping, or 16.6 percent of world tonnage, as of the Convention date (1974), had ratified the Code, while another 17 nations with 35 million tons (48.1 percent) showed an interest in ratifying the Convention. The breakdown of nations[13] is shown in Table 6-1, which indicates 41 nations as yet undecided on ratification. It is interesting to note the inconsistent pattern of ratification or intention to ratify. While the Soviet Union, for example, ratified the Code (excepting all government cargoes), the Ukrainian SSR, an integral part of the USSR, did not. Likewise, the People's Republic of China, Taiwan, the United States, South Africa, and many Arab countries did not ratify the Code. Most importantly, countries of flags of convenience will obviously not ratify it, because it restricts the participation of carriers under open registry in liner trade.

The Code, as the title implies, regulates liner shipping conferences, although some developing countries have recently advocated the extension of the coverage to include bulk carriers or the framing of a similar Code for bulk shipping and other tramp services in international trade. One of the Code's fundamental issues includes the right of each nation to participate in its own trade. It uses as a basis the existence of viable conference arrangements for its ef-

Table 6–1 Ratification Status, by Country, of UNCTAD Code of Conduct for Liner Conferences

By 1 June 1980, 46 countries had made definitive signatures* (s), approved (app), accepted (acc), ratified (r), or acceded to (a) the Convention. The countries, arranged in chronological order of signature, are:

Ghana	24 June 1975	r
Chile	25 June 1975	s
Pakistan	27 June 1975	s
Gambia	30 June 1975	s
Sri Lanka	30 June 1975	s
Venezuela	30 June 1975	s
Bangladesh	24 July 1975	a
Nigeria	10 September 1975	a
Benin	27 October 1975	a
United Republic of Tanzania	3 November 1975	a
Niger	13 January 1976	r
Philippines	2 March 1976	r
Guatemala	3 March 1976	r
Mexico	6 May 1976	a
United Republic of Cameroon	15 June 1976	a
Cuba	23 July 1976	a
Indonesia	11 January 1977	r
Ivory Coast	17 February 1977	r
Central African Republic	13 May 1977	a
Senegal	20 May 1977	r
Zaire	25 July 1977	a
Madagascar	23 December 1977	a
Togo	12 January 1978	r
Cape Verde	13 January 1978	a
India	14 February 1978	r
Kenya	27 February 1978	a
Mali	15 March 1978	a
Sudan	16 March 1978	a
Gabon	5 June 1978	r
Ethiopia	1 September 1978	r
Iraq	25 October 1978	a
Costa Rica	27 October 1978	r
Peru	21 November 1978	a
Egypt	25 January 1979	a
Tunisia	15 March 1979	a
Republic of Korea	11 May 1979	a
Czechoslovakia	4 June 1979	app
Honduras	12 June 1979	a
Union of Soviet Socialist Republics	28 June 1979	acc
German Democratic Republic	9 July 1979	r

* A "definitive signature" without reservation as to ratification is understood as having the same binding international legal effect as ratification.

Table 6–1   (continued)

Sierra Leone	9 July 1979	a
Uruguay	9 July 1979	a
Bulgaria	12 July 1979	a
Guyana	7 January 1980	a
Morocco	11 February 1980	a
Jordan	17 March 1980	a

On or prior to June 30, 1975, the Convention had been signed by a number of countries which by June 1, 1980 had not yet deposited with the Secretary-General of the United Nations an instrument of ratification, acceptance, or approval. The countries, arranged in chronological order of signature, are:

Iran	7 August 1974
Ecuador	22 October 1974
Yugoslavia	17 December 1974
Malta	15 May 1975
Brazil	23 June 1975
Algeria	27 June 1975
France	30 June 1975
Belgium	30 June 1975
Germany, Federal Republic of	30 June 1975
Turkey	30 June 1975

fective implementation and control; it does, however, allow for participation of nonconference shipping within the environment agreed upon by the liner conferences in the trade. The Code consists of 145 articles which cover economic, regulatory, consultative, and operational issues.

Under the terms of Article 49 of the Convention, the Code is to enter into force six months after 24 countries with a combined gross tonnage of at least 25 percent of world liner tonnage ratify the Convention. Tonnages (72.9 million) are based on gross tons of liners in existence in 1973, exclusive of ships in the U.S. National Defense Reserve Fleet. The nations that had ratified the Convention or indicated their intention to ratify it by mid-1980 accounted for approximately 65 percent of total world gross liner tonnage.

6.2.1.   EEC Ratification of the UNCTAD Code

As of 1979, the European Economic Commission (EEC) was close to a compromise ratification of the Code. They made several reservations, one of which exempts OECD trade with reciprocating nations from the cargo-sharing provisions of the Code. It appears that the EEC countries will move toward ratification of the Code independent of U.S. action, unless the United States moves quickly to at least take a formal position toward the Code. The EEC countries formulated a joint agreement called the Brussels Agreement on May 15, 1979, which defines their joint stand with regard to the Code and includes the following major terms.

Article I. Each member state that ratifies does so in accordance with the reservation exempting OECD trade from the Code's cargo-sharing provision.

Article II. Each group of shipping lines of the same nationality within a conference will decide by commercial negotiation whether another line of the same nationality may be admitted to membership; or, if a new conference is created, what lines of that nationality may carry a share of the trade.

Article III. Where a liner conference participates in a cargo-sharing agreement, the share of cargo to which any group of national lines is entitled under the 40–40–20 provision of the Code will be redistributed among all the conference members. The redistribution will be determined by:

- The volume of cargo carried by the conference and generated by the member states whose trade is served by it;
- Past performance of the shipping lines in the trade covered by the pool;
- The volume of cargo carried by the conference and shipper through ports of member states; and,
- The needs of the shippers whose cargoes are carried by the conference.

Article IV. Additional reservations state that:

- In conference trade between a member state and a state that is party to the Code and not an OECD country, another member state of the OECD may participate in the redistribution outlined in Article III.
- The 40–40–20 cargo-sharing provision of the Code does not apply to trade between member states. This does not affect the opportunity of these states to participate as third-country lines under Code.
- The Code's decision-making and certain of its rate-setting provisions will not apply in trade between member states.
- In trade between member states and between these states and other OECD countries, ship owners will not insist on using dispute settlement procedures under the Code.

Article V. The national lines of a member state that are conference members will consult all other community lines before making a decision related to a conference matter concerning the trade of a member state.

With the likely ratification by Japan, the United Kingdom, Germany, France, Denmark, Belgium, Luxemburg, Italy, and the Netherlands, the Code will come into effect as an international instrument with the force of law among the ratifying states.

6.3   Provisions of the UNCTAD Code and Their Effects on U.S. Trade

This section considers the main provisions covered by the Code of Conduct for Liner Conferences and how U.S. trade might be affected by each provision therein. The effects will be different under conditions where the Code comes into force with or without U.S. agreement and/or ratification, as well as that of major U.S. trading partners.

The following are the main subjects to be covered by the Code of Conduct for Liner Conferences:

Relations between Member Lines:
   Membership
   Share of Trade
   Pooling
   Decision-making Procedures
   Sanctions
   Self-Policing
   Conference Agreements

Relations with Shippers:
   Loyalty Arrangements
   Dispensation
   Availability of Tariffs and Related Regulations
   Annual Reports
   Consultation Machinery

Freight rates:
   Criteria for Freight Rate Determination
   Conference Tariffs
   General Freight Rate Increase
   Promotional Freight Rates
   Surcharges
   Currency Changes

Other Matters:
   Fighting Ships
   Adequacy of Service

Provisions and Machinery for Settlement of Disputes:
Each subject and Article will be considered in turn, followed by a discussion of its putative effects on U.S. trade.

6.3.1. Relations between Member Lines

Articles 1 through 6 of the Code of Conduct relate to member relations in areas such as membership rules, trade shares, decision making, and policing.

6.3.1.1. Article 1—Membership

The Code provides that any national shipping line will have the right to be a full member of a conference that serves the foreign trade of its country, subject to certain criteria. These criteria are that the shipping line furnish evidence of its ability and intention to operate a regular, adequate, and efficient service on a long-term basis; that it undertakes to abide by the conference agreement; and that it deposits a financial guarantee. Basically the conference is open to any shipping line of the country being served by the conference.

It is more difficult for a third-party line to become a member of the conference. It must meet the same criteria as a shipping line of the country being served. In addition, the conference may take into account the volume of trade and the adequacy of service on the route covered, and other factors indicating the need for a third-party line. The conference need not admit the third-party line to membership in the conference.

The membership policy provided by the Code is essentially open membership for the national shipping lines of the countries whose trade is being served and closed membership for third-party lines.

This membership policy is contrary to that currently required by U.S. law wherein any conference operating in the U.S. foreign trade must have an open membership policy. That is, the conference must "provide reasonable and equal terms and conditions for admission and readmission to conference membership of the qualified carriers in the trade."[14]

6.3.1.2. Article 2—Share of Trade

Article 2 provides that any member of the conference will have sailing and loading rights in the trade covered by the conference. The group of national shipping lines of each of the two trading countries will have *equal* rights to share in the trade. However, third-country shipping lines, *if any*, will only have a right to share a significant part, such as 20 percent of the trade.

This method of dividing trade, known as the 40–40–20 rule, would have a vast, and perhaps detrimental, effect on U.S. shipping. For a discussion of the impact of the 40–40–20 rule on U.S. trade, see Section 6.10 of this chapter.

6.3.1.3. Pooling

Article 2(2) provides that when a conference operates a pool, all the members of the conference that serve the trade covered by the pool will have a right to join the pool. The pool shares will then be divided according to the 40–40–20 rule. If there is no pooling, berthing, sailing, or other trade participation agreement in a conference, either group of national shipping lines of the country whose trade is being served may require that a pool be introduced.

6.3.1.4. Article 3—Decision-Making Procedures

The Code provides that each full member of a conference must have an equal voice in decision-making procedures. However, a decision regarding trade between two countries is subject to the veto power of the shipping lines of those two countries. But because so many of the decisions made by a conference relate to the trade between two countries, each member of the conference would actually have an equal vote in very few decisions.

This veto power is a departure from the present system of conference decision making where each shipping line has one vote. It would seem to give too much shipping regulatory power to a shipping line, sometimes merely a private company. The veto power may conflict with the U.S. prohibition against a conference agreement that is "unjustly discriminatory or unfair as between carriers, shippers, exporters, importers, or ports."[15]

6.3.1.5. Article 4—Sanctions

Article 4 provides that conference members will be entitled to secure their release from the terms of the conference agreement after three months' notice, without penalty, unless the conference agreement provides otherwise. The member is required to fulfill its responsibilities to the conference until the date of withdrawal. Upon withdrawal, the member must pay any outstanding financial obligations to the conference.

The conference may expel a member for failure to abide by the conference agreement. The expulsion will not be effective, however, until after a notice and a hearing.

The Shipping Act of 1916 requires that U.S. conference agreements provide that any member may withdraw from membership upon reasonable notice without penalty for withdrawal. This Code provision would not disturb present U.S. practice; three months may be considered reasonable notice.

6.3.1.6. Article 5—Self-Policing

Article 5 provides that conferences must adopt an illustrative list of practices regarded as breaches of the conference agreement and should provide effective self-policing machinery to deal with malpractices, with specific provisions requiring:

- The fixing of penalties for the designated offenses, to be commensurate with their seriousness;
- The establishment of machinery for the examination and impartial adjudication of complaints against malpractices by a person or body unconnected with any of the conference member lines or affiliates;
- The reporting on the disposition of complaints against malpractices to governments, upon request, whose shipping and trade are involved and to shipping lines that are members of the conference.

At the present time, the FMC will not approve a conference agreement unless it provides for adequate policing of the obligations under it. As a result, most conferences in the U.S. trades provide machinery for dealing with malpractices. The FMC reviews and approves the self-policing procedures of conferences operating in the United States trade.

Under this Code, the self-policing is left up to the conferences, with no government involvement. A conference is free to adopt a limited list of malpractices but lacks machinery for dealing with them. Under present Code provisions, there is no government review to ensure adequate policing.

6.3.1.7. Article 6—Conference Agreements

Article 6 provides that all conference agreements—pooling, berthing, and sailing rights agreements—will be available on request to all appropriate government authorities of the countries whose trade is being served.

At the present time all agreements of this type in the U.S. foreign trade must be filed with and approved by the FMC, and the FMC does not approve an agreement that would be detrimental to the standards set forth in Section 15 of the Shipping Act (46 U.S.C. 814). If the United States becomes a member of the Code, it may no longer have the sole right to approve or disapprove conference and other agreements.

6.3.2. Relations with Shippers

Relations between liner conferences and shippers are covered by Articles 7 through 11 of the Code, which define the permissible types of loyalty arrangements and the negotiating and consultation procedures to be followed.

6.3.2.1. Article 7—Loyalty Arrangements

The Code governs the use of loyalty arrangements by conference members. The form and terms of these arrangements will be decided by consultations between the conference and shippers' organizations. The rate they decide upon will be within a fixed range of percentages of the freight rate applicable to other shippers. If a change in the differential causes an increase in the rates, the change may be implemented only after 150 days' notice to the shippers or according to regional practice or by agreement.

The loyalty arrangements must contain provisions to safeguard the rights of the shippers and of the shipping lines. For example, the shipper is bound in respect to any cargo whose shipment is controlled by him; he may not divert the cargo by subterfuge. The loyalty contract must explicitly state what damages will be incurred in the event of a breach. If a shipper does breach, he is entitled to reassume full loyalty status subject to the fulfillment of certain conditions.

The loyalty arrangement must provide a list of cargo excluded from the arrangement, methods of dispute settlement and termination, and terms for granting dispensation.

Generally, carriers in the United States trade are prohibited from charging rates that are unjustly discriminatory between shippers.[16] They may, however, subject to the approval of the FMC, use dual-rate contracts.[17] This system provides lower rates to a shipper or consignee who agrees to give all or any fixed portion of his patronage to a given carrier or conference.

The dual-rate system is different from that provided by the Code because the contract is subject to FMC approval, and the FMC will not approve a contract that is detrimental to the commerce of the United States or that is unfair or discriminatory. No such review exists for the arrangements under the Code that result from consultations between shipping lines and shippers. As a result, if the United States ratifies the Code, the FMC may lose its present power to approve dual-rate contracts.

Many of the Code requirements for loyalty arrangements, however, are the same as or similar to present United States require-ments for dual-rate contracts. For example, when the tariff rate for goods under the contract increases, it may not be implemented until after a reasonable notice to the shippers, and the notice period must be at least 90 days, a shorter period than the 150 days required by the Code.

Under United States law, as under the Code, a shipper may not divert cargo, of which he has the right to control shipment, by subterfuge to another carrier. It also requires damages to be specified in the contract. Unlike the Code, U.S. law provides that the contract will cover only cargo, for which the shipper has the right to choose a carrier at the time of shipment. The contract may not require the shipper to divert the shipment of goods from natural routings.

U.S. law also provides specifically that the shipper may terminate without penalty upon 90 days' notice and provides for the exclusion of certain cargo.

Under the Code, the FMC would probably lose its power to approve dual-rate contracts. However, the Code provides that car-riers and shippers may agree on any lawful loyalty agreement. This suggests that the respective governments will retain authority to legislate regarding loyalty arrangements.

6.3.2.2. Article 8—Dispensation

The Code requires that conferences examine requests from shippers for a dispensation from loyalty arrangements. If the request is denied, the reasons must be given in writing.

In two instances the shipper is automatically released from the loyalty arrangement. The first is where a conference fails to confirm, within a time specified by the arrangement, sufficient space to ac-commodate the shipper's cargo. The second is where conference services are arranged on inducement, but either the shipping line does not call, despite due notice by shippers, or the shipping line does not reply within an agreed time to the notice given by shippers.

United States law does not provide for an examination of shippers' requests for dispensation. Instead, it provides that a shipper may terminate without penalty upon 90 days' notice. While this allows shippers the freedom to withdraw from the dual-rate contract for any reason, it may be a more lengthy process than that required by the Code.

Under United States law, a carrier must give the shipper 90 days notice of a rate increase and a shipper must give a carrier 90 days notice to terminate. In this way a shipper could give notice to ter-minate as soon as he learned of a rate increase and so not be required to pay the higher rate. There is no assurance under the Code that a shipper would be allowed to terminate during the 150-days-notice period before a rate increase.

United States law provides for release of the shipper from the contract when the carrier cannot provide as much space as required by the shipper upon reasonable notice. This provision coincides with the automatic dispensation in the Code if failure to provide space is synonymous with failure to confirm space.

6.3.2.3. Article 9—Availability of Tariffs and Related Regulations

The Code provides that tariffs, related regulations, and any amendments thereto should be made available upon request to all shippers and their councils at reasonable cost. The related regulations should spell out all conditions relating to the application of freight rates and to the carriage of cargoes.

This provision does not differ greatly from the present U.S. law wherein carriers and conferences must file their tariffs with the FMC and keep them open to public inspection.

6.3.2.4. Article 10—Annual Reports

The Code would require that conferences submit annual reports to shippers' organizations that would also be available to the appropriate authorities of countries whose trade is covered by the conference concerned.

This Code requirement would bring changes in current United States practice. Shippers' organizations are currently outlawed in the United States as being contrary to the antitrust laws. If the Code is ratified by the United States, it will be necessary for Congress to grant antitrust immunity for shippers' organizations. The requirement of reports to a government authority, however, parallels to some extent the current requirement that conferences file minutes with the FMC.

6.3.2.5. Article 11—Consultation Machinery

The Code provides for consultation betweeen a conference, a shippers' organization, representatives of shippers, and shippers. Any of the parties may request a consultation. They may discuss *inter alia:*

- Changes in general tariff conditions and related regulations;
- Changes in the general level of tariff rates and rates for major commodities;

- Promotional and/or special freight rates;
- Imposition of, and related changes in, surcharges;
- Loyalty arrangements, their establishment or changes in their form and general conditions;
- Changes in the tariff classification of ports;
- Procedure for the supply of necessary information by shippers concerning the expected volume and nature of their cargoes; and,
- Presentation of cargo for shipment and the requirements regarding notice of cargo availability.

If they fall within the activity of the conference, the consultation may also discuss:

- Operation of cargo inspection services;
- Changes in the pattern of services;
- Effects of the introduction of new technology, unitization in particular, in the carriage of cargo, with consequent reduction of conventional service or loss of direct service; and,
- Adequacy and quality of shipping services, including the impact of pooling, berthing, or sailing arrangements on the availability of shipping services and freight rates at which shipping services are provided; as well as changes in the areas served and in the regularity of calls by conference vessels.

Consultations must be held before a final decision can be made on any of these matters. Each of the parties participating is responsible for providing any relevant information and to make an effort to clarify any matters under discussion. Appropriate government authorities may participate in these consultations upon request but do not necessarily play a decision-making role.

As in the section on Annual Reports, shippers' organizations would need to be allowed in the United States before this section of the Code could be implemented. Currently, decisions on most of these subjects are made by the conferences subject to the approval or review of the FMC. The shipper has very little, if any, input in these decisions at the conference level, but has a full range of remedies before the FMC. Under the Code's system, the role of the shipper would be greatly increased while that of the FMC would be greatly decreased.

6.3.3. Freight Rates

Articles 12 through 17 concern conference tariffs, rate making procedures, and other aspects of freight charges made to shippers.

6.3.3.1. Article 12—Criteria for Freight Rate Determination

The Code provides that in deciding questions of tariff policy, the following criteria must be taken into account:

- Freight rates shall be fixed at as low a level as is feasible from the commercial point of view and shall permit a reasonable profit for ship owners;
- The cost of operations of conference shall, as a rule, be evaluated for the round-trip voyage of ships, with the outbound and inbound directions considered as a single case. Where applicable, the outbound and inbound voyages should be considered separately. The freight rates should take into account, among other factors, the nature of cargoes, the interrelation between weight and cargo measurement, as well as the value of cargoes;
- In fixing promotional freight rates and/or special freight rates for specific goods, the conditions of trade for these goods in the countries served by the conference, particularly in developing and land-locked countries, shall be taken into account.

In the United States, carriers must file proposed tariffs with the FMC for approval. The FMC may disapprove a rate if, after notice and hearing, it is found to be so unreasonably high or low as to be detrimental to the commerce of the United States.

Currently, conferences are free to use whatever criteria they choose in setting freight rates. The rates are subject only to FMC's subsequent challenge that they are detrimental to U.S. commerce.

If the United States ratifies the Code, the economic well being of the United States will no longer be a criterion for rate-setting decisions.

6.3.3.2. Article 13—Conference Tariffs

The Code provides that conference tariffs should be drawn up simply and clearly and contain as few classes or categories as possible. U.S. law does not now address this problem. The Code also provides that the tariffs may not unfairly differentiate between shippers similarly situated and that shipping lines must adhere to published tariffs.

These requirements coincide with the U.S. prohibitions against unjust discrimination between shippers and against charging any rate other than that filed with and approved by the FMC (46 U.S.C. §§ 816, 817).

6.3.3.3. *Article 14—General Freight Rate Increases*

The Code provides that a conference should give shippers notice of not less than 150 days of its intention to effect a general increase in freight rates. The shippers may then request a consultation to discuss the increase which should be held within 30 days of the notice.

The conference may submit to the shippers, upon request or on its own initiative, a report from independent accountants which should include the relevant costs and revenues the conference feels necessitate an increase.

If the consultation reaches an agreement, the increase takes effect on the date set in the notice, unless a later date is agreed upon. But if no agreement is reached within 30 days of giving the notice, the matter must be submitted to international mandatory conciliation. If the parties accept the conciliator's decision, it will be binding on them and effective from the date mentioned in the conciliator's recommendation.

If a conference refuses to abide by the conciliator's recommendation, the shippers are not bound by their loyalty arrangements. Shippers must give 30 days' notice that they are no longer bound, and the conference may not retaliate by refusing to pay any deferred rebates that are owed to the shipper.

Unless otherwise agreed, a conference may not give another notice of intention to increase rates for at least 10 months after an increase has become effective; rate increases must be at least fifteen months apart.

At the present time, the FMC reviews shipping rates filed by common carriers.

If a carrier wants to raise its rates or institute a new rate, it must file the new tariff with the FMC and publish notice of the change at least 30 days before the new rate becomes effective. The FMC may, upon a showing of good cause, allow a rate to become effective in less than 30 days. If a rate increase is filed by a carrier in the context of an approved dual rate contract system, the carrier must give 90 days notice. If a non-state-controlled carrier chooses to decrease its rates, the new rate is effective immediately upon publication and filing. Controlled carriers must give 30 days notice before effectuating a rate decrease.

Under the Code, the power of the FMC to regulate liner shipping through the approval or disapproval of section 15 agreements will change, or even disappear.

6.3.3.4. Article 15—Promotional Freight Rates

The Code provides that conferences institute promotional freight
rates for nontraditional exports. The procedure for this is as follows:
the shippers submit a request for the promotional rates, together
with relevant information to the conference; and the conference must
make a decision on it within 30 days. In making its decision, the
conference should balance the need to promote the product and the
impact such a promotion may have on a competitor's product. Once
the conference establishes a promotional rate, it will be in effect for
12 months, unless otherwise agreed by the parties. Each member
of the conference should accept its fair share of the cargo for which
a promotional rate has been established.

In the United States, if a conference chooses to decrease any of
its rates, the new rate becomes effective upon the publication and
filing with the FMC. It is not required that a lowered rate remain
in effect for any mandatory period of time.

6.3.3.5. Article 16—Surcharges

Conferences may impose a temporary surcharge to cover a sudden
or extraordinary increase in costs or loss of revenue. Before a surcharge is imposed, notice must be given and a consultation held
between the conference and the parties affected by the surcharge.
In an emergency, a surcharge may be imposed without a consultation, but one must be held as soon as possible thereafter. If the
conference incurs any loss through a delay in consultation, it may
recoup the loss by prolonging the surcharge. Conversely, if a conference imposes a surcharge which a later consultation agrees is
unfounded, the conference must refund the money to the shippers.

Under the present United States system, a conference may file
a surcharge with the FMC, to become effective on 30 or 90 days
notice. In an emergency situation, the FMC has discretion to allow
the increased rates to become effective in less than the statutory
notice requirement. At the present time conferences are not required
to consult with shippers regarding these increases. However, conferences must establish procedures for promptly hearing and considering shippers' requests and complaints (46 U.S.C. 814).

If the United States ratifies the Code, the new procedure for
raising rates would certainly be cumbersome for U.S. shipping lines.
The role of the shipper in rate increases would grow, while the
FMC's role would diminish or disappear completely.

6.3.3.6. Article 17—Currency Changes and Resulting Charges

The formal devaluation or revaluation of a conference's tariff currency provides a *de facto* reason for the introduction of a surcharge or a freight rate adjustment reflecting the actual change in ship owner's costs or the reduction in value of their freight earnings directly resulting from such a devaluation or revaluation.

The adjustment should be such that, in the aggregate, the shipping line neither gains nor loses as a result of the surcharge. A surcharge or adjustment necessitated by a currency change calls for the same consultation procedure as for other types of surcharges.

6.3.4. Other Matters

The use of "fighting ships" by conferences and the adequacy of service to be provided on conference trade routes are covered by Articles 18 and 19, respectively.

6.3.4.1. Article 18—Fighting Ships

The use of "fighting ships" by a conference is prohibited; American conferences are currently prohibited from using fighting ships by 46 U.S.C. 812. However, some foreign conferences occasionally use fighting ships to prevent or eliminate outside competition. This provision would therefore not change present American practice, but it would harmonize practices of American and foreign conferences.

6.3.4.2. Article 19—Adequacy of Service

The Code directs conferences to ensure that their members provide regular, adequate, and efficient service on their trade routes. In doing this, the conferences should also consider any seasonal variations in their cargo volumes. In the situation where a carrier will call at a port only if a specified minimum of cargo is available, that minimum should be specified in the tariff. U.S. regulations do not specifically address this issue except to encourage rate parity within U.S. coastal areas (§205 Merchant Marine Act of 1936, 46 U.S.C. §1115).

6.3.5. Provisions and Machinery for Settlement of Disputes[18]

The Code provides machinery for the settlement of disputes arising from the application of Code provisions. This machinery may be utilized to settle disputes between the following parties:

- A conference and a shipping line;
- The shipping line members of a conference;
- A conference or a shipping line member thereof and a shippers' organization or representatives of shippers or shipper; and,
- Two or more conferences.

The parties are encouraged to settle their differences through direct negotiations. But if this is not successful, disputes on the following subjects may be referred to international mandatory conciliation:

- Refusal of admission of a national shipping line to a conference serving the foreign trade of the country of that shipping line;
- Refusal of admission of a third-country shipping line to a conference;
- Expulsion from a conference;
- Inconsistency of a conference agreement with this Code;
- A general freight-rate increase;
- Surcharges;
- Changes in freight rates or the imposition of a currency adjustment factor due to exchange rate changes;
- Participation in trade; and,
- The form and terms of proposed loyalty arrangements.

The Code provides rules for requests for conciliation and notice to the other party. Where conciliation proceedings are initiated, they will have precedence over national law. The parties are not bound to use the conciliation procedure, however, and may agree to use a different method to settle their disputes.

Under the Code, a panel of conciliators will be established consisting of experts of high repute or experience in the fields of law, economics of sea transport, or foreign trade and finance. The Code stipulates a procedure by which the parties to the dispute will choose one or an uneven number of conciliators. After hearing the case, the conciliators will make a recommendation in accordance with the provisions of the Code. If the Code is not applicable, the conciliators may apply whatever law is agreed upon by the parties or is most closely connected with the dispute.

If the parties accept the recommendation, it will constitute a final determination of the dispute.

The process of conciliation is not very different from the present system of using arbitration to settle disputes. As in arbitration, the conciliators hear the case and make a recommendation. In the end, however, they have no power to enforce their recommendation. If the parties, or one of them, chooses to ignore the recommendation, the process will have been without effect, as well as being time-consuming and costly. This expense is borne by the parties to the dispute.

The conciliation process does offer the parties a forum in which to voice their differences. It also offers other concerned parties the opportunity to make known their opinions regarding disagreements, as well as providing for recommendations from objective experts. These same advantages are obtained through the present use of negotiation and arbitration.

The FMC, of course, provides judicial remedies, including reparations, for violations of the Shipping Act.

6.4. Impact of the Code on U.S. Shipping Regulation

Implementation of the UNCTAD Code, if ratified by the United States, will involve changes in the regulatory role of the FMC in key areas such as review of rate agreements and rate changes, conference self-policing, and law enforcement. The extent of change in each case, however, will depend on the interpretation given to the relevant articles, as discussed in the following sections.

6.4.1. Impact of the Code on the Role of the Federal Maritime Commission

The Federal Maritime Commission (FMC) is the institution in the United States charged with regulating common carriers by water, both individual carriers and those joined in conferences. Generally the duties of the FMC are to regulate the rates charged for shipping in domestic commerce, to license ocean freight forwarders, to permit shipping companies to form rate-setting conferences that would otherwise be in violation of antitrust statutes, to review rates filed by common carriers and to ensure that carriers adhere to the rates on file, and to investigate charges of discriminating practices in ocean shipping.[19]

If the Code of Conduct for Liner Conferences is ratified by the United States, the present role of the FMC in regulating conferences will undoubtedly change. It is not certain, however, what the new role would be.

The Code initiated by the United Nations Conference on Trade and Development (UNCTAD) seeks to regulate shipping conferences. Shipping conferences are defined by UNCTAD as groups of shipping lines operating with basic agreements for charging uniform rates, for allocating routes, berthing and sailing rights, and for pooling cargo and revenues, and intended to shut out nonconference competition.[20]

The role of the FMC in international liner shipping is to balance the interests of the liner shipping companies and shippers, the American importers and exporters who use liner services. To do this, the FMC grants antitrust immunity to carriers where it decides that such restraints on competition will operate in the public interest, and it tries to prevent undue discrimination among shippers, carriers, and ports.[21]

The FMC derives its authority to regulate liner conferences from the Shipping Act of 1916.[22] Section 15 of the Shipping Act grants to the FMC its most important power, the power to approve anticompetitive agreements between common carriers by water. Any anticompetitive agreements between common carriers, including those affecting rates, accommodations, competition, pooling, sailings, cargo movement or working arrangements must be filed with and approved by the FMC.

The proponents of the agreement must show that the proposed agreement is neither "unjustly discriminatory (nor) unfair as between carriers, shippers, exporters, importers, or ports, or between exporters from the United States and their foreign competitors, (nor) to operate to the detriment of the commerce of the United States, (nor) to be contrary to the public interest."[23] An approved section 15 agreement is exempt from the antitrust laws of the United States.

It is illegal for any carrier to act on an agreement that has not been approved by the FMC and it may be fined up to $1000 per day for doing so.

Apart from economic considerations, there are certain standards that agreements must meet in order to merit FMC approval. For example, the FMC may approve only those conference agreements that allow open membership. That is, the agreement must provide for reasonable and equal terms and conditions for admission and readmission to the conference of any qualified carrier in the trade. It must also provide that any member may withdraw from membership upon a reasonable notice without penalty.

6.4.2. Enforcement of Conference Agreements

The Commission enforces conference agreements, in part, by disapproving any agreement that does not adequately provide for self-policing of obligations under the agreement. As a result, every conference agreement contains a list of prohibited malpractices. A malpractice is generally any action by a member of the conference that violates the terms of the conference agreement or of the requirements imposed on conferences and carriers by the regulatory authorities and which may result in that member gaining an undue advantage over other members, or may give an undue advantage to particular shippers as compared with other shippers.

6.4.2.1. Rate Agreements

The FMC reviews shipping rates filed by common carriers. Every common carrier by water and every conference which operates in the foreign trade must file its rates with the FMC. The tariffs are kept open to the public and must contain the following:

- The places between which freight is carried;
- The classification of freight in force;
- Other services and charges rendered;
- Any rules and regulations affecting rates; and
- Examples of rate documents.

A conference may charge only those rates published in the tariffs.

Under the Code, the power of the FMC to regulate liner shipping through the approval or disapproval of section 15 agreements will change, or even disappear.

Currently, the Shipping Act requires that anticompetitive agreements be filed with the FMC so that they can be evaluated and approved or disapproved on their economic merits. According to the FMC, "(t)he current case-by-case approach . . . recognizes the complexity of U.S. international trading patterns which extend from our several coasts to virtually every nation on the globe."[24]

Under the UNCTAD Code, there is no government oversight of these anticompetitive agreements.[25] If the agreements are filed with an international organization, presumably they would be reviewed to ensure conformity to the applicable Code provisions.[26]

The present FMC review of agreements, with the objective of ensuring the economic well-being of the United States, may give way to review by an international body. To that body, the United States would be one country among many, and our economic welfare would certainly not be a primary consideration in its review of agreements.

If the FMC loses its power to approve or disapprove anticompetitive agreements, it loses its most important power, and would consequently be much less effective in the regulation of liner conferences than it is now. If the FMC retains power to approve or disapprove agreements, its standards of review will change. The factors to consider would be determined by the requirements of the Code.

At the very least, however, the FMC would have access to the agreements. Article 6 provides that the agreements will be made available on request to the appropriate authorities of the countries whose trade is served by the conference and of the countries whose shipping lines are members of the conference.

All conference agreements under the Code must conform to the applicable requirements of the Code.[27] This applies to Code provisions regarding conference membership. At the present time, the FMC approves only those conference agreements that provide for open membership to the conference. Under Article 1 of the Code, conference membership may be closed to non-national countries. Basically, any national shipping line will have the right to be a member of a conference that serves the foreign trade of its country. Third-party lines will sometimes be allowed membership but it is not a guaranteed right. All agreements under the Code must conform to this requirement. Thus, another important responsibility of the FMC—to ensure that conferences operating in the U.S. trades maintain open membership—is lost.

6.4.3. Self-Policing of Conferences

Requirements for self-policing of conferences would be much less stringent under the Code than they currently are in the United States under the Shipping Act. At the present time, the FMC will not approve a conference agreement unless it contains a list of malpractices and the procedure for dealing with them. Under the Code, conferences are directed to adopt a list of malpractices and machinery to deal with them.[28] There is no requirement, however, that the malpractice list and machinery be included in the conference agreement. As there is no review by a government authority, a conference may take a very lax attitude toward self-policing.

The government authorities, presumably the FMC in the United States, will be allowed very little interference in the self-policing procedure. Article 5 provides only that the authority of a country whose trade is served may request a report of any action taken on a malpractice. The report will be given but the parties concerned will remain anonymous.

The present requirement that tariffs be filed with the FMC and open to the public need not change under the Code. The proposed Code requires that tariffs and related regulations be published and made available to all shippers and their councils at a reasonable cost. The regulations must contain conditions relating to the application of freight rates, loading and unloading areas, and the carriage of specific cargo. In the United States, the shipping companies could still be required to file their tariffs with the FMC. However, the present power of the FMC to specify the form and content of tariffs and to disapprove rates under very limited circumstances would change.

6.4.4. Notice of Rate Change

As noted before in Section 6.3.2 and 6.3.3, under the Code a conference is required to give shippers notice of not less than 150 days of its intention to effect a general increase in freight rates. Shippers may then request a consultation within 30 days of the notice.[29] The consultation is designed to review the reasons and justifications for the increase. The conference is also encouraged to submit a report from independent accountants. Shippers may request such a report which should include the relevant costs and revenues which, according to the conference, justify imposition of an increase.

Only if an agreement is reached between conference and shipper does the increase take effect on the date set in the notice, unless a later date is agreed upon. According to the proposed Code, failure to reach an agreement within 30 days of giving the notice requires that the matter be submitted to international mandatory conciliation. If the parties accept the conciliator's decision, it will be binding on them, effective from the date mentioned in the conciliator's recommendation. This would require a change in U.S. law under which the FMC rules on the reasonableness of the proposed rate.

Should a conference refuse to abide by the conciliator's recommendation, then shippers are not bound by their loyalty arrangements and may take other actions as well. They must, however, give 30 days' notice that they are no longer parties to the agreement, and the Code explicitly forbids conferences to retaliate against such shippers by refusing to pay any deferred rebates that are owed.

The time before notices of intention to increase rates must be at least 10 months after the last increase has become effective. In other words, rate increases cannot be introduced less than fifteen months apart.

6.4.5. Law Enforcement

The FMC is responsible for enforcing laws regulating conference activity in the United States. Several of these laws regulate the way in which a common carrier, operating between a United States port and a foreign port, may operate. (A number of quite specific requirements are mentioned in Appendix 3A.)

The use of certain ships, called fighting ships, to undercut competitors' rates is against U.S. law, as is the unfair discrimination of a conference against a shipper who has given business to a competitor. Carriers regulated by the FMC may not refuse to carry the shipper's cargo unless they can show that it is beyond their capacity. Similarly, it is illegal for a carrier to unfairly or unjustly discriminate between customers based on the volume of freight offered.

While dual-rate contracts are permitted, after filing with the FMC for the right to use them, the full rate may be charged to shippers who do not give the carrier all, or a specified part, of their business, while lower rates are applied to exclusive shippers or shippers who undertake to give the conference or carrier a fixed amount of their cargo.

The authority to investigate any violation by a carrier of these provisions rests with the FMC. Should the FMC find that a foreign carrier has violated the law, or that it has combined with other carriers to break the law or to exclude American carriers, the FMC may notify the Commissioner of Customs, and request that vessels of such carriers be denied entry to U.S. ports until the violation ceases. Should an American carrier violate one of these provisions, it may be subject to a fine, imposed by the FMC. The FMC responsibility for enforcing the laws regulating competition may not be changed by the Code. The Code agrees with United States law in that it outlaws fighting ships.

Under the Code, the shipping lines may negotiate with the shippers as to the terms of loyalty agreements. Article 7 provides that the arrangement may be based on any lawful system. This implies that the United States could, by means of legislation, continue to regulate the types of loyalty arrangements used in the U.S. trades. The Code differs from present U.S. law in that it permits the use of deferred rebates.[30] A deferred rebate means that the carrier returns part of the freight money to the shipper in consideration for receiving the shipper's business.

The FMC is also responsible for enforcing laws prohibiting discriminatory behavior by carriers. The thrust of these laws is that carriers must charge the same rates to all shippers. It is illegal for a carrier to use any means to transport goods at less than the established rate. It is also illegal for the carrier to give preference to any person, locality, or description.

A carrier operating in foreign commerce may not discriminate between shipper or ports. It is also prohibited from charging a rate that is unjustly prejudicial to United States exporters compared to their foreign competitors. If the FMC finds that an unjustly discriminatory or prejudicial rate has been charged, it may alter the rate. These FMC responsibilities regarding the investigation of discrimination by carriers would probably remain unchanged under the new Code.

If the United States signs and ratifies the Code, it will be necessary to change some of the United States shipping laws and regulations to conform to the provisions of the Code.[31] As it is now the duty of the FMC to make rules and regulations affecting shipping in the foreign trade, it may be the responsibility of the FMC to make the rules implementing the UNCTAD Code if the United States signs it and it is ratified.

The Code makes numerous references to "appropriate authorities." Although one purpose of the Code was to reduce direct government control over shipping and to increase commercial control, some government involvement in international shipping will still be necessary. In some ways, Chapters III, IV, and V of the Code simply extend the regulation the FMC has practiced on a unilateral basis to an international level.[32]

If the United States ratifies the Code, it must provide for an appropriate authority to work with conferences and shipping councils as required by the Code. Quite possibly the new responsibility would be delegated to the FMC.

Government involvement is mandated by various articles of the Code governing such areas as agreements (made available under the terms of Article 6), tariffs (Articles 9, 14, 15), consultation machinery (Article 11), and service adequacy (Article 19).[33]

The potential for continued government involvement also exists in the following areas:[34]

- Bilateral agreements, since they would probably be excluded from the scope of the Code, thereby requiring government supervision.
- *Ex post* review of cargo allocations for conformity to Code requirements.
- Settlement of disputes if the results of conciliation are rejected by one of the parties.
- Activities which are deemed serious breaches of our antitrust laws. A government entity may be required to serve as a watchdog against abuses of the antitrust laws. The question of antitrust immunity may be especially relevant in intermodal transportation.
- Protection of U.S.-flag operators from undue discrimination where other governments play a dominant role in either supporting their liner operators or where they control the national shippers' council.
- Regulation of controlled carriers that do not join conferences.
- Authority over the entire sector of services provided by non-state-controlled independents may in fact be required since they are not covered by the terms of the Code. The increased potential monopoly power of conferences under the Code may be channeled into producing lower costs through rationalization, the benefits of which should be shared with shippers, as alluded to in Article 19 of the Code. Nevertheless, the existence of a certain degree of nonconference competition can act as a safety valve against unwarranted abuses of power. Some organization will have to make the determination of how much nonconference competition is required and will have to protect these carriers from conference attempts to drive them from the trade.

If the United States signs the UNCTAD Code and it is ratified, the responsibilities of the FMC will change. It will lose one of its most important powers, the power to approve anticompetitive agreements between common carriers. FMC approval presently confers antitrust immunity to these carriers. If the FMC no longer approves the agreements, it will be necessary to change the antitrust laws to except carrier agreements from its provisions.

The FMC will also lose the power to survey and approve the rates of common carriers engaged in foreign commerce, but will probably retain its power to regulate loyalty arrangements and discriminatory practices among carriers engaged in foreign commerce.

If the United States ratifies the Code, the FMC will probably assume the responsibilities delegated to an "appropriate government authority" by the Code. It will, of course, continue its present responsibilities of regulating the practices of common carriers in domestic commerce. It may also be assigned to arbitrate in the settlement of disputes and may continue to provide antitrust exemptions. In all, we would expect the responsibilities of the FMC to be greater under the Code.

6.5. Regulatory Impact of Code Acceptance on Carriers

Liner conferences in the U.S. foreign trade are presently governed by the Federal Maritime Commission (FMC), implementing the Shipping Act of 1916. If the United States ratifies the UNCTAD Code, the FMC may still be the government body in the United States that ensures that carriers are complying with the law. The law being complied with, however, will change. For the most part, the regulation of carriers would increase under the Code. Conferences would lose some of their present decison-making discretion and would be responsible for meeting more requirements.

Under the Shipping Act, all anticompetitive agreements between carriers, including conference agreements, must be filed with and approved by the FMC. The Act requires that conference agreements contain certain provisions—open-membership, withdrawal without penalty, self-policing machinery, and a procedure to consider shippers' requests and complaints.

The FMC will approve any conference agreement that is not unjustly discriminatory or unfair as between carriers, shippers, or ports, that is not detrimental to the commerce of the United States, and that is not contrary to the public interest or in violation of the Shipping Act. Once the conference agreement has been approved, the conference is generally free to set rates and to organize pools and pool shares. The resulting pooling agreements and the rates must be approved by the FMC, but the conference uses its discretion in setting rates and organizing pools.

Under the UNCTAD Code, the conferences would lose much of their present discretion, as the Code would establish the machinery for setting rates and organizing pools. The Code provides that if a pool does not exist in a conference, either a group of national shipping lines or members of the conference may require that a pool be introduced. Once the pool is introduced, the Code determines the share of the trade to be carried by each party to the pool. The Code also provides that the national shipping lines of two trading countries will have veto power regarding any decision relating to the trading countries.

A conference is now free to set its own freight rates, subject to the approval of the FMC. Under the Code, instead of submitting proposed freight rates to the FMC for approval, the conference must negotiate with government and shippers' representatives and then submit to international conciliation if an agreement can not be reached.

There would probably be decreased regulation for the conferences in the area of self-policing. Under the Shipping Act, each conference agreement must provide for adequate policing of obligations under it. The FMC reviews and approves these provisions when it approves the conference agreement. The Code mandates that the conferences establish a self-policing machinery, but it does not provide for any review of the procedure. Therefore, self-policing is left up to the individual conferences.

The Code provides for a working mechanism by which shippers may consult with the conferences. A conference would be required to maintain, in the countries served by its vessels, full-time conference representatives or committees having power to negotiate with shippers and to make decisions on important matters of common interest. This consultation mechanism would be expensive, burdensome, and time-consuming for the conferences.

In all, the Code would impose more supervision of carrier rates and terms of affreightment. It would also reduce the incentives for carriers to rationalize their individual or combined operations. As a result, rates would generally be higher with the Code.

6.6. Impact of Code Acceptance on Shippers

The major effect of the UNCTAD Code will be the reduction of competition between liner carriers. This, of course, will tend to allow freight rates to rise to a level above that produced by competition, and the shippers will be forced to pay the higher rates.

In an effort to keep the freight rates from escalating, the Code provides that the conferences negotiate with the affected governments and shippers' councils prior to setting their rates. If an agreement cannot be reached, the matter is submitted to international arbitration. Once a rate becomes effective, the conference may not publish an intent to raise rates again for 10 months. The result would be that the conference would try to implement huge rate increases every 15 months in an effort to anticipate future costs. Because it is doubtful that the shippers' input could keep the rates low, each 15 months shippers would be faced with a large jump in freight rates.

If the conference faces an unexpected decrease in revenue or increase in costs, it may impose a surcharge. Usually the conference must consult with shippers before imposing such a surcharge. In an emergency situation, however, it may charge first and consult later. Shippers argue that this does not offer them adequate protection from surcharges.

Should Code acceptance result in consolidation of mainline vessel calls to a smaller number of ports served, shippers using the ports losing service may be adversely affected through increased overland/feeder transport costs.

At the present time antitrust laws prevent shippers of the United States from forming a United States Shippers' Council. The Code would provide for such a council to consult and negotiate with carriers and conferences of carriers providing liner services in the United States international trade.

A shippers' council could, of course, be granted antitrust immunity without passage of the Code. With the passage of the Code, the negotiating stance of the shippers' council vis-à-vis the conference would be weaker than without it because the reduction of competition would remove some of the conference's motivation to negotiate.

U.S. shippers are currently protected from conference discrimination by the Shipping Act of 1916. The Code is silent as to the concept of discrimination, but Article 13, paragraph 1, states that "tariffs shall not unfairly differentiate between shippers similarly situated." In effect, this affords shippers the same protection as the Shipping Act.

6.7. Effect of Code Adoption on U.S. Cargo Preference

Under current U.S. law,[35] government-owned and government-sponsored cargoes are reserved for U.S bottoms. Implementation of the Code would imply cessation of cargo preference on the liner-carried segment of such cargoes. Military cargo is excluded from Code coverage.

6.8. Implications of the Code for U.S. Ports

Imposition of the Code on various routes is expected to reduce significantly the number of ports served in a particular trade as a result of the lack of incentive to serve any but the primary ports. The Code can be expected to reduce competition in the liner trade as well as service to shippers. The elimination of some ports in a given trade will not only reduce service and affect the economic viability of such by-passed routes, but can be expected to also greatly increase point-to-point cost to shippers as a result of the addition of further feeder costs.

6.9. Other Potential Impacts of the Code

Since the introduction of the Code, there has been a marked increase in the move of pseudo bulk or neo bulk cargoes traditionally carried on liner vessels to parcel bulk carriers. This move toward specialized shipping to avoid potential or real implications of the imposition of the Code may cause major future loss of liner cargo to U.S. operators. An increasing number of cargo brokers are now in the business of space chartering on dry and liquid bulk carriers—a trend that is expected to continue, particularly if the imposition of the Code results in deterioration of reliability, frequency, and quality of service and/or a large increase in freight rates.

Intermodal transport is essential for effective containerized-liner operations. The Code makes no provisions for intermodal operations and would encourage only national-flag operators to invest in intermodal facilities.

The impact of the Code on freight rates will depend on many factors such as:

- Reservation of cargo may induce introduction of cheap, inefficient, high-operating cost tonnage that would drive up conference rates.
- Closed conferences will reduce competition and thereby drive up rates, while at the same time permitting more rationalization on a bilateral basis, which might reduce freight rates. Effective rationalization, however, is generally not found possible in bilateral liner trades, particularly if containerized. Therefore introduction of closed bilateral conferences is expected to have no appreciable effect on freight rates.
- The imposition of explicit shipper (council) consultation in rate setting may result in a downward pressure on rates.

- Restriction on third-party carriage will reduce competition and efficiency, thus raising freight rates.
- The 15-month rate freeze imposed by the Code will induce conferences to "play it safe" and introduce rate increases far above those required to cover expected near-term cost increases. As no rate adjustment is allowed for 15 months, rates will generally be significantly higher than necessary.
- The extent to which rates will change obviously depends on the degree of reallocation of tonnage vis-à-vis current allocation.
- The Code merely reserves equal shares for trading partners and a 'significant' portion for third-party nations which in most cases has been interpreted as 'no more' than 20 percent for third parties. Furthermore, third-party shares can be adjusted by national-flag carriers, which would result in participating third-party carriers allocating only inefficient tonnage to the trade.

6.10. Impacts of Cargo Sharing on U.S. Trade

Prior sections of this chapter have largely concentrated on a discussion of the impacts of the UNCTAD Code, with special concern to its cargo sharing provisions. There are, however, as mentioned earlier, other cargo-sharing arrangements that could be considered. Cargo-sharing agreements generally limit supply of capacity, which may affect cost and quality of shipping, by restricting rate-setting activity. The effect of cargo-sharing agreements on rates will be influenced by the method used to limit competition and the supply of vessels. This is important because it affects the setting of rates through control of the availability of lower-priced marginal tonnage.

The transport charges incurred by exporters/importers are the rates charged for shipping services. The relationship between these rates and the actual costs of supplying transport is determined by the mechanism of rate setting. These rates have a number of forms—conference rates, bilateral shipping arrangements, short- and long-term charter rates, and nonconference liner rates.

While conference rates and bilateral arrangements must be reviewed by the Federal Maritime Commission, charter rates are determined in an open market with free competition, with prices based on marginal costs. Nonconference liner services usually offer rates set below those of the conference lines. (Some nonconference lines are operated by subsidized national fleets and offer rates below marginal costs.)

The method for setting rates and allocating cargoes will have a significant effect on the changes in transport costs. The relationship between shipping freight rates and the costs of providing freight transport are often obscured by the methods used for calculating the costs and setting the rates.

A more severe constraint may arise where the existing shipping capacity of agreement partners is inadequate to carry their share. Should general multilateral cargo-sharing agreements come into force, the United States and many less developed countries (LDCs) lack sufficient fleet capacity to carry their share of their trade. Since the demand for marine transport is subject to fairly wide swings, especially in bulk commodity shipments, the supply of vessels can vary from being a condition of scarcity to one of excess capacity in a relatively short time. The limitation of fleet capacity to the national fleets of the partners to bilateral or multilateral cargo-sharing agreements will expose them to even greater fluctuations in demand and therefore available capacity. Many countries, particularly LDCs which find themselves in a position of insufficient capacity to carry "their share" under the agreement (or Code), resort to various interpretations of "national shipping" by in-charter or space charter of capacity, joint venturing, or other methods which provide them with an increase of capacity without investment in additional tonnage.

The major operational areas in which the stipulations of cargo-sharing agreements may require specification are chartering, routing, scheduling, and vessel characteristics. Lines that currently charter in order to fulfill their conference/pooling agreements, or to gain time while contemplating new buildings or conversions, may find that future cargo-sharing agreements may require them to own their tonnage. This has obvious implications for the structure of the liner industry and the pace and scope of decision-making processes.

Liners, as part of conferences, usually follow a fixed route and schedule, with minor variations in the sequence and number of port calls, including the number of times a port is visited during a round-trip voyage. On many trade routes calls are made at a port either outbound or inbound.

If control of market share is attempted through operational regulation, the routes and schedules of the participants will have to be supervised. The trans-shipment role of participants would also require supervision, which is not attempted at the present time.

Practically all U.S. liner services include liner services to more than one country or trading partner. Bilateral cargo sharing agreements could seriously affect the ability of liner operators to schedule and allocate capacity effectively for optimum utilization on all legs of the route, particularly when (1) cargo-sharing agreements exist between the United States and some or all of the countries served by a particular liner trade route, or (2) bilateral cargo-sharing agreements are in force between all countries on the liner trade route on a bilateral basis.

Routing and scheduling of liner services subject to several cargo-sharing agreements may become quite difficult unless the cargo-sharing agreements include revenue sharing. On the other hand, revenue sharing, as a part of a bilateral cargo-sharing agreement itself, introduces many drawbacks.

There are a number of alternatives to a bilateral cargo-sharing system which facilitate multilateral liner operation; these include the pooling of tonnage of all the countries involved in a trade route, in proportion to their entitlements under a multilateral cargo sharing agreement, and operation of the pooled fleet as one. Charges on any leg are as per agreement, and pool revenues are shared in proportion to the agreed upon cargo-share entitlement. This approach has some similarity to the multinational containership pooling practiced by several consortia in Northern Europe.

Instead of a closed consortium type of tonnage pooling under a multilateral cargo-sharing agreement, open entry by national-flag vessels can also be used. Here each country obtains a share of cargo for each leg of the multinational trade route. Countries or shipping companies can then trade their share entitlements to improve the balance of their trade route or schedule. Another important operational consideration not usually included under cargo-sharing agreements is the role and entitlement of trans-shipment countries.

Fleet and route rationalization, based on fixed market shares negotiated in bilateral cargo-sharing agreements, would be difficult if the United States maintains free competition for the U.S. market share among U.S.-flag lines. Rationalization would be even more difficult if all countries involved in a multinational route had separate bilateral agreements with few, if any, cross-trade markets left open to U.S.-flag liners serving the route.

Endnotes

1. 46 U.S.C. §814 (1976).
2. 46 C.F.R. §522.6.
3. 46 C.F.R. §522.2.
4. 46 C.F.R. §522.2(a)(3).
5. This does not apply to Argentinian pools where the national-flag lines may carry more than their allotted 80 percent.
6. 46 U.S.C. §814 (1976).
7. After the carrier joins the pool, its participation is not complete until it enters into an association agreement with the other carrier(s) of its flag. Such an association agreement provides the mechanism for dividing the involved flag share of the basic pool.
8. UNCTAD, *The Liner Conference System* (1970), p. 92.
9. Id. at 95.

10. 46 C.F.R. §522.2(4).
11. 46 C.F.R. §522.2(5).
12. Whitehurst, C. H. Jr., "Convention on a Code of Conduct for Liner Conference," Center for the Study of Marine Policy Reports, Vol. 3, No. 1, September 1980.
13. *Ibid.*
14. U.S.C. §814 (1976).
15. 46 U.S.C. §814 (1976).
16. 46 U.S.C. §816 (1976).
17. 46 U.S.C. §813a (1976).
18. See Shah, "The Dispute Settlement Machinery of the U.N. Convention on a Code of Conduct for Liner Conferences," 7. *J. Mar. L. & Comm.*, October 1975, pp. 127–168.
19. *Federal Regulatory Directory*, p. 508, 1980–81.
20. UNCTAD Secretariat, *The Regulation of Liner Conferences: A Code of Conduct for the Liner Conference System* (1972).
21. L. Kanuk, Statement before the House Merchant Marine and Fisheries Committee, April 2, 1981.
22. Shipping Act, 1976, §§14–20, 22–23, 46 U.S.C. §§812–819, 821–832.
23. Shipping Act, 1916, Sec. 15, 46 U.S.C. §814 (1976).
24. L. Kanuk, *op. cit.*, p. 7.
25. *Ibid.*
26. Ch. V, Art. 22, Convention on a Code of Conduct for Liner Conference (Code).
27. Ch. V, Art. 22, Code.
28. Ch. II, Art. 5, Code.
29. Ch. IV, Art. 14(2), Code.
30. Ch. IV, Art. 14(7), Code.
31. Ch. VII, Art. 47(1), Code.
32. L. Kanuk, *op. cit.*, p. 12.
33. *Ibid.*
34. *Id.* at 13–14.
35. Cargo Preference Legislation—(1) Public Resolution No. 17 (1934), goods financed with Export-Import Bank loans to be carried in U.S.-flag vessels; (2) Cargo Preference Act of 1954: at least 50 percent of government-financed cargo must use American-flag ships; (3) PL–480.

Appendix 6A

SUGGESTED LANGUAGE FOR A FREIGHT CONFERENCE AGREEMENT

AGREEMENT NO. _____
(Name of Conference)

This agreement[1] was entered into by and between the parties on
_____. The undersigned, common carriers of freight by water
in the foreign commerce of the United States (hereinafter referred to as
"Members"), in consideration of the benefits, advantages, and privileges
to be severally and collectively derived from this agreement, hereby associate themselves in a conference to be known as _____ (hereinafter referred to as "the Conference") to govern their transportation of
freight from _____to_____ (or between_____
and_____).[2]

AUTHORITY UNDER THIS AGREEMENT

Subject to applicable provisions of law, the Conference is authorized to:
1. Agree upon and establish rates and charges for the carriage of cargo

---

1. If the intention is that the conference rates should apply whether the service
is direct or with trans-shipment, the following provision should be included: to the
extent that rates established under this agreement include service by way of trans-
shipment, as well as direct service by the members, approval of this agreement
does not encompass approval of any trans-shipment arrangement which would otherwise require section 15 approval.
2. 46 C.F.R. §522.6(a).

and rules and regulations governing the application thereof and defining the service to be rendered therefor;

2. Declare rates for specified commodities to be "open," with or without agreed minimum, and thereafter declare the rates for such commodities to be "closed";

3. Agree upon and establish tariffs, tariff amendments, and supplements;

4. Make rules and regulations for the handling and carriage of cargo;

5. Provide for use of a contract/noncontract rate system for filing with the Commission for approval pursuant to section 14b of the Shipping Act, 1916;

6. Agree on amounts of brokerage and/or compensation to forwarders and the conditions for the payment thereof as permitted by applicable law;

7. Keep such records and statistics as may be required by the parties or deemed helpful to their interests.

ADMISSION

Any common carrier by water, as defined in section 1 of the Shipping Act, 1916, which has been regularly covered by this Agreement, or which furnishes evidence of ability and intention in good faith to institute and maintain such a common carrier service between ports within the scope of this Agreement, and which agrees in good faith to abide by all the terms and conditions of this Agreement, may hereafter become a party to this agreement by affixing its signature thereto. Every application for membership shall be acted upon promptly. No carrier that has complied with the conditions set forth in this paragraph shall be denied admission or readmission to membership.

Prompt notice of admission to membership shall be furnished to the Federal Maritime Commission and no admission shall be effective prior to the postmark date of such notice. Advice of any denial of admission to membership, together with a complete statement of the reasons therefor, shall be furnished promptly to the Federal Maritime Commission. (Other conditions of membership not inconsistent with the foregoing, including payment of a reasonable admission fee, payment of any outstanding financial obligations arising out of prior membership, or the posting of a security bond or deposit may be included.)

WITHDRAWAL

Any Member may withdraw from the Conference without penalty by giving the Conference at least _____ days written notice of intention to withdraw: Provided, however, that action taken by the Conference to compel the payment of outstanding financial obligations by the resigning

Member shall not be construed as a penalty for withdrawal. Notice of the withdrawal shall be furnished promptly to the Federal Maritime Commission.

EXPULSION

No Member may be expelled against its will from this Conference except for failure to maintain a common carrier service between the ports within the scope of this Agreement (said failure to be determined according to the minimum sailing requirements set forth in this Agreement) or for failure to abide by the terms and conditions of this agreement. No expulsion shall become effective until a detailed statement setting forth the reason or reasons therefor has been furnished the expelled Member and a copy of the statement submitted to the Federal Maritime Commission.

ABANDONMENT OF SERVICE

Membership in the Conference shall cease when service is abandoned. A Member's failure to have a sailing in the trade for a period of _____ consecutive months shall be regarded as an abandonment. If war, strikes, force majeure, or other circumstances beyond its control compel a Member to suspend service, it may apply for inactive status, provided that application is made prior to termination of membership. Notice of termination of membership shall be furnished promptly to the Federal Maritime Commission.

OFFICERS, ORGANIZATION, AND ADMINISTRATION

The Members shall select a Chairman and/or Secretary to serve for _____ . The Chairman (or Secretary), when available, shall preside at Conference meetings. He (or she) shall have full authority to carry out the decisions of the Conference and perform such duties and appoint such committees as may be directed by the Conference. In the absence of the Chairman (or Secretary) at any meeting, an Acting Chairman may be selected by the Members present to conduct the meeting. The Chairman (or Secretary) shall keep a record of the proceedings of all Conference meetings, whether formal or otherwise, and of the actions taken by the Conference. Information and statistics required by the Chairman (or Secretary) in making or carrying out decisions of the Conference shall be made available by the Conference members.

The Members may select a Vice Chairman (or Assistant Secretary) and such other assistants as may be required to assist the Chairman (or Secretary) in the performance of his (or her) duties.

The Conference office shall be located at _____ . This office may compile cargo statistics required or necessary to the carrying out of Conference decisions; compile data relating to rate applications; issue dockets for meetings; maintain contract lists and files of all conference tariffs (copies of such tariffs shall be filed with the Federal Maritime Commission in conformity with the provisions of section 18(b)(1) of the Shipping Act, 1916); and perform such other duties as are prescribed by this Agreement, directed by the Members and specifically recorded in the minutes of Conference meetings.

The expense of annual Conference maintenance, as determined by the Conference Members or by a committee established or appointed for the purpose, shall be divided among the Members of the Conference in a manner to be agreed upon. Bills for such expenses shall be paid promptly upon receipt thereof.

MEETINGS[3]

Regular Conference meetings shall be held _____ upon not less than _____ notice from the Chairman (Secretary) unless such notice is unanimously waived. Advance notice of all matters requiring Conference action shall be given each Member.

Special Conference meetings may be requested by any Member upon application to the Conference office together with an explanation of the reason or reasons therefor. The special meeting shall be called by the Chairman (Secretary) and adequate notice thereof shall be given all Members. The notice shall indicate the subject matter and reason for the meeting.

Special Conference meetings may be requested by any Member upon application to the Conference office together with an explanation of the reason or reasons therefor. The special meeting shall be called by the Chairman (Secretary), and adequate notice thereof shall be given all Members. The notice shall indicate the subject matter and reason for the meeting.

If it is required or necessary that the Conference take emergency action with respect to rates or other matters and there is not time to convene a special meeting, the Members may be polled by the Chairman (Secretary) by telephone, and such action authorized by the consent of _____ of the Members. All such telephone calls, the subject matter thereof, and the

---

3. Every agreement should contain a provision stating the manner in which the joint business of the parties may be carried out—i.e., full membership meeting, agents' meeting, principals' meeting, owners' meeting—through committees or subcommittees, telephone or oral polls, or through any other procedure by which the joint business of the parties may be conducted.

action taken by the Conference shall be reported in the Minutes of the next regular Conference meeting.

Meetings of such committees as are appointed by the Conference in the conduct of its affairs shall be held at times and places as may be decided by such committees and a record shall be made of proceedings of all such committee meetings, whether formal or otherwise, including the results of all actions taken.

VOTING RIGHTS

Each Member shall be entitled to vote, with the following exceptions:

1. Any Member who has given notice of withdrawal shall not, while such notice is outstanding, be entitled to vote on any Conference matter, rate, rule, or regulation that is to continue in effect or become effective after the effective date of such withdrawal;

2. Any inactive Member whose service has been suspended shall not be entitled to vote on any matter except (a) amendment of the Conference agreement, and (b) dissolution of the Conference;

3. No Member shall be entitled to vote on the expulsion of another Member if it is a parent, subsidiary, or associated company of the Member complained against.

A quorum at any meeting shall consist of _____, and no meeting shall be held unless a quorum is present. Voting on any matter regularly before the Conference shall be by those present (or by proxy) and entitled to vote.

(1) Unanimous consent shall be required to:

_____

_____

(2) An affirmative vote of not less than _____ of the Members shall be required to authorize the taking of the following action: _____

_____

_____

Appendix 6B

SUGGESTED LANGUAGE FOR A POOLING AGREEMENT[1]

AGREEMENT NO. _____
(Name of Agreement)

This agreement was entered into by and between the parties on
_____ . The undersigned, common carriers of freight by water
in the foreign commerce of the United States (hereinafter referred to as
"parties"), agree that in the trade from _____ to _____
(or between _____ and _____), they will pool (or
apportion) the revenues earned by, or losses of, each party for the carriage
of (all cargoes, specific commodities, etc.) (if the pool is for traffic only to
so specify).

The pool to be established pursuant to this agreement will operate as
follows:

[List in lettered subparagraphs the exact method or procedure under
which the pool will operate. Show percentage formula for division of revenue; deductions prior to division; expenses to be shared, with share to
each party; division of carryings, if any; allocation by each party of space
and/or vessels; and so forth.]

---

1. C.F.R. §522.6(c).

Appendix 6C

SUGGESTED LANGUAGE FOR A JOINT SERVICE AGREEMENT[1]

AGREEMENT NO. _____
(Name of Agreement)

This agreement was entered into by and between the parties on _____ . The undersigned, common carriers of freight by water in the foreign commerce of the United States (hereinafter referred to as "parties"), agree that in the trade from _____ to _____ (or between _____ and _____), they will establish and maintain a joint cargo service to be known as _____ . (Insert name of new service.)

1. The joint service may become a member of, and may resign, or withdraw from any lawful conference, pooling arrangement, or other agreement subject to the Shipping Act, 1916, as amended, that may operate in the whole or any portion of the trades covered hereby. The joint service shall act as a single member or party to such agreements and shall be represented for such conference, pooling or other purposes by _____ which (or who) shall have full authority with respect to all matters coming before the conference. The signature to such conference, pooling or other arrangements shall be in the following form:

_____
Name of New Service

By _____

_____
Title or Authority

_____

1. C.F.R. §522.6(d).

2. In the case of any trades or traffic within the scope of this agreement where the rates, charges, and practices are not prescribed by any conference of which the joint service is a member, the new service shall establish and maintain its own rates, charges, and practices covering such trades or traffic. The joint service shall file a tariff containing such rates, rules, and regulations with the Federal Maritime Commission in accordance with the provisions of section 18(b) of the Shipping Act, 1916, as amended;

3. The parties shall cooperate to supply tonnage for this joint service as their owned or chartered vessels are available (or _____). It is intended to have a sailing approximately at least _____ ;

4. The parties shall contribute to and share in any and all deposits, costs, expenses, profits, and losses incurred by and derived from this joint service in the following proportions;

5. Copies of bills of lading of the joint service, showing the name of the new service and the names of the companies which are parties to this agreement, shall be furnished promptly to the Federal Maritime Commission;

6. The parties shall establish and maintain at (_____) an office from which the operations of the joint service will be directed;

7. This agreement may be canceled by any party giving _____ months written notice to the other party, and to the Federal Maritime Commission. Notice of resignation or withdrawal from every conference, pooling or other agreement of which the joint service is a member or party shall also be given, so that such resignations or withdrawals shall become effective simultaneously or as near thereto as possible, with the termination of this agreement; provided, however, that this agreement shall remain in full force and effect until all such resignations and withdrawals become effective.

Appendix 6D

SUGGESTED LANGUAGE FOR A SAILING AGREEMENT[1]

AGREEMENT NO. _____
(Name of Agreement)

This agreement was entered into by and between the parties on _____ . The undersigned, common carriers of freight by water in the foreign commerce of the United States (hereinafter referred to as the "parties"), agree that in the trade from _____ to _____ (or between _____ and _____), they will space their sailings in accordance with the following provisions of this agreement.

1. This agreement shall apply to the berth services operated or to be operated by the parties in the above-named trade(s);

2. Each of the parties hereto will furnish equivalent tonnage as regards type and capacity, and will maintain alternate (or specify other arrangement) sailings in the trade mentioned above, with a minimum of _____ sailings each annually, so far as practicable and subject to such charges as may be instituted by cargo requirements or other factors. The parties will cooperate to arrange advertising and sailing schedules so as to avoid conflicting dates;

3. There shall be no pooling or sharing of profits or losses. Revenues earned by the vessels employed under this agreement shall accrue to the operator thereof;

4. Each party shall manage and operate its own vessels at its own risk and expense, each party being responsible for the manning, navigation, etc., of its own vessels, the solicitation and booking of cargoes, collection

---

1. 46 C.F.R. §522.6(e).

of freight, appointment and removal of agents, settlement of cargo claims and all other activities required in the maintenance of service and sailings covered by this agreement;

5. The parties may advertise their respective services separately but in the event that such services are advertised in a single newspaper advertisement, or other medium, the full corporate or trade name of each party shall be shown in a manner to reflect their separate interests (for example, XYZ Line, Inc.) (for example, ABC Lines);

ALTERNATE SERVICES

6. Each of the parties hereto shall, as a member of any conference, exercise its rights, independent of the other, in voting on freight rates or on any other matter or thing within the scope of the agreement of such conference;

7. This agreement shall continue in effect until

(a) Cancelled by mutual consent to be evidenced in writing; or

(b) By the giving of _____ (   ) months written notice by either party to the other;

8. If in the opinion of a party to this agreement one of the parties hereto has committed a breach of this agreement, the matter of whether such breach has occurred shall be left to the determination of three (3) arbitrators, one to be nominated by the complaining party within thirty (30) days after his giving written notice to the party charged of demand for arbitration, a second to be nominated by the party charged within thirty (30) days after receipt by him of notice of demand for arbitration, and the third to be appointed by agreement of the two so nominated or, failing agreement thereon, by (a recognized arbitration body). The arbitrators so chosen shall, after hearing both parties, make their award in writing. The decision of the arbitrators shall be final and binding on the parties hereto and there shall be no appeal against the award of the arbitrators. All expenses in connection with any complaint made under this agreement shall be borne equally by all parties hereto. Nothing contained in this agreement shall interfere with the rights of any party hereto under the provisions of the Shipping Act of 1916, as amended.

Chapter 7

U.S. INLAND WATER TRANSPORTATION

U.S. inland water transport, in terms of tons of commerce moved per year, has doubled almost every 20 years since 1940 and is growing at a compound rate of nearly 5 percent per year. It is currently in excess of 624 million tons per year. The ton-mile transport effort in inland water transport has increased at an even greater rate and is now in excess of 290 billion ton miles with the average transport distance in excess of 460 miles as shown in Tables 7-1 and 7-2. Distribution of inland commerce by arrival and departure, as well as by type of vessel used, is presented in Table 7-3. The composition and growth of the inland water fleet for the years 1975-1978 is shown in Table 7-4. Table 7-5 shows the fleet characteristics for 1978 subdivided by major areas of operations. Most components of the inland waterway system network are natural waterways or well over 50 years old. Table 7-6 presents the distribution of lengths and depths of the major waterways of the United States. The overall length of navigable inland waterways has remained nearly constant for over 50 years. However, the energy and economic efficiency of inland water transportation is expected to result in significant future investments in inland waterways improvements and extensions.

The freight carried on U.S. rivers and canals by U.S. inland water transportation as a percentage of ton miles carried by all U.S. domestic transport carriers (rail, road, pipeline, and inland water) has increased from 3.7 percent in 1940 to 51 percent in 1950, 9.2 percent in 1960, 10.5 percent in 1970 and 12.2 percent in 1976. Table 7-7 shows the freight distribution by transport mode for 1978. Inland water transportation is expected to account for 14 percent of all U.S domestic transport in ton miles by 1980. Inland water transport is used primarily for the movements of bulk or bulkable commodities. About one third of the goods carried are crude oil or petroleum

Table 7–1 Traffic Transported on Inland Waterways of the United States (Exclusive of Great Lakes)

Year	Net Tons of 2,000 Pounds*	Ton Miles
1940	183,417,791	22,411,961,000
⋮	⋮	⋮
1965	472,480,483	152,812,240,000
1966	489,066,210	164,528,798,000
1967	500,912,733	174,582,978,000
1968	520,904,639	179,336,707,000
1969	548,481,358	187,666,323,000
1970	553,598,222	204,084,966,000
1971	560,470,417	210,003,291,000
1972	597,255,337	229,754,230,000
1973	596,459,513	232,307,988,000
1974	599,219,554	247,430,888,000
1975	582,211,482	243,038,688,000
1976	607,703,665	267,216,851,000
1977	612,149,130	277,580,717,000
1978	624,015,527	290,396,521,000

SOURCE: American Waterways Operators Inc., 1981.

* Known duplications resulting from reporting of identical shipments over two or more waterways have been eliminated except that the figures for 1965 and subsequent years represent originated traffic.

Table 7–2 U.S. Coastal and Coastwise Traffic

Year	Net Tons of 2,000 Pounds	Ton Miles
1958	194,050,174	304,770,000,000
⋮	⋮	⋮
1965	201,508,107	302,545,000,000
1966	208,374,966	306,766,000,000
1967	214,646,527	310,429,000,000
1968	214,250,535	304,480,000,000
1969	216,707,773	300,948,000,000
1970	238,440,385	359,784,000,000
1971	242,916,056	360,205,000,000
1972	242,660,087	351,509,000,000
1973	236,794,660	327,649,000,000
1974	233,358,124	322,802,209,000
1975	231,932,437	315,845,946,000
1976	236,278,624	322,932,250,000
1977	248,083,336	343,536,591,000
1978	305,342,824	540,373,236,000

SOURCE: American Waterway Operators Inc., 1981.

Note: This table applies to domestic traffic receiving a carriage over the ocean or the Gulf of Mexico, e.g., New Orleans to Baltimore, New York to Puerto Rico, San Francisco to Hawaii, or Puerto Rico to Hawaii. Traffic between Great Lakes ports and seacoast ports, when having a carriage over the ocean, is also termed coastwise.

Table 7-3   U.S. Inland Water Commerce (1978) (thousands of short tons)

		North Eastern	Atlantic IW*	Gulf IW*	Lower Miss.	Upper Miss.	Ohio and Tributaries	California	Pacific NW	Great Lakes	Total
Self-Propelled	In	9,686	2,612	5,556	279	237	—	4,501	199	—	22,834
	Out	9,686	2,612	5,632	203	237	—	4,501	199	—	22,834
Dry	In	337	1,823	5,017	117	237	—	984	134	—	8,413
	Out	337	1,823	5,010	124	237	—	984	134	—	8,413
Tank	In	9,349	789	539	162	—	—	3,517	65	—	14,421
	Out	9,349	789	622	79	—	—	3,517	65	—	14,421
Non-Self-Propelled	In	58,372	63,672	94,380	139,066	38,405	127,152	8,538	38,629	14,245	582,459
	Out	58,461	63,672	115,761	82,553	75,261	133,794	8,538	38,629	5,791	582,459
Dry	In	9,499	15,594	43,331	89,076	24,191	103,447	1,266	30,983	9,992	327,379
	Out	9,499	15,594	44,009	39,112	64,181	119,929	1,266	30,983	2,807	327,379
Tank	In	48,873	48,077	51,049	49,990	14,214	23,705	7,272	7,646	4,253	255,080
	Out	48,962	48,078	71,752	43,441	11,080	13,865	7,272	7,646	2,984	255,080
Totals	In	68,058	66,284	99,936	139,345	38,642	127,152	13,039	38,828	14,245	605,293
	Out	68,147	66,284	121,393	82,756	75,498	133,794	13,039	38,828	5,791	605,293

SOURCE: American Waterway Operators Inc., 1981.

* Inland Waterways.

Table 7–4 Number of U.S. Towing Vessels and Barges Operated for the Transportation of Freight, 1975–1978

Types of Vessels	1975	1976	1977	1978
Self-Propelled				
Towboats and tugs				
Number of Vessels	4,100	4,240	4,379	4,380
Horsepower	5,088,221	5,585,891	6,161,348	6,390,438
Non-Self-Propelled				
Dry Cargo Barges and Scows				
Number of vessels	21,876	23,164	24,937	24,037
Cargo capacity (net tons)	25,525,996	27,135,336	29,454,921	29,838,851
Tank Barges				
Number of vessels	3,534	3,623	3,770	3,946
Cargo capacity (net tons)	8,201,561	8,510,016	9,519,840	9,467,565
Total Non-Self-Propelled				
Number of vessels	25,410	26,787	28,707	27,983
Cargo capacity (net tons)	33,727,557	35,645,352	38,974,761	39,306,416

SOURCE: U.S. Army Corps of Engineers, Inland Water Transport, Superintendent of Documents, 1979.

Table 7-5 Number of U.S. Towing Vessels and Barges Operated for the Transportation of Freight as of October 1, 1978

Types of Vessels	Mississippi River System and Gulf Intracoastal Waterway	Atlantic, Gulf, and Pacific Coasts	Great Lakes System	Total
Self-Propelled				
Towboats and Tugs				
Number of vessels	2,632	1,602	146	4,380
Horsepower	4,072,634	2,162,459	155,345	6,390,438
Non-Self-Propelled				
Dry Cargo Barges and Scows				
Number of vessels	19,809	4,040	188	24,037
Cargo capacity (net tons)	25,149,335	4,387,597	301,919	29,838,851
Tank Barges				
Number of vessels	3,250	622	74	3,946
Cargo capacity (net tons)	6,717,435	2,595,757	154,373	9,467,565
Total Non-Self-Propelled				
Number of vessels	23,059	4,662	262	27,983
Cargo capacity (net tons)	31,866,770	6,983,354	456,282	39,306,416

SOURCE: U.S. Army Corps of Engineers, Inland Water Transport, Superintendent of Documents, 1979.

Table 7–6 Commercially Navigable Waterways of the United States by Lengths and Depths*

Group	Lengths in Miles of Waterways					
	Under 6 ft	6 to 9 ft	9 to 12 ft	12 to 14 ft	14 ft and Over	Total
Atlantic Coast Waterways	1,426	1,241	584	938	1,581	5,770
Atlantic Intracoastal Waterway— Norfolk, Va. to Key West, Fla.	—	65	65	1,104	—	1,234
Gulf Coast Waterways	2,055	647	1,133	79	378	4,292
Gulf Intracoastal Waterway—St. Marks, Fla., to the Mexican Border	—	—	—	1,137	—	1,137
Mississippi River System	2,020	969	4,957	740	268	8,954
Pacific Coast Waterways	730	498	237	26	2,084	3,575
Great Lakes	45	89	—	8	348	490
All Other Waterways	76	7	—	1	7	91
Total	6,352	3,516	6,976	4,033	4,666	25,543

SOURCE: Department of Transportation, *National Transportation Statistics.*

* The mileages in this table represent the lengths of all navigable channels of the United States, including those improved by the federal government, other agencies, and those which have not been improved but are usable for commercial navigation.

Table 7–7 1978 U.S. Freight Ton Miles by Mode (in millions)

Mode	1978 Ton Miles		Percent
Air carrier	4,371		0.2
Oil pipeline	585,200	p	25.0
Rail	858,105		36.7
Highway	602,000	p	25.7
Inland waterways	290,397		12.4
Total	2,340,073		100.0

SOURCE: Department of Transportation, *National Transportation Statistics.*

p = preliminary.

Table 7–8   Commodity Composition of Shallow-Draft U.S. Waterborne Carriage—1976

	Millions of Tons	*Percent*
Bituminous coal	128.0	24.4
Crude oil	47.5	9.1
Gasoline and fuel oil	103.3	19.7
Other petroleum products	17.6	3.4
Building materials	60.6	11.6
Miscellaneous minerals	17.5	3.3
Chemicals and allied products	31.6	6.0
Primary metal products	7.4	1.4
Farm products	47.8	9.1
Foods and kindred products	9.7	1.9
Marine products	13.6	2.6
Rafted logs	15.3	2.9
Waste and scrap metals	13.2	2.5
All other commodities	10.9	2.1
Total	524.0	100.0

SOURCE: U.S. Army Corps of Engineers, Inland Water Transport, Part 2, 1955 and 1976.

products. The rest consist of coal, grain, building materials, and other goods, as shown in Table 7–8. While energy products (coal and petroleum) constitute more than half the total goods carried, this percentage has declined over the last 20 years.

7.1.   Reasons for Growth of U.S. Inland Water Transportation

The consistent growth of the inland water industry and its participation in U.S. domestic transportation is largely the result of increased productivity resulting from the growing power of tugboats in use. More powerful towboats are used for tows of greater tonnage. This results in lower fuel consumption and decreased use of supplies, labor, and overhead. On the upper Mississippi River, for example, the average tow in 1950 was 1,200 tons of cargo, while in 1976 tows averaged 4,100 tons of cargo. Table 7–9 presents the long-term growth in towboat power.

These larger tows result in significant labor-cost savings. Similarly, improved automation permits effective towboat control with a minimum crew. Larger locks constructed on the Ohio and Mississippi Rivers since the 1950s have eliminated much of the time-consuming process of double-locking.

Revenue ton miles per man hour has increased by 50 percent

Table 7–9   **Average Horsepower per Towboat on U.S. Inland and Intracoastal Waterways**

Jan. 1	Horsepower per Towboat	
	Mississippi River System and Gulf Intracoastal Waterway	Other U.S Inland Waterways
1950	466.7	420.1
1955	551.4	479.2
1960	699.8	593.1
1965	847.6	715.7
1970	990.2	908.3
1975	1,342.2	1,241.0
1976	1,406.9	1,317.4

SOURCE: U.S. Army Corps of Engineers, *Summary of United States Flag Passenger and Cargo Vessels Operating or Available for Operation* (Annual), Waterborne Commerce Statistics Center (New Orleans, Louisiana).

Table 7–10   **U.S. Revenue Ton Miles Carried per Man Hour by Water* and Rail†**

	Class A & B Carriers by Water (Miss. River and Tributaries)	Class I Railroads
1965	4,171.6	445.9
1970	6,487.6	554.6
1974	7,336.4	655.6
1975	6,602.5	644.7

SOURCES: * Interstate Commerce Commission, *Transport Statistics in the United States*, Part 5, "Carriers by Water," and Statement No. 650, *Revenue and Traffic of Class A & B Water Carriers*, respective years.
     † *Moody's Transportation Manual*, Moody's Investors Service, Inc., New York, 1977, pp. A26–A27.

between 1965 and 1975 (as shown in Table 7–10). Comparable data for railways show a similar increase; water transport consistently carries ten times as much per man hour as rail transport.

7.1.1.   The Composition of the U.S. Inland Waterway

The most important issue driving the growth of inland waterway transport is its economics. An industry with a wide ownership distribution, over 1,850 companies are engaged in commercial barge transport on U.S. inland waterways, of which 185 are certified by the Interstate Commerce Commission (ICC) to provide regular service as common carriers, with 31 companies serving shipper contracts and able to operate as both contract and common carriers. The bulk of the industry, though, or about 1,630 companies, operates as contract carriers under contracts exempt from ICC regulation under the Interstate Commerce Acts.

Well over 400 companies with over 30 percent of the total barge capacity, or about 6,800 barges, transport their own goods in private transportation. The total U.S. inland water transport industry comprises over 23,000 barges with a capacity of nearly 32 million tons or a capacity 50 percent larger than that of the U.S. oceangoing fleet (Table 7–5; see also Table 2–2).

Similarly, the combined horsepower of all towboats operating on inland waterways is over 5 million SHP now and therefore nearly 50 percent of that installed in U.S. oceangoing vessels.

The manpower employed in inland water transport is 80,000—nearly four times the number of seafarers employed on U.S. oceangoing vessels. A major reason for the recent rapid growth of inland water transport is its low cost, particularly its low energy cost.

7.1.2. U.S. Great Lakes Domestic Water Transport

Great Lakes shipping is unique in the technology used and method of carriage. The amount of goods carried in U.S. Great Lakes water transport has remained virtually constant over the last 10 years, at 150 million tons per year. Additionally, 60–70 million tons per year are carried in translake and other foreign (mainly between the United States and Canada) transport, 80–85 percent of which involves carriage of iron ore, concentrates, limestone, and coal. The amount of wheat carried is insignificant.

This transport will probably increase in the future as a result of the superior fuel efficiency of Great Lakes shipping, performed by specially designed Great Lake carriers, most of which are self-propelled dry bulk carriers. Interlake locks impose severe beam constraints and less severe length constraints on Great Lakes vessels. Table 7–11 is a summary of the principal commodities carried in U.S. Great Lakes traffic.

Table 7–11 Summary of Principal Commodities Carried in U.S. Great Lakes Domestic Waterborne Commerce (000s of short tons and percentage of total)

Commodity	1972	1973	1974	1975	1976
Iron Ore and concentrates	69,818 (45%)	79,903 (48%)	74,903 (48%)	66,177 (48%)	68,595 (49%)
Limestone	29,509 (19%)	34,000 (20%)	33,210 (21%)	26,653 (19%)	27,546 (20%)
Coal and lignite	25,272 (16%)	23,908 (14%)	22,005 (14%)	21,967 (16%)	21,818 (16%)
Sand, gravel, and crushed stone	5,316 (4%)	5,958 (4%)	5,343 (4%)	4,443 (3%)	3,950 (3%)
Building cement	3,748 (3%)	3,326 (2%)	3,339 (2%)	3,090 (2%)	3,116 (2%)
Distillate fuel oil	3,065 (3%)	2,603 (2%)	2,487 (2%)	1,926 (2%)	2,098 (1%)
Gasoline	2,500 (1%)	2,517 (2%)	1,769 (1%)	1,604 (1%)	1,474 (1%)
Residual fuel oil	2,372 (1%)	2,127 (1%)	2,151 (1%)	2,143 (2%)	2,549 (2%)
Nonmetallic minerals	1,527 (1%)	1,630 (1%)	1,724 (1%)	1,422 (1%)	1,366 (1%)
Wheat	1,400 (1%)	1,385 (1%)	1,107 (1%)	1,455 (1%)	1,528 (1%)
All other commodities	9,315 (6%)	7,786 (5%)	7,246 (5%)	6,208 (5%)	6,273 (4%)
Total	153,842 (100%)	165,143 (100%)	155,284 (100%)	137,088 (100%)	140,313 (100%)
U.S. Great Lakes Domestic and Foreign Waterborne Commerce					
Domestic	153,842 (72%)	165,143 (71%)	155,284 (75%)	137,088 (71%)	140,313 (68%)
Translakes (U.S. and Canada)	44,213 (21%)	51,425 (22%)	42,370 (20%)	46,829 (24%)	53,896 (26%)
Other foreign	15,919 (7%)	15,333 (7%)	9,092 (5%)	9,930 (5%)	11,761 (6%)
Total	213,974 (100%)	231,901 (100%)	206,746 (100%)	193,847 (100%)	205,971 (100%)

SOURCE: U.S. Army Corps of Engineers, Domestic Waterborne Commerce, Superintendent of Documents, 1978.

7.2.   Investment Costs and Revenues of U.S. Inland Water Transport

Private investment in inland water transport during the period 1969–1979 amounted to $3.32 billion, compared to private investment in railways of $31.23 billion. Public investment, on the other hand, was $2.158 billion for water transportation. Practically all public investment was for canal improvement, locks, and navigational aids. A comparative estimate of public investment in railways is not available. The ton miles of transport supplied by these two competing transport systems during this 10-year period was nearly the same— 967 billion for rail and 801 billion for inland water.

Examination of the revenues per ton mile of various transport modes (Table 7–12) reveals that inland water transport costs are about equal to those of oil pipelines, less than 23 percent of rail and 5 percent of those for road transport. Pipelines, on the other hand, are highly specialized and their use requires the movement of large consignments of identical commodities in continuous flow.

Table 7–12   Revenue per Ton Mile of Freight Carried, 1976

Method of Carriage	Mills Per* Ton Mile
Class I Intercity Motor Carriers	99.7
Class I Railroads	22.0
Oil Pipelines	4.1
Classes A & B Carriers by Water—Mississippi River and Tributaries	5.1

SOURCE: Interstate Commerce Commission, Bureau of Economics, *Transport Economics*, Vol. V, No. 1, 1978, p. 11, and Statement No. 650, "Revenue and Traffic of Class A and B Water Carriers," Washington D.C., 1977.

* A mill is 1/10 of a cent, and a ton mile is one ton carried one mile.

7.3.   Inland Water Transport Policy Issues

Consideration of policy issues in inland water transport within the framework of national transportation policy is affected by the modal aspects of national inland water shipping, as well as requirements introduced by interstate commerce and federal power or energy policy.

Many changes have occurred recently in public interest, setting of national priorities, congressional approach, and administrative execution of transport issues. Some historic developments such as defense transport are now no longer relevant. Changes in economic factors and technological capability have introduced new opportunities. Further new opportunities are produced by demand for the transport of goods in bulk or pseudo-bulk carriers and the public, congressional, and administrative desire for less regulation. These changes are of increasing interest as more commodities move in integrated intermodal transportation. Grain, for example, is barged on inland waterways to a port where these same barges are loaded onto a barge-carrying ship.

A major policy problem of major bulk transport modes is limited analytical and conceptual capability and experience in the water resource and transport policy area. This situation exists because Congress has long assumed a direct role in investment decisions, policy strategy formulation, and implementation of modal projects without requiring concerned federal agencies to perform proper evaluations of the public benefits of the projects.

Another problem confronting bulk transport modes is multiple federal agency involvement in inland water transport, ports, shipping, and pipeline transport. Overcoming a long-accepted policy generated by modal and agency separation is becoming increasingly difficult, although some policy coherence is emerging. One difficulty is the functional separation of advocacy and regulation by federal agencies. This includes the functions of various government departments, such as the Departments of Transportation, Interior, Commerce, State, Justice, Health and Human Services, Housing and Urban Development, and such agencies as the Environmental Protection Agency.

There appear to be major conflicts in agency interest and interpretation of function and, as a result, interpretation of national transportation policy. National modal transport policy is generally interpreted by modal advocacy agencies in a narrow sense, and Congress has done little to remove this impediment to effective national transportation policy enactment and implementation although it has often supported modal advocacy by legislation. Because transportation technology and the form of commodities in transport are changing rapidly, and the interdependence of transport modes is increasing, it is imperative for national transportation policy to be defined by a national transportation plan and implemented by related programs.

As noted in Chapter 5, the United States has the world's second largest network of navigable inland waterways. These waterways are largely developed and maintained by the U.S. Army Corps of Engineers and the resulting costs paid for by the federal government. It is claimed that these extensive waterways usually benefit irrigation, flood control, and other water resources. Total federal inland waterway and intracoastal construction expenditures are a fraction of those expended for right of ways of other modes, with local (state, mu-

nicipal, private, etc.) expenditures often exceeding those of the federal government for waterway construction and operations.

The major developments affecting waterway transportation are tied
to the requirements of the rapidly changing environment and method
of operations of the inland water transport industry, such as:

- Changing inland water transport technology and its effects on
  cargo form, cargo handling, and cargo stowage methods;
- Changing economies of inland water transport and resulting
  changes in service demand;
- Increased demand for bulk commodities originating in the major
  U.S. inland waterway basin or its tributaries;
- Improved inland water terminal capacity and resulting inter-
  modal transfer capability; and
- Improvements in material handling capability that allow different
  types of cargoes to be handled efficiently.

As pointed out in Chapter 5, many policy issues emanate from these
developments. The policy issues discussed are all based on or affected
by the above-mentioned developments.

The most important policy issue is the proposed imposition of user
charges. This would have very broad impacts, and can be expected
to materially affect barge transportation costs. Because barge transportation costs are so low, the percentage increase resulting from
user charges would be quite significant. User charges would have
to be calculated on the basis of barge-service cost and, in fact, added
to it.

Another issue is the regulation of nonregulated contract carriers.
Although the regulation is designed to promote regular service, the
very nature of the majority of goods transported on U.S. inland
waterways benefits by the flexibility and low cost of unregulated
carriage.

From the discussion of pertinent inland water transport (IWT)
policy issues, it is apparent that no cohesive national water policy
exists and, concomitantly, no national transport objectives within
which IWT policy issues can be evaluated.

Generally IWT policy develops from decisions on individual issues
and projects. Choices are considered on an economic, political, strategic, environmental, or other basis and seldom on merit alone.
Neither are policy issues resolved on the basis of integrated transport
needs independent of a national transportation policy.

In mid-1981 Congress was considering new, expensive user-charge
legislation for users of inland, coastal, and Great Lakes waterways.
One bill (S.810–H.R.2962) directs the Army Corps of Engineers to
impose user charges "sufficient to recover the full cost of operation
and maintenance (O&M) of locks, dams, and maintained channels,

including amortized costs of new construction on inland waterways." A similar bill (S.809–H.R.2959) applies the same philosophy on users of coastal ports and deep-draft channels. There appears to be great pressure to single out domestic users on the issue of full cost recovery for federal government–provided facilities and services.

7.4. The Regulation of Inland Domestic Water Carriers

Regulation of carriers by water proceeded piece-meal until 1940. The original Interstate Commerce Act[1] applied

> *to any common carrier or carriers engaged in the transportation of passengers or property wholly by railroad, or partly by water, when both are used, under a common control, management or arrangement, for a continuous carriage of shipment. . . .*

More than practical continuity in transportation was required.[2] If the common arrangement was demonstrated, only the traffic transported by water under the common arrangement was regulated.[3]

The Hepburn Act[4] gave the ICC the power to prescribe through-routes utilizing different railroads or railroads and water carriers. In 1912 the Panama Canal Act[5] added a power to prescribe through-routes, the power to require physical connection between railroads and water carriers, an absolute prohibition against railroads owning carriers operating through the Panama Canal, and a prohibition against railroads controlling any water carrier unless the ICC approved of the control.

Maximum rate filing for common carriers by water in interstate or foreign commerce on the high seas or the Great Lakes was introduced in the Shipping Act of 1916.[6] The agency preceding the Federal Maritime Commission (FMC) received the rate filing.

The Transportation Act of 1920[7] included a declaration of support for water transportation[8] which led to the development of a "demonstration" barge line operated by the government.[9] In 1928 Congress provided that common carriers by water should obtain a certificate of public convenience and necessity before engaging in operations on the Mississippi or its tributaries. Once a carrier was certified, the ICC would require other carriers to connect with it.[10]

Beginning in 1933[11] common and contract carriers-by-water operating through the Panama Canal, between U.S. points, were required to file actual rates with the FMC. The requirement was extended to coastwise and Great Lakes carriers in 1938, with the FMC obtaining the power to set maximum or minimum rates.[12]

The First Annual Report (1886) of the ICC recommended that

regulation of water carriers require them to publish and adhere to fixed rates so that the railroads would know the competitor's rates.[13] Congress, however, waited more than 50 years to pass legislation subjecting domestic water carriers to regulation.

In 1940 Part III was added to the Interstate Commerce Act to regulate all interstate carriers by water (comprising common carriers and contract carriers), except those regulated as railroads because controlled by railroads.[14] Prior laws regulating interstate commerce by water carriers were repealed only if inconsistent with Part III.[15] The ICC now regulates the entry of carriers into the business, areas of operation, mergers, rates, and through-routes.

One author has commented on the addition of Part III as follows:[16]

The circumstances surrounding the enactment of the statute were similar to those leading up to the Motor Carrier Act of 1935; the debate centered about the question of how far water carriers should be regulated in order to protect railroads from unregulated competition.

A District Court declared that the purposes of regulating transportation by water were to preserve the earning capacity of the carrier and to prevent ruinous competition.[17] Here the Court borrowed words the Supreme Court had used in explaining the purposes of regulation under earlier portions of the Interstate Commerce Act.

Also added in 1940 was a statement of national transportation policy which was to guide the ICC in all its decisions. The policy is, in part,[18] "to provide for fair and impartial regulation of all modes of transportation subject to the provisions of this Act, so administered as to recognize and preserve the inherent advantages of each." This policy prompted the Supreme Court to find that the purpose of the 1940 Act, together with the old laws, was "to provide a completely integrated interstate regulatory system over motor, railroad, and water carriers."[19]

7.4.1. Extent of Federal Regulation

Significant exemptions from Part III of the 1940 Interstate Commerce Act limit the extent of federal regulation. Some figures from the 83rd Annual Report of the ICC for 1969 demonstrate this and suggest the importance of water transportation in the transportation system.

In 1967 13 percent of intercity ton miles carried over water was federally regulated, compared with 36 percent carried by motor, 86 percent carried by pipeline, and 100 percent for ton miles carried by rail and air; only railroads carried more ton miles. While the regulated water ton miles were less than half the regulated motor ton miles, the unregulated water ton miles alone were more than all the motor ton miles. Ton miles by water included coastal, inland waterways, intercoastal, and Great Lakes traffic.[20] On the inland waterways and Great Lakes taken separately, it has been estimated that up to 95 percent of the ton miles carried are exempt from federal regulation.[21]

With such significant exemptions the ICC is not busy regulating water carriers: in fiscal 1969 the Commission closed 7,810 cases, of which 26 involved water carriers. Out of 256,000 common carrier tariffs received, only 4,000 were from water carriers and 726 were from pipeline companies; of 20,000 tariffs criticized, 165 were from water carriers and 55 were from pipeline companies; and of 3,200 tariffs rejected, only eight were from water carriers and nine were from pipeline companies.[22]

As of June 30, 1969, 92 water carriers and 96 oil pipelines were required to file annual and periodic reports and to follow the uniform system of accounts. An additional 103 water carriers with less than $100,000 in gross revenues were required to file annual reports, but they were not subject to the uniform system of accounts.[23] The latter figure suggests an industry with a huge number of small operations. Revenues of water carriers with revenues over $100,000 constitute 1.4 percent of operating revenues of all surface carriers for 1968; their share of investment in operating property and equipment was only 0.8 percent. Pipelines accounted for 4.4 percent of the revenue but 9.8 percent of the investment.[24]

7.5. ICC Regulation of Domestic Carriers by Water—Overview

Domestic water carriers operate between points in the United States in five general geographic areas of service—along the inland waterways, along either the Gulf or Atlantic intracoastal waterway, between ports along one coast (coastwide trade), on the Great Lakes, and on intercoastal routes via the Panama Canal.[25] This classification is introduced mainly for clarity in discussing different types of service. Where the type of operation has an effect on the regulations imposed, it will be noted.

The Interstate Commerce Commission (ICC) regulates interstate transportation of goods by water, indicated by a movement from a point in one state to a point in another state (except between Alaska or Hawaii and the mainland).[26] Interstate transportation includes transportation on a route which merely passes through the waters of another state,[27] on a route from one state to another state via a foreign port,[28] or on a through-route from state to state even though the water portion is entirely within one state.[29] However, the ICC has no authority to regulate intrastate rates, even if they discriminate against interstate commerce.[30] The ICC also regulates movement, within the United States, of goods in foreign commerce, either prior to trans-shipment for a foreign port, or subsequent to such trans-shipment at the U.S port after movement from a foreign port.[31] The FMC regulates the transportation of goods between a foreign port and the United States.[32]

Since ICC jurisdiction over goods in foreign commerce requires a finding of trans-shipment, the use of lighter-aboard-ship (LASH) barges within the United States posed a regulatory problem. LASH barges are carried fully loaded aboard a "mother ship" from a foreign port to the United States, then lowered into the water to be towed to inland destinations.[33] The ICC claimed grounds that the effect of lowering the barges into the water was the same as trans-shipment by transfer of lading.[34] In upholding the ICC's determination, the District Court[35] observed that technological advances should not defeat the ICC's jurisdiction.

7.5.1. Common vs. Contract Carriers

Regulated water carriers fall into two classes—common carriers and contract carriers. Section 310[36] generally precludes a carrier from being both. As previously noted, however, the greater portion of transportation by water is exempt from regulation.

A water common carrier is defined as "a person holding itself out to the general public to provide water transportation for compensation."[37] The critical factor is that the carrier must be willing to engage in transportation for anyone to be judged a common carrier. A regulated common carrier is issued a "certificate of public convenience and necessity" and is thereafter required to provide transportation "on reasonable request."[38]

The contract carrier, on the other hand, does not make his services generally available to the public. He engages in transportation for compensation (other than as a common carrier) of passengers or property in interstate or foreign commerce under individual contracts or agreements.[39] "Transportation includes furnishing a vessel, for compensation, to a person not a carrier regulated by the Act, unless the ICC determines that regulation of such person is not necessary to effectuate the National Transportation Policy (NTP), resulting in his receiving an exemption."[40] The exemption may later be revoked by the ICC, if necessary. Vessel furnishing is considered distinct from other contract carrier operations; authority to furnish vessels to noncarriers does not include authority to engage in other contract carrier operations.[41] The authority to engage in contract carrier operations is embodied in a permit containing a description of the authorized operations, together with any restrictions.

Contract carriers of cargo serve only a small number of shippers (rather than the general public) under individual contracts (rather than fixed tariffs) on an irregular or as-needed basis (rather than on a schedule). They frequently deal only in full-cargo shipments for one shipper per voyage or large shipments for a very few shippers. Since the distinctions between common carriers and contract carriers are not precise, restrictions may be placed on the contract carrier's permit to preclude it from competing with the common carriers,[42] or the authority may be denied altogether if the existing carriers can provide the needed service.[43]

7.5.2. Exempt Operations

Much of the domestic transportation by water is exempt from regulation. Some exceptions are absolute, while others are within the discretion of the ICC.

7.5.2.1. Absolute Exemptions

Two absolute exemptions exist which are available to any carrier; a third is available only to contract carriers passing through international waters. A brief description of each follows.

Bulk Commodities. Section 303(b)[44] provides that transportation of certain commodities carried without wrappers or containers in 1939[45] is exempt from regulation unless the route followed passes through the Panama Canal. The exemption is not lost if other commodities are carried at the same time, although the other commodities are still regulated. "Bulk commodities are usually fungible goods such as grains, coal, or ore. Any water carrier can engage in the transportation of bulk commodities throughout the entire inland waterways without requesting any grant of authority from the ICC."[46] Additional bulk commodities are alumina[47] and phosphate rock.[48]

Liquid Cargoes. Section 303(d)[49] exempts transportation by water of liquid cargoes in tank vessels designed and used exclusively for such service and approved by the Coast Guard.

Great Lakes Bulk Commodities. Section 303(c)[50] exempts transportation by water of not more than three commodities in bulk (not restricted as in 303(b)) on a nonoceangoing vessel through waters made international by treaty. This provision applies to the Great Lakes.[51]

7.5.2.2. Discretionary Exemptions

Four additional exemptions are discretionary with the ICC.
Discontinuous Transport. Section 303(g)(1)[52] permits the ICC to

exempt transportation within a harbor that is not part of a continuous through-movement in interstate commerce.

Private Carriers. Section 303(h)[53] permits the ICC to exempt a carrier that transports only property of the person controlling the carrier. (Such a carrier is also known as a private carrier.)

Noncompetitive Contract Carriage. Section 303(e)[54] permits the ICC (in accordance with the declared policy of Congress) to exempt transportation by water by contract carriers,[55] which is not actually and substantially competitive with transportation by any common carrier because of the inherent nature of the commodities transported—that is, their requirement for special equipment or transportation in bulk. In granting this exemption, the ICC need not consider its effect on the national transportation policy under which competition is to be encouraged.[56] This exemption may be revoked by the ICC, but the ICC must authorize the previously exempt transportation without further proceeding if such authority is sought.[57]

By order,[58] the ICC has exempted all transportation of oil field equipment in Gulf states' marshlands. A District Court approved the exemption of "transportation by water of contractor's equipment, materials, and supplies incidental to and used with such equipment in construction work on the Mississippi River and its tributaries. . . ."[59]

In another case, the carrier proposed to carry regulated cargoes on the decks of vessels carrying petroleum products in tanks, which meant losing the Section 303(d) exemption. However, the transportation of the petroleum products was exempted under §303(e)(2) as being not substantially competitive with transportation by any common carrier by rail or motor because transportation by water was so cheap that the other common carriers were, as a practical matter, excluded from that trade.[60]

The ICC elaborated somewhat on the criteria for exemption in *Bulk Food Carriers, Inc.,—Exemption Application.*[61] An exemption was granted for the bulk transportation of phosphate rock from Florida to California,[62] even though the inherent nature of the commodity (that is, a requirement for special equipment or shipment in bulk) did not demonstrate that shipment by the protesting railroads was infeasible. But from evidence of the unwillingness of the railroads to provide this service,[63] the ICC inferred that transportation by rail was impractical or unattractive and therefore that the proposed service by water would not be actually or substantially competitive.[64]

Vessel Furnishers. Section 302(e)[65] permits the ICC to exempt from regulation the furnishing of a vessel when the user uses the vessel to transport its own property and regulation thereof is not necessary to effectuate the national transportation policy. The purpose of regulating vessel furnishers is to prevent shippers from using the pool of vessels available from the furnishers to enforce unreasonable demands on the common and contract carriers,[66] or to prevent the vessel furnishers from offering rates low enough to attract shippers away from the regulated carriers.[67] Since vessel furnishing should be exempted only when the person obtaining the vessel could not use it in substitution for (or competition with) common or contract carriers, the criteria for exempting vessel furnishers should be quite similar to the criteria for exempting contract carriers under §303(e)(2).[68] However, under §302(e), the effect on the national transportation policy must be assessed; either a permit or an exemption must be obtained[69] and willful failure to obtain a permit subjects a person to criminal sanctions under §317(a).[70]

7.6. ICC Regulation of Entry

Carrier entry regulations vary according to the type of service to be provided by the prospective entrant. The following sections describe the applicable regulations governing entry of contract carriers, common carriers, dual operators, and temporary services.

7.6.1. *Common Carrier Certification*

A person desiring to be a common carrier in interstate commerce must apply for a certificate of public convenience and necessity. He bears the burden of convincing the ICC that he is able to perform the proposed service and that the service is or will be required by the present or future public convenience and necessity.[71] A competitor is entitled to intervene in these proceedings to oppose the grant of authority by disputing the showing necessary to entitle the applicant to a certificate.[72] The granting of a certificate was found[73] not to be subject to the National Environment Policy Act (NEPA) of 1969.[74]

Rarely will an applicant be found unqualified simply for lack of financial resources.[75] Even if an applicant holds authorities under which operations are not being conducted (dormant authorities), this does not preclude a finding by the ICC that an applicant is willing and able to conduct the proposed service.[76]

Litigation usually erupts over the contents of the term "public convenience and necessity." Probably the most quoted enumeration of factors considered in making findings of public convenience of necessity appears in *Nashua Motor Express, Inc. v. United States:*[77]

> (I)nadequacy of present service is not a term which is convertible with that of public convenience and necessity but is, rather, only one element to be considered in arriving at the broader determination of public

convenience and necessity. . . . Other elements of importance appear
to be the desirability of different kinds of service, and the desirability
of improved service.

These factors will be elaborated on in the order given to convey the pivotal considerations in a particular case.

The applicant may attempt to demonstrate that the present service is inadequate[78] or nonexistent.[79] The ICC may be very liberal in granting authority to operate on newly completed waterways on the grounds that it can remove any surplus of authorities by revoking dormant authorities.[80]

If there is no showing that the present service is inadequate, the application for a new service is not necessarily denied.[81] This is true even if the proposed service does not constitute an improvement over existing service.[82] A certificate need not be denied merely because there is adequate existing rail and motor service.[83]

It is stated frequently that adequate present service cannot preclude award of a certificate because that would read "convenience" out of the statute.[84] The ICC may consider future shipping needs[85] and grant applications without finding that existing carriers would be unable to expand to meet future demand.

The ICC has broad discretion to determine the public interest when looking at the total situation. It may decide that future shipping needs should be assured, not left uncertain.[86] The ICC may also consider the argument that providing quality service by water will lead to the development and location of industry along the waterway, thus ensuring the future demand necessary to justify the present grant of authority.[87]

Of course, in a given situation, the applicant may be unable to prove the need for his service,[88] or the protesting carriers may claim that apparent inadequacy of present service is due to operating conditions which could not be affected by authorizing another carrier to operate in the area.[89]

The ICC, not the courts, determines how much competition is in the public interest.[90] A certified water carrier may not complain about competition that arises through granting a certificate to an applicant; the certificate grants no exclusive right to use the waterway[91] nor immunity against competition.[92] A certificate may be granted if it is in the public interest to do so, even if existing carriers will have to share the tonnage with the applicant.[93] On the other hand, "(E)xisting carriers are entitled to transport all of the traffic they can handle adequately, efficiently, economically without the competition of a new service in the considered territory."[94] (This may only be another way of saying that in the quoted case the applicant failed to show a need for the service.) Increasing competition may be one factor in favor of granting a certificate.[95] Allegations of antitrust violations are disposed of by ruling on the basic issues of the applicant's fitness to conduct the service and the public need for it.[96]

A certificate may be approved, in part, because the applicant proposes a different kind of service.[97] The proposed service may be different simply because it is provided by a water carrier; in such a case, shippers may be found to be entitled to the "inherent advantages" of transportation by water,[98] even where other transportation is available, if a need for transportation by water is shown.[99] The major advantage of transportation by water is low transportation charges.[100] If this were the only reason for granting a certificate, it might be necessary to actually inquire into comparative rates.[101] Where there are other reasons for the grant of authority, such an inquiry is not necessary.[102]

A carrier proposal to render more efficient[103] service or some other improved service[104] may be a factor favoring award of a certificate. The decision as to whether a proposed service is economically sound is made by management in the first instance; an application need not be denied merely because the service is of unproven economic soundness where a need for the service has been shown.[105]

Where a certificate is sought, it will not be denied because the operations resemble the operations of a contract carrier since the applicant will have to hold himself out to performance transportation for the general public, not just the shipper he currently has in mind.[106]

The certificate granted specifies the areas to be served and the conditions of operation. The ICC may impose conditions or limitations on the carrier's operations, but may not restrict the carrier in adding equipment or in extending its operations to include uncompleted portions of waterways if it is authorized to operate on the completed portions.[107]

The type of service permitted is specified according to the type of equipment used. If the carrier tows its own barges, it is engaged in freighting[108] and its authority will read (in part), "by non-self-propelled vessels with separate towing vessels." If, however, the carrier operates by towing only barges owned by shippers, it is engaged in general towage. This is a different service and must be specifically authorized in the certificate.[109] Certificates routinely include both authorities.

"There is no requirement in Part III that a water carrier must own or actually operate vessels. The statutory requirement is use of the vessel irrespective of ownership."[110] Thus a person is engaged in transportation by towage if he either charters tugs to tow shippers' barges or hires space in another carrier's tow. Such a person is a carrier and such hiring of towage is not unlawful.[111]

7.6.2. Contract Carriers

An applicant desiring to conduct contract carrier operations must obtain a permit to operate as a contract carrier in a certain area.[112] The applicant must demonstrate his entitlement to the permit by showing that he is able to perform the proposed service, that the service is in the public interest, and that approval is consistent with the National Transportation Policy.[113] This last showing is not required of a common carrier, although it may not be much different from a showing of need for the service.

In the case of an application by a subsidiary of U.S. Steel, which desired to transport its steel to Cape Canaveral for use in the space program, the following general summary of contract carrier applications appears.[114]

> *Under the contract carrier provision of Part III, applications have generally been denied upon showing that existing carriers could provide the shipper with the type of service it requires. See* Indian Towing Company, Inc. Contract Carrier Application *(309 ICC 473 (1970)). On the other hand, contract carriers by water have been granted extensions of authority in cases of shipper-owned carriers which gear their services to their parent companies in the interest of efficiency and economy.* Ohio Barge Line, Inc., Extension—Pig Tin, 285 ICC 5. *Contract Carrier authorities also have been granted where the showing is made that low-cost transportation would be provided by the applicant and that an applicant's equipment is especially adapted to the shippers' needs and protestant has not furnished a reasonably adequate service.* Marine Transport Lines, Inc. Extension—Los Angeles, 285 ICC 655, Hanson-Towing Company Contract Carrier Application, 311 ICC 609, McGehee Contract Carrier Applications, 285 ICC 107.

The permit granted specifies the scope of the business permitted, but no condition in the permit may limit the carrier's right to substitute or change contracts, or to add to his service or equipment within the scope of the permit and as business requires.[115]

7.6.3. Dual Operations

Section 310[116] prohibits any carrier or person controlling, controlled by, or under common control with such carrier from holding both a certificate and a permit unless the ICC finds that holding both authorizations is consistent with the public interest and the National Transportation Policy (NTP). Operations as both a common carrier and a contract carrier are called dual operations.

Such operations are consistent with the public interest and the NTP when they are not competitive with each other[117] or are conducted separately,[118] or when the contract carrier operations are exempted under 303(e)(2).[119] Possible conflict with §310 may be prevented through certificate restrictions.[120] Even if the reasons are not given for the grant of permission to engage in dual operations, the authorization is subject to the retained right of the ICC to reconsider the decision if a change brings about "an improper competitive situation, discrimination, or preference."[121]

7.6.4. Temporary Operations

If there is an immediate or urgent need for service[122] by a common carrier or a contract carrier in a given area, the ICC may authorize such service for up to 180 days without a hearing. If such authority is granted, there is no presumption that permanent authority will thereafter be granted.[123] However, the operations may continue until the ICC rules on an application for permanent authority which was submitted in a timely manner.[124]

7.6.5. Dormant Authorities and Revocation

No authorization from the ICC is necessary for a carrier by water to cease operations. Of course, if a common carrier ceases operations, it violates its duty to provide transportation on reasonable request and, therefore, 305(a).[125] No penalty appears to attach to this violation, however. Thus, a certificate or permit may very easily become dormant. "Operations under dormant rights may be revived by the holder at any time."[126]

Under the regulations, dormant rights may not be transferred unless the dormancy is for reasons beyond the carrier's control.[127] Under a 1965 statutory change[128] the ICC has acquired specific authority to cancel dormant authorities.[129]

7.7. Merger and Transfer of Authority

Regulations governing mergers and transfer of operating authority have far-reaching effects on the size of inland waterway operators, the intensity of competition among them, and the efficiency and adequacy of service provided to users. In the following sections we examine the various criteria used by the ICC when deciding on permit transfers and intramodal or intermodal mergers.

7.7.1. Transfer to Noncarriers

The transfer of a certificate or permit under Section 312[130] to any person who is not already a carrier is largely governed by regulations[131] issued to protect the public interest and ensure compliance with the law and regulations. If the transaction involves two carriers, different standards under §5(2)[132] apply. The primary showing necessary under the regulations is that[133]

(T)he proposed transferee is fit, willing, and able properly to perform the service authorized by the certificate or permit sought to be transferred and to conform to the provisions of Part III of the Interstate Commerce Act and the requirements, rules, and regulations of the Commission thereunder.

Transactions under Section 312 are usually routine, such as transfer from a subsidiary corporation to its parent.[134] One ill-fated transfer from an individual to an allegedly formed corporation was also made under this section, however.[135] Failure to conform to the regulations concerning such transfer, if deemed an attempt to evade the regulations, may lead to denial of the transfer on the grounds that the proposed transferee has been shown unable to conform to the regulations of the ICC.[136]

If operations have been suspended under the certificate or permit to be transferred, the transfer will be approved only on the additional showings that the suspension was beyond the holder's control and that the water-carrier operations under the authority to be transferred will be consistent with the public interest.[137]

7.7.2. Intramodal Merger

If a proposed transaction will result in control or common ownership of two or more carriers, the transaction must be approved by the ICC under §5(2);[138] if it is not, the control or power to exercise control is unlawful.[139] The ICC may approve the transaction together with such conditions as it may find reasonable if it is found to be in the public interest.[140] Four statutory factors are to be included in the determination of whether to approve the transaction:[141]

1. The effect on adequate transportation service to the public;
2. The effect on the public interest of including or not including other area carriers;
3. The total fixed charges to result; and
4. The interest of the carrier employees.

The term "carrier" (for the purposes of §5(2)) includes railroads, express companies, sleeping car companies, motor carriers, and water carriers subject to the Act.[142] Mergers in which at least one carrier is a water carrier are discussed here. If all the carriers involved are water carriers, the transaction is referred to as "intramodal"; if at least one carrier is not a water carrier, the transaction is termed "intermodal." A water carrier may have been exempted by the ICC

from regulation but it is still a carrier subject to regulation so that
the acquisition of control by another carrier is subject to §5(2).[143]

Certain equipment arrangements between carriers are not subject
to §5(2). Purchase or operation of a carrier's equipment is not subject
to ICC approval as long as the transaction does not put the other
carrier out of business;[144] but if the effect of the transaction, whether
in equipment or otherwise, is to put a competitor out of business
or otherwise effect control over two or more carriers, approval under
§5(2) is required.[145]

In a merger of two large water carriers[146] into Union Mechling
Corp., the ICC commented on their approval criteria as follows:[147]

> *Among the factors to be considered in determining the question of
> consistency with the public interest are (1) the needs of the shippers,
> (2) the ability of the carrier to provide the proposed service, (3) the
> effects of the proposed service on existing carriers, and (4) the economic
> soundness of the water carrier industry as a result of the approval of
> the transaction.*

Thereupon, the ICC made the following findings: that Union Mechling was financially able to meet the fixed costs arising from the
transaction;[148] that the merger would result in substantial savings;[149]
that the merged corporation would provide more frequent sailings
than either presently provided;[150] that it was unimportant that the
transaction involved the merger of two financially healthy carriers;[151]
that there would be no substantial reduction in total transportation
service in the affected region;[152] and that on balance, including the
competitive effect of a larger carrier, the transaction was consistent
with the National Transportation Policy (NTP). The last point bears
some elaboration.

Despite the large size of the resulting carrier, in an industry where
two constituents were part of the "Big Five,"[153] little was said directly
about the effect of the merger on the remaining water carriers. The
ICC noted that the competitive effect would be just one factor to
be weighed against the advantages of improved service, safer operation, and reduced costs to determine whether the consolidation
would help effectuate the National Transportation Policy (NTP).
While carte blanche to approve any merger was not granted, the
ICC felt that the transportation acts and the NTP contemplated
national systems of a limited number of entities in each mode, adding
that,[154] "A reduction in intramodal competition and an increase in
the size of those carriers which survive consolidation was contemplated." It does not appear that "bigness" is much of a bar to intramodal mergers of water carriers.

In intramodal mergers of motor carriers[155] and railroads,[156] the
Supreme Court explicitly said that the ICC need not deny a §5(2)

application, even if it could be found to violate the antitrust laws, if the merger is in the public interest. The anticompetitive effect is one factor to weigh in determining the public interest. One justification advanced by the Court for not giving antitrust considerations controlling weight is that rates are regulated thus reducing one of the evils that antitrust laws sought to attack.[157]

7.7.3. Intermodal Merger

If the acquisition is intermodal, the findings discussed above in the intramodal situation remain valid. It appears, however, that the ICC takes much more seriously the question of the anticompetitive effect in an intermodal than in an intramodal merger. If this apparent difference actually exists and is a principled distinction, it probably stems from the fear that an intermodal merger might operate to the detriment of the "inherent advantage" of the constituent modes, contrary to the National Transportation Policy. Thus, while saying that acquisition of a motor carrier by a water carrier is not subject to antitrust complaints, the ICC was careful to consider whether the transaction would seriously disrupt competition by improving either company's finances in an anticompetitive manner, by eliminating a service competitive with one mode, or by instituting a coordinated service to the detriment of competition in one mode or the other.[158]

If either a water carrier or a motor carrier is the acquiring carrier, it need only show that acquisition is consistent with the public interest.[159] However, if the acquiring carrier is a railroad, the applicant must affirmatively show that the public interest will be served by approving the merger and that competition (in the mode acquired) will not be reduced.[160] This policy is seen to reflect long-standing congressional concern that the railroads not be permitted to dominate the other modes of transportation.[161] With regard to transportation by water, this policy first found expression in the Panama Canal Act of 1912, one provision of which prohibited a railroad or pipeline company from controlling a water carrier utilizing the Panama Canal.[162] Another provision permitted any railroad or pipeline company to control any water carrier not utilizing the Panama Canal with which it does or may compete. Permission would be granted if it appeared that the railroad would not prevent the water carrier from operating in the public interest and that approval would not reduce competition on the water route.[163]

Shortly after the passage of the Panama Canal Act, the ICC forced eastern railroads to give up their control of boats plying the Great Lakes.[164] The ICC believed that the railroad-dominated lines were stifling competition, and that divestiture would revive competition.

One source cites an ICC study which concluded that not only did the decision fail to revive competition, but it also resulted in a substantial decline in the package freight service on the Great Lakes. This source goes on to point out that the ICC frequently did permit railroad control of water carriers; in these cases, control had the support of shippers and other interested groups.[165]

In 1962 the ICC denied the application of the Illinois Central and Southern Railroads to jointly control John I. Hay Co., a barge line.[166] The ICC was not satisfied that control of Hay by the railroads would not reduce competition. Since the explanation of how competition might be reduced is not entirely consistent, the case may help illustrate a strong aversion to railroad control of water carriers. On the other hand, the ICC noted that the barge routes were substantially parallel to the rail routes and inferred from the evidence that the operation would be conducted to maximize all-rail routes; this finding appears to explain the decision.[167] On the other hand, the ICC expressed solicitude for Hay's competitors by suggesting that Hay's access to capital and the larger sales force provided by affiliation with the railroads would potentially reduce competition by driving Hay's competitors out of business.[168] This apparent inconsistency is not entirely inappropriate insofar as it indicates the railroads' failure to relieve the ICC's doubts concerning the effect of the transaction on competition; the decision may indicate, however, how heavy a burden this can be.

In 1972, however, the ICC authorized Southern Railway to operate a subsidiary to ship coal from new mines by barge via the Ohio and Tennessee rivers and by rail from Sheffield, Alabama to landlocked utility companies.[169] The ICC ruled that permission would be granted unless: (1) the railroad and the controlled carrier served two or more common points; and (2) the two carriers do, or would but for common ownership, compete for the same traffic. The ICC found that there were no facilities for loading railroad cars at the mine; interline railroad service[170] in this case was not available and therefore the two carriers did not serve two common points. The ICC also found that if an all-rail route was established, it would be unlikely to be competitive with the water-rail route, satisfying the second part of the test.[171]

It should not be surprising that hearings on repeal of §5(16) provoked adverse comments from the representatives of common carriers by water.[172] One statement was careful to distinguish integrated transportation from common ownership of several modes of transportation.[173]

In sum, operating authority may be transferred to a noncarrier merely by showing that the transferee is able to lawfully provide service. If two or more regulated carriers combine, the result must be consistent with the public interest, and anticompetitive effect is merely one factor in considering the result. Railroad control of any other mode of transportation may not be approved except on an express finding that competition in the other mode will not be reduced.

7.8.   Rate Regulation

The rates of common carriers by water are regulated much like those of other carriers subject to the Rate Regulation Act. The common carrier must provide transportation for just and reasonable charges, all unjust and unreasonable charges being unlawful.[174] Discrimination against persons, ports, connecting carriers, and so forth is forbidden, but lower rates than another carrier are not discrimination against such other carrier.[175] Rates may not be lower for a longer than for a shorter distance over the same route unless the lower rates are authorized by the ICC and are compensatory.[176] Tariffs showing all charges must be filed with the ICC and the carrier may not charge other than the lawful, filed rates; but the ICC may reject a tariff rendering it void and unlawful.[177] Complaints of unlawful rates may be heard by the ICC which may then prescribe the lawful rate, or maximum or minimum rates.[178] Any new rate may be suspended for not more than seven months to permit investigation, but it goes into effect thereafter, whether or not the investigation is concluded.[179]

In prescribing rates and regulations relating thereto,[180]

> "(T)he Commission shall give due consideration, among other factors, to the effect of rates upon the movement of traffic by the carrier or carriers for which the rates are prescribed; to the need, in the public interest, of adequate and efficient water transportation service at the lowest cost consistent with the furnishing of such service; and to the need of revenues sufficient to enable water carriers, under honest, economical, and efficient management, to provide such service."

In ruling on rates, the ICC may not take into consideration any evidence of the value of the carrier's goodwill, earning power, or certificate.[181]

Contract carriers are required to establish reasonable minimum rates.[182] The ICC may require that actual contracts be filed with it,[183] but it has declined to do so.[184] The ICC may prescribe a minimum charge if a minimum rate contravenes the National Transportation Policy (NTP) and may suspend a minimum rate for seven months to permit a hearing.[185]

7.8.1. Intermodal Routes and Rates

The ICC has some statutory guidance with respect to through-routes by rail and water, the division of rates over through-routes, and competitive rates in different modes.

Common carriers by water must establish through-routes with other water carriers and with railroads; railroads must also establish through-routes with water carriers.[186] If there is a through-route, a joint rate may be (but need not be) charged which is less than the sum of the several local rates over the route travelled.[187] If the carriers do not establish through-routes on their own, the ICC may order them to establish them and may order establishment of joint rates over those routes when they are considered to be in the public interest.[188] Carriers are also required to provide the facilities for interchange of traffic without preferring some connecting carriers over others.[189] Under part of the Panama Canal Act, the ICC can order the establishment of a physical connection between a railroad and a common carrier by water.[190]

The problems that common carriers by water have had in establishing through-routes with railroads and joint rates over those through-routes was summed up by the Supreme Court: "This (case) . . . is but another episode in the long and continued struggle between the railroads and competing barge lines."[191]

The conflict between water carriers and railroads over joint routes takes many forms. The first problem a water carrier faces is the establishment of a through-route. Of course, a railroad may not refuse to establish a through-route with a water carrier, but railroads have attempted to discourage the establishment or use of through-routes by other devices. The Pennsylvania Railroad interchanged cars with Seatrain for carriage to Havana and back, but refused permission for use of its cars when Seatrain announced a service between New Jersey and Louisiana via Havana. The ICC, under its power to prescribe through-routes, ordered the interchange of railroad cars with Seatrain. The Supreme Court sustained the order, declaring in passing that the National Transportation Policy (NTP) required the interchange lest the inherent advantage of Seatrain's service be lost.[192]

Even if there is a through-route, the railroad may, by lowering the all-rail through-rate, and holding up the rate for the rail portion of a barge-rail rate, attempt to make the barge-rail rate unattractive. When the ICC in such a situation dismissed the barge lines' request for establishment of a joint barge-rail rate (i.e. lower than the sum of the local rates between the points served), the Supreme Court ruled that the ICC must establish a joint rate under §307(d) whenever a joint rate (the all-rail rate) is used "to favor rail carriers over carriers by water and to deprive the latter of their 'inherent advantages.' "[193]

In prescribing a joint rate, the ICC must preserve the inherent advantages of each mode, including cost advantage. A differential between local and through rates may not discriminate against connecting carriers unless justified by different costs.[194] But barge rates lower than railroad rates because of the inferior service by barge do not constitute unlawful discrimination against railroads, if the rates are compensatory.[195]

Grain shipped from Chicago to New York by rail arrives in Chicago by rail, barge, and lake steamer. When the railroads were unable to discourage barge traffic by charging higher rates for ex-barge grain,[196] they sought permission (under §4)[197] to charge a lower rate for transporting grain to Kankakee (and then to New York) than for transporting grain to Chicago (and then New York). The purpose was to lower the all-rail rate to New York to the level of the barge-rail rate via Chicago. The Supreme Court found that the ICC's order granting §4 relief was unsupported by the record and erroneously arrived at because the ICC failed to consider whether the rates violated other sections of the Rate Regulation Act or the National Transportation Policy (NTP).[198]

Historically, then, it has at times been difficult for water carriers to establish through-routes with railroads and to obtain nondiscriminatory joint rates with the railroads.

When two different modes of transportation are competing for the same traffic, the ICC has the problem of defining what its objectives should be in assessing the evidence supporting a rate filing. Section 15a(3)[199] was added in 1958 because the railroads felt that the ICC had maintained railroad rates at an artifically high level to prevent competing modes from being driven out of business.[200] This section provides in part:

> *Rates of a carrier shall not be held up to a particular level to protect the traffic of any other mode of transportation, giving due consideration to the objectives of the National Transportation Policy declared in this Act.*

Dissatisfied with ICC activity under §15a(3), the Congress in 1976 amended[201] the section to make it inapplicable to railroads and added new §§15a(4)[202] and (5)[203] to apply to railroads. In addition, new §1(5)(b)[204] redefines the reasonable rates for railroads.

Taken together, the amendments appear to wipe out a history of deciding intermodal competitive rate cases by reference to the inherent cost and service advantages of each mode and to whether those advantages were destroyed by the proposed rates. The Senate Committee expressed its desire that the changes have this effect.[205]

As a result of the changes, the ICC is to consider the competitive effect of the rate with respect to shippers, commodities, ports, and the like and not with respect to other modes of transportation.[206] A railroad rate that covers variable costs will not usually be considered unreasonably low. Therefore, it appears that railroads may cut their rates to compete with barge lines to levels that cover variable costs, and the barge line may not object to the effect this competition has on its business, except to the extent that such rates are contrary to §§2, 3, or 4 of the Act. It is doubtful that the barge line may object that the effect of a reduced rate on its business is contrary to the National Transportation Policy.[207]

7.9. Recent Legislation, Legislative Proposals, and Related Developments Affecting Domestic Shipping

As previously noted, the Railroad Revitalization and Regulatory Reform Act of 1976[208] altered the basis of railroad rate making. Part of the change limited the ICC's power to consider the competitive effect of railroad rates on other modes of transportation. This will undoubtedly have some effect on inland water carriers' rate making, though it is impossible to predict the effect. Presumably, the inland water carriers remain apprehensive about predatory or discriminatory rates, geographic discrimination in rates, or "sharpshooting," that is, rate reductions in a narrow area designed to drive a specific competitor out of business.

Apparently no specific legislation has been introduced to deal with the specific concerns of the inland water carriers. One other concern that surfaced in testimony on comprehensive transportation reform bills was with the impact of private carriers on the common carriers. Since some private carriers hold certificates or permits, they may carry proprietary cargoes one way without regulation and then bid for regulated cargo on the return trip. It is argued that private carriage skims off the most profitable traffic leaving the dregs for the common carriers.

General reform for all modes of transportation apparently has not been acted upon because of the pressure of passing railroad regulatory reform. One prior attempt to alter the regulation of all modes was the Surface Transportation Act of 1971. One provision of this bill would have required the unregulated bulk carriers to file their rates with the ICC along with other reports.

The only known pending proposal relating directly to the inland water carriers is a proposal to establish a Federal Inland Waterways Administration in the Department of Transportation. No action has been taken on this proposal. A bill to extend the coastwise laws to the Virgin Islands "with respect to the transportation of crude oil, residual fuel oil, and refined petroleum products" was the subject of a hearing before the Senate Commerce Committee on February 25, 1976.

The ICC recently held that all grain transportation in bulk on the inland waterways was exempt from regulation. The legislative history of the 1973 amendment to §303(b) was relied on and interpreted to express a legislative intent that retention of the custom-of-the-trade provision (as of 1939) was intended to deny only to sugar the exemption of §303(b). However, the case has not been concluded, as the ICC issued a general order to show cause why this interpretation should not be adopted, and it is reasonable to assume protests will be filed.

The ICC granted an exemption under §302(e) to a shipper who chartered a fully manned towboat because the shipper would control the use of the ship and would suffer the gains and losses (rebutting the claim that an affreightment charter was involved) and because no protestant had shown a willingness to perform the requested service, which was of a different type from that previously performed by a common carrier (showing the charter was not substantially competitive).

7.10. Cabotage Laws

Cabotage laws are laws designed to reserve to a nation's own ships the coastwise trade between a nation's ports. The chief cabotage law of the United States, known as the Jones Act,[209] provides that merchandise transported between points in the United States must be transported in vessels built in the United States, documented under the laws of the United States,[210] and owned by citizens of the United States;[211] if not so transported, the merchandise is subject to forfeiture.

Two provisos are designed to help alleviate burdens that might be placed on shipping as a result of development of new technologies of transportation. Empty LASH and Seabee barges, containers, and equipment other than propulsion equipment for use with such barges or containers may be transported between U.S. points in nonqualified vessels. In addition, one nonqualified barge belonging to the same company or consortium as the "mother-ship" may transfer cargo to another nonqualified barge for further movement in U.S. foreign commerce, as long as the country of the "mother-ship" registry permits reciprocal privileges in its waters to barges registered in the United States.[212] In 1973, the Secretary of the Treasury reported to Congress no developments in reciprocity under the law.[213]

Other exemptions from the coastwise laws exist and are potentially lucrative, although they are not of general application. An attempt to obtain an exemption for the tanker *Sansinena* in 1970 under the emergency legislation dating back to the Korean conflict met with such an uproar that the exemption was withdrawn six days after it was announced.[214]

A vessel may lose its entitlement to engage in the coastwise trade if it is ever sold foreign or placed under foreign registry, or rebuilt anywhere other than the United States, with major components built anywhere other than in the United States.[215]

7.11.   Conclusions

U.S. domestic and inland water shipping has grown into a major transportation industry that will continue to grow, particularly in view of escalating energy costs. Deregulation is making inroads into most transport modes and will increasingly affect domestic and inland water shipping by permitting more freedom in the terms of operations and carriage of goods.

Endnotes

1. Ch. 104, Pt. I, §1, 24 Stat. 379 (1887), *as amended*, 49 U.S.C. §1(1)(a) (1970), quoted in Zoll, *The Development of Federal Regulatory Control Over Water Carriers*, 12 *ICC Prac. J.* 522, 552–53 (1945) [hereinafter cited as Zoll].
2. *United States v. Munson SS Line*, 283 U.S. 43 (1931)
3. Zoll at 553.
4. Ch. 3591, §4, 34 Stat. 589 (1906), *as amended*, 49 U.S.C. §15(3) (1970).
5. 37 Stat. 560 (1912), *as amended*, 49 U.S.C. §§5(14)–(16), 6(11), (12). The ICC read this Act as encouraging competition between rail and water carriers and preventing railroads from stifling competition through common ownership. Zoll at 559.
6. 39 Stat. 728 (1916), *as amended*, 46 U.S.C. §§801–842 (1976 and Supp. II 1978).
7. 41 Stat. 456 (1920) (codified in scattered sections of 49 U.S.C. (1976 and Supp. II 1978).
8. 15 U.S.C. §1528 (Supp. II 1978) currently provides:

   It is declared to be the policy of Congress to promote, encourage, and develop water transportation, service, and facilities in connection with the commerce of the United States, and to foster and preserve in full vigor both rail and water transportation.

9. Zoll at 566.
10. Denison Act, Ch. 891, 45 Stat. 978 (1928).
11. Intercoastal Shipping Act, Ch. 199, 47 Stat. 1425 (1933), *as amended*, 46 U.S.C. §§843–844 (1976 and Supp. II 1978).

12. 46 U.S.C. §§845a, 845b (1976 and Supp. II 1978).
13. Zoll at 448. In its 1932 Annual Report, the ICC summarized its existing jurisdiction over water carriers:

> There is some demand for the further regulation of the rates and charges of water carriers. Their joint rates with connecting rail lines are under our jurisdiction, but not their port-to-port rates, except in instances where we have permitted rail carriers under the Panama Canal Act to continue in control of water carriers.

Annual Report of the ICC, 1932, pp. 20, 21, quoted in Zoll at 561 n.39.
14. Transportation Act of 1940, ch. 722, title II, §201, 34 Stat. 929 (1949), *as amended*, 49 U.S.C. §§901–923 (1976 and Supp. II 1978). Throughout the text, sections of part III will be referred to by their section numbers in part III of the Interstate Commerce Act. Thus, §301 corresponds to 49 U.S.C. §901, and so forth.
15. 49 U.S.C. §920 (1976) (repealed because executed, 1978). This preserves FMC jurisdiction where not inconsistent with ICC jurisdiction; see discussion of Alaska and Hawaii statehood acts, *infra*, note 26.
16. W. Jones, *Cases and Materials on Regulated Industries* 510 (2d ed., 1976).
17. *Detroit & C. Nav. Co. v. United States*, 57 F. Supp. 81, 82–83 (E.D. Mich. 1944), *rev'd on other grounds*, 326 U.S. 236 (1945), quoting from *Texas & P.R.R. Co. v. Gulf, C. & S.F. R.R. Co.*, 270 U.S. 266, 277 (1925).
18. Act. Sept. 18, 1940, ch. 722, title I, §1, 54 Stat. 899, codified at 49 U.S.C. §10101 (Supp. II 1978) amended the Interstate Commerce Act by inserting before part I thereof the following provision entitled "National Transportation Policy":

> It is hereby declared to be the national transportation policy of the Congress to provide for fair and impartial regulation of all modes of transportation subject to the provisions of this act, so administered as to recognize and preserve the inherent advantages of each; to promote safe, adequate, economical and efficient service and foster sound economic conditions in transportation and among the several carriers; to encourage the establishment and maintenance of reasonable charges for transportation services, without unjust discriminations, undue preferences or advantages, or unfair or destructive competitive practices; to cooperate with the several States and the duly authorized officials thereof; and to encourage fair wages and equitable working conditions—all to the end of developing, coordinating, and preserving a national transportation system by water, highway, and rail, as well as other means, adequate to meet the needs of the commerce of the United States, of the Postal Service, and of the national defense. All of the provisions of this act shall be administered and enforced with a view to carrying out the above declaration of policy.

The origin of the term "inherent advantages" is discussed in McGehee, "The Inherent Advantages of Carrier Modes Under the National Transportation Policy," 34 *ICC Prac J*. 722 (1967).
19. *United States v. Pennsylvania R.R. Co.*, 323 U.S. 612, 618–19 (1944).
20. 83 *ICC Annual Report* 88 (1969).

21. Great Lakes: Statement of Gilbert R. Johnson, Counsel, Lake Carriers' Association, *Common Ownership by Regulated Carriers: Hearing on S.452, S. 1353, S. 1354, S. 1355 and S. 2189, before the Surface Transportation Sub. Comm. of the Senate Comm. on Interstate and Foreign Commerce,* 86th Cong., 1st Sess., 68 (Comm. Print 1961) [hereinafter *Common Ownership—Hearing*]. Inland waterways: *Union Mechling v. United States,* 390 F. Supp. 391, 402 (W.D. Pa. 1974).

22. 83 *ICC Annual Report* 122 (1969) (Appendix B, Table 4).

23. *Id.* 131 (Appendix G, Table 1).

24. *Id.* 132 (Appendix G, Table 2).

25. D. Locklin, *Economics of Transportation* 37 (7th ed., 1972) [hereinafter cited as Locklin].

26. By the Alaska Statehood Act §27(b), Act of July 7, 1958, Pub. L. No. 85–508, §27(b), 72 Stat. 339 (printed as a note before 48 U.S.C. §21 (1970)), and by the Hawaii Statehood Act, Act of Mar. 18, 1959, Pub. L. No. 86–3, §18, 73 Stat. 4 (printed as a note before 48 U.S.C. §491 (1970)), transportation to or from Alaska or Hawaii remains subject to regulation by the FMC. See *Alaska S.S. Co, Alaska "Grandfather" Appl.,* 325 ICC 196 (1965); *L. E. Erickson & Ed. W. Wolf Alaska "Grandfather" Appl.,* 325 ICC 276 (1965) (interpreting "high seas"). The ICC does regulate interstate commerce not on the high seas between points in Alaska. 49 U.S.C. §909(a) (1970(repealed because expired, 1978). However, under Pub. L. No. 87–595 (1962), common carriers by motor vehicle may establish interstate motor-water through-routes between Alaska or Hawaii and any other state, notwithstanding that the water carrier might be regulated by the FMC. 49 U.S.C. §10703 (Supp. II 1978).

27. *Cornell Steamboat Co. v. United States,* 53 F. Supp. 349 (S.D.N.Y. 1943) *aff'd,* 321 U.S. 634.

28. *Pennsylvania R.R. Co. v. United States,* 55 F. Supp. 473 (D.N.J. 1943), *aff'd in part, rev'd in part,* 323 U.S. 612 (1944).

29. 49 U.S.C. §10541(a)(2)(Supp. II 1978) covering such a combined shipment does not expressly require the water portion be from a point in one state to a point in another state.

30. 49 U.S.C. §10541 (Supp. II 1978).

31. *Id.*

32. 46 U.S.C. §§801 et seq. (1976 and Supp. II 1978).

33. See 40 *ICC Prac. J.* 52 (1972). The LASH System is briefly discussed in joint release no. 132–72, May 12, 1972, by the FMC and the ICC is quoted. The statement provided that the ocean carrier must file the rates for the entire service from port-to-port with the FMC, even though some part of the service might be provided by a carrier subject to the ICC. The inland carrier doing the towing, if not controlled by the ocean carrier, will be subject to the ICC's regulations because trans-shipment will have occurred.

34. *Port Royal Marine Corp.—Declaratory Order—"LASH" Operations,* 344 ICC 876 (1974).

35. *Port Royal Marine Corp. v. United States,* 378 F. Supp. 345 (S.D. Ga. 1974), *aff'd mem.,* 420 U.S. 901 (1975). Both the ICC and the court relied heavily on the earlier ICC case of *Sacramento-Yolo Port District, Petition for Declaratory Order,* 341 ICC 105 (1972) which held that lifting containers off a ship and onto a barge was transshipment, subjecting the person towing the barge

to ICC regulation. The outcome in the specific factual setting of the *Sacramento* case, that of a municipal port authority providing towing in lieu of a port call by the oceangoing vessel, was overturned legislatively, jurisdiction over such towage being vested in the FMC. 46 U.S.C. §804 (1976 and Supp. II 1978).

The court also observed that the Departments of Justice and Transportation and the FMC contended the ICC was without jurisdiction over LASH operations. 378 F. Supp. at 347 n.1.

36. 49 U.S.C. §10930 (Supp. II 1978).

37. 49 U.S.C. §10102(27)(Supp. II 1978).

38. 49 U.S.C. §11101(a)(Supp. II 1978).

39. 49 U.S.C. §10102(1), (12), (28) (Supp. II 1978).

40. 49 U.S.C. §10544 (Supp. II 1978).

41. *Barrett Line, Inc. v. United States*, 326 U.S. 179 (1945) (5–4 decision). The decision recounts the history of the provision, which passed through a stage in which furnishing vessels to any person was regulated (abandoned because of fears that the regulation of lessor would be influenced by lessee-carrier's operations), another stage in which furnishing vessels was not transportation and was therefore exempt, and finally entered its final form by which the furnisher is regulated (unless exempt) if the vessel is furnished to a noncarrier (under §302(e)), but the carrier is regulated if the vessel is furnished to a carrier (under §303(f)(2)). *Accord, DeBardeleben Coal Corp. v. United States* 54 F. Supp. 643 (W.D. Pa. 1944). See also note 120 *infra*.

42. In *American Range Lines, Inc., Contract Carrier Application* 260 ICC 362 (1944), a carrier that had contracts with 13 shippers and claimed that it carried full cargoes for one shipper or large shipments for a few shippers was granted a "grandfather" permit (based on pre-1940 operations) because it did not hold itself out to the public. However, it was restricted to carrying specific commodities in lots of 500 tons or more for not more than three shippers on any one voyage.

The factors in the text are a synthesis of factors mentioned in the above case and elements of service discussed in common carrier cases.

43. *Indian Towing Co., Contract Carrier Application*, 309 ICC 473 (1960).

44. 49 U.S.C. §10542(a)(Supp. II 1978). This section was amended in 1973, Act of Dec. 27, 1973, Pub. L. 93–201, §1, 87 Stat. 838, to eliminate a limitation of three commodities per vessel where a vessel included all vessels constituting a tow, and to eliminate an interpretation that the exemption was lost when a single nonexempt commodity was also transported. The Senate Report on the bill, Senate Report # 93–513, 93d Cong., 1st Sess., is printed in [1970] *U.S. Code Cong. and Ad. News* 2923. This report indicates that sugar is the only major commodity not transported in bulk in 1939. It also indicates that the ICC sought to require filing of rates for the transportation of commodities in bulk. Additional background is found at [1970] *U.S. Code Cong. and Ad. News* 5155 and 40 *ICC Prac. J.* 636 (1973).

45. Bulk transportation in 1939 need not have been by water; in *A.L. Mechling Barge Lines, Inc., Investigation of Operations*, 325 ICC 745 (1965), the company convinced the ICC that carriage of alumina was exempt because alumina was transported in bulk in 1939, although by rail and not by water; therefore the carrier was not engaging in any unauthorized transportation. The purpose of the restriction was to prevent shifting of in-container transportation to in-bulk

transportation in order to escape regulation or to prevent shifting modes in another manner to escape regulation. The latter reason is not very persuasive, for the result of the decision is to shift alumina from regulated (rail) transportation to exempt water transportation.

46. *Union Mechling Corp. v. United States*, 390 F. Supp. 411, 415 (W.D. Pa. 1974).

47. *Id.*

48. *Bulk Food Carriers, Inc.—Exemption Application*, 326 ICC 106 (1965).

49. 49 U.S.C. §10542(c)(Supp. II 1978).

50. 49 U.S.C. §10542(b)(Supp. II 1978).

51. Comment, Regulation of Water Carriers by the Interstate Commerce Commission, 50 *Yale L.J.* 654, 659 (1941).

52. 49 U.S.C. §10544(a)(Supp. II 1978). Order exempting portions of New York and Philadelphia harbors, 49 C.F.R. §1070.1 (1975). Such exemptions may be revoked as indicated in text at note 57 *infra*.

53. 49 U.S.C. §10544(f)(Supp. II 1978).

54. 49 U.S.C. §10544(c)(Supp. II 1978).

55. The restriction to contract carriers appears to have been read out of the statute by the ICC in Pan-Atlantic S.S. Corp.—Exemption, Section 303(e), 285 ICC 752 (1956), *affd.*, 355 U.S. 181 (1957). There, the ICC exempted certain operations of a common carrier and found that §310, prohibiting dual operating authority, did not apply because under the exemption, the carrier did not receive contract carrier operating authority. 285 ICC at 755.

56. *Seatrain Lines, Inc. v. United States*, 152 F. Supp. 619 (D. Del.), *affd.*, 355 U.S. 181 (1957).

57. §303(ℓ), 49 U.S.C. §10929 (Supp. II 1978)(applies to exemptions under Section 10544(a)-(c).

58. 49 C.F.R. §§1011.1 et seq. (1975).

59. *Warner v. United States*, 97 F. Supp. 580, 582 (W.D. Tenn., 1950), *aff'd mem.*, 341 U.S. 907 (1951).

60. *Pan-Atlantic S.S. Corp.—Exemption, Section 303(e)*, 285 ICC 752 (1956), *aff'd sub nom. Seatrain Lines, Inc. v. United States*, 152 F. Supp. 619 (D. Del.), *aff'd* mem., 355 U.S. 181 (1957). It is amusing that the Pan-Atlantic exemption was granted based on the findings made in granting Seatrain a similar exemption several years earlier, 285 ICC at 755, yet Seatrain was one of the protestants in the *Pan-Atlantic* case.

61. 326 ICC 106 (1965).

62. If the shipment was not intercoastal (i.e., through the Panama Canal) the carrier would be entitled to the bulk commodities exemption of §303(b). *Id.*, at 109 n. 3.

63. The ICC noted that there was no existing rail tariff for carrying the commodity and no evidence that it ever had been carried by rail except experimentally. Though the railroads did carry the commodity from Wyoming to California, this was not deemed competitive with carriage from Florida to California.

64. The ICC relied on the earlier case of *Pan-Atlantic S.S. Corp Exemption, §303(e)*, 285 ICC 752 (1956), discussed *supra*, text at n. 60. In another case, the ICC decided it was not possible to find that transporting loaded truck trailers by water was not substantially competitive with another mode of transportation. *H.E. Savage, Jr., Application*, 260 ICC 603 (1945), *mod.*, 265 ICC 137 (1947).

65. 49 U.S.C. §10544(e)(Supp. II 1978).

66. *G. M. Cox Shipyard, Inc., Applications*, 260 ICC 20 (1943). "Regulation of applicant and other furnishers of vessels, as contemplated by section 302(e), results from their position in the national transportation system. They provide a pool of equipment from which other carriers draw during emergencies and peak-load periods. Unregulated use of this pool of equipment by shippers well might place them in the position of being able to use the charter market as leverage to enforce their demands for unreasonable rates and discriminatory service from common and contract carriers."

67. *Boylan v. United States*, 310 F. 2d 493 (9th Cir. 1962), *cert. denied*, 372 U.S. 935 (1963). See also note 69, *infra*.

68. The cases seem to bear out the similarity. Compare *A.J. Cenac and O.J. Cenac Applications*, 260 ICC 818 (1943) ("Furnishing of vessels to persons other than carriers subject to the act, for use by them in marine construction between points in Louisiana and Texas exempted from the provisions of part III of the act.") with *Warner v. United States*, 97 F. Supp. 580 (W.D. Tenn. 1950), text at note 59 *supra* (transportation for waterway construction).

69. *Boylan v. United States*, 310 F. 2d 493 (9th Cir. 1952), upheld a conviction under §317(a) for willful failure to obtain a permit for furnishing a tug to a construction company to tow its materials interstate to its construction site. Regulating vessel furnishers is not unconstitutional, as the law is reasonably related to the purpose of preventing pressure on the regulated carriers. Such regulation to achieve the National Transportation Policy is warranted even if the only beneficiaries of the regulation are the certified common and contract carriers.

70. 49 U.S.C. §11914(c)(Supp. II 1978).

71. 49 U.S.C. §10922(a)(Supp. II 1978). When Part II was enacted and established entry requirements for water carriers, existing businesses were given an opportunity to obtain authorization to continue service without any showing of need for the service. These were so-called grandfather rights. Similar rights were later included when Alaska became a state. In passing on "grandfather" applications, the ICC limited the authority granted in terms of kind of service and area of service to the service proven to exist on the data specified and continuously thereafter. Since the prior service was not conducted with an eye on the statutory scheme, the effort to fit a variety of services into the regulatory mold sometimes provides the best indication of the scope of the statutory categories.

72. *Mississippi Valley Barge Line Co. v. United States*, 56 F. Supp. 1 (W.D. Pa. 1944).

73. *Union Mechling Corp. v. United States*, 390 F. Supp. 391 (W.D. Pa. 1974).

74. 42 U.S.C. §§4331 et seq. (1976 and Supp. II 1978).

75. Cf. *H. E. Savage, Jr., Application*, 260 ICC 603 (1945) (Application for permit denied for failure to show financial fitness; §303(e) exemption also denied).

76. *Newtex S.S. Corp. v. United States*, 107 F. Supp 388 (S.D.N.Y.), *aff'd mem.*, 344 U.S. 901 (1952).

77. 230 F. Supp. 646, 652 (D.N.H. 1964).

78. *Union Mechling Corp. v. United States*, 390 F. Supp 391 (W.D. Pa. 1974) (shippers' complaints plus shortage of barges at peak harvest season).

79. *Atlantic Coast Line RR Co. v. United States*, 202 F. Supp. 456 (S.D. Fla.

1962); *accord, Frank E. Woods Common Carrier Application,* 303 ICC 158 (1958) (absence of prior service by water carrier explains limited shipper support). See text at notes 98–102 *infra.*

80. *Igert Extension—Arkansas River,* 332 ICC 696, 705 (1968), *mod.,* 335 ICC 225 (1969) states:

> In reaching the conclusion that certain additional applicants should be authorized to conduct regulated transportation in the Waterway we have given consideration to the fact that should a plethora of operating authorities occur and result in non use of certificates we are now empowered under section 312(a) of the act, in circumstances therein set forth, to suspend, change or revoke, in whole or in part, a water carrier certificate for non use, should an applicant fail to conduct operations pursuant to certificate terms or the provisions of law. John J. Mulqueen Revocation of Certificate, 332 ICC 389.

81. *Union Mechling Corp. v. United States,* 390 F. Supp. 391 (W.D. Pa. 1974).
82. *Union Mechling Corp. v. United States,* 390 F. Supp. 411 (W. D. Pa. 1974).
83. *Atchison, T. & S.F. Ry. Co. v. United States,* 300 F. Supp. 1339 (N.D. Ill, 1969), *aff'd mem.,* 396 U.S. 275 (1970) (different kind of service proposed).
84. *Ohio River Co., Extension—Lower Mississippi River,* 343 ICC 509 (1973). *Hall & Sons v. United States,* 88 F. Supp. 596, 602 (D. Mass. 1950) is quoted in *Norfolk S. Bus Corp. v. United States,* 96 F. Supp. 756, 761, affd. 340 U.S. 802 (1950) as follows:

> The word "necessity" in the broad statutory formula must not be taken too literally . . . as implying that a transportation crisis of major proportions would ensue unless the application were granted. If that were the meaning, the use of the word 'convenience' would be an obvious superfluity.

85. *Union Mechling Corp. v. United States,* 390 F. Supp. 391 (W.D. Pa. 1974); *Ohio River Co. Extension—Lower Mississippi River,* 343 ICC 509 (1973) (showing made that traffic on lower Mississippi expected to double by 1980).
86. *United States v. Detroit & C. Nav. Co.,* 326 U.S. 236 (1945). The case dealt with authority to carry new automobiles over the Great Lakes on resumption of new car production, interrupted by World War II.
87. *Union Mechling Corp. v. United States,* 390 F. Supp. 411 (W.D. Pa. 1974), *aff'd Sioux City & N.O. Barge Lines Inc., Extension—Mississippi River, System,* 343 ICC 412 (1973).
88. *A.L. Mechling Barge Lines, Inc. Extension—Gulf Intracoastal Waterway,* 306 ICC 223 (1959). See discussion at note 95 *infra.*
89. *Union Mechling Corp. v. United States,* 390 F. Supp. 411 (W.D. Pa. 1974) (claim that present delays were the result of weather conditions and not an indication of inadequate service).
90. *Id.*
91. 49 U.S.C. §10922(f)(Supp. II 1978). *DeBardeleben Coal Corp. v. United States,* 54 F. Supp. 643 (W.D. Pa. 1944).
92. *Coyle Lines v. United States,* 115 F. Supp. 272 (E.D. La. 1953)
93. *Lukenback S.S. Co. v. United States,* 122 F. Supp. 824 (S.D.N.Y.), *aff'd mem.,* 347 U.S. 984 (1954).
94. *Indian Towing Co., Contract Carrier Application,* 309 ICC 473, 478 (1960).
95. *Ohio River Co., Extension—Lower Mississippi River,* 343 ICC 509 (1973).

Granting Ohio authority might increase competition with the "Big Five": American Commercial Barge Lines, Federal Barge Lines, Mississippi Valley Barge Line, A. L. Mechling, and Union Barge Line (the last two having merged into Union-Mechling prior to the decision in this case). The Big Five were said to carry an overwhelming portion of the regulated traffic on the lower Mississippi.

Increasing competition may, on the other hand, conflict with other policies, see A.L. Mechling Barge Lines, Inc. Extension—Gulf Intracoastal Waterway, 306 ICC 223 (1959), although with amendment of §303(b) (see note 44 supra), the precise holding of this case probably is no longer viable.

96. Igert Extension—Arkansas River, 332 ICC 696 (1968), mod., 335 ISS 225 (1969).

97. Atchison, T. & S. F. Ry. Co. v. United States, 300 F. Supp. 1339 —N.D. Ill. 1969), aff'd mem., 396 U.S. 275 (1970). The proposed service was a Pacific coastwise service utilizing containers filled by the shipper and transported by truck and ship. The last prior service had ended in 1959. Sea-Land Service, Inc., Extension—Pacific Coastwise, 329 ICC 447 (1967).
Accord, Ohio River Co. Extension—Lower Mississippi River, 343 ICC 509 (1973) (applicant evinced willingness to tow LASH barges; competing carriers did not appear to be willing to tow them).

98. The quoted phrase is a reference to the National Transportation Policy, Note before 49 U.S.C. §10101 (Supp. II 1978), quoted at note 18 supra.

99. Frank E. Woods Common Carrier Application, 303 ICC 158 (1958); John I. Hay Co. Extension—Milwaukee, 285 ICC 472 (1945); Atchison, T. & S.F. Ry Co. v. United States, 300 F. Supp. 1339, 1342 (N.D. Ill, 1969) citing the National Transportation Policy that different modes should be developed and stating: "[S]hippers should not be denied the inherent advantages of water transportation merely because of the presence and adequacy of existing motor and rail services."

100. McAllister Brothers, Inc. Extension—Steel, 332 ICC 505 (1968), modified 335 ICC 52 (1969).

101. Schaffer Transportation Co. v. United States, 355 U.S. 83 (1957).

102. Atlantic Coast Line R. Co. v. United States, 202 F. Supp. 456 (S.D. Fla. 1962); McAllister Brothers, Inc. Extension—Steel, 335 ICC 52(1969).

103. Union Mechling Corp. v. United States, 390 F. Supp. 411 (W.D. Pa. 1974). The National Transportation Policy, supra note 18, includes promotion of "efficient service."

104. Ohio River Co. Extension—Lower Mississippi River, 343 ICC 509 (1973) (single line service more efficient than joint line; also decided that grant would make more barges available to shippers).

105. Sea-Land Service Inc. Extension—Pacific Coastwise, 329 ICC 447 (1967), aff'd sub nom. Atchison, T. & S.F. Ry. Co. v. United States, 300 F. Supp. 1339 (N.D. Ill. 1969), aff'd mem., 396 U.S. 275 (1970); New England Forwarding Co., Extension—Import Export, 335 ICC 58, 73 (1969).

106. McAllister Brothers, Inc., Extension—Steel, 335 ICC 52 (1969). The extension was sought to ship steel from the West Coast to New York for use in the World Trade Center. The railroads protested (to no avail) that contract carriage was involved since the project would end and the application should be therefore denied.

107. 49 U.S.C. §10922(e) (Supp. II 1978). When a new portion of a waterway is

completed, a common carrier wishing to extend its operations must apply for a certificate authorizing such extension no later than the date on which extended operations are instituted. 49 C.F.R. §1140.1 et seq. (1975). See also note 120, *infra*.

108. " 'Freighting' is a term used to denote transportation by a water carrier when such carrier supplies the cargo space, such as a barge, and also the motive power, such as a tugboat or towboat." *Indian Towing Co., Contract Carrier Application*, 309 ICC 473, 473 n.1 (1960). The distinction between freighting and general towage applies alike to common and contract carriers.

109. *Campbell Trans. Co. Comm. Carr. Appl.*, 260 ICC 107 (1943). "Authority to perform such towage [providing motive power for propulsion of non-self-propelled vessels furnished by shipper] is not included in the authority granted to water carriers to engage in the transportation of commodities with the use of separate towing vessels. Towage is a distinct type of service or field of operation. Many carriers perform only towage . . . Carriers whose certificates or permits do not specifically authorize the performance of towage are without authority to engage in such services." *Id.* at 110.

The general transporter of commodities in freighting service who is obliged to furnish equipment to transport the freight may use shippers' barges as part of its equipment, "so long as it used them for its freighting purposes and did not merely transport them as service to the owners." *Callahan Road Imp. Co. v. United States*, 107 F. Supp. 184, 187 (N.D.N.Y. 1952), affd., 345 U.S. 507 (1953). This distinction is a reasonable classification under §304(c). *Id.*

110. *Pittsburgh Towing Co.—Cert. Transfer—Charles Zubik*, 317 ICC 661, 668 (1963), affd., 325 ICC 460 (1965). (citations omitted).

111. *Id.*

112. 49 U.S.C. §10921 (Supp. II 1978).

113. 49 U.S.C. §10923(a) (Supp. II 1978). *Warner v. United States*, 97 F. Supp. 580 (W.D. Tenn. 1950), *aff'd* 341 U.S. 907 (1951). See also, on financial ability, note 75, *supra*.

114. *Warrior & Gulf Nav. Co. Extension—Cape Canaveral*, 322 ICC 261, 264 (1964). See also, discussing regulation of vessel furnishers, text at notes 65–68 *supra*.

115. 49 U.S.C. §10923(d) (Supp.) (1978). See also, note 108, *supra*.

116. 49 U.S.C. §10930(a) (Supp. II 1978).

117. *Warrior & Gulf Nav. Co. Extension—Cape Canaveral*, 322 ICC 261 (1964).

118. *Ingram Corp—Purchase—The Barrett Line Inc.*, 325 ICC 263 (1965) (purchase of contract carrier by company with a common carrier as a subsidiary.)

119. *Pan-Atlantic S.S. Corp.—Exemption, Section 303(e)* 285 ICC 752, 755 (1956), *aff'd.*, 355 U.S. 181 (1957), discussed *supra* notes 55, 60.

120. *Portland Tug & Barge Co. v. United States*, 55 F. Supp. 723 (D. Ore. 1944). A common carrier's certificate was restricted so that it was authorized to furnish barges only to other carriers (§303(f)(2), see note 41 *supra*) rather than being also authorized to engage in the contract carrier activity of furnishing barges to noncarriers, §302(e), thus avoiding dual operations.

121. *Warrior & Gulf Nav. Co. Extension—Cape Canaveral*, 322 ICC 261, 266 (1964); *Igert Extension—Arkansas River*, 322 ICC 696, 709 (1968) *mod.*, 335 ICC 225 (1969) (reserving right in ICC to impose conditions "to insure that said carrier's operations conform to the provisions of section 310 of the act").

122. In *Seatrain Lines, Inc., Temporary Authority Application*, 285 ICC 83 (1951), the urgent need for service was that service to Savannah had been interrupted by World War II and had not been reinstituted thereafter. Temporary authority was granted after temporary authority to purchase a certificate [§ 311(b), 49 U.S.C.A. § 911(b)] covering New York to Savannah service was denied. In view of the fact that final favorable disposition of the application for permanent authority occurred over three years later, it may be that the showing of urgency in instituting service need not be particularly striking. In *Bulk Food Carrier, Inc.—Exemption Application*, 326 ICC 106 (1965), it was noted that temporary authority had been granted pending outcome of the permit or exemption application. Nevertheless, there was some indication no other carrier was willing to perform the transportation described there. See also text at notes 61–64, *supra*.

123. 49 U.S.C. §10928 (Supp. II 1978).

124. *Pan-Atlantic S.S. Corp. v. Atlantic Coast Line R.R. Co.*, 353 U.S. 436 (1957). *See* 49 C.F.R. § 1131a.1 et seq. (1975) (applications for temporary authority); 49 C.F.R§§ 1101.1 et seq. (1975) (extension of temporary operating authority).

125. 49 U.S.C. §11101(a) (Supp. II 1978).

126. *Pittsburgh Towing Company—Certificate Transfer—Charles Zubik*, 325 ICC 460, 471 (1965), *rev'd on other grounds, sub nom. Mississippi Valley Barge Line Co. v. United States*, 252 F. Supp. 162 (E.D. Mo. 1966), *appeal dismissed* 385 U.S. 32.

127. 49 C.F.R. §1141.9 (1975).

128. 49 U.S.C. §10925(b)(Supp. II 1978). Dormant authority may be cancelled for willful failure to comply with §305(a) concerning furnishing transportation on request after a demand for compliance from the ICC and a hearing. Legislative history is found at [1965] *U.S. Code Cong. and Adm. News* 2923.

129. *Mulqueen Revocation of Certificate*, 332 ICC 389 (1968)(ordering transportation service be resumed in 90 days or authority would be revoked). See also note 80, *supra*.

130. 49 U.S.C. §10926 (Supp. II 1976).

131. 49 C.F.R. §§1141.1 et seq. (1975).

132. 49 U.S.C. §§11343–11345, 11347 (Supp. II 1978).

133. 49 C.F.R. §1141.3(0) (1975).

134. *United States Lines Company (Panama Pacific Line) Certificate Transfer*, 260 ICC 355 (1944).

135. *Pittsburgh Towing Co.—Certificate Transfer—Charles Zubik*, 317 ICC 661 (1963), *aff'd* 324 ICC 460 (1965), *rev'd sub. nom. Mississippi Valley Barge Line Co. v. United States*, 252 F. Supp. 162 (E.D. Mo. 1966), *appeal dismissed sub nom. Pittsburgh Towing Co. v. Mississippi Valley Barge Line Co.*, 385 U.S. 32 (late filing), *rehearing den.*, 385 U.S. 995.

136. *Mississippi Valley Barge Line Co. v. United States*, 252 F. Supp. 162 (E.D. Mo. 1966).

The ICC's view (four of eleven Commissioners dissenting) was that failure to follow the regulations in applying for the transfer was harmless because following the regulations would have had no effect on the outcome.

The case involved the transfer by Zubik of a dormant certificate. The ICC described the intent of §312 as being "to facilitate transfer not subject to section 5" (325 ICC at 466) and noted that operations may be revived at any time without a showing of need for the service. If the transferor could revive operations without a showing of need and then transfer the certificate, the ICC apparently saw little reason to require the transferee to demonstrate consistency with the public interest in his acquisition of the certificate preliminary to reviving operations. (See note 137, *infra*.) If it did not matter who revived the operations, then failure to disclose an option contract to sell the certificate, even though required to be disclosed by the regulations (49 C.R.F §1141.4(b) (1975)), could not affect the outcome.

The Court's view was that the record did not indicate that the proposed recipient of the certificate (Pittsburgh Towing) was financially fit to carry on the operations and that the decision authorizing transfer should be reversed for violation of the regulations by the applicant and for the ICC's failure to follow its own regulations.

Thereafter, since the transfer was ineffective, one Osbourne, with whom Zubik had had the undisclosed option contract, attempted to operate under the certificate in Zubik's name and on behalf of his estate (Zubik having died). Osbourne was enjoined from continuing to evade the regulations. *Mississippi Valley Barge Line Co. v. United States*, 273 F. Supp. 1 (E.D. Mo. 1967), *aff'd mem.*, *sub nom.* Osbourne v. Mississippi Valley Barge Line Co., 389 U.S. 579 (1968).

137. 49 C.F.R. §1141.9 (1975).
138. 49 U.S.C. §11343 (Supp. II 1978).
139. 49 U.S.C. §11343(b)(Supp. II 1978). But see *Ingram Corp.—Purchase—The Barrett Line, Inc.*, 324 ICC 263 (1965)(transfer of most of Barrett's properties in good faith and under misinterpretation of §5(a) no bar to approval of control under §5(2)); *McAllister Bros. Inc.—Control & Merger-Russell Bros. Towing Co. Inc.*, 317 ICC 459 (1962)(similar).
140. 49 U.S.C. §11344(c)(Supp. II 1978). A condition may be imposed on a merger that arguably might be prohibited in granting a permit under §309(g). *Ingram Corp.—Purchase—The Barrett Line, Inc.*, 324 ICC 263 (1965). The ICC has claimed the authority, without exercising it, to approve the merger of parallel lines conditioned on the transfer of the one operating authority to a third carrier. *Union Mechling Corp—Merger—Union Barge Line Corp & A.L. Mechling Barge Lines, Inc.*, [hereinafter, *Union-Mechling Corp.—Merger*], 342 ICC 874 (1973) (dictum). See also note 95, *supra*.
141. 49 U.S.C. §11344(b)(Supp. II 1978).
142. 49 U.S.C. §11343(a)(Supp. II 1978).
143. *Valley Line Co. v. United States*, 390 F. Supp. 435 (W.D. Pa. 1975), *rev'g*, *Katy Industries, Inc.—Control—Cenac Towing Co.*, 342 ICC 666 (1973). Control of Cenac Towing Co. was sought by the corporation controlling the Missouri-Kansas-Texas Railroad. Cenac derived 5 percent of its revenues from renting tugs and barges to the petroleum industry, exempted from regulation under §302(e), see note 68, *supra*. The remainder of its revenues were derived from transportation exempt under §303(d) (see text at note 49, *supra*). Cenac was found to be a carrier subject to the Act. The Court's reasoning probably would apply only to discretionary exemptions; thus, a carrier exempt under §303(b)–(d) would probably not be deemed a carrier subject to the Act for purposes of §5(2), although the opinion is susceptible to a contrary interpretation.
144. "We hold that Section 5(2) is not applicable to interchanges of carrier equip-

ment which do not effect control of two or more carriers in a common interest."
Railway Labor Exec. Ass'n v. United States, 151 F. Supp. 108, 113 (D.D.C
1957), *aff'd Railway Labor Exec. Ass'n v. Chicago & N.W. Ry. Co.,* 298 ICC
69 (1956); see *McAllister Light. Line, Inc. Purchase,* 265 ICC 483 (1948) (no
authority needed to buy tug from carrier which was liquidating).

145. "Transactions within the scope of that section [§5(2)], whereby carriers are
divested of their ability to continue their operations, including those putting
a competitor out of business, and terminating his authority . . . may not
lawfully be consummated without our prior approval." *Bekins Moving & Storage Co.—Purchase—A.C. Farrington,* 65 M.C.C. 56, 59 (1955). See also note
139, *supra.*

146. Union Barge Line Co. & A.L. Mechling Barge Lines, Inc.; see note 95, *supra.*

147. *Union Mechling Corp—Merger,* 342 ICC 874, 881 (1973). Additional criteria
mentioned may relate to the reasonableness of the terms of the agreement,
McAllister Bros. Inc.—Control & Merger—Russell Bros. Towing Co., 317
ICC 459 (1962) or the reasonableness of the purpose of the merger, *Weyer-
haeuser Co. Merger, Weyerhaeuser S.S. Co.,* 317 ICC 434 (1962), *rev'g* 312
ICC 778 (1962) (tax saving is a proper objective).

148. *Accord, McAllister Bros. Inc.—Control & Merger—Russell Bros. Towing Co.,*
317 ICC 459 (1962) (no evidence of increased fixed costs); see text at note
140, *supra.*

149. Estimates of the savings ranged from $500,000 to $1,000,000 per year.

150. Each company provided sailings every six days averaging out to one sailing
every three days. The merged company would provide one sailing every four
days. The ICC noted that a shipper could not take advantage of the average
interval of three days because he had to commit his freight to a given carrier.
Thus, sailings every four days (merged carrier) was an improvement over
sailings every six days (either carrier individually).

151. The ICC cited *Northern Lines Merger Cases,* 396 U.S. 491, 509 (1970), noting
that mergers should not be limited to preserving "the halt and the lame."
The ICC, 342 ICC at 885, also quoted *Seaboard Air Line R.R. Co.—Merger—
Atlantic Coast Line,* 320 ICC 122 129 (1963) as follows:

> There, however, is no provision in the act which expressly or by implication
> prohibits the merger of financially strong railroads. The act draws no dis-
> tinction as between competitive and non-competitive railroads. There is no
> requirement in either the statute or judicial precedent which limits the
> Commission's authority to approve mergers to those involving carriers which
> are insolvent or on the brink of bankruptcy.

152. Four water carriers and a newly merged railroad (Illinois Central Gulf RR)
would operate in the lower Mississippi area. See note 95, *supra,* authorizing
a fifth water carrier for the lower Mississippi. The Administrative Law Judge
also considered the effect on unregulated traffic and found there would be
454 carriers after the merger against 455 before.

153. See note 95 *supra.*

154. 342 ICC at 885.

155. *McLean Trucking Co. v. United States,* 321 U.S. 67 (1944).

156. See, e.g., *Northern Lines Merger Cases,* 396 U.S. 491, 506–514 (1970).

157. *McLean Trucking Co. v. United States,* 321 U.S. 67, (1944).

158. *TTC Corp.—Purchase—Terminal Trans. Co.*, 97 MCC 380 (1965), *aff'd sub. nom. Atlantic Coast Line RR Co. v. United States*, 265 F. Supp. 549 (N.D. ILL. 1966).
159. *Id.*
160. *Id.*, 49 U.S.C. §§5(2)(b) (railroad acquiring motor carrier) and 5(16)(railroad acquiring water carrier not operating through the Panama Canal) (1970).
161. *TTC Corp.—Purchase—Terminal Trans. Co.*, 97 MCC 380 (1965).
162. 49 U.S.C. §11321(b)(Supp. II 1978).
163. *Id.*
164. *Lake Line Applications under Panama Canal Act*, 31 ICC 699 (1965), discussed in Delisi, *Coordinated Freight Transportation Service: Legal and Regulatory Aspects*, pt. 2, 34 ICC Prac. J. 548, 557–58 (1967) [hereinafter cited as Delisi and part number], and in Locklin, *supra* note 25, at 863.
165. Delisi pt. 2, *supra* note 164, at 558.
166. *Illinois C. RR Co.—Control—John I. Hay Co.*, 317 ICC 39 (1962).
167. The ICC considered it likely that Hay's officers would yield to directions from the railroad's directors. "Control, within the meaning of the act, is defined to be the power or authority to manage, direct, superintendend, restrict, govern, administer, or oversee. *New York C. & St. L.R. Co. Control*, 295 ICC 703. An affirmative demonstration of the power to dominate or influence is not necessary. In our opinion, a finding is warranted that Hay would be under the complete domination and control of its parent railroads, and that insofar as its overall policies are concerned it would not be 'independent' as contended by applicants." 317 ICC at 52–53. Operating a barge line only for the benefit of two railroads would be contrary to the National Transportation Policy preserving the inherent advantages of each mode and the statute permitting railroad control. 49 U.S.C. §11321(b)(Supp. II 1978).
168. This finding is presumably motivated by the statutory standard that operation of the water carrier "will still allow competition without reduction on the water route in question." 49 U.S.C. §11321(b)(Supp. II 1978).
169. *Southern Ry. Co. §5(15) Application*, 342 ICC 416 (1972), *aff'd sub. nom. American Waterways Operators Inc. v. United States*, 386 F. Supp. 799 (D.D.C. 1974), *affd.* 421 U.S. 1006 (1975).
170. [C]ompletion [for traffic] can be found to exist where the railroad affiliated with the water carrier does not provide a single-line route in competition with the water carrier but has an interline route with a subsidiary or other railroads. 342 ICC at 433.
171. The ICC also canvassed many of its prior cases including *Illinois C. R.R. Co.—Control—John I. Hay Co.*, 317 I.CC 39 (1962) and decided that the cases had consistently found competition would be precluded only when parallel rail and water routes were involved. In these cases, the railroad appeared to have an effective monopoly on the parallel water route thus preventing or excluding competition and depriving the public of the advantages of active competition.
172. *Common Ownership Hearing*, *supra* note 21, statement of Braxton B. Carr, President, The American Waterways Operators, Inc. at 25; statement of George Peterkin, Pres. Dixie Lines, Inc. for the Inland Waterways Common Carriers Assoc. at 51; statement of Gilbert R. Johnson, Counsel, Lake Carriers' Assoc. at 68.

173. *Id.*, statement of Braxton B. Carr at 25.
174. 49 U.S.C. §10701 (Supp. II 1978).
175. 49 U.S.C. §10701, 10741 (Supp. II 1978).
176. 49 U.S.C. §10726 (Supp. II 1978).
177. 49 U.S.C. §§10761–10762 (Supp. II 1978).
178. 49 U.S.C. §§10704, 11701 (Supp. II 1978).
179. 49 U.S.C. §10708 (Supp. II 1978).
180. 49 U.S.C. §907(f)(1970), for the same substance expressed in different words see the present law 49 U.S.C. §10704 (Supp. II 1978).
181. 49 U.S.C. §10701(d)(Supp. II 1978).
182. 49 U.S.C. §10702(b) (Supp. II 1978).
183. 49 U.S.C. §10764 (Supp. II 1978).
184. *Filing of Contracts by Contract Carriers by Water* (ex parte No. 161), 285 I.C.C. 450 (1953).
185. 49 U.S.C. §§10704, 10708 (Supp. II 1978).
186. 49 U.S.C. §10703 (Supp. II 1978). Water carriers may establish through routes with motor carriers, and water carriers to Alaska or Hawaii, but are not required to establish such rates. *Id.*
187. See *ICC v. Mechling*, 330 U.S. 567 (1947); M. Fair and J. Guandolo, Transportation Regulation 190 (7th ed. 1972) citing *Through Routes & Through Rates*, 12 ICC 164, 166 (1907).
188. 49 U.S.C. §10705 (Supp. II 1978).
189. 49 U.S.C. §10701(cf)(Supp. II 1978).
190. 49 U.S.C. §10503(a)(Supp. II 1978).
191. *A.L. Mechling Barge Lines, Inc. v. United States*, 376 U.S. 375, 376 (1964).
192. *United States v. Pennsylvania RR Co.*, 323 U.S. 612 (1945). The Court also argued that the railroad could not discriminate against Seatrain by not interchanging cars while interchanging cars with other water carriers.
193. *Dixie Carriers, Inc. v. United States*, 351 U.S. 56, 60 (1956). Dixie proposed a joint barge-rail rate, lower than the all-rail rate, by which the connecting railroad would charge the same rate for its services in either the all-rail or barge-rail rate with the barge line absorbing the differential.
194. *ICC v. Mechling*, 330 U.S. 567 (1947). The railroads in 1939 began charging the local rate between Chicago and New York for ex-barge grain but not for grain arriving by Great Lakes steamer or railroad. The local rate was 8½¢ per hundred pounds, higher than the through rate. The rate was allowed to go into effect, *ICC v. Inland Waterways Corp.*, 319 U.S. 671 (1943) (reversing District Court injunction), but was challenged in a rate proceeding leading to this appeal. The ICC declared the proper differential was 3¢ which the Supreme Court held was not justified by different costs, noting that ex-lake grain required reshipping at Chicago but moved at the same rate as ex-rail grain.
195. *Alabama Gt. S. RR Co. v. United States*, 340 U.S. 216 (1951). An eight-year investigation into joint rail-barge differentials from all-rail traffic encompassing water carriers operating on the Mississippi and Warrior Rivers culminated in an order that the connecting railroad would receive the same amount for its services whether it was an all-rail or rail-barge route, the barges absorbing the differential. The railroads claimed to be the low-cost mode, that permitting the barges to charge less than railroads destroyed the inherent advantage of

the railroads, and, therefore, barges should not be permitted to charge less. The Court declared that even if the railroads were the low cost mode, that fact would provide no justification for raising the rates of a competing mode.

196. *ICC v. Mechling*, 330 U.S. 567 (1947), note 194 *supra.*

197. 49 U.S.C. §4(1)(1970), now 49 U.S. §10726 (Supp. II 1978), text at note 176, *supra.*

198. *A.L. Mechling Barge Lines, Inc. v. United States*, 376 U.S. 375 (1964). The Court said that it was not mandatory to rule on all objections to a rate in a §4 proceeding, but that the ICC should realize that it would make good sense in some cases by preventing the spawning of new hearings. This was such a case: the proceeding was in its seventh year, the rates were in effect, and yet the validity of the rate had not yet been considered by the ICC. The Court held there were insufficient facts to support the finding that the through-rate to the East was reasonably compensatory and no lower than necessary to meet competition. The Court cited evidence that traffic had not diverted from barges with no evidence of additional traffic or profit for the railroads east of Kankakee and Chicago.

199. 49 U.S.C. §15a(3)(1970), now 49 U.S.C. §10704(d)(Supp. II 1978). The legislative history of §15a(3) is briefly recounted in *ICC v. New York, N.H. & H. R.R. Co.*, 372 U.S. 744, 753–58 (1963).

200. See *American Commercial Lines, Inc. v. Louisville & N. R. Co.*, 392 U.S. 571, 580 (1968).

201. Act of Feb. 5, 1976, Pub. L. No. 94–120, 90 Stat. 31 (known as the Railroad Revitalization and Regulation Reform Act).

202. *Id.*, §205.

203. *Id.*, §203(b).

204. *Id.*, §202(b).

205. Sen. Rep. No. 94–499, 94th Cong., 2d Sess. 48 (1976), reprinted in [1976] *U.S. Code Cong. and Ad. News* 31, 54.
   "[T]he Committee wishes it to be clearly understood that it is not endorsing or ratifying the decisions under Section 15a(3) that have been made by the Commission to date. In particular, [the amendments] should not be construed to countenance the Commission's practice of allocating "fair shares" of the transportation market among several modes.
   It is not the Committee's intent that the Commission engage as a "giant handicapper" in surface transportation.

206. Act of February 5, 1976, Pub. L. No. 94–120, §203(b), 90 Stat. 39; Sen. Conf. Rep. No. 94–595, 94th Cong., 2d Sess. 150, reprinted in [1976] *U.S. Code Cong. and Ad. News* at 157.

207. This analysis would end speculation created by *American Lines v. Louisville & N. R.R. Co.*, 392 U.S. 571 (1968), better known as the *Ingot Molds* case, and *ICC v. New York, N.H. & H. R.R. Co.*, 372 U.S. 744 (1963), whether the cost advantage of a carrier was to be determined by comparing variable or fully distributed costs. For analysis of the experience under §15a(3), see, e.g., Ross, "Regulation of Intermodal Rate Competition in Transportation," 69 *Mich. L.R.* 1011 (1971); Coyle, *The Compatibility of the Rule of Rate Making and the National Transportation Policy*, 38 ICC Prac. J. 340 (1971); McCarney, *ICC Rate Regulation & Railmotor Carrier Pricing Behavior: A Reappraisal*, 35 *ICC Prac J.* 707 (1968).

See *Lake Carriers' Ass'n. v. United States*, 399 F. Supp. 386 (N.D. Ohio 1975) (failure to offer unit train service to lake ports similar to service to Michigan utilities violates §3(1) as "undue or unreasonable preference" of carrier's traffic over competing mode's traffic; case remanded to ICC to prescribe joint rate for unit train service to ports).

208. Pub. L. 94–21, 90 Stat. 31 (codified in scattered sections of Title 15, 31, 45, and 49).
209. Merchant Marine Act of 1920, §27, 46 U.S.C. §883 (1970).
210. For the purposes of the coastwise trade documented under the laws of the United States refers to enrollment within the meaning of Chap. 12, Title 46 §251 et seq.
211. Citizenship of a corporation is defined at 49 U.S.C. §802. American subsidiaries of foreign corporations meeting statutory criteria may operate vessels in the coastwise trade. 49 U.S.C. §883–1 (1970).
212. The Secretary of Treasury is given discretionary authority to suspend the application of the Jones Act with respect to the vessels of any country granting reciprocal privileges. This was designed to meet three problems: first, to provide assurance of reciprocal treatment for American vessels before suspension of the effect of the Jones Act; second, to surmount a difficulty that if reciprocal privileges were granted to any nation to whom the United States owed Most Favored Nation (MFN) obligations, the privileges would have to be granted to all other nations to which MFN obligations were owed; third, to prevent the intended effect from being dissipated by granting reciprocal privileges for operations in the waters of a flag of convenience (based on a vessel's registry) and not in the waters at the foreign end of a trade route. 1971 *U.S. Code Cong. and Ad. News* 1950, 1755. The Senate Committee report offers an example of the operations necessitating the legislation. *Id.* at 1751–52.
213. 119 *Cong. Rec.* 5092 (1973).
214. Lowry III, *Jones Act*, 40 *ICC Prac. J.* 779, 779 n.2, 790–92 (1973).
215. 49 U.S.C. §883 (1970).

Chapter 8

SUMMARY AND CONCLUSIONS

The United States is at a critical crossroad in its economic development. After years of leadership in most aspects of a modern economy, there are now few markets in which our technology, manufactured goods, and transportation are not challenged. With few exceptions, American leadership reigns supreme only in agriculture. During periods when the United States was self-sufficient in most products and dependent on international trade for barely 3 to 4 percent of its gross domestic product (GDP), the United States maintained its leadership and competitiveness. At those times, U.S. foreign trade exports consisted largely of goods the whole world wanted and only we could supply. Today, U.S. international trade has assumed nearly 9 percent of our GDP and is rapidly growing.

Our increasing dependence on foreign trade and declining competitiveness in some major markets make this dependence even more serious. Nowhere is this more obvious than in American shipping. Our merchant fleet today is smaller and older than at any time in recent history. Our vessels, liners, and bulk carriers alike have increasing difficulty in maintaining their market share, even in our own foreign trade.

Apart from the goverment umbrella protecting our domestic shipping from foreign competition, there is little protection of an incentive for investment in U.S. foreign-trade shipping. Our liner shipping has difficulty maintaining its share of our own commerce, while U.S.-flag bulk carriers are carrying an ever-declining share of U.S. foreign trade.

While the United States was among the first nations to legislate a formal policy of government aid to merchant shipping, and particularly its liner industry serving essential trade routes, these programs have become ineffective and, in many aspects, counterproductive. Our shipbuilding productivity is no longer among the highest in the world and our ship-operating productivity is only held

317

at a somewhat reasonable level as a result of technological and management ingenuity. Neither construction nor operating differential subsidies provide a really significant benefit to U.S. shipping or assure its parity with foreign competitors in terms of costs, management decision-making ability, freedom of operation, and other critical factors.

Government aid and advocacy has become a controversial issue, with many claiming that it does more harm than good. A major complaint concerns the restrictions imposed on operational and financial shipping management decision making, which puts U.S.-flag operators at a disadvantage compared to their foreign competitors. These restrictions vary, from the need for authorization of frequency and route of services offered by subsidized liner operators to various financing and regulatory restrictions.

Restrictions are imposed on U.S. shipping under antitrust laws, in the import or export of vessels, in the manning of U.S.-flag vessels, on vessel ownership, on terms of affreightment, and others. Most of these restrictions are generally not subscribed to by other maritime nations. These, more than any differences in manning costs, are the reasons for the increasing lack of competitiveness of U.S. shipping.

Fuel costs, for example, are today an overriding element in ship-operating costs, yet, even now, eight years after the oil crisis of 1973, and the subsequent rapid escalation of bunker prices, U.S. ships are still being equipped with steam plants that have a higher consumption than comparable diesel-engine plants installed in most foreign-built vessels. Among the reasons for this was, until recently, the unavailability of large output U.S.-manufactured marine diesels. A temporary reinterpretation of the "Buy American" clauses permitting installation of foreign-built diesels into U.S.-built ships might have resulted in the introduction of programs for diesel marine engineers and provided an earlier incentive for U.S. manufacturers to build large marine diesel engines.

Although federally guaranteed construction and mortgage loans offer buyers of U.S. ships competitive financing by U.S. standards, recent skyhigh U.S. interest rates make even government-guaranteed rates noncompetitive with those obtainable by buyers of foreign-built ships. If we add to this better financing terms, the much better delivery schedule, and greater choice of efficient propulsion plant offered by many foreign yards, it is easy to see why even subsidized U.S. construction (based on cost parity) is not attractive to many U.S. buyers. The above are just a few examples of the issues facing policy makers charged with the goal of revitalizing the U.S. merchant marine.

8.1. Recent Developments

American foreign-going shipping is an international industry and must operate under terms similar to those prevalent in world shipping to achieve competitiveness. Shipping companies abroad increasingly are now entering into joint venture, joint service, or other types of pooling agreements often involving several flags of registry and multinational ownerships to achieve both financial and operational rationalization. Quite a number of shipping services are now truly multinational. U.S.-flag owners are among the few who generally do not participate in these "joint ventures."

Space chartering started in the bulk trades with partial ship capacities chartered for use by pseudo-bulk shippers. This has severely curtailed the pseudo-bulk cargo offered to liner shipping. Space chartering in liner trade, on the other hand, is concerned with the provision of control of liner capacity without ownership or operating responsibility. All of these and other types of arrangements have been practiced for some time by foreign operators.

While most foreign countries have more restrictive conditions under which alien workers can be employed in the domestic economy, the majority of maritime nations recognize that similar terms cannot be imposed on international shipping. We are among the few who, while fairly flexible in the terms under which aliens can work in the United States, restrict employment on U.S.-flag vessels to U.S. citizens. This policy, while designed to maintain U.S. seafaring employment, has actually been one reason for the reduction in U.S. seafaring jobs.

Although transportation and other services today account for 46 percent of our gross national product (GNP) and contribute nearly 33 percent of our export revenues, the international economic policy of the United States is still largely or nearly exclusively structured around the needs of the manufacturing and producing industries.

Transportation and other services provide the major portion of net foreign exchange earnings, yet they play a minor role in the formulation of U.S. trade policy. In fact, it is the large balance-of-payment surpluses earned by U.S transportation and other services that permit the offsetting of a major part of the deficit in the U.S. international trade of manufacturing and other goods.*

Major technological developments affecting shipping originated in the United States. While other maritime nations readily adopted

---

* Robinsky, J. D., "A Full Partnership for Services," *Business Week*, June 29, 1981.

such U.S. innovations, we appear to be much more reluctant in accepting technological, operational, or managerial advances developed elsewhere. This has permitted many of our foreign competitors to leapfrog U.S. developments.

Entrepreneurship built America, but few opportunities are left for the exercise of entrepreneurship in U.S. shipping. Since the Shipping Act of 1916, U.S. maritime policy evolved largely in the form of amendments to or variations of this basic act. The role of the United States in the world economy and its trade and strategic position have changed radically in the intervening years and most importantly during the last decade. It therefore appears relevant to reconsider our maritime policy and devise a maritime policy based on the needs of the future rather than on past policy.

While it is important not to forget the past, its main relevance lies in serving as a lesson for the future. Our economic and strategic needs are different now and will be significantly changed again before long. U.S. maritime policy must allow the U.S. shipping industry to follow the challenges and opportunities of changing conditions by providing meaningful government support and minimum government involvement.

8.2. Conclusions

Various policy issues have been addressed in our discussions. The overriding issue is obviously the lack of national transportation planning or, for that matter, long-range planning in general at the federal government level. This, in turn, has led to a general lack of a sense of direction. True, we still have the old basic premises on which our shipping laws are founded and which are used to justify our continued "commitment" to a viable U.S. merchant marine. Yet are these premises still valid, or, if valid, are they really the primary issues?

There are increasing uncertainties in economic resource availability and in our technological, social, strategic, and political posture. The traditional government decision-making processes appear to work less and less effectively. A general feeling of lack of defined goals, lack of goal-tending strategies, and lack of defined process is pervasive. This is particularly true in the case of shipping policy, where neither mission nor objective are effectively specified.

The goals of U.S. shipping policy are only vaguely defined and are, in part, not even meaningful. The proposed methods for implementing U.S. shipping policy are largely unrealistic. We need a new and global projection of the role of U.S. shipping, as well as defined realistic goals, not generalized and unachievable policy.

Goals and policy must view the United States in its proper economic and strategic perspective vis-à-vis its trading partners, competitors, and potential adversaries. Similarly, U.S. shipping must be viewed in its relation to the U.S transportation industry and U.S. economy as a whole.

Shipping policymaking takes place in a political environment and is largely a bargaining process in which parochial and other interests are felt. Implementation of policy often suffers under lack of interagency coordination and interagency rivalry.

In many countries transportation planning and policymaking form an integral part of national economic planning and are considered complementary to the development of other sectors of the economy, while, at the same time, permitting freedom of structure and implementation. It appears that at this critical time in U.S. economic development, the complementarity of the producing and service industries must be recognized and policies developed that permit farsighted decision making designed to rekindle entrepreneurship, development of imaginative technology, novel financing approaches, efficient management, and operation of U.S shipping. This, though, will only materialize if and when we eliminate our parochial approaches to shipping policymaking, unshackle the industry from unnecessary regulation, eliminate government involvement (or interference) in shipping management, and permit U.S shipping to operate under truly competitive conditions in relation to world shipping.

BIBLIOGRAPHY

General Shipping

Abrahamsson, B. J. "The Marine Environment and Ocean Shipping: Some Implications for a New Law of the Sea." *International Organization*, Spring 1977.

Abrahamsson, B. J. *International Ocean Shipping: Current Concepts and Principles*. Boulder, Col.: Westview Press, 1980.

Alexanderson, G. and Norstrom, G., *World Shipping*. New York: John Wiley and Sons, 1963.

Bess, D. *Marine Transportation*. Danville, Ill.: Interstate Printers and Publishers, Inc., 1976.

Branch, A. E. *The Elements of Shipping*. 4th ed. London: Chapman and Hall, 1977.

Bross, S. *Ocean Shipping*. Cambridge, Md.: Cornell Maritime Press, 1956.

Couper, A. D. *The Geography of Sea Transport*. London: Hutchinson and Co., 1972.

Gilman, S. "Optimal Shipping Technologies for Routes to Developing Countries," *Journal of Transportation Economics and Policy*, January 1977.

"Far East Shipping 1980/1981," *Seatrade Magazine*, December 1980.

Hanson, P. "Soviet Union and World Shipping," *Journal of Soviet Studies*, July 1970.

Lawrence, S. A. *International Sea Transport: The Years Ahead*. Lexington, Mass.: D. C. Heath and Company, 1972.

Ram, M. S. *Shipping*. New York: Asia Publishing House, 1969.

Rinman, T., and Linden, R. *Shipping—How it Works*. Gothenburg, Sweden: 1978.

Seatrade U.S. Yearbook 1980, Seatrade Magazine, 1980.

Seaward, N., et al., "Shipper Report," *Seatrade*, October 1980, pp. 105–123.

Shipping Statistics Yearbook (Annual). Bremen: Institute for Shipping Economics.

Simat, Helliesen and Eichner, Inc., "The Competitive Position of the U.S.-Flag Shipping Industry." Prepared for the Maritime Administration, December 1979.

Simon, W. M. "Foreign Trade Elasticities for Twenty Industries," United States International Trade Commission Publication 738, August 1975.

Stoneham, P. E. "New Directions for Research in Shipping Companies," *Maritime Policy and Management*, Vol. 7, No. 3, 1980, pp. 185–191.

Tanker Register. London: E. Clarkson & Co. 1970.

UNCTAD. Commodity Survey 1968. TD/B/C.1/150.

UNCTAD. Consultation in Shipping. TD/B/C.4/20, 1965.

UNCTAD. Containers, Pallets, and Other Unitized Methods for the Intermodal Movement of Freight. New York. St/Eca/120.

UNCTAD. Development of Expansion of Merchant Marine in Developing Countries. TD/B/C.4/42, 1966.

UNCTAD. Establishment or Expansion of Merchant Marines in Developing Countries. 69.II.D.1.1968.

UNCTAD. Formation and Strengthening of Shippers' Commodity Groups, TD/B/C.4/188, November 1979.

UNCTAD, The Generalized System of Preferences and the Multilateral Trade Negotiations, TD/B/C.1/52/Rev. 1, 1978.

UNCTAD. *Handbook of International Trade and Development.* HF495.U54a.

UNCTAD. The Impact on World Seaborne Trade of Changes in Shipping Costs, TD/B/C.4/76, November 1970.

UNCTAD. Improved Methods of Financing Ship Acquisition by Developing Countries, TD/B/C.4/179, July 1978.

UNCTAD. International Transoceanic Transport and Economic Development, TD/B/C.4/46, 1968.

UNCTAD. Liberalization of Terms and Conditions of Assistance, TD/B/C.3/77. January 1970.

UNCTAD. Maritime Transport and Economic Development. September 1969.

UNCTAD. Measures for the Promotion, Expansion, and Diversification of Manufactures and Semi-Manufactures from Developing Countries.

UNCTAD V. Merchant Fleet Development, TD 222, and supplements 1–5, May 1979.

UNCTAD. Port Administration and Legislation Handbook, ST/E/108.

UNCTAD. Program for the Liberation and Expansion of Trade in the Commodities of Interest in Developing Countries, TD/B/C.1/32.

UNCTAD. Protection of Shipper Interests, TD/B/C.4/1976, 1978.

UNCTAD. The Relationships between Shippers at Both Ends of a Trade, TD/B/C.4/180, August 1978.

UNCTAD. Review of International Trade and Development 1969. TD/B/257/Rev. 1.

UNCTAD. Review of Maritime Transport (Annual).

UNCTAD. Review of Maritime Transport 1969. TD/B/C.4/66.

UNCTAD. Shipping and the World Economy—Report of a Seminar on Shipping Economics. 67.II.D.12.

UNCTAD. Shipping in the Seventies. UN Sales No. 72, II.D.15.

UNCTAD. Technical Assistance in Shipping and Ports. TD/B/C.4/48. February 1969.

UNCTAD. Terms of Shipment. TD/B/C.4/36, 1969.

UNCTAD. Trade Expansion and Economic Integration Among Developing Countries. TD/B/85.

UNCTAD. Trade Projections for 1975 and 1980. TD/B.264. 1969.

UNCTAD. Trade Relations Among Countries Having Different Economic and Social Systems. TD/B/251. July 1969.

UNCTAD. A Transport Strategy for Landlocked Developing Countries, TD/B/453/Add. 1 Rev. 1, 1974.

UNCTAD. Transportation Modes and Technologies for Development, 1975.

UNCTAD. The World Commodity Situation and Outlook, TD/B/C.1/207, March 1979.

U.S., Congress, House, Committee on Merchant Marine and Fisheries. Third Flag. Hearings before the Subcommittee on the Merchant Marine, 94th Cong., 1st and 2d Sess., serial no. 95–35, 1977.

U.S. Department of Commerce, International Trade Administration, "World Trade Outlook for the Far East and South Asia," *Overseas Business Report*, September 1980.

U.S. Department of Commerce, International Trade Administration, "Market Profiles for Asia and Oceania," *Overseas Business Report*, December 1980.

U.S. Department of Commerce, Maritime Administration. *A Statistical Analysis of the World's Merchant Fleet* (Annual).

U.S. Department of Commerce, Maritime Commission, "Foreign Flag Merchant Ships Owned by U.S. Parent Companies, as of December 31, 1973," April 1979.

U.S. Department of Commerce, Maritime Administration, "Vessel Inventory Report," March and October 1980.

U.S. Department of Commerce, Maritime Administration, "United States' Ocean-borne Foreign Trade Routes," October 1979, March 1978.

U.S. Department of Transportation, "Potential Economic Impacts of Nonmarket Cargo Allocation in U.S. Foreign Trade," July 1976.

Government Aids to Shipping

Balassa, B. "Export Incentives and Export Performance in Developing Countries: A Comparative Analysis." World Bank Reprint Series, Number 59.

Balassa, B. "Export Subsidies by Developing Countries." World Bank Reprint Series, Number 51.

Balassa, B. "Intra-Industry Trade and the Integration of Developing Countries in the World Economy." World Bank Reprint Series, Number 113.

Balassa, B. "Prospects for Trade in Manufactured Goods between Industrial and Developing Countries, 1978–1990". World Bank Reprint Series, Number 156.

Balassa, B. "Structural Change in Trade in Manufactured Goods Between Industrial and Developing Nations." World Bank Staff Working Paper No. 396, June 1980.

Balassa, B. "The Tokyo Round and the Developing Countries." World Bank Reprint Series, Number 134.

Bale, M. D., and Lutz, E. "Trade Restrictions and International Price Stability." World Bank Staff Working Paper No. 303, October 1978.

Chenery, H. B. "Interactions between Industrialization and Exports." World Bank Reprint Series, Number 150.

Cizaukas, A. C. "The Nature of Export Credit Finance and Its Implications for Developing Countries." World Bank Staff Working Paper No. 409, July 1980.

Committee of American Steamship Lines. *Government Aids to Foreign Competitors*. Washington, D.C. 1964.

Eversheim, F. *Effects of Shipping Subsidization*. Bremen, 1958.

U.S. Department of Defense Sealife Procurement and National Security Study (1972).

"U.S. Maritime Objectives Continue to be Elusive," *Shipping World*, No. 49, December 2, 1976.

Wijkman, P. M. "Effects of Cargo Reservation: A Review of UNCTAD Code of Conduct for Liner Conferences," *Marine Policy*, October 1981, pp. 271–289.

Shipping Policy

Barker, J., and Brandwein, R. *The U.S. Merchant Marine in National Perspective*. Lexington, Mass.: D. C. Heath and Co., 1970.

Bennathan, E., and Walters, A. A. *Port Pricing and Investment Policy for Developing Countries*. Oxford: Oxford University Press, 1979.

Committee of American Steamship Lines. *Studies Re-examining National Maritime Policies and Requirements*. 6 Vols. Washington, 1964–65.

Coyle. The Compatibility of the Rule of Rate-Making and the National Transportation Policy, 38 *ICC Prac. J.* 340 (1971).

Dabrowski, K. "Internal and External Shipping Policy Measures," *Maritime Policy and Management*, Vol. 6, No. 2, 1979, pp. 81–92.

Darling, H. J. *The Elements of an International Shipping Policy for Canada*. Ottawa: Transport Canada Marine, 1974.

Doganis, R. S., and Metaxas, B. N. "The Impact of Flags of Convenience." Research Report No. 3, September 1976. London: Transport Studies Group, Polytechnic of Central London, 1976. (This report was followed by a discussion paper by Ken Grundey.)

Federal Maritime Commission, "East Asian Trade Study," Staff Report, August 1980.

Federal Maritime Commission, "North Atlantic Trade Study," Staff Report, April 1979.

Federal Maritime Commission, "South American Trade Study," Staff Report, February 1980.

Flemming, D. K. "The Role of the Federal Government in U.S. Marine Transportation," *Maritime Policy and Management*, Vol. 6, No. 4, 1979, pp. 253–267.

Frankel, E. G. "U.S. Shipping Policy and Conditions of a New World Economic and Political Environment," *Maritime Policy and Management*, Vol. 7, No. 1, 1980.

Gorter, W. *United States Shipping Policy*. New York: Harper Brothers, 1956.

Grundey, K. "Flags of Convenience in 1978." Discussion Paper No. 8, November 1978. London: Transport Studies Group, Polytechnic of Central London, 1978. (This is a follow-up of the study by Doganis and Metaxas.)

Horn, J. "Nationalism and Internationalism in Shipping." *Journal of Transportation Economics and Policy*, September 1969.

Kilgour, J. G. *The U.S. Merchant Marine: National Maritime Policy and Industrial Relations*. New York: Praeger, 1975.

Larner, R., "Public Policy in the Ocean Freight Industry" in *Promoting Competition in Regulated Markets*, A. Phillips, ed. Washington, D.C.: Brookings Institution, 1975.

Lawrence, S. A., *International Shipping: The Years Ahead*. Lexington, Mass.: Lexington Books, 1972.

Lawrence, S. *United States Merchant Shipping Policies and Politics*. Washington, D.C.: Brookings Institution, 1966.

Metaxas, B. N. "Notes on the Internationalization Process in the Maritime Sectors." *Maritime Policy and Management*, January 1978.

Morris, M. A. *International Policies and the Sea: The Case of Brazil*. Boulder, Col.: Westview Press, 1978.

Moyer, C. "A Critique of the Rationales for Present U.S. Maritime Programs." *Transportation Journal*, Winter 1974.

Naess, E. D. *The Great PanLibHon Controversy*. London: Gower Press, 1972.

Northwestern University Transportation Center Forum Proceedings, "In Search of a Rational Liner Shipping Policy." March 13–14, 1978. Evanston, Ill.: Northwestern University Transportation Center, 1978.

OECD. Export Cartels. Paris, 1974.

OECD. Maritime Transport (Annual). Paris.

OECD. Ocean Freight Rates as Part of Total Transport Costs. Paris, 1967.

Pearson, C. S. *International Marine Environment Policy: The Economic Dimension*. Baltimore: John Hopkins University Press, 1975.

Reese, H. C., ed. *Merchant Marine Policy*. Proceedings of the Symposium of the Fifteenth Ocean Shipping Management Institute of the American University's School of Business Administration. Cambridge, Md: Cornell Maritime Press, 1963.

Sturmey, S. G., *British Shipping and World Competition*. London: The Athlone Press, 1962.

Sturmey, S. G. *A Consideration of the Ends and Means of National Shipping Policy*. Bergen, Norway: Institute for Shipping Research, 1965.

Zeis, P. M. *American Shipping Policy*. Princeton, N.J.: Princeton University Press, 1938.

Shipping Regulation

Committee of American Steamship Lines. *Studies Re-examining National Maritime Policies and Requirements*. 6 Vols. Washington, 1964–65.

Coyle. "The Compatibility of the Rule of Rate-Making and the National Transportation Policy," 38 *ICC Prac. J.* 340 (1971).

Cunningham, J. C. "The Administrative History of the Federal Maritime Commission's Self-Policing Rules (Parts I and II)." *Journal of Maritime Law and Commerce*, 43 (1979) and Vol. 11, No. 2, 1980.

Deakin, B. M. "Shipping Conferences: Some Economic Aspects of International Regulations." *Maritime Studies and Management*, July 1974.

Doganis, R. S. and Metaxas, B. N. "The Impact of Flags of Convenience." Research Report No. 3, September 1976. London: Transport Studies Group, Polytechnic of Central London, 1976. (This report was followed by a discussion paper by Ken Grundey.)

Federal Regulatory Directory, 1980–1981.

Federal Maritime Commission, "18th Annual Report" (Fiscal year ended September 30, 1979).

Grundey, K. "Flags of Convenience in 1978." Discussion Paper No. 8, November 1978. London: Transport Studies Group, Polytechnic of Central London, 1978. (This is a follow-up of the study by Doganis and Metaxas.)

Maritime Matters, Agreement Between the United States of America and the Union of Soviet Socialist Republics, December 29, 1975, Department of State, Treaties and Other International Acts Series 8195.

OECD. Export Cartels. Paris: 1974.

UNCTAD. Economic Consequences of the Existence or Lack of a Genuine Link Between Vessel and Flag of Registry. TD/B/C.4/168, March 10, 1977.

UNCTAD. Rules of Origin in the General Scheme of Preferences in Favor of the Developing Countries. TD/B/AC.5/3, 1969.

UNCTAD. West African Shipping Range. D. Tresselt, TD/B/C.4/32. Prepared for the Institute of Shipping Research, Bergen, Norway.

U.S. Department of Commerce, Maritime Administration. "Effective U.S. Control of Merchant Ships: A Statistical Study."

U.S. Department of Commerce, Maritime Administration. "Foreign-Flag Ships Owned by U.S. Parent Companies" (Annual).

Shipping Conferences

Bush, W. L. "Steamship Conference Contract Rate Agreements and the Dual Rate System." *ICC Practitioner's Journal*, November–December 1972.

Canadian Transport Commission. "Study of the Economic Implications of the International Convention on a Code of Conduct for Liner Conferences." Ottawa: ESAB 76–13, February 1976.

Croner's Directory of Freight Conferences.

Davies, J. "The Competitive Environment of Liner Conferences," *Maritime Policy and Management*, No. 5, 1978, pp. 97–106.

Davies, J. E. "The Economics of the Open-Conference System," *Maritime Policy and Management*, Vol. 7, No. 2, 1980, pp. 85–102.

Deakin, B. M., and Seward, T. *Shipping Conferences: A Study of Their Origins, Destinations, and Economic Practices*. Cambridge, England: Cambridge University Press, 1973.

Department of Trade, United Kingdom. "Implementation of the United Nations Convention on a Code of Conduct for Liner Conferences," Annex I, "Convention on a Code of Conduct for Liner Conferences."

Devanney, J. W., Livanos, V. M., and Stewart, R. J. "Conference Rate Making and the West Coast of South America," Massachusetts Institute of Technology, Technical Report No. 72–1, January 1972.

Ellsworth, R. A. "Competition or Rationalization in the Liner Industry?" *Journal of Maritime Law and Commerce*, Vol. 10, No. 4, July 1979, pp. 497–517.

Evans, J. J., and Behnam, A. "A Fork Tariff System for Liner Freight Rates," *Journal of Transport Economics and Policy*, January 1975, pp. 62–66.

Evans, J. J. "Liner Freight Rates, Discrimination, and Cross-Subsidization," *Maritime Management and Policy*, No. 4, 1977, pp. 227–233.

Federal Maritime Commission. Fact Finding Investigation No. 6: The Effect of Steamship Conference Organization, Rules, Regulations, and Practices Upon the Foreign Commerce of the U.S., 1965.

Frankel, E. G., Testimony on behalf of U.S. Lines before the Maritime Subsidy Board, Maritime Administration, U.S. Department of Commerce, February 6, 1979.

Frankel, E. G., Arnold, J. H., and Read, P. G. "Impact of Cargo Sharing on U.S. Liner Trade," *Marine Policy*, January 1981, pp. 23–39.

Future of Liner Shipping. International Symposium in Bremen, September 23–25, 1975. Bremen: Institute for Shipping Economics, 1975.

Gardner, B., Evans, J., Davies, J., and Lowe, E. "Liner Shipping in the U.S. Trades," *Maritime Policy and Management*, No. 5, 1978, pp. 141–266.

Harbridge House, Inc., "The U.S. Merchant Marine and the International Conference System," prepared for the Maritime Administration, August 1978.

Heaver, T. D. "A Theory of Shipping Conference Pricing and Policies," *Maritime Studies and Management*, No. 1, 1973.

Heaver, T. D. "The Structure of Liner Conference Rates," *Journal of Industrial Economics*, 1973.

Heaver, T. D. "TransPacific Trade Liner Shipping and Conference Rates," *Transportation and Logistics Reviews*, Spring 1972.

Kanuk, L. Statement before the House Merchant Marine and Fisheries Committee, April 2, 1981.

Laing, E. T. "Shipping Freight Rates for Developing Countries," *Journal of Transport Economics and Policy*, September 1977, pp. 262–276.

Laing, E. T. "The Rationality of Conference Pricing and Output Policies," Part I, Maritime Studies and Management, No. 3, 1975. Part II, Maritime Studies and Management, No. 3, 1976 (see Schneerson's commentary in the latter issue).

"Liner Shipping in the U.S. Trades." *Maritime Policy and Management*, July 1978. (This is a special issue and is an answer to the 1977 report by the U.S. Department of Justice, "The Regulated Ocean Shipping Industry.")

Lopatine, "The UNCTAD Code of Conduct for Liner Conferences: Time for a U.S. Response," 22 *Harv. Int. L. J.*, 1981.

Manalytics, Inc., "The Impact of Bilateral Shipping Agreements in the U.S. Liner Trade," Maritime Administration, Office of Commercial Development, May 1979.

Manalytics, Inc., "Implementation of Rationalized Ocean Liner Service," a report prepared for the Federal Maritime Commission, October 1980.

Manalytics, Inc. "Limited Rationalization of Liner Ship Service, United States Atlantic and Gulf Ports to Northern Europe," Federal Maritime Commission, Bureau of Industry Economics, September 1979.

Manalytics, Inc. "Rationalized and Induced Transatlantic Liner Shipping Services and Costs," A Report to the Federal Maritime Commission, Bureau of Industry Economics, June 1980.

Marx, D. *International Shipping Cartels*. Princeton, N.J.: Princeton University Press, 1953.

McLachlen, D. L. "The Price Policy of Liner Conferences." *Scottish Journal of Political Economy*, November 1963.

Neff, S. C. "The UN Code of Conduct for Liner Conferences," *Journal of World Trade Law*, Vol. 14, No. 5, September–October 1980, pp. 398–423.

Northwestern University Transportation Center Forum Proceedings, "In Search of a Rational Liner Shipping Policy." March 13–14, 1978. Evanston, Ill.: Northwestern University Transportation Center, 1978.

"Rate Regulation in Ocean Shipping," 78 *Harv. L. Rev.* 635 (1965).

Restrictive Trade Practices Commission (Canada). Shipping Conferences, Arrangements, and Practices. Ottawa: Queen's Printers, 1966.

Sampson, G. P., and Yeats, A. J. "Tariff and Transport Barriers Facing Australian Exports," *Journal of Transport Economics and Policy*, May 1977, pp. 141–154.

Schmeltzer, E., and Weiner, G. J. "Liner Shipping in the 1980's: Competitive Patterns and Legislative Initiatives in the 96th Congress," *Journal of Maritime Law and Commerce*, Vol. 12, No. 7, October 1980, pp. 25–45.

Schmidt, L. "The International Shipping Policy Issues at UNCTAD V, Manila, May 1979," *Maritime Policy and Management*, Vol. 6, No. 4, 1979, pp. 269–279.

Schneerson, D. "The Rationality of Conference Pricing and Output Policies: Commentary." *Maritime Studies and Management*, No. 3, 1976.

Shah, M. J. "The Implementation of the UN Convention on a Code of Conduct for Liner Conferences 1974," *Journal of Maritime Law and Commerce*, Vol. 9, No. 1, October 1977, pp. 79–110.

Shipping Conferences Rate Policy and Developing Countries. Hamburg: Institute for International Economics, 1973.

Sturmey, S. G. "The Development of the Code of Conduct for Liner Conferences," *Marine Policy*, April 1979.

Svendsen, A. S. "Liner Conferences and the Determinationa of Freight Rates," Paper No. 5. The Institute of Economics, 1957, Bergen, Norway.

UNCTAD. Conference Practices and Adequacy of Shipping Services, TD/B/C.4/62, January 1970.

UNCTAD. Convention on a Code of Conduct for Liner Conferences. UN Document, TD/CODE/11/Rev., April 6, 1974.

UNCTAD. Level and Structure of Freight Rates Conference Practices and Adequacy of Shipping Services. TD/B/C.4/47.

UNCTAD. Level and Structure of Freight Rates Conference Practices and Adequacy of Shipping Services. TD/B/C.4/38, 1969.

UNCTAD. The Liner Conference System, TD/B/C4/62, 1970.

UNCTAD. Liner Shipping in India's Overseas Trade. Sarangan. TD/B/C.4/31, 1967.

UNCTAD. The Regulation of Liner Conferences, A Code of Conduct for the Liner Conference System, TD/104, 1972.

U.S. Congress, Senate, Committee on Commerce, Science, and Transportation. Illegal Rebating in the U.S. Ocean Commerce. Hearings before the Subcommittee on Merchant Marine and Tourism. 95th Cong., 1st sess., serial no. 95–13, 1977.

Zerby, J. A. "Impact of New Maritime Legislative Proposals: Potential Change in the Structure of the Shipping Industry," report to the Federal Maritime Commission, Bureau of Industry Economics, June 1, 1980.

Zerby, J. A. "Issues in Liner Regulation for the 1980's: Recommendations for Long-Range Planning Efforts by the FMC", Vol. 4, Preliminary report and recommendation to the Federal Maritime Commission, November 1980.

Zerby, J. A. "On the Practicality of the UNCTAD 40–40–20 Code for Liner Conferences," *Maritime Policy and Management*, Vol. 6, 1979, pp. 241–251.

Zerby, J. A. and Conlon, R. M. "An Analysis of Capacity Utilization in Liner Shipping," *Journal of Transport Economics and Policy*, January 1978, pp. 27–46.

Maritime Law

Anand, R. P. Legal Regime of the Sea-Bed and the Developing Countries (1976).

Atherley-Jones, L. A. *Commerce in War* (1907).

Barros, J. and Johnson, D. M. *The International Law of Pollution*. New York: Free Press, 1974.

Bilder, The Canadian Arctic Waters Pollution Prevention Act: New Stresses on the Law of the Sea, 69 *Mich. L. Rev.* 1 (197–71).

Blackwell, R. J. "Implementation of the Merchant Marine Act of 1970." *Journal of Maritime Law and Commerce*, January 1974.

Blood, D. *Inland Waterway Policy in the U.S.* (1972).

Boczek, B. A. *Flags of Convenience: An International Legal Study*. Cambridge, Mass.: Harvard University Press, 1962.

Bouchez, L. J. The Future of the Law of the Sea (1972).

British Shipping Laws. London: Stevens and Sons, various years. (This is a set of volumes each by a different author on a different subject. Volume 13 gives much information on international organizations and classification agencies in shipping.)

Carver, *Carriage by Sea* (1963).

Churchill, R., and Nordquist, M. *New Directions in the Law of the Sea*. Dobbs Ferry, N.Y.: Oceana Publications, 1973. (This set, in many volumes, gives the original texts of conventions and amendments.)

Colombos, C. J. *The International Law of the Sea* (1967).

Comite Maritime International. International Conventions on Maritime Law (texts). Secretariat of the International Maritime Committee. (This can be obtained by writing c/o Henry Voet-Genicot, 17 Borzestraat, B2000 Antwerp, Belgium.)

Comment, "Regulation of Water Carriers by the Interstate Commerce Commission," 50 *Yale L. J.* 654 (1941).

Extavour, W. C. *The Exclusive Economic Zone: A Study of the Evolution and Progressive Development of the International Law of the Sea*. Rockville, Md.: Sijthoff and Noordhoff, 1979.

Gilmore, G. *The Law of Admiralty* (1957).

Gilmore, G., and Black. *The Law of Admiralty* (2nd ed. 1975).

Gold, E. *Canadian Admiralty Law: Introductory Materials*. 2nd ed. Halifax: Dalhousie University, Faculty of Law, 1978.

Gold, E., ed. *New Directions in Maritime Law 1978*. Halifax: Dalhousie University, Faculty of Law, 1978.

Hale, W. B. *Hand-book on the Law of Bailments and Carriers* (1896).

Healy, N. J. and Sharpe, D. J. *Admiralty: Cases and Materials*. American Casebook Series. St. Paul, Minn.: West Publishing Co., 1974.

Jantscher, G. R., *Bread upon the Waters: Federal Aids to the Maritime Industries*. Washington, D.C.: Brookings Institution, 1975.

Jessup, D. *The Law of Territorial Waters and Maritime Jurisdiction*. Millwood, N.Y.: Kraus Reprint, 1927.

Jones, W. *Cases and Materials on Regulated Industries* (2nd ed. 1976).

Knight, H. G. *The Law of the Sea* (1976).

Lowe, "The Right of Entry into Maritime Ports in International Law," 14 *San Diego L. Rev.* 597 (1976–77).

McCarney, "ICC Rate Regulation and Rail Motor Carrier Pricing Behavior: A Reappraisal," 35 *ICC Prac. J.* 707 (1968).

McDougal, M. and Burke, W. *The Public Order of the Oceans*. Yale University Press, New Haven, Conn.: 1962.

McGenee, "The Inherent Advantages of Carrier Modes Under the National Transportation Policy," 34 *ICC Prac. J.* 722 (1967).

Meyers, H. *The Nationality of Ships* (1967).

Note, "Rate Regulation in Ocean Shipping," 78 *Harv. L. Rev.* 635 (1965).

Parks, A. L. *Law of Tug, Tow, and Pilotage*. Centerville, Md.: Cornell Maritime Press, 1971.

Reiff, H. *The United States and the Treaty Law of the Sea* (1959).

"Role, Regulation of Intermodal Rate Competition in Transportation," 69 *Mich. L. R.* 101 (1971).

Shah, M. J. "The Dispute Settlement Machinery of the U.N. Convention on a Code of Conduct for Liner Conferences," 7 *Journal of Maritime Law and Commerce*, October 1975, pp. 127–168.

Shah, M. J. "The Implementation of the UN Convention on a Code of Conduct for Liner Conferences 1974," *Journal of Maritime Law and Commerce*, Vol. 9, No. 1, October 1977, pp. 79–110.

Shipping Act of 1916, §§14–20, 22–23, 46 U.S.C. §§812–819, 821–832.

Singh, N. *International Conventions of Merchant Shipping* (1963).

Singh, N. *International Conventions of Merchant Shipping*. 2nd ed. London: Stevens and Sons, 1973. (This is volume 8 of British Shipping Laws.)

Smith, The Politics of Lawmaking: Problems in International Maritime Regulation—Innocent Passage v. Free Transit," 37 *Pitt. L. Rev.* 487 (1976).

Swartztrauber, S. *The Three-Mile Limit of Territorial Seas* (1972).

Totland, T. "Protectionism in International Shipping and Some Economic Effects," *Maritime Policy and Management*, Vol. 7, No. 2, 1980, pp. 103–114.

UNCTAD. Economic Consequences of the Existence or Lack of a Genuine Link Between Vessel and Flag of Registry, TD/B/C.4/AC.1/8, 1980.

UNCTAD. Legal Mechanisms for Regulating the Operations of Open-Registry Fleets During the Phasing-out Period, TD/B/C.4/AC.1/8, 1980.

UNCTAD. The Repercussions of Phasing-Out Open Registries, TD/B/C.4/AC.1/5, September 24, 1979.

United Nations. *The Sea: Legal and Political Aspects, a Select Bibliography* (1974).

U.S., Department of Justice, Antitrust Division. The Regulated Ocean Shipping Industry. Report, 1977 (stock #027–000–00474–1).

Van Doren, L. O. *The Law of Shipment* (1932).

White, I. L. *Decision-Making for Space: Law and Politics in Air, Sea, and Outer Space* (1970).

Zerby, J. A. "Impact of New Maritime Legislative Proposals: Potential Change in the Structure of the Shipping Industry," A report to the Federal Maritime Commission, Bureau of Industry Economics, June 1, 1980.

Zoll, "The Development of Federal Regulatory Control Over Water Carriers," 12 *ICC Prac. L.* 552 (1945).

INDEX